Samuel P. Huntington

The Clash of Civilizations and the Remaking of World Order

SIMON & SCHUSTER
New York   London   Toronto   Sydney

SIMON & SCHUSTER
Rockefeller Center
1230 Avenue of the Americas
New York, NY 10020

First Simon & Schuster trade paperback edition 2003

SIMON & SCHUSTER and colophon are registered trademarks
of Simon & Schuster, Inc.

For information regarding special discounts for bulk purchases,
please contact Simon & Schuster Special Sales at
1-800-456-6798 or business@simonandschuster.com

Designed by Karolina Harris

Manufactured in the United States of America

25   27   29   30   28   26   24

The Library of Congress has cataloged the hardcover edition as follows:
Huntington, Samuel P.
The clash of civilizations and the remaking of world order /
Samuel P. Huntington.
p.   cm.
Includes index.
1. World politics—1989–   2. Post-communism.
3. Civilization, Modern—1950–   I. Title.
D860.H86   1996
909.82'9—dc20   96-31492
ISBN 0-684-81164-2
0-684-84441-9 (Pbk)

To Nancy,
who has endured "the clash" with a smile

Contents

List of Illustrations: Tables, Figures, Maps   11
Preface   13

I. A World of Civilizations

1. The New Era in World Politics   19
   INTRODUCTION: FLAGS AND CULTURAL IDENTITY   19
   A MULTIPOLAR, MULTICIVILIZATIONAL WORLD   21
   OTHER WORLDS?   29
   COMPARING WORLDS: REALISM, PARSIMONY, AND PREDICTIONS   36

2. Civilizations in History and Today   40
   THE NATURE OF CIVILIZATIONS   40
   RELATIONS AMONG CIVILIZATIONS   48

3. A Universal Civilization? Modernization and Westernization   56
   UNIVERSAL CIVILIZATION: MEANINGS   56
   UNIVERSAL CIVILIZATION: SOURCES   66
   THE WEST AND MODERNIZATION   68
   RESPONSES TO THE WEST AND MODERNIZATION   72

II. The Shifting Balance of Civilizations

4. The Fading of the West: Power, Culture, and Indigenization   81
   WESTERN POWER: DOMINANCE AND DECLINE   81
   INDIGENIZATION: THE RESURGENCE OF
      NON-WESTERN CULTURES   91
   LA REVANCHE DE DIEU   95

5. Economics, Demography, and the Challenger Civilizations   *102*
   THE ASIAN AFFIRMATION   *103*
   THE ISLAMIC RESURGENCE   *109*
   CHANGING CHALLENGES   *120*

III. The Emerging Order of Civilizations

6. The Cultural Reconfiguration of Global Politics   *125*
   GROPING FOR GROUPINGS: THE POLITICS OF IDENTITY   *125*
   CULTURE AND ECONOMIC COOPERATION   *130*
   THE STRUCTURE OF CIVILIZATIONS   *135*
   TORN COUNTRIES: THE FAILURE OF CIVILIZATION SHIFTING   *139*

7. Core States, Concentric Circles, and Civilizational Order   *155*
   CIVILIZATIONS AND ORDER   *155*
   BOUNDING THE WEST   *157*
   RUSSIA AND ITS NEAR ABROAD   *163*
   GREATER CHINA AND ITS CO-PROSPERITY SPHERE   *168*
   ISLAM: CONSCIOUSNESS WITHOUT COHESION   *174*

IV. Clashes of Civilizations

8. The West and the Rest: Intercivilizational Issues   *183*
   WESTERN UNIVERSALISM   *183*
   WEAPONS PROLIFERATION   *186*
   HUMAN RIGHTS AND DEMOCRACY   *192*
   IMMIGRATION   *198*

9. The Global Politics of Civilizations   *207*
   CORE STATE AND FAULT LINE CONFLICTS   *207*
   ISLAM AND THE WEST   *209*
   ASIA, CHINA, AND AMERICA   *218*
   CIVILIZATIONS AND CORE STATES: EMERGING ALIGNMENTS   *238*

10. From Transition Wars to Fault Line Wars   *246*
    TRANSITION WARS: AFGHANISTAN AND THE GULF   *246*
    CHARACTERISTICS OF FAULT LINE WARS   *252*

INCIDENCE: ISLAM'S BLOODY BORDERS 254
CAUSES: HISTORY, DEMOGRAPHY, POLITICS 259

11. The Dynamics of Fault Line Wars 266
IDENTITY: THE RISE OF CIVILIZATION CONSCIOUSNESS 266
CIVILIZATION RALLYING: KIN COUNTRIES AND DIASPORAS 272
HALTING FAULT LINE WARS 291

V. The Future of Civilizations

12. The West, Civilizations, and Civilization 301
THE RENEWAL OF THE WEST? 301
THE WEST IN THE WORLD 308
CIVILIZATIONAL WAR AND ORDER 312
THE COMMONALITIES OF CIVILIZATION 318

Notes 323
Index 353

List of Illustrations

•

Tables

2.1. Use of Terms: "Free World" and "the West," p. 55

3.1. Speakers of Major Languages, p. 60

3.2. Speakers of Principal Chinese and Western Languages, p. 61

3.3. Proportion of World Population Adhering to Major Religious Traditions, p. 65

4.1. Territory Under the Political Control of Civilizations, 1900–1993, p. 84

4.2. Populations of Countries Belonging to the World's Major Civilizations, 1993, p. 85

4.3. Shares of World Population Under the Political Control of Civilizations, 1900–2025, p. 85

4.4. Shares of World Manufacturing Output by Civilization or Country, 1750–1980, p. 86

4.5. Civilization Shares of World Gross Economic Product, 1950–1992, p. 87

4.6. Civilization Shares of Total World Military Manpower, p. 88

5.1. Youth Bulge in Muslim Countries, p. 119

8.1. Selected Chinese Arms Transfers, 1980–1991, p. 189

8.2. U.S. Population by Race and Ethnicity, p. 205

10.1. Ethnopolitical Conflicts, 1993–1994, p. 258

10.2. Ethnic Conflicts, 1993, p. 258

10.3. Militarism of Muslim and Christian Countries, p. 258

10.4. Possible Causes of Muslim Conflict Propensity, p. 263

Figures

2.1. Eastern Hemisphere Civilizations, p. 49

3.1. Alternative Responses to the Impact of the West, p. 75

3.2. Modernization and Cultural Resurgence, p. 76
 5.1. The Economic Challenge: Asia and the West, p. 104
 5.2. The Demographic Challenge: Islam, Russia, and the West, p. 118
 5.3. Muslim Youth Bulge by Region, p. 120
 9.1. The Global Politics of Civilizations: Emerging Alignments, p. 245
10.1. Sri Lanka: Sinhalese and Tamil Youth Bulges, p. 260
11.1. The Structure of a Complex Fault Line War, p. 274

Maps

1.1. The West and the Rest: 1920, pp. 22–23
1.2. The Cold War World: 1960s, pp. 24–25
1.3. The World of Civilizations: Post-1990, pp. 26–27
7.1. The Eastern Boundary of Western Civilization, p. 159
7.2. Ukraine: A Cleft Country, p. 166
8.1. The United States in 2020: A Cleft Country? p. 205

Preface

In the summer of 1993 the journal *Foreign Affairs* published an article of mine titled "The Clash of Civilizations?". That article, according to the *Foreign Affairs* editors, stirred up more discussion in three years than any other article they had published since the 1940s. It certainly stirred up more debate in three years than anything else I have written. The responses and comments on it have come from every continent and scores of countries. People were variously impressed, intrigued, outraged, frightened, and perplexed by my argument that the central and most dangerous dimension of the emerging global politics would be conflict between groups from differing civilizations. Whatever else it did, the article struck a nerve in people of every civilization.

Given the interest in, misrepresentation of, and controversy over the article, it seemed desirable for me to explore further the issues it raised. One constructive way of posing a question is to state an hypothesis. The article, which had a generally ignored question mark in its title, was an effort to do that. This book is intended to provide a fuller, deeper, and more thoroughly documented answer to the article's question. I here attempt to elaborate, refine, supplement, and, on occasion, qualify the themes set forth in the article and to develop many ideas and cover many topics not dealt with or touched on only in passing in the article. These include: the concept of civilizations; the question of a universal civilization; the relation between power and culture; the shifting balance of power among civilizations; cultural indigenization in non-Western societies; the political structure of civilizations; conflicts generated by Western universalism, Muslim militancy, and Chinese assertion; balancing and bandwagoning responses to the rise of Chinese power; the causes and dynamics of fault line wars; and the futures of the West and of a world of civilizations. One major theme absent from the article concerns the crucial impact of population growth on instability and the balance of power. A second important theme absent from the article is summarized in the book's title and final sentence: "clashes of civilizations are the greatest threat to world peace, and an international order based on civilizations is the surest safeguard against world war."

This book is not intended to be a work of social science. It is instead meant to be an interpretation of the evolution of global politics after the Cold War. It aspires to present a framework, a paradigm, for viewing global politics that will be meaningful to scholars and useful to policymakers. The test of its meaningfulness and usefulness is not whether it accounts for everything that is happening in global politics. Obviously it does not. The test is whether it provides a more meaningful and useful lens through which to view international developments than any alternative paradigm. In addition, no paradigm is eternally valid. While a civilizational approach may be helpful to understanding global politics in the late twentieth and early twenty-first centuries, this does not mean that it would have been equally helpful in the mid-twentieth century or that it will be helpful in the mid-twenty-first century.

The ideas that eventually became the article and this book were first publicly expressed in a Bradley Lecture at the American Enterprise Institute in Washington in October 1992 and then set forth in an Occasional Paper prepared for the Olin Institute's project on "The Changing Security Environment and American National Interests," made possible by the Smith Richardson Foundation. Following publication of the article, I became involved in innumerable seminars and meetings focused on "the clash" with academic, government, business, and other groups across the United States. In addition, I was fortunate to be able to participate in discussions of the article and its thesis in many other countries, including Argentina, Belgium, China, France, Germany, Great Britain, Korea, Japan, Luxembourg, Russia, Saudi Arabia, Singapore, South Africa, Spain, Sweden, Switzerland, and Taiwan. These discussions exposed me to all the major civilizations except Hinduism, and I benefitted immensely from the insights and perspectives of the participants in these discussions. In 1994 and 1995 I taught a seminar at Harvard on the nature of the post-Cold War world, and the always vigorous and at times quite critical comments of the seminar students were an additional stimulus. My work on this book also benefitted greatly from the collegial and supportive environment of Harvard's John M. Olin Institute for Strategic Studies and Center for International Affairs.

The manuscript was read in its entirety by Michael C. Desch, Robert O. Keohane, Fareed Zakaria, and R. Scott Zimmerman, and their comments led to significant improvements in both its substance and organization. Throughout the writing of this book, Scott Zimmerman also provided indispensable research assistance; without his energetic, expert, and devoted help, this book would never have been completed when it was. Our undergraduate assistants, Peter Jun and Christiana Briggs, also pitched in constructively. Grace de Magistris typed early portions of the manuscript, and Carol Edwards with great commitment and superb efficiency redid the manuscript so many times that she must know large portions of it almost by heart. Denise Shannon and Lynn Cox at Georges Borchardt and Robert Asahina, Robert Bender, and Johanna Li at Simon & Schuster have cheerfully and professionally guided the manuscript through the publication process. I am immensely grateful to all these individuals for their help in bringing this book into being. They have made it much better than it would have been otherwise, and the remaining deficiencies are my responsibility.

My work on this book was made possible by the financial support of the John M. Olin Foundation and the Smith Richardson Foundation. Without their assistance, completion of the book would have been delayed for years, and I greatly appreciate their generous backing of this effort. While other foundations have increasingly focused on domestic issues, Olin and Smith Richardson deserve accolades for maintaining their interest in and support for work on war, peace, and national and international security.

S . P . H .

I

·

A

World

of

Civilizations

Chapter 1

•

The New Era in World Politics

On January 3, 1992, a meeting of Russian and American scholars took place in the auditorium of a government building in Moscow. Two weeks earlier the Soviet Union had ceased to exist and the Russian Federation had become an independent country. As a result, the statue of Lenin which previously graced the stage of the auditorium had disappeared and instead the flag of the Russian Federation was now displayed on the front wall. The only problem, one American observed, was that the flag had been hung upside down. After this was pointed out to the Russian hosts, they quickly and quietly corrected the error during the first intermission.

The years after the Cold War witnessed the beginnings of dramatic changes in peoples' identities and the symbols of those identities. Global politics began to be reconfigured along cultural lines. Upside-down flags were a sign of the transition, but more and more the flags are flying high and true, and Russians and other peoples are mobilizing and marching behind these and other symbols of their new cultural identities.

On April 18, 1994, two thousand people rallied in Sarajevo waving the flags of Saudi Arabia and Turkey. By flying those banners, instead of U.N., NATO, or American flags, these Sarajevans identified themselves with their fellow Muslims and told the world who were their real and not-so-real friends.

On October 16, 1994, in Los Angeles 70,000 people marched beneath "a sea of Mexican flags" protesting Proposition 187, a referendum measure which would deny many state benefits to illegal immigrants and their children. Why are they "walking down the street with a Mexican flag and demanding that this country give them a free education?" observers asked. "They should be waving the American flag." Two weeks later more protestors did march down the street carrying an American flag — upside down. These flag displays ensured victory for Proposition 187, which was approved by 59 percent of California voters.

In the post–Cold War world flags count and so do other symbols of cultural identity, including crosses, crescents, and even head coverings, because culture counts, and cultural identity is what is most meaningful to most people. People are discovering new but often old identities and marching under new but often old flags which lead to wars with new but often old enemies.

One grim *Weltanschauung* for this new era was well expressed by the Venetian nationalist demagogue in Michael Dibdin's novel, *Dead Lagoon*: "There can be no true friends without true enemies. Unless we hate what we are not, we cannot love what we are. These are the old truths we are painfully rediscovering after a century and more of sentimental cant. Those who deny them deny their family, their heritage, their culture, their birthright, their very selves! They will not lightly be forgiven." The unfortunate truth in these old truths cannot be ignored by statesmen and scholars. For peoples seeking identity and reinventing ethnicity, enemies are essential, and the potentially most dangerous enmities occur across the fault lines between the world's major civilizations.

The central theme of this book is that culture and cultural identities, which at the broadest level are civilization identities, are shaping the patterns of cohesion, disintegration, and conflict in the post–Cold War world. The five parts of this book elaborate corollaries to this main proposition.

Part I: For the first time in history global politics is both multipolar and multicivilizational; modernization is distinct from Westernization and is producing neither a universal civilization in any meaningful sense nor the Westernization of non-Western societies.

Part II: The balance of power among civilizations is shifting: the West is declining in relative influence; Asian civilizations are expanding their economic, military, and political strength; Islam is exploding demographically with destabilizing consequences for Muslim countries and their neighbors; and non-Western civilizations generally are reaffirming the value of their own cultures.

Part III: A civilization-based world order is emerging: societies sharing cultural affinities cooperate with each other; efforts to shift societies from one civilization to another are unsuccessful; and countries group themselves around the lead or core states of their civilization.

Part IV: The West's universalist pretensions increasingly bring it into conflict with other civilizations, most seriously with Islam and China; at the local level fault line wars, largely between Muslims and non-Muslims, generate "kin-country rallying," the threat of broader escalation, and hence efforts by core states to halt these wars.

Part V: The survival of the West depends on Americans reaffirming their Western identity and Westerners accepting their civilization as unique not universal and uniting to renew and preserve it against challenges from non-Western societies. Avoidance of a global war of civilizations depends on world leaders accepting and cooperating to maintain the multicivilizational character of global politics.

A MULTIPOLAR, MULTICIVILIZATIONAL WORLD

In the post–Cold War world, for the first time in history, global politics has become multipolar *and* multicivilizational. During most of human existence, contacts between civilizations were intermittent or nonexistent. Then, with the beginning of the modern era, about A.D. 1500, global politics assumed two dimensions. For over four hundred years, the nation states of the West — Britain, France, Spain, Austria, Prussia, Germany, the United States, and others — constituted a multipolar international system within Western civilization and interacted, competed, and fought wars with each other. At the same time, Western nations also expanded, conquered, colonized, or decisively influenced every other civilization (Map 1.1). During the Cold War global politics became bipolar and the world was divided into three parts. A group of mostly wealthy and democratic societies, led by the United States, was engaged in a pervasive ideological, political, economic, and, at times, military competition with a group of somewhat poorer communist societies associated with and led by the Soviet Union. Much of this conflict occurred in the Third World outside these two camps, composed of countries which often were poor, lacked political stability, were recently independent, and claimed to be nonaligned (Map 1.2).

In the late 1980s the communist world collapsed, and the Cold War international system became history. In the post–Cold War world, the most important distinctions among peoples are not ideological, political, or economic. They are cultural. Peoples and nations are attempting to answer the most basic question humans can face: Who are we? And they are answering that question in the traditional way human beings have answered it, by reference to the things that mean most to them. People define themselves in terms of ancestry, religion, language, history, values, customs, and institutions. They identify with cultural groups: tribes, ethnic groups, religious communities, nations, and, at the broadest level, civilizations. People use politics not just to advance their interests but also to define their identity. We know who we are only when we know who we are not and often only when we know whom we are against.

Nation states remain the principal actors in world affairs. Their behavior is shaped as in the past by the pursuit of power and wealth, but it is also shaped by cultural preferences, commonalities, and differences. The most important groupings of states are no longer the three blocs of the Cold War but rather the world's seven or eight major civilizations (Map 1.3). Non-Western societies, particularly in East Asia, are developing their economic wealth and creating the basis for enhanced military power and political influence. As their power and self-confidence increase, non-Western societies increasingly assert their

The West and the Rest: 1920

Ruled by the West

Actually or Nominally Independent of the West

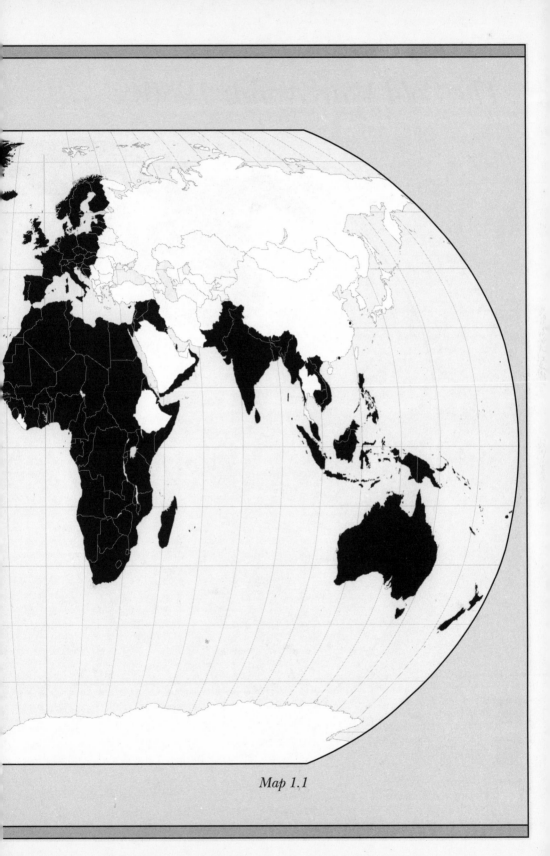

Map 1.1

The Cold War World: 1960s

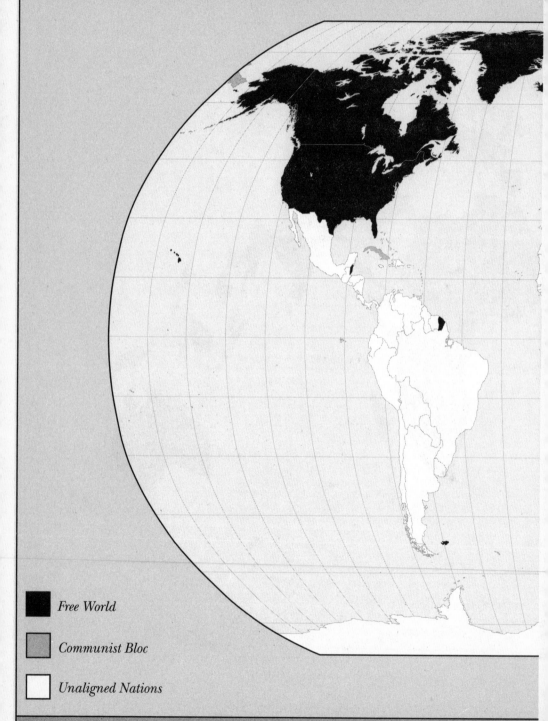

Free World

Communist Bloc

Unaligned Nations

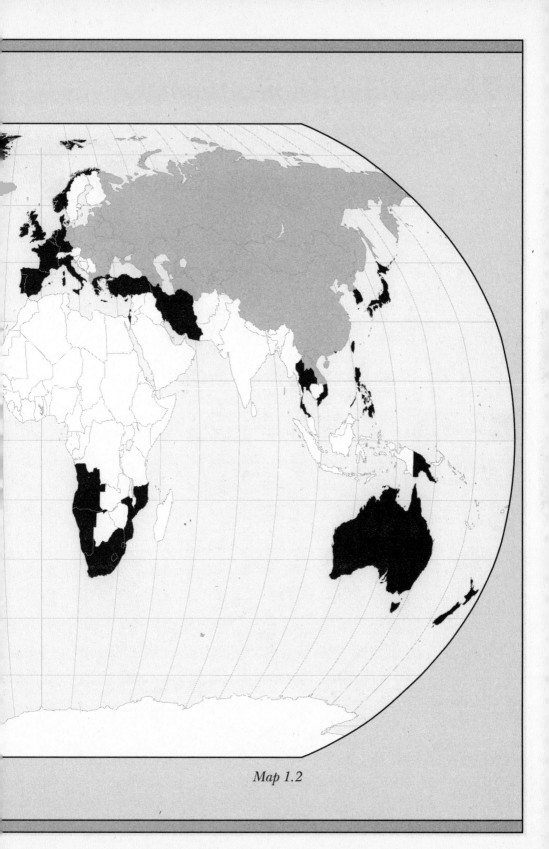

Map 1.2

The World of Civilizations:
Post-1990

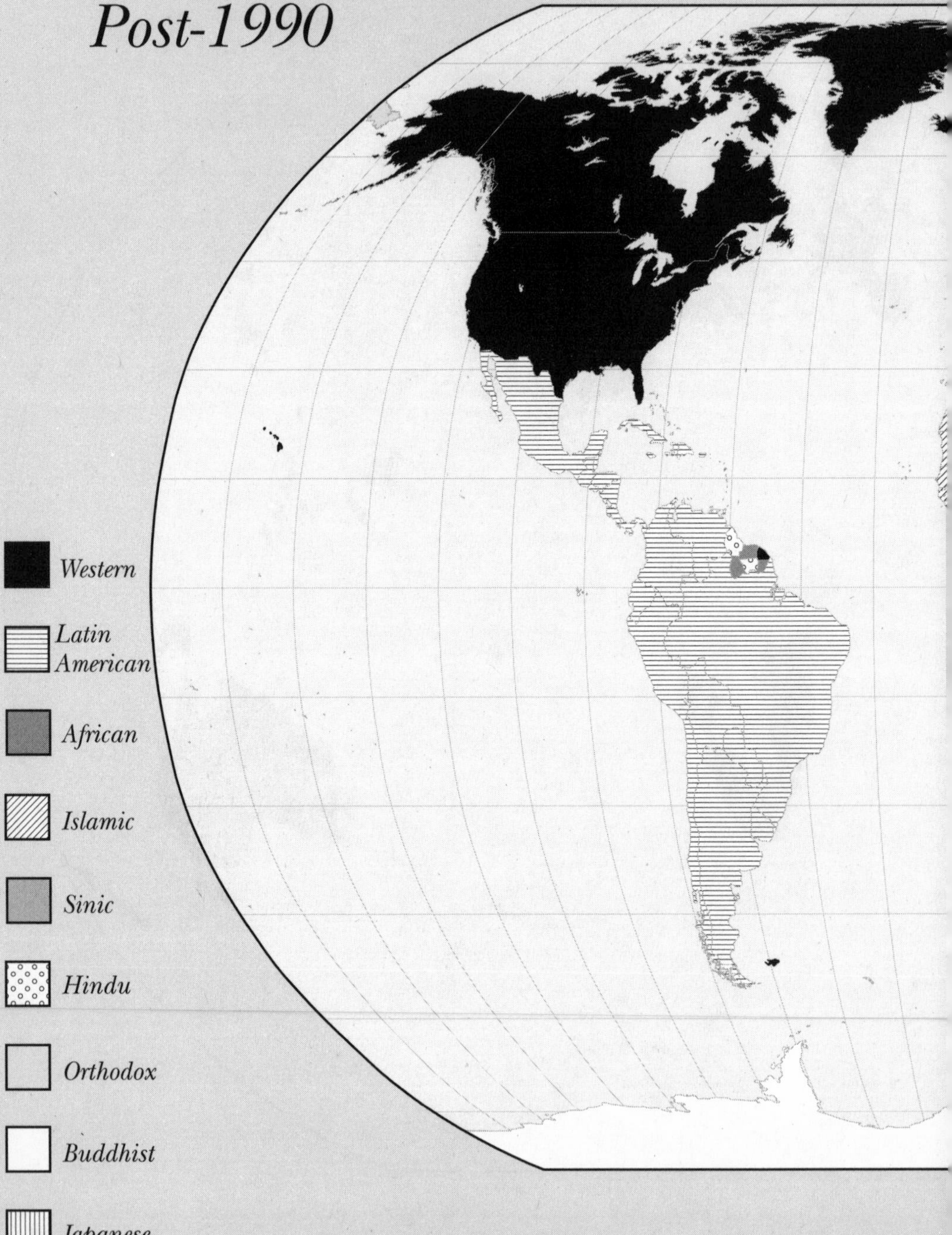

Western

Latin American

African

Islamic

Sinic

Hindu

Orthodox

Buddhist

Japanese

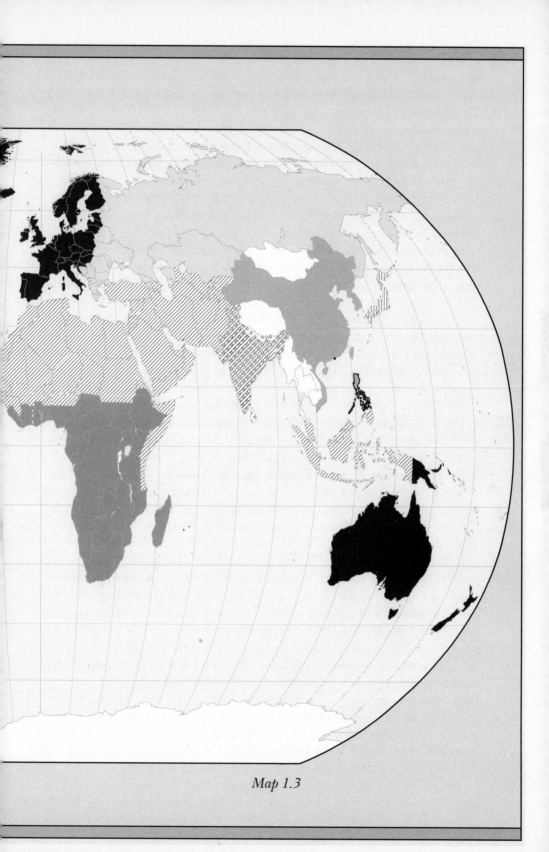

Map 1.3

own cultural values and reject those "imposed" on them by the West. The "international system of the twenty-first century," Henry Kissinger has noted, ". . . will contain at least six major powers — the United States, Europe, China, Japan, Russia, and probably India — as well as a multiplicity of medium-sized and smaller countries."[1] Kissinger's six major powers belong to five very different civilizations, and in addition there are important Islamic states whose strategic locations, large populations, and/or oil resources make them influential in world affairs. In this new world, local politics is the politics of ethnicity; global politics is the politics of civilizations. The rivalry of the superpowers is replaced by the clash of civilizations.

In this new world the most pervasive, important, and dangerous conflicts will not be between social classes, rich and poor, or other economically defined groups, but between peoples belonging to different cultural entities. Tribal wars and ethnic conflicts will occur within civilizations. Violence between states and groups from different civilizations, however, carries with it the potential for escalation as other states and groups from these civilizations rally to the support of their "kin countries."[2] The bloody clash of clans in Somalia poses no threat of broader conflict. The bloody clash of tribes in Rwanda has consequences for Uganda, Zaire, and Burundi but not much further. The bloody clashes of civilizations in Bosnia, the Caucasus, Central Asia, or Kashmir could become bigger wars. In the Yugoslav conflicts, Russia provided diplomatic support to the Serbs, and Saudi Arabia, Turkey, Iran, and Libya provided funds and arms to the Bosnians, not for reasons of ideology or power politics or economic interest but because of cultural kinship. "Cultural conflicts," Vaclav Havel has observed, "are increasing and are more dangerous today than at any time in history," and Jacques Delors agreed that "future conflicts will be sparked by cultural factors rather than economics or ideology."[3] And the most dangerous cultural conflicts are those along the fault lines between civilizations.

In the post–Cold War world, culture is both a divisive and a unifying force. People separated by ideology but united by culture come together, as the two Germanys did and as the two Koreas and the several Chinas are beginning to. Societies united by ideology or historical circumstance but divided by civilization either come apart, as did the Soviet Union, Yugoslavia, and Bosnia, or are subjected to intense strain, as is the case with Ukraine, Nigeria, Sudan, India, Sri Lanka, and many others. Countries with cultural affinities cooperate economically and politically. International organizations based on states with cultural commonality, such as the European Union, are far more successful than those that attempt to transcend cultures. For forty-five years the Iron Curtain was the central dividing line in Europe. That line has moved several hundred miles east. It is now the line separating the peoples of Western Christianity, on the one hand, from Muslim and Orthodox peoples on the other.

The philosophical assumptions, underlying values, social relations, customs, and overall outlooks on life differ significantly among civilizations. The revitalization of religion throughout much of the world is reinforcing these cultural differences. Cultures can change, and the nature of their impact on politics and economics can vary from one period to another. Yet the major differences in political and economic development among civilizations are clearly rooted in their different cultures. East Asian economic success has its source in East Asian culture, as do the difficulties East Asian societies have had in achieving stable democratic political systems. Islamic culture explains in large part the failure of democracy to emerge in much of the Muslim world. Developments in the postcommunist societies of Eastern Europe and the former Soviet Union are shaped by their civilizational identities. Those with Western Christian heritages are making progress toward economic development and democratic politics; the prospects for economic and political development in the Orthodox countries are uncertain; the prospects in the Muslim republics are bleak.

The West is and will remain for years to come the most powerful civilization. Yet its power relative to that of other civilizations is declining. As the West attempts to assert its values and to protect its interests, non-Western societies confront a choice. Some attempt to emulate the West and to join or to "bandwagon" with the West. Other Confucian and Islamic societies attempt to expand their own economic and military power to resist and to "balance" against the West. A central axis of post–Cold War world politics is thus the interaction of Western power and culture with the power and culture of non-Western civilizations.

In sum, the post–Cold War world is a world of seven or eight major civilizations. Cultural commonalities and differences shape the interests, antagonisms, and associations of states. The most important countries in the world come overwhelmingly from different civilizations. The local conflicts most likely to escalate into broader wars are those between groups and states from different civilizations. The predominant patterns of political and economic development differ from civilization to civilization. The key issues on the international agenda involve differences among civilizations. Power is shifting from the long predominant West to non-Western civilizations. Global politics has become multipolar and multicivilizational.

OTHER WORLDS?

Maps and Paradigms. This picture of post–Cold War world politics shaped by cultural factors and involving interactions among states and groups from different civilizations is highly simplified. It omits many things, distorts some things, and obscures others. Yet if we are to think seriously about the world, and act effectively in it, some sort of simplified map of reality, some theory, concept, model, paradigm, is necessary. Without such intellectual constructs, there is, as William James said, only "a bloomin' buzzin' confusion." Intellectual and scientific advance, Thomas Kuhn showed in his classic *The Structure of Scientific Revolutions*, consists of the displacement of one paradigm, which has become increasingly incapable of explaining new or newly discovered facts, by a new paradigm, which does account for those facts in a more satisfactory fashion. "To be accepted as a paradigm," Kuhn wrote, "a theory must seem better than its competitors, but it need not, and in fact never does, explain all the facts with which it can be confronted."[4] "Finding one's way through unfamiliar terrain," John Lewis Gaddis also wisely observed, "generally requires a map of some sort. Cartography, like cognition itself, is a necessary simplification that allows us to see where we are, and where we may be going." The Cold War image of superpower competition was, as he points out, such a model, articulated first by Harry Truman, as "an exercise in geopolitical cartography that depicted the international landscape in terms everyone could understand, and so doing prepared the way for the sophisticated strategy of containment that was soon to follow." World views and causal theories are indispensable guides to international politics.[5]

For forty years students and practitioners of international relations thought and acted in terms of the highly simplified but very useful Cold War paradigm of world affairs. This paradigm could not account for everything that went on in world politics. There were many anomalies, to use Kuhn's term, and at times the paradigm blinded scholars and statesmen to major developments, such as the Sino-Soviet split. Yet as a simple model of global politics, it accounted for more important phenomena than any of its rivals, it was an essential starting point for thinking about international affairs, it came to be almost universally accepted, and it shaped thinking about world politics for two generations.

Simplified paradigms or maps are indispensable for human thought and action. On the one hand, we may explicitly formulate theories or models and consciously use them to guide our behavior. Alternatively, we may deny the need for such guides and assume that we will act only in terms of specific "objective" facts, dealing with each case "on its merits." If we assume this, however, we delude ourselves. For in the back of our minds are hidden assumptions, biases, and prejudices that determine how we perceive reality, what facts we look at, and how we judge their importance and merits. We need explicit or implicit models so as to be able to:

1. order and generalize about reality;
2. understand causal relationships among phenomena;
3. anticipate and, if we are lucky, predict future developments;
4. distinguish what is important from what is unimportant; and
5. show us what paths we should take to achieve our goals.

Every model or map is an abstraction and will be more useful for some purposes than for others. A road map shows us how to drive from A to B, but will not be very useful if we are piloting a plane, in which case we will want a map highlighting airfields, radio beacons, flight paths, and topography. With no map, however, we will be lost. The more detailed a map is the more fully it will reflect reality. An extremely detailed map, however, will not be useful for many purposes. If we wish to get from one big city to another on a major expressway, we do not need and may find confusing a map which includes much information unrelated to automotive transportation and in which the major highways are lost in a complex mass of secondary roads. A map, on the other hand, which had only one expressway on it would eliminate much reality and limit our ability to find alternative routes if the expressway were blocked by a major accident. In short, we need a map that both portrays reality and simplifies reality in a way that best serves our purposes. Several maps or paradigms of world politics were advanced at the end of the Cold War.

One World: Euphoria and Harmony. One widely articulated paradigm was based on the assumption that the end of the Cold War meant the end of significant conflict in global politics and the emergence of one relatively harmonious world. The most widely discussed formulation of this model was the "end of history" thesis advanced by Francis Fukuyama.* "We may be witnessing," Fukuyama argued, ". . . the end of history as such: that is, the end point of mankind's ideological evolution and the universalization of Western liberal democracy as the final form of human government." To be sure, he said, some conflicts may happen in places in the Third World, but the global conflict is over, and not just in Europe. "It is precisely in the non-European world" that the big changes have occurred, particularly in China and the Soviet Union. The war of ideas is at an end. Believers in Marxist-Leninism may still exist "in places like Managua, Pyongyang, and Cambridge, Massachusetts," but overall liberal democracy has triumphed. The future will be devoted not to great exhilarating struggles over ideas but rather to resolving mundane economic and technical problems. And, he concluded rather sadly, it will all be rather boring.[6]

The expectation of harmony was widely shared. Political and intellectual leaders elaborated similar views. The Berlin wall had come down, communist regimes had collapsed, the United Nations was to assume a new importance, the former Cold War rivals would engage in "partnership" and a "grand bargain," peacekeeping and peacemaking would be the order of the day. The President of the world's leading country proclaimed the "new world order"; the president of, arguably, the world's leading university vetoed appointment of a professor of security studies because the need had disappeared: "Hallelujah! We study war no more because war is no more."

The moment of euphoria at the end of the Cold War generated an illusion of harmony, which was soon revealed to be exactly that. The world became different in the early 1990s, but not necessarily more peaceful. Change was inevitable; progress was not. Similar illusions of harmony flourished, briefly, at

* A parallel line of argument based not on the end of the Cold/War but on long-term economic and social trends producing a "universal civilization" is discussed in chapter 3.

the end of each of the twentieth century's other major conflicts. World War I was the "war to end wars" and to make the world safe for democracy. World War II, as Franklin Roosevelt put it, would "end the system of unilateral action, the exclusive alliances, the balances of power, and all the other expedients that have been tried for centuries — and have always failed." Instead we will have "a universal organization" of "peace-loving Nations" and the beginnings of a "permanent structure of peace."[7] World War I, however, generated communism, fascism, and the reversal of a century-old trend toward democracy. World War II produced a Cold War that was truly global. The illusion of harmony at the end of that Cold War was soon dissipated by the multiplication of ethnic conflicts and "ethnic cleansing," the breakdown of law and order, the emergence of new patterns of alliance and conflict among states, the resurgence of neo-communist and neo-fascist movements, intensification of religious fundamentalism, the end of the "diplomacy of smiles" and "policy of yes" in Russia's relations with the West, the inability of the United Nations and the United States to suppress bloody local conflicts, and the increasing assertiveness of a rising China. In the five years after the Berlin wall came down, the word "genocide" was heard far more often than in any five years of the Cold War. The one harmonious world paradigm is clearly far too divorced from reality to be a useful guide to the post–Cold War world.

Two Worlds: Us and Them. While one-world expectations appear at the end of major conflicts, the tendency to think in terms of two worlds recurs throughout human history. People are always tempted to divide people into us and them, the in-group and the other, our civilization and those barbarians. Scholars have analyzed the world in terms of the Orient and the Occident, North and South, center and periphery. Muslims have traditionally divided the world into *Dar al-Islam* and *Dar al-Harb*, the abode of peace and the abode of war. This distinction was reflected, and in a sense reversed, at the end of the Cold War by American scholars who divided the world into "zones of peace" and "zones of turmoil." The former included the West and Japan with about 15 percent of the world's population, the latter everyone else.[8]

Depending upon how the parts are defined, a two-part world picture may in some measure correspond with reality. The most common division, which appears under various names, is between rich (modern, developed) countries and poor (traditional, undeveloped or developing) countries. Historically correlating with this economic division is the cultural division between West and East, where the emphasis is less on differences in economic well-being and more on differences in underlying philosophy, values, and way of life.[9] Each of these images reflects some elements of reality yet also suffers limitations. Rich modern countries share characteristics which differentiate them from poor traditional countries, which also share characteristics. Differences in wealth may lead to conflicts between societies, but the evidence suggests that this happens primarily when rich and more powerful societies attempt to conquer and colonize poor and more traditional societies. The West did this for four hundred years, and then some of the colonies rebelled and waged wars of liberation against the colonial powers, who may well have lost the will to empire. In the current world, decolonization has occurred and colonial wars of liberation have been replaced by conflicts among the liberated peoples.

At a more general level, conflicts between rich and poor are unlikely because, except in special circumstances, the poor countries lack the political unity, economic power, and military capability to challenge the rich countries. Economic development in Asia and Latin America is blurring the simple dichotomy of haves and have-nots. Rich states may fight trade wars with each other; poor states may fight violent wars with each other; but an international class war between the poor South and the wealthy North is almost as far from reality as one happy harmonious world.

The cultural bifurcation of the world division is still less useful. At some level, the West is an entity. What, however, do non-Western societies have in common other than the fact that they are non-Western? Japanese, Chinese, Hindu, Muslim, and African civilizations share little in terms of religion, social structure, institutions, and prevailing values. The unity of the non-West and the East-West dichotomy are myths created by the West. These myths suffer the defects of the Orientalism which Edward Said appropriately criticized for promoting "the difference between the familiar (Europe, the West, 'us') and the strange (the Orient, the East, 'them')" and for assuming the inherent superiority of the former to the latter.[10] During the Cold War the world was, in considerable measure, polarized along an ideological spectrum. There is, however, no single cultural spectrum. The polarization of "East" and "West" culturally is in part another consequence of the universal but unfortunate practice of calling European civilization Western civilization. Instead of "East and West," it is more appropriate to speak of "the West and the rest," which at least implies the existence of many non-Wests. The world is too complex to be usefully envisioned for most purposes as simply divided economically between North and South or culturally between East and West.

184 States, More or Less. A third map of the post–Cold War world derives from what is often called the "realist" theory of international relations. According to this theory states are the primary, indeed, the only important actors in world affairs, the relation among states is one of anarchy, and hence to insure their survival and security, states invariably attempt to maximize their power. If one state sees another state increasing its power and thereby becoming a potential threat, it attempts to protect its own security by strengthening its power and/or by allying itself with other states. The interests and actions of the more or less 184 states of the post–Cold War world can be predicted from these assumptions.[11]

This "realist" picture of the world is a highly useful starting point for analyzing international affairs and explains much state behavior. States are and will remain the dominant entities in world affairs. They maintain armies, conduct diplomacy, negotiate treaties, fight wars, control international organizations, influence and in considerable measure shape production and commerce. The governments of states give priority to insuring the external security of their states (although they often may give higher priority to insuring their security as a government against internal threats). Overall this statist paradigm does provide a more realistic picture of and guide to global politics than the one- or two-world paradigms.

It also, however, suffers severe limitations.

It assumes all states perceive their interests in the same way and act in the same way. Its simple assumption that power is all is a starting point for understanding state behavior but does not get one very far. States define their interests in terms of power but also in terms of much else besides. States often, of course, attempt to balance power, but if that is all they did, Western European countries would have coalesced with the Soviet Union against the United States in the late 1940s. States respond primarily to perceived threats, and the Western European states then saw a political, ideological, and military threat from the East. They saw their interests in a way which would not have been predicted by classic realist theory. Values, culture, and institutions pervasively influence how states define their interests. The interests of states are also shaped not only by their domestic values and institutions but by international norms and institutions. Above and beyond their primal concern with security, different types of states define their interests in different ways. States with similar cultures and institutions will see common interest. Democratic states have commonalities with other democratic states and hence do not fight each other. Canada does not have to ally with another power to deter invasion by the United States.

At a basic level the assumptions of the statist paradigm have been true throughout history. They thus do not help us to understand how global politics after the Cold War will differ from global politics during and before the Cold War. Yet clearly there are differences, and states pursue their interests differently from one historical period to another. In the post–Cold War world, states increasingly define their interests in civilizational terms. They cooperate with and ally themselves with states with similar or common culture and are more often in conflict with countries of different culture. States define threats in terms of the intentions of other states, and those intentions and how they are perceived are powerfully shaped by cultural considerations. Publics and statesmen are less likely to see threats emerging from people they feel they understand and can trust because of shared language, religion, values, institutions, and culture. They are much more likely to see threats coming from states whose societies have different cultures and hence which they do not understand and feel they cannot trust. Now that a Marxist-Leninist Soviet Union no longer poses a threat to the Free World and the United States no longer poses a countering threat to the communist world, countries in both worlds increasingly see threats coming from societies which are culturally different.

While states remain the primary actors in world affairs, they also are suffering losses in sovereignty, functions, and power. International institutions now assert the right to judge and to constrain what states do in their own territory. In some cases, most notably in Europe, international institutions have assumed important functions previously performed by states, and powerful international bureaucracies have been created which operate directly on individual citizens. Globally there has been a trend for state governments to lose power also through devolution to substate, regional, provincial, and local political entities. In many states, including those in the developed world, regional movements exist promoting substantial autonomy or secession. State governments have in considerable measure lost the ability to control the flow of money in and out of their country and are having increasing difficulty controlling the flows of ideas, technology, goods, and people. State borders, in short, have become increasingly permeable. All these developments have led many to see the gradual end of the hard, "billiard ball" state, which purportedly has been the norm since the Treaty of Westphalia in 1648,[12] and the emergence of a varied, complex, multilayered international order more closely resembling that of medieval times.

Sheer Chaos. The weakening of states and the appearance of "failed states" contribute to a fourth image of a world in anarchy. This paradigm stresses: the breakdown of governmental authority; the breakup of states; the intensification of tribal, ethnic, and religious conflict; the emergence of international criminal mafias; refugees multiplying into the tens of millions; the proliferation of nuclear and other weapons of mass destruction; the spread of terrorism; the prevalence of massacres and ethnic cleansing. This picture of a world in chaos was convincingly set forth and summed up in the titles of two penetrating works published in 1993: *Out of Control* by Zbigniew Brzezinski and *Pandaemonium* by Daniel Patrick Moynihan.[13]

Like the states paradigm, the chaos paradigm is close to reality. It provides a graphic and accurate picture of much of what is going on in the world, and unlike the states paradigm, it highlights the significant changes in world politics that have occurred with the end of the Cold War. As of early 1993, for instance, an estimated 48 ethnic wars were occurring throughout the world, and 164 "territorial-ethnic claims and conflicts concerning borders" existed in the former Soviet Union, of which 30 had involved some form of armed conflict.[14] Yet it suffers even more than the states paradigm in being too close to reality. The world may be chaos but it is not totally without order. An image of universal and undifferentiated anarchy provides few clues for understanding the world, for ordering events and evaluating their importance, for predicting trends in the anarchy, for distinguishing among types of chaos and their possibly different causes and consequences, and for developing guidelines for governmental policy makers.

COMPARING WORLDS: REALISM, PARSIMONY, AND PREDICTIONS

Each of these four paradigms offers a somewhat different combination of realism and parsimony. Each also has its deficiencies and limitations. Conceivably these could be countered by combining paradigms, and positing, for instance, that the world is engaged in simultaneous processes of fragmentation and integration.[15] Both trends indeed exist, and a more complex model will more closely approximate reality than a simpler one. Yet this sacrifices parsimony for realism and, if pursued very far, leads to the rejection of all paradigms or theories. In addition, by embracing two simultaneous opposing trends, the fragmentation-integration model fails to set forth under what circumstances one trend will prevail and under what circumstances the other will. The challenge is to develop a paradigm that accounts for more crucial events and provides a better understanding of trends than other paradigms at a similar level of intellectual abstraction.

These four paradigms are also incompatible with each other. The world cannot be both one and fundamentally divided between East and West or North and South. Nor can the nation state be the base rock of international affairs if it is fragmenting and torn by proliferating civil strife. The world is either one, or two, or 184 states, or potentially an almost infinite number of tribes, ethnic groups, and nationalities.

Viewing the world in terms of seven or eight civilizations avoids many of these difficulties. It does not sacrifice reality to parsimony as do the one- and two-world paradigms; yet it also does not sacrifice parsimony to reality as the statist and chaos paradigms do. It provides an easily grasped and intelligible framework for understanding the world, distinguishing what is important from what is unimportant among the multiplying conflicts, predicting future developments, and providing guidelines for policy makers. It also builds on and incorporates elements of the other paradigms. It is more compatible with them than they are with each other. A civilizational approach, for instance, holds that:

- The forces of integration in the world are real and are precisely what are generating counterforces of cultural assertion and civilizational consciousness.
- The world is in some sense two, but the central distinction is between the West as the hitherto dominant civilization and all the others, which, however, have little if anything in common among them. The world, in short, is divided between a Western one and a non-Western many.
- Nation states are and will remain the most important actors in world affairs, but their interests, associations, and conflicts are increasingly shaped by cultural and civilizational factors.
- The world is indeed anarchical, rife with tribal and nationality conflicts, but the conflicts that pose the greatest dangers for stability are those between states or groups from different civilizations.

A civilizational paradigm thus sets forth a relatively simple but not too simple map for understanding what is going on in the world as the twentieth century ends. No paradigm, however, is good forever. The Cold War model of world politics was useful and relevant for forty years but became obsolete in the late 1980s, and at some point the civilizational paradigm will suffer a similar fate. For the contemporary period, however, it provides a useful guide for distinguishing what is more important from what is less important. Slightly less than half of the forty-eight ethnic conflicts in the world in early 1993, for example, were between groups from different civilizations. The civilizational perspective would lead the U.N. Secretary-General and the U.S. Secretary of State to concentrate their peacemaking efforts on these conflicts which have much greater potential than others to escalate into broader wars.

Paradigms also generate predictions, and a crucial test of a paradigm's validity and usefulness is the extent to which the predictions derived from it turn out to be more accurate than those from alternative paradigms. A statist paradigm, for instance, leads John Mearsheimer to predict that "the situation between Ukraine and Russia is ripe for the outbreak of security competition between them. Great powers that share a long and unprotected common border, like that between Russia and Ukraine, often lapse into competition driven by security fears. Russia and Ukraine might overcome this dynamic and learn to live together in harmony, but it would be unusual if they do."[16] A civilizational approach, on the other hand, emphasizes the close cultural, personal, and historical links between Russia and Ukraine and the intermingling of Russians and Ukrainians in both countries, and focuses instead on the civilizational fault line that divides Orthodox eastern Ukraine from Uniate western Ukraine, a central historical fact of long standing which, in keeping with the "realist" concept of states as unified and self-identified entities, Mearsheimer totally ignores. While a statist approach highlights the possibility of a Russian-Ukrainian war, a civilizational approach minimizes that and instead highlights the possibility of Ukraine splitting in half, a separation which cultural factors would lead one to predict might be more violent than that of Czechoslovakia but far less bloody than that of Yugoslavia. These different predictions, in turn, give rise to different policy priorities. Mearsheimer's statist prediction of possible war and Russian conquest of Ukraine leads him to support Ukraine's having nuclear weapons. A civilizational approach would encourage cooperation between Russia and Ukraine, urge Ukraine to give up its nuclear weapons, promote substantial economic assistance and other measures to help maintain Ukrainian unity and independence, and sponsor contingency planning for the possible breakup of Ukraine.

Many important developments after the end of the Cold War were compatible with the civilizational paradigm and could have been predicted from it. These include: the breakup of the Soviet Union and Yugoslavia; the wars going on in their former territories; the rise of religious fundamentalism throughout the world; the struggles within Russia, Turkey, and Mexico over their identity;

the intensity of the trade conflicts between the United States and Japan; the resistance of Islamic states to Western pressure on Iraq and Libya; the efforts of Islamic and Confucian states to acquire nuclear weapons and the means to deliver them; China's continuing role as an "outsider" great power; the consolidation of new democratic regimes in some countries and not in others; and the developing arms competition in East Asia.

The relevance of the civilizational paradigm to the emerging world is illustrated by the events fitting that paradigm which occurred during a six-month period in 1993:

• the continuation and intensification of the fighting among Croats, Muslims, and Serbs in the former Yugoslavia;

• the failure of the West to provide meaningful support to the Bosnian Muslims or to denounce Croat atrocities in the same way Serb atrocities were denounced;

• the unwillingness of Russia to join other U.N. Security Council members in getting the Serbs in Croatia to make peace with the Croatian government, and the offer of Iran and other Muslim nations to provide 18,000 troops to protect Bosnian Muslims;

• the intensification of the war between Armenians and Azeris, Turkish and Iranian demands that the Armenians surrender their conquests, the deployment of Turkish troops to and Iranian troops across the Azerbaijan border, and Russia's warning that the Iranian action contributes to "escalation of the conflict" and "pushes it to dangerous limits of internationalization";

• the continued fighting in central Asia between Russian troops and *mujahedeen* guerrillas;

• the confrontation at the Vienna Human Rights Conference between the West, led by U.S. Secretary of State Warren Christopher, denouncing "cultural relativism," and a coalition of Islamic and Confucian states rejecting "Western universalism";

• the refocusing in parallel fashion of Russian and NATO military planners on "the threat from the South";

• the voting, apparently almost entirely along civilizational lines, that gave the 2000 Olympics to Sydney rather than Beijing;

• the sale of missile components from China to Pakistan, the resulting imposition of U.S. sanctions against China, and the confrontation between China and the United States over the alleged shipment of nuclear technology to Iran;

• the breaking of the moratorium and the testing of a nuclear weapon by China, despite vigorous U.S. protests, and North Korea's refusal to participate further in talks on its own nuclear weapons program;

• the revelation that the U.S. State Department was following a "dual containment" policy directed at both Iran and Iraq;

• the announcement by the U.S. Defense Department of a new strategy of preparing for two "major regional conflicts," one against North Korea, the other against Iran or Iraq;

• the call by Iran's president for alliances with China and India so that "we can have the last word on international events";

• the new German legislation drastically curtailing the admission of refugees;

• the agreement between Russian President Boris Yeltsin and Ukrainian President Leonid Kravchuk on the disposition of the Black Sea fleet and other issues;

• the bombing of Baghdad by the United States, its virtually unanimous support by Western governments, and its condemnation by almost all Muslim governments as another example of the West's "double standard";

• the United States' listing Sudan as a terrorist state and indicting Egyptian Sheik Omar Abdel Rahman and his followers for conspiring "to levy a war of urban terrorism against the United States";

• the improved prospects for the eventual admission of Poland, Hungary, the Czech Republic, and Slovakia into NATO;

• the 1993 Russian parliamentary election which demonstrated that Russia was indeed a "torn" country with its population and elites uncertain whether they should join or challenge the West.

A comparable list of events demonstrating the relevance of the civilization paradigm could be compiled for almost any other six-month period in the early 1990s.

In the early years of the Cold War, the Canadian statesman Lester Pearson presciently pointed to the resurgence and vitality of non-Western societies. "It would be absurd," he warned, "to imagine that these new political societies coming to birth in the East will be replicas of those with which we in the West are familiar. The revival of these ancient civilizations will take new forms." Pointing out that international relations "for several centuries" had been the relations among the states of Europe, he argued that "the most far-reaching problems arise no longer between nations within a single civilization but between civilizations themselves."[17] The prolonged bipolarity of the Cold War delayed the developments which Pearson saw coming. The end of the Cold War released the cultural and civilizational forces which he identified in the 1950s, and a wide range of scholars and observers have recognized and highlighted the new role of these factors in global politics.[18] "[A]s far as anyone interested in the contemporary world is concerned," Fernand Braudel has sagely warned, "and even more so with regard to anyone wishing to act within it, it 'pays' to know how to make out, on a map of the world, which civilizations exist today, to be able to define their borders, their centers and peripheries, their provinces and the air one breathes there, the general and particular 'forms' existing and associating within them. Otherwise, what catastrophic blunders of perspective could ensue!"[19]

Chapter 2

●

Civilizations in History and Today

The Nature of Civilizations

Human history is the history of civilizations. It is impossible to think of the development of humanity in any other terms. The story stretches through generations of civilizations from ancient Sumerian and Egyptian to Classical and Mesoamerican to Christian and Islamic civilizations and through successive manifestations of Sinic and Hindu civilizations. Throughout history civilizations have provided the broadest identifications for people. As a result, the causes, emergence, rise, interactions, achievements, decline, and fall of civilizations have been explored at length by distinguished historians, sociologists, and anthropologists including, among others, Max Weber, Emile Durkheim, Oswald Spengler, Pitirim Sorokin, Arnold Toynbee, Alfred Weber, A. L. Kroeber, Philip Bagby, Carroll Quigley, Rushton Coulborn, Christopher Dawson, S. N. Eisenstadt, Fernand Braudel, William H. McNeill, Adda Bozeman, Immanuel Wallerstein, and Felipe Fernández-Armesto.[1] These and other writers have produced a voluminous, learned, and sophisticated literature devoted to the comparative analysis of civilizations. Differences in perspective, methodology, focus, and concepts pervade this literature. Yet broad agreement also exists on central propositions concerning the nature, identity, and dynamics of civilizations.

First, a distinction exists between civilization in the singular and civilizations in the plural. The idea of civilization was developed by eighteenth-century French thinkers as the opposite of the concept of "barbarism." Civilized society differed from primitive society because it was settled, urban, and literate. To be civilized was good, to be uncivilized was bad. The concept of civilization provided a standard by which to judge societies, and during the nineteenth century, Europeans devoted much intellectual, diplomatic, and political energy to elaborating the criteria by which non-European societies might be judged sufficiently "civilized" to be accepted as members of the European-dominated international system. At the same time, however, people increasingly spoke of civilizations in the plural. This meant "renunciation of a civilization defined as an ideal, or rather as the ideal" and a shift away from the assumption there was a single standard for what was civilized, "confined," in Braudel's phrase, "to a few privileged peoples or groups, humanity's 'elite.' " Instead there were many civilizations, each of which was civilized in its own way. Civilization in the singular, in short, "lost some of its cachet," and a civilization in the plural sense could in fact be quite uncivilized in the singular sense.[2]

Civilizations in the plural are the concern of this book. Yet the distinction between singular and plural retains relevance, and the idea of civilization in the singular has reappeared in the argument that there is a universal world civilization. This argument cannot be sustained, but it is useful to explore, as will be done in the final chapter of this book, whether or not civilizations are becoming more civilized.

Second, a civilization is a cultural entity, outside Germany. Nineteenth-century German thinkers drew a sharp distinction between civilization, which involved mechanics, technology, and material factors, and culture, which involved values, ideals, and the higher intellectual artistic, moral qualities of a society. This distinction has persisted in German thought but has not been accepted elsewhere. Some anthropologists have even reversed the relation and conceived of cultures as characteristic of primitive, unchanging, nonurban societies, while more complex, developed, urban, and dynamic societies are civilizations. These efforts to distinguish culture and civilization, however, have not caught on, and, outside Germany, there is overwhelming agreement with Braudel that it is "delusory to wish in the German way to separate *culture* from its foundation *civilization*."[3]

Civilization and culture both refer to the overall way of life of a people, and a civilization is a culture writ large. They both involve the "values, norms, institutions, and modes of thinking to which successive generations in a given society have attached primary importance."[4] A civilization is, for Braudel, "a space, a 'cultural area,' " "a collection of cultural characteristics and phenomena." Wallerstein defines it as "a particular concatenation of worldview, customs, structures, and culture (both material culture and high culture) which forms some kind of historical whole and which coexists (if not always simultaneously) with other varieties of this phenomenon." A civilization is, according to Dawson, the product of "a particular original process of cultural creativity which is the work of a particular people," while for Durkheim and Mauss, it is "a kind of moral milieu encompassing a certain number of nations, each national culture being only a particular form of the whole." To Spengler a civilization is "the inevitable *destiny* of the Culture . . . the most external and artificial states of which a species of developed humanity is capable . . . a conclusion, the thing-become succeeding the thing-becoming." Culture is the common theme in virtually every definition of civilization.[5]

The key cultural elements which define a civilization were set forth in classic form by the Athenians when they reassured the Spartans that they would not betray them to the Persians:

> For there are many and powerful considerations that forbid us to do so, even if we were inclined. First and chief, the images and dwellings of the gods, burnt and laid ruins: this we must needs avenge to the utmost of our power, rather than make terms with the man who has perpetrated such deeds. Secondly, the Grecian race being of the same blood and the same language, and the temples of the gods and sacrifices in common; and our similar customs; for the Athenians to become betrayers of these would not be well.

Blood, language, religion, way of life, were what the Greeks had in common and what distinguished them from the Persians and other non-Greeks.[6] Of all the objective elements which define civilizations, however, the most important usually is religion, as the Athenians emphasized. To a very large degree, the major civilizations in human history have been closely identified with the world's great religions; and people who share ethnicity and language but differ in religion may slaughter each other, as happened in Lebanon, the former Yugoslavia, and the Subcontinent.[7]

A significant correspondence exists between the division of people by cultural characteristics into civilizations and their division by physical characteristics into races. Yet civilization and race are not identical. People of the same race can be deeply divided by civilization; people of different races may be united by civilization. In particular, the great missionary religions, Christianity and Islam, encompass societies from a variety of races. The crucial distinctions among human groups concern their values, beliefs, institutions, and social structures, not their physical size, head shapes, and skin colors.

Third, civilizations are comprehensive, that is, none of their constituent units can be fully understood without reference to the encompassing civilization. Civilizations, Toynbee argued, "comprehend without being comprehended by others." A civilization is a "totality." Civilizations, Melko goes on to say,

> have a certain degree of integration. Their parts are defined by their relationship to each other and to the whole. If the civilization is composed of states, these states will have more relation to one another than they do to states outside the civilization. They might fight more, and engage more frequently in diplomatic relations. They will be more interdependent economically. There will be pervading aesthetic and philosophical currents.[8]

A civilization is the broadest cultural entity. Villages, regions, ethnic groups, nationalities, religious groups, all have distinct cultures at different levels of cultural heterogeneity. The culture of a village in southern Italy may be different from that of a village in northern Italy, but both will share in a common Italian culture that distinguishes them from German villages. European communities, in turn, will share cultural features that distinguish them from Chinese or Hindu communities. Chinese, Hindus, and Westerners, however, are not part of any broader cultural entity. They constitute civilizations. A civilization is thus the highest cultural grouping of people and the broadest level of cultural identity people have short of that which distinguishes humans from other species. It is defined both by common objective elements, such as language, history, religion, customs, institutions, and by the subjective self-identification of people. People have levels of identity: a resident of Rome may define himself with varying degrees of intensity as a Roman, an Italian, a Catholic, a Christian, a European, a Westerner. The civilization to which he belongs is the broadest level of identification with which he strongly identifies. Civilizations are the biggest "we" within which we feel culturally at home as distinguished from all the other "thems" out there. Civilizations may involve a large number of people, such as Chinese civilization, or a very small number of people, such as the Anglophone Caribbean. Throughout history, many small groups of people have existed possessing a distinct culture and lacking any broader cultural identification. Distinctions have been made in terms of size and importance between major and peripheral civilizations (Bagby) or major and arrested or abortive civilizations (Toynbee). This book is concerned with what are generally considered the major civilizations in human history.

Civilizations have no clear-cut boundaries and no precise beginnings and endings. People can and do redefine their identities and, as a result, the composition and shapes of civilizations change over time. The cultures of peoples interact and overlap. The extent to which the cultures of civilizations resemble or differ from each other also varies considerably. Civilizations are nonetheless meaningful entities, and while the lines between them are seldom sharp, they are real.

Fourth, civilizations are mortal but also very long-lived; they evolve, adapt, and are the most enduring of human associations, "realities of the extreme *longue duree*." Their "unique and particular essence" is "their long historical continuity. Civilization is in fact the longest story of all." Empires rise and fall, governments come and go, civilizations remain and "survive political, social, economic, even ideological upheavals."[9] "International history," Bozeman concludes, "rightly documents the thesis that political systems are transient expedients on the surface of civilization, and that the destiny of each linguistically and morally unified community depends ultimately upon the survival of certain primary structuring ideas around which successive generations have coalesced and which thus symbolize the society's continuity."[10] Virtually all the major civilizations in the world in the twentieth century either have existed for a millennium or, as with Latin America, are the immediate offspring of another long-lived civilization.

While civilizations endure, they also evolve. They are dynamic; they rise and fall; they merge and divide; and as any student of history knows, they also disappear and are buried in the sands of time. The phases of their evolution may be specified in various ways. Quigley sees civilizations moving through seven stages: mixture, gestation, expansion, age of conflict, universal empire, decay, and invasion. Melko generalizes a model of change from a crystallized feudal system to a feudal system in transition to a crystallized state system to a state system in transition to a crystallized imperial system. Toynbee sees a civilization arising as a response to challenges and then going through a period of growth involving increasing control over its environment produced by a creative minority, followed by a time of troubles, the rise of a universal state, and then disintegration. While significant differences exist, all these theories see civilizations evolving through a time of troubles or conflict to a universal state to decay and disintegration.[11]

Fifth, since civilizations are cultural not political entities, they do not, as such, maintain order, establish justice, collect taxes, fight wars, negotiate treaties, or do any of the other things which governments do. The political composition of civilizations varies between civilizations and varies over time within a civilization. A civilization may thus contain one or many political units. Those units may be city states, empires, federations, confederations, nation states, multinational states, all of which may have varying forms of government. As a civilization evolves, changes normally occur in the number and nature of its constituent political units. At one extreme, a civilization and a political entity may coincide. China, Lucian Pye has commented, is "a civilization pretending to be a state."[12] Japan is a civilization that *is* a state. Most civilizations, however, contain more than one state or other political entity. In the modern world, most civilizations contain two or more states.

Finally, scholars generally agree in their identification of the major civilizations in history and on those that exist in the modern world. They often differ, however, on the total number of civilizations that have existed in history. Quigley argues for sixteen clear historical cases and very probably eight additional ones. Toynbee first placed the number at twenty-one, then twenty-three; Spengler specifies eight major cultures. McNeill discusses nine civilizations in all of history; Bagby also sees nine major civilizations or eleven if Japan and Orthodoxy are distinguished from China and the West. Braudel identifies nine and Rostovanyi seven major contemporary ones.[13] These differences in part depend on whether cultural groups such as the Chinese and the Indians are thought to have had a single civilization throughout history or two or more closely related civilizations, one of which was the offspring of the other. Despite these differences, the identity of the major civilizations is not contested. "Reasonable agreement," as Melko concludes after reviewing the literature, exists on at least twelve major civilizations, seven of which no longer exist (Mesopotamian, Egyptian, Cretan, Classical, Byzantine, Middle American, Andean) and five which do (Chinese, Japanese, Indian, Islamic, and Western).[14] To these five civilizations it is useful in the contemporary world to add Orthodox Latin American, and, possibly, African civilizations.

The major contemporary civilizations are thus as follows:

Sinic. All scholars recognize the existence of either a single distinct Chinese civilization dating back at least to 1500 B.C. and perhaps to a thousand years earlier, or of two Chinese civilizations one succeeding the other in the early centuries of the Christian epoch. In my *Foreign Affairs* article, I labeled this civilization Confucian. It is more accurate, however, to use the term Sinic. While Confucianism is a major component of Chinese civilization, Chinese civilization is more than Confucianism and also transcends China as a political entity. The term "Sinic," which has been used by many scholars, appropriately describes the common culture of China and the Chinese communities in Southeast Asia and elsewhere outside of China as well as the related cultures of Vietnam and Korea.

Japanese. Some scholars combine Japanese and Chinese culture under the heading of a single Far Eastern civilization. Most, however, do not and instead recognize Japan as a distinct civilization which was the offspring of Chinese civilization, emerging during the period between A.D. 100 and 400.

Hindu. One or more successive civilizations, it is universally recognized, have existed on the Subcontinent since at least 1500 B.C. These are generally referred to as Indian, Indic, or Hindu, with the latter term being preferred for the most recent civilization. In one form or another, Hinduism has been central to the culture of the Subcontinent since the second millennium B.C. "[M]ore than a religion or a social system; it is the core of Indian civilization."[15] It has continued in this role through modern times, even though India itself has a substantial Muslim community as well as several smaller cultural minorities. Like Sinic, the term Hindu also separates the name of the civilization from the name of its core state, which is desirable when, as in these cases, the culture of the civilization extends beyond that state.

Islamic. All major scholars recognize the existence of a distinct Islamic civilization. Originating in the Arabian peninsula in the seventh century A.D., Islam rapidly spread across North Africa and the Iberian peninsula and also eastward into central Asia, the Subcontinent, and Southeast Asia. As a result, many distinct cultures or subcivilizations exist within Islam, including Arab, Turkic, Persian, and Malay.

Orthodox. Several scholars distinguish a separate Orthodox civilization, centered in Russia and separate from Western Christendom as a result of its Byzantine parentage, distinct religion, 200 years of Tatar rule, bureaucratic

[margin note: Modern Civilz. Views]

despotism, and limited exposure to the Renaissance, Reformation, Enlightenment, and other central Western experiences.

Western. Western civilization is usually dated as emerging about A.D. 700 or
800. It is generally viewed by scholars as having three major components, in
Europe, North America, and Latin America.

Latin American. Latin America, however, has a distinct identity which differ-
entiates it from the West. Although an offspring of European civilization, Latin
America has evolved along every different path from Europe and North
America. It has had a corporatist, authoritarian culture, which Europe had to
a much lesser degree and North America not at all. Europe and North America
both felt the effects of the Reformation and have combined Catholic and
Protestant cultures. Historically, although this may be changing, Latin America
has been only Catholic. Latin American civilization incorporates indigenous
cultures, which did not exist in Europe, were effectively wiped out in North
America, and which vary in importance from Mexico, Central America, Peru,
and Bolivia, on the one hand, to Argentina and Chile, on the other. Latin
American political evolution and economic development have differed
sharply from the patterns prevailing in the North Atlantic countries. Subjec-
tively, Latin Americans themselves are divided in their self-identifications.
Some say, "Yes, we are part of the West." Others claim, "No, we have our
own unique culture," and a large literature by Latin and North Americans
elaborates their cultural differences.[16] Latin America could be considered either
a subcivilization within Western civilization or a separate civilization closely
affiliated with the West and divided as to whether it belongs in the West. For
an analysis focused on the international political implications of civilizations,
including the relations between Latin America, on the one hand, and North
America and Europe, on the other, the latter is the more appropriate and useful
designation.

The West, then, includes Europe, North America, plus other European
settler countries such as Australia and New Zealand. The relation between the
two major components of the West has, however, changed over time. For
much of their history, Americans defined their society in opposition to Europe.
America was the land of freedom, equality, opportunity, the future; Europe
represented oppression, class conflict, hierarchy, backwardness. America, it was
even argued, was a distinct civilization. This positing of an opposition between
America and Europe was, in considerable measure, a result of the fact that at
least until the end of the nineteenth century America had only limited contacts
with non-Western civilizations. Once the United States moved out on the world
scene, however, the sense of a broader identity with Europe developed.[17] While
nineteenth-century America defined itself as different from and opposed to
Europe, twentieth-century America has defined itself as a part of and, indeed,
the leader of a broader entity, the West, that includes Europe.

The term "the West" is now universally used to refer to what used to be
called Western Christendom. The West is thus the only civilization identified

by a compass direction and not by the name of a particular people, religion, or geographical area.* This identification lifts the civilization out of its historical, geographical, and cultural context. Historically, Western civilization is European civilization. In the modern era, Western civilization is Euroamerican or North Atlantic civilization. Europe, America, and the North Atlantic can be found on a map; the West cannot. The name "the West" has also given rise to the concept of "Westernization" and has promoted a misleading conflation of Westernization and modernization: it is easier to conceive of Japan "Westernizing" than "Euroamericanizing." European-American civilization is, however, universally referred to as Western civilization, and that term, despite its serious disabilities, will be used here.

African (possibly). Most major scholars of civilization except Braudel do not recognize a distinct African civilization. The north of the African continent and its east coast belong to Islamic civilization. Historically, Ethiopia constituted a civilization of its own. Elsewhere European imperialism and settlements brought elements of Western civilization. In South Africa Dutch, French, and then English settlers created a multifragmented European culture.[18] Most significantly, European imperialism brought Christianity to most of the continent south of the Sahara. Throughout Africa tribal identities are pervasive and intense, but Africans are also increasingly developing a sense of African identity, and conceivably sub-Saharan Africa could cohere into a distinct civilization, with South Africa possibly being its core state.

Religion is a central defining characteristic of civilizations, and, as Christopher Dawson said, "the great religions are the foundations on which the great civilizations rest."[19] Of Weber's five "world religions," four — Christianity, Islam, Hinduism, and Confucianism — are associated with major civilizations. The fifth, Buddhism, is not. Why is this the case? Like Islam and Christianity, Buddhism early separated into two main subdivisions, and, like Christianity, it did not survive in the land of its birth. Beginning in the first century A.D., Mahayana Buddhism was exported to China and subsequently to Korea, Vietnam, and Japan. In these societies, Buddhism was variously adapted, assimilated to the indigenous culture (in China, for example, to Confucianism and Taoism), and suppressed. Hence, while Buddhism remains an important component of their cultures, these societies do not constitute and would not identify themselves as part of a Buddhist civilization. What can legitimately be de-

---

* The use of "East" and "West" to identify geographical areas is confusing and ethnocentric. "North" and "south" have universally accepted fixed reference points in the poles. "East" and "west" have no such reference points. The question is: east and west of what? It all depends on where you stand. "West" and "East" presumably originally referred to the western and eastern parts of Eurasia. From an American viewpoint, however, the Far East is actually the Far West. For most of Chinese history the West meant India, whereas "In Japan 'the West' usually meant China." William E. Naff, "Reflections on the Question of 'East and West' from the Point of View of Japan," *Comparative Civilizations Review*, 13–14 (Fall 1985 & Spring 1986), 228.

scribed as a Therevada Buddhist civilization, however, does exist in Sri Lanka, Burma, Thailand, Laos, and Cambodia. In addition, the populations of Tibet, Mongolia, and Bhutan have historically subscribed to the Lamaist variant of Mahayana Buddhism, and these societies constitute a second area of Buddhist civilization. Overall, however, the virtual extinction of Buddhism in India and its adaptation and incorporation into existing cultures in China and Japan mean that Buddhism, although a major religion, has not been the basis of a major civilization.[20] *

RELATIONS AMONG CIVILIZATIONS

Encounters: Civilizations Before A.D. 1500. The relations among civilizations have evolved through two phases and are now in a third. For more than three thousand years after civilizations first emerged, the contacts among them were, with some exceptions, either nonexistent or limited or intermittent and intense. The nature of these contacts is well expressed in the word historians use to describe them: "encounters."[21] Civilizations were separated by time and space. Only a small number existed at any one time, and a significant difference exists, as Benjamin Schwartz and Shmuel Eisenstadt argued, between Axial Age and pre-Axial Age civilizations in terms of whether or not they recognized a distinction between the "transcendental and mundane orders." The Axial Age civilizations, unlike their predecessors, had transcendental myths propagated by a distinct intellectual class: "the Jewish prophets and priests, the Greek philosophers and sophists, the Chinese Literati, the Hindu Brahmins, the Buddhist Sangha and the Islamic Ulema."[22] Some regions witnessed two or three generations of affiliated civilizations, with the demise of one civilization and interregnum followed by the rise of another successor generation. Figure 2.1 is a simplified chart (reproduced from Carroll Quigley) of the relations among major Eurasian civilizations through time.

Civilizations were also separated geographically. Until 1500 the Andean and Mesoamerican civilizations had no contact with other civilizations or with each

---

* What about Jewish civilization? Most scholars of civilization hardly mention it. In terms of numbers of people Judaism clearly is not a major civilization. Toynbee describes it as an arrested civilization which evolved out of the earlier Syriac civilization. It is historically affiliated with both Christianity and Islam, and for several centuries Jews maintained their cultural identity within Western, Orthodox, and Islamic civilizations. With the creation of Israel, Jews have all the objective accoutrements of a civilization: religion, language, customs, literature, institutions, and a territorial and political home. But what about subjective identification? Jews living in other cultures have distributed themselves along a continuum stretching from total identification with Judaism and Israel to nominal Judaism and full identification with the civilization within which they reside, the latter, however, occurring primarily among Jews living in the West. See Mordecai M. Kaplan, *Judaism as a Civilization* (Philadelphia: Reconstructionist Press, 1981; originally published 1934), esp. 173–208.

other. The early civilizations in the valleys of the Nile, Tigris-Euphrates, Indus, and Yellow rivers also did not interact. Eventually, contacts between civilizations did multiply in the eastern Mediterranean, southwestern Asia, and northern India. Communications and commercial relations were restricted, however, by the distances separating civilizations and the limited means of transport available to overcome distance. While there was some commerce by sea in the Mediterranean and Indian Ocean, "Steppe-traversing horses, not ocean-traversing sailing ships, were the sovereign means of locomotion by which the separate civilizations of the world as it was before A.D. 1500 were linked together — to the slight extent to which they did maintain contact with each other."[23]

Ideas and technology moved from civilization to civilization, but it often took centuries. Perhaps the most important cultural diffusion not the result of conquest was the spread of Buddhism to China, which occurred about six hundred years after its origin in northern India. Printing was invented in China in the eighth century A.D. and movable type in the eleventh century, but this technology only reached Europe in the fifteenth century. Paper was introduced into China in the second century A.D., came to Japan in the seventh century, and was diffused westward to Central Asia in the eighth century, North Africa in the tenth, Spain in the twelfth, and northern Europe in the thirteenth. Another Chinese invention, gunpowder, made in the ninth century, disseminated to the Arabs a few hundred years later, and reached Europe in the fourteenth century.[24]

FIGURE 2.1
EASTERN HEMISPHERE CIVILIZATIONS

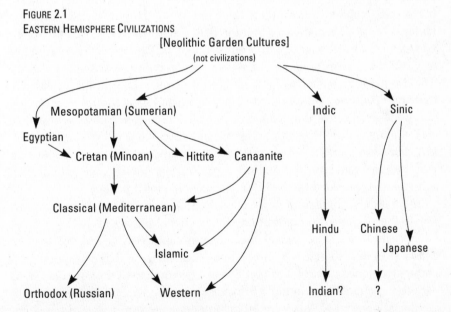

Source: Carroll Quigley, *The Evolution of Civilizations: An Introduction to Historical Analysis* (Indianapolis: Liberty Press, 2nd ed., 1979), p. 83.

The most dramatic and significant contacts between civilizations were when people from one civilization conquered and eliminated or subjugated the people of another. These contacts normally were not only violent but brief, and they occurred only intermittently. Beginning in the seventh century A.D., relatively sustained and at times intense intercivilizational contacts did develop between Islam and the West and Islam and India. Most commercial, cultural, and military interactions, however, were within civilizations. While India and China, for instance, were on occasion invaded and subjected by other peoples (Moguls, Mongols), both civilizations also had extensive times of "warring states" within their own civilization. Similarly, the Greeks fought each other and traded with each other far more often than they did with Persians or other non-Greeks.

Impact: The Rise of the West. European Christendom began to emerge as a distinct civilization in the eighth and ninth centuries. For several hundred years, however, it lagged behind many other civilizations in its level of civilization. China under the T'ang, Sung, and Ming dynasties, the Islamic world from the eighth to the twelfth centuries, and Byzantium from the eighth to the eleventh centuries far surpassed Europe in wealth, territory, military power, and artistic, literary, and scientific achievement.[25] Between the eleventh and thirteenth centuries, European culture began to develop, facilitated by the "eager and systematic appropriation of suitable elements from the higher civilizations of Islam and Byzantium, together with adaptation of this inheritance to the special conditions and interests of the West." During the same period, Hungary, Poland, Scandinavia, and the Baltic coast were converted to Western Christianity, with Roman law and other aspects of Western civilization following, and the eastern boundary of Western civilization was stabilized where it would remain thereafter without significant change. During the twelfth and thirteenth centuries Westerners struggled to expand their control in Spain and did establish effective dominance of the Mediterranean. Subsequently, however, the rise of Turkish power brought about the collapse of "Western Europe's first overseas empire."[26] Yet by 1500, the renaissance of European culture was well under way and social pluralism, expanding commerce, and technological achievements provided the basis for a new era in global politics.

Intermittent or limited multidirectional encounters among civilizations gave way to the sustained, overpowering, unidirectional impact of the West on all other civilizations. The end of the fifteenth century witnessed the final reconquest of the Iberian peninsula from the Moors and the beginnings of Portuguese penetration of Asia and Spanish penetration of the Americas. During the subsequent two hundred fifty years all of the Western Hemisphere and significant portions of Asia were brought under European rule or domination. The end of the eighteenth century saw a retraction of direct European control as first the United States, then Haiti, and then most of Latin America revolted against European rule and achieved independence. In the latter part of the nineteenth century, however, renewed Western imperialism extended Western rule over almost all of Africa, consolidated Western control in the Subcontinent and elsewhere in Asia, and by the early twentieth century subjected virtually the entire Middle East except for Turkey to direct or indirect Western control. Europeans or former European colonies (in the Americas) controlled 35 percent of the earth's land surface in 1800, 67 percent in 1878, and 84 percent in 1914. By 1920 the percentage was still higher as the Ottoman Empire was divided up among Britain, France, and Italy. In 1800 the British Empire consisted of 1.5 million square miles and 20 million people. By 1900 the Victorian empire upon which the sun never set included 11 million square miles and 390 million people.[27] In the course of European expansion, the Andean and Mesoamerican civilizations were effectively eliminated, Indian and Islamic civilizations along with Africa were subjugated, and China was penetrated and subordinated to Western influence. Only Russian, Japanese, and Ethiopian civilizations, all three governed by highly centralized imperial authorities, were able to resist the onslaught of the West and maintain meaningful independent existence. For four hundred years intercivilizational relations consisted of the subordination of other societies to Western civilization.

The causes of this unique and dramatic development included the social structure and class relations of the West, the rise of cities and commerce, the relative dispersion of power in Western societies between estates and monarchs and secular and religious authorities, the emerging sense of national consciousness among Western peoples, and the development of state bureaucracies. The immediate source of Western expansion, however, was technological: the invention of the means of ocean navigation for reaching distant peoples and the development of the military capabilities for conquering those peoples. "[I]n large measure," as Geoffrey Parker has observed, " 'the rise of the West' depended upon the exercise of force, upon the fact that the military balance between the Europeans and their adversaries overseas was steadily tilting in favour of the former; . . . the key to the Westerners' success in creating the first truly global empires between 1500 and 1750 depended upon precisely those improvements in the ability to wage war which have been termed 'the military revolution.' " The expansion of the West was also facilitated by the superiority in organization, discipline, and training of its troops and subsequently by the superior weapons, transport, logistics, and medical services resulting from its leadership in the Industrial Revolution.[28] The West won the world not by the superiority of its ideas or values or religion (to which few members of other civilizations were converted) but rather by its superiority in applying organized violence. Westerners often forget this fact; non-Westerners never do.

By 1910 the world was more one politically and economically than at any other time in human history. International trade as a proportion of the gross world product was higher than it had ever been before and would not again approximate until the 1970s and 1980s. International investment as a percentage of total investment was higher then than at any other time.[29] Civilization meant Western civilization. International law was Western international law coming out of the tradition of Grotius. The international system was the Western Westphalian system of sovereign but "civilized" nation states and the colonial territories they controlled.

The emergence of this Western-defined international system was the second major development in global politics in the centuries after 1500. In addition to interacting in a domination-subordination mode with non-Western societies, Western societies also interacted on a more equal basis with each other. These interactions among political entities within a single civilization closely resembled those that had occurred within Chinese, Indian, and Greek civilizations. They were based on a cultural homogeneity which involved "language, law, religion, administrative practice, agriculture, landholding, and perhaps kinship as well." European peoples "shared a common culture and maintained extensive contacts via an active network of trade, a constant movement of persons, and a tremendous interlocking of ruling families." They also fought each other virtually without end; among European states peace was the exception not the rule.[30] Although for much of this period the Ottoman empire controlled up to one-fourth of what was often thought of as Europe, the empire was not considered a member of the European international system.

For 150 years the intracivilizational politics of the West was dominated by the great religious schism and by religious and dynastic wars. For another century and a half following the Treaty of Westphalia, the conflicts of the Western world were largely among princes — emperors, absolute monarchs, and constitutional monarchs attempting to expand their bureaucracies, their armies, their mercantilist economic strength, and, most important, the territory they ruled. In the process they created nation states, and beginning with the French Revolution the principal lines of conflict were between nations rather than princes. In 1793 as R. R. Palmer put it, "The wars of kings were over; the wars of peoples had begun."[31] This nineteenth-century pattern lasted until World War I.

In 1917, as a result of the Russian Revolution, the conflict of nation states was supplemented by the conflict of ideologies, first among fascism, communism, and liberal democracy and then between the latter two. In the Cold War these ideologies were embodied in the two superpowers, each of which defined its identity by its ideology and neither of which was a nation state in the traditional European sense. The coming to power of Marxism first in Russia and then in China and Vietnam represented a transition phase from the European international system to a post-European multicivilizational system. Marxism was a product of European civilization, but it neither took root nor succeeded there. Instead modernizing and revolutionary elites imported it into non-Western societies; Lenin, Mao, and Ho adapted it to their purposes and used it to challenge Western power, to mobilize their people, and to assert the national identity and autonomy of their countries against the West. The collapse of this ideology in the Soviet Union and its substantial adaptation in China and Vietnam does not, however, necessarily mean that these societies will import the other Western ideology of liberal democracy. Westerners who assume that it does are likely to be surprised by the creativity, resilience, and individuality of non-Western cultures.

Interactions: A Multicivilizational System. In the twentieth century the relations among civilizations have thus moved from a phase dominated by the unidirectional impact of one civilization on all others to one of intense, sustained, and multidirectional interactions among all civilizations. Both of the central characteristics of the previous era of intercivilizational relations began to disappear.

First, in the favorite phrases of historians, "the expansion of the West" ended and "the revolt against the West" began. Unevenly and with pauses and reversals, Western power declined relative to the power of other civilizations. The map of the world in 1990 bore little resemblance to the map of the world in 1920. The balances of military and economic power and of political influence shifted (and will be explored in greater detail in a later chapter). The West continued to have significant impacts on other societies, but increasingly the relations between the West and other civilizations were dominated by the reactions of the West to developments in those civilizations. Far from being simply the objects of Western-made history, non-Western societies were increasingly becoming the movers and shapers of their own history and of Western history.

Second, as a result of these developments, the international system expanded beyond the West and became multicivilizational. Simultaneously, conflict among Western states — which had dominated that system for centuries — faded away. By the late twentieth century, the West has moved out of its "warring state" phase of development as a civilization and toward its "universal state" phase. At the end of the century, this phase is still incomplete as the nation states of the West cohere into two semiuniversal states in Europe and North America. These two entities and their constituent units are, however, bound together by an extraordinarily complex network of formal and informal institutional ties. The universal states of previous civilizations are empires. Since democracy, however, is the political form of Western civilization, the emerging universal state of Western civilization is not an empire but rather a compound of federations, confederations, and international regimes and organizations.

The great political ideologies of the twentieth century include liberalism, socialism, anarchism, corporatism, Marxism, communism, social democracy, conservatism, nationalism, fascism, and Christian democracy. They all share one thing in common: they are products of Western civilization. No other civilization has generated a significant political ideology. The West, however, has never generated a major religion. The great religions of the world are all products of non-Western civilizations and, in most cases, antedate Western civilization. As the world moves out of its Western phase, the ideologies which typified late Western civilization decline, and their place is taken by religions and other culturally based forms of identity and commitment. The Westphalian separation of religion and international politics, an idiosyncratic product of Western civilization, is coming to an end, and religion, as Edward Mortimer suggests, is "increasingly likely to intrude into international affairs."[32] The intracivilizational clash of political ideas spawned by the West is being supplanted by an intercivilizational clash of culture and religion.

Global political geography thus moved from the one world of 1920 to the three worlds of the 1960s to the more than half-dozen worlds of the 1990s. Concomitantly, the Western global empires of 1920 shrank to the much more limited "Free World" of the 1960s (which included many non-Western states opposed to communism) and then to the still more restricted "West" of the 1990s. This shift was reflected semantically between 1988 and 1993 in the decline in the use of the ideological term "Free World" and the increase in use of the civilizational term "the West" (see Table 2.1). It is also seen in increased references to Islam as a cultural-political phenomenon, "Greater China," Russia and its "near abroad," and the European Union, all terms with a civilizational content. Intercivilizational relations in this third phase are far more frequent and intense than they were in the first phase and far more equal and reciprocal than they were in the second phase. Also, unlike the Cold War, no single cleavage dominates, and multiple cleavages exist between the West and other civilizations and among the many non-Wests.

An international system exists, Hedley Bull argued, "when two or more states have sufficient contact between them, and have sufficient impact on one another's decisions, to cause them to behave — at least in some measure — as parts of a whole." An international society, however, exists only when states in an international system have "common interests and common values," "conceive themselves to be bound by a common set of rules," "share in the working of common institutions," and have "a common culture or civilization."[33] Like its Sumerian, Greek, Hellenistic, Chinese, Indian, and Islamic predecessors, the European international system of the seventeenth to the nineteenth centuries was also an international society. During the nineteenth and twentieth centuries the European international system expanded to encompass virtually all societies in other civilizations. Some European institutions and practices were also exported to these countries. Yet these societies still lack the common culture that underlay European international society. In terms of British international relations theory, the world is thus a well-developed international system but at best only a very primitive international society.

Every civilization sees itself as the center of the world and writes its history

TABLE 2.1
USE OF TERMS
"FREE WORLD" AND "THE WEST"

	Number of References 1988	1993	% Change in References
New York Times			
Free World	71	44	−38
The West	46	144	+213
Washington Post			
Free World	112	67	−40
The West	36	87	+142
Congressional Record			
Free World	356	114	−68
The West	7	10	+43

Source: *Lexis/Nexis*. Reference numbers are numbers of stories about or containing the terms "free world" or "the West." References to "the West" were reviewed for contextual appropriateness to insure that the term referred to "the West" as a civilization or political entity.

as the central drama of human history. This has been perhaps even more true of the West than of other cultures. Such monocivilizational viewpoints, however, have decreasing relevance and usefulness in a multicivilizational world. Scholars of civilizations have long recognized this truism. In 1918 Spengler denounced the myopic view of history prevailing in the West with its neat division into ancient, medieval, and modern phases relevant only to the West. It is necessary, he said, to replace this "Ptolemaic approach to history" with a Copernican one and to substitute for the "empty figment of one *linear* history, the drama of a *number* of mighty cultures."[34] A few decades later Toynbee castigated the "parochialism and impertinence" of the West manifested in the "egocentric illusions" that the world revolved around it, that there was an "unchanging East," and that "progress" was inevitable. Like Spengler he had no use for the assumption of the unity of history, the assumption that there is "only one river of civilization, our own, and that all others are either tributary to it or lost in the desert sands."[35] Fifty years after Toynbee, Braudel similarly urged the need to strive for a broader perspective and to understand "the great cultural conflicts in the world, and the multiplicity of its civilizations."[36] The illusions and prejudices of which these scholars warned, however, live on and in the late twentieth century have blossomed forth in the widespread and parochial conceit that the European civilization of the West is now the universal civilization of the world.

Chapter 3

•

A Universal Civilization? Modernization and Westernization

UNIVERSAL CIVILIZATION: MEANINGS

Some people argue that this era is witnessing the emergence of what V. S. Naipaul called a "universal civilization."[1] What is meant by this term? The idea implies in general the cultural coming together of humanity and the increasing acceptance of common values, beliefs, orientations, practices, and institutions by peoples throughout the world. More specifically, the idea may mean some things which are profound but irrelevant, some which are relevant but not profound, and some which are irrelevant and superficial.

First, human beings in virtually all societies share certain basic values, such as murder is evil, and certain basic institutions, such as some form of the family. Most peoples in most societies have a similar "moral sense," a "thin" minimal morality of basic concepts of what is right and wrong.[2] If this is what is meant by universal civilization, it is both profound and profoundly important, but it is also neither new nor relevant. If people have shared a few fundamental values and institutions throughout history, this may explain some constants in human behavior but it cannot illuminate or explain history, which consists of changes in human behavior. In addition, if a universal civilization common to all humanity exists, what term do we then use to identify the major cultural groupings of humanity short of the human race? Humanity is divided into subgroups—tribes, nations, and broader cultural entities normally called civilizations. If the term civilization is elevated and restricted to what is common to humanity as a whole, either one has to invent a new term to refer to the largest cultural groupings of people short of humanity as a whole or one has to assume that these large but not-humanity-wide groupings evaporate. Vaclav Havel, for example, has argued that "we now live in a single global civilization," and that this "is no more than a thin veneer" that "covers or conceals the immense variety of cultures, of peoples, of religious worlds, of historical traditions and historically formed attitudes, all of which in a sense lie 'beneath' it."³ Only semantic confusion, however, is gained by restricting "civilization" to the global level and designating as "cultures" or "subcivilizations," those largest cultural entities which have historically always been called civilizations.*

Second, the term "universal civilization" could be used to refer to what civilized societies have in common, such as cities and literacy, which distinguish them from primitive societies and barbarians. This is, of course, the eighteenth century singular meaning of the term, and in this sense a universal civilization is emerging, much to the horror of various anthropologists and others who view with dismay the disappearance of primitive peoples. Civilization in this sense has been gradually expanding throughout human history, and the spread of civilization in the singular has been quite compatible with the existence of many civilizations in the plural.

Third, the term "universal civilization" may refer to the assumptions, values, and doctrines currently held by many people in Western civilization and by some people in other civilizations. This might be called the Davos Culture. Each year about a thousand businessmen, bankers, government officials, intellectuals, and journalists from scores of countries meet in the World Economic Forum in Davos, Switzerland. Almost all these people hold university degrees in the physical sciences, social sciences, business, or law, work with words and/ or numbers, are reasonably fluent in English, are employed by governments, corporations, and academic institutions with extensive international involvements, and travel frequently outside their own country. They generally share beliefs in individualism, market economies, and political democracy, which are also common among people in Western civilization. Davos people control virtually all international institutions, many of the world's governments, and the bulk of the world's economic and military capabilities. The Davos Culture hence is tremendously important. Worldwide, however, how many people share this culture? Outside the West, it is probably shared by less than 50 million people or 1 percent of the world's population and perhaps by as few as one-tenth of 1 percent of the world's population. It is far from a universal culture, and the leaders who share in the Davos Culture do not necessarily

* Hayward Alker has accurately pointed out that in my *Foreign Affairs* article I "definitionally disallowed" the idea of a world civilization by defining civilization as "the highest cultural grouping of people and the broadest level of cultural identity people have short of that which distinguishes humans from other species." This is, of course, the way the term has been used by most civilization scholars. In this chapter, however, I relax that definition to allow the possibility of peoples throughout the world identifying with a distinct global culture which supplements or supplants civilizations in the Western, Islamic, or Sinic sense.

have a secure grip on power in their own societies. This "common intellectual culture exists," as Hedley Bull pointed out, "only at the elite level: its roots are shallow in many societies . . . [and] it is doubtful whether, even at the diplomatic level, it embraces what was called a common moral culture or set of common values, as distinct from a common intellectual culture."[4]

Fourth, the idea is advanced that the spread of Western consumption patterns and popular culture around the world is creating a universal civilization. This argument is neither profound nor relevant. Cultural fads have been transmitted from civilization to civilization throughout history. Innovations in one civilization are regularly taken up by other civilizations. These are, however, either techniques lacking in significant cultural consequences or fads that come and go without altering the underlying culture of the recipient civilization. These imports "take" in the recipient civilization either because they are exotic or because they are imposed. In previous centuries the Western world was periodically swept by enthusiasms for various items of Chinese or Hindu culture. In the nineteenth century cultural imports from the West became popular in China and India because they seemed to reflect Western power. The argument now that the spread of pop culture and consumer goods around the world represents the triumph of Western civilization trivializes Western culture. The essence of Western civilization is the Magna Carta, not the Magna Mac. The fact that non-Westerners may bite into the latter has no implications for their accepting the former.

It also has no implications for their attitudes toward the West. Somewhere in the Middle East a half-dozen young men could well be dressed in jeans, drinking Coke, listening to rap, and, between their bows to Mecca, putting together a bomb to blow up an American airliner. During the 1970s and 1980s Americans consumed millions of Japanese cars, TV sets, cameras, and electronic gadgets without being "Japanized" and indeed while becoming considerably more antagonistic toward Japan. Only naive arrogance can lead Westerners to assume that non-Westerners will become "Westernized" by acquiring Western goods. What, indeed, does it tell the world about the West when Westerners identify their civilization with fizzy liquids, faded pants, and fatty foods?

A slightly more sophisticated version of the universal popular culture argument focuses not on consumer goods generally but on the media, on Hollywood rather than Coca-Cola. American control of the global movie, television, and video industries even exceeds its dominance of the aircraft industry. Eighty-eight of the hundred films most attended throughout the world in 1993 were American, and two American and two European organizations dominate the collection and dissemination of news on a global basis.[5] This situation reflects two phenomena. The first is the universality of human interest in love, sex, violence, mystery, heroism, and wealth, and the ability of profit-motivated companies, primarily American, to exploit those interests to their own advantage. Little or no evidence exists, however, to support the assumption that the emergence of pervasive global communications is producing significant convergence in attitudes and beliefs. "Entertainment," as Michael Vlahos has said, "does not equate to cultural conversion." Second, people interpret communications in terms of their own preexisting values and perspectives. "The same visual images transmitted simultaneously into living rooms across the globe," Kishore Mahbubani observes, "trigger opposing perceptions. Western living rooms applaud when cruise missiles strike Baghdad. Most living outside see that the West will deliver swift retribution to non-white Iraqis or Somalis but not to white Serbians, a dangerous signal by any standard."[6]

Global communications are one of the most important contemporary manifestations of Western power. This Western hegemony, however, encourages populist politicians in non-Western societies to denounce Western cultural imperialism and to rally their publics to preserve the survival and integrity of their indigenous culture. The extent to which global communications are dominated by the West is, thus, a major source of the resentment and hostility of non-Western peoples against the West. In addition, by the early 1990s modernization and economic development in non-Western societies were leading to the emergence of local and regional media industries catering to the distinctive tastes of those societies.[7] In 1994, for instance, CNN International estimated that it had an audience of 55 million potential viewers, or about 1 percent of the world's population (strikingly equivalent in number to and undoubtedly largely identical with the Davos Culture people), and its president predicated that its English broadcasts might eventually appeal to 2 to 4 percent of the market. Hence regional (i.e., civilizational) networks would emerge broadcasting in Spanish, Japanese, Arabic, French (for West Africa), and other languages. "The Global Newsroom," three scholars concluded, "is still confronted with a Tower of Babel."[8] Ronald Dore makes an impressive case for the emergence of a global intellectual culture among diplomats and public officials. Even he, however, comes to a highly qualified conclusion concerning the impact of intensified communications: "*other things being equal*[italics his], an increasing density of communication should ensure an increasing basis for fellow-feeling between the nations, or at least the middle classes, or at the very least the diplomats of the world," but, he adds, "some of the things that may not be equal can be very important indeed."[9]

Language. The central elements of any culture or civilization are language and religion. If a universal civilization is emerging, there should be tendencies toward the emergence of a universal language and a universal religion. This claim is often made with respect to language. "The world's language is English," as the editor of the *Wall Street Journal* put it.[10] This can mean two things, only one of which would support the case for a universal civilization. It could mean that an increasing proportion of the world's population speaks

English. No evidence exists to support this proposition, and the most reliable evidence that does exist, which admittedly cannot be very precise, shows just the opposite. The available data covering more than three decades (1958–1992) suggest that the overall pattern of language use in the world did not change dramatically, that significant declines occurred in the proportion of people speaking English, French, German, Russian, and Japanese, that a smaller decline occurred in the proportion speaking Mandarin, and that increases occurred in the proportions of people speaking Hindi, Malay-Indonesian, Arabic, Bengali, Spanish, Portuguese, and other languages. English speakers in the world dropped from 9.8 percent of the people in 1958 speaking languages spoken by at least 1 million people to 7.6 percent in 1992 (see Table 3.1). The proportion of the world's population speaking the five major Western languages (English, French, German, Portuguese, Spanish) declined from 24.1 percent in 1958 to 20.8 percent in 1992. In 1992 roughly twice as many people spoke Mandarin, 15.2 percent of the world's population, as spoke English, and an additional 3.6 percent spoke other versions of Chinese (see Table 3.2).

In one sense, a language foreign to 92 percent of the people in the world cannot be the world's language. In another sense, however, it could be so described, if it is the language which people from different language groups and cultures use to communicate with each other, if it is the world's lingua franca, or in linguistic terms, the world's principal Language of Wider Communication (LWC).[11] People who need to communicate with each other have to find means of doing so. At one level they can rely on specially trained professionals who have become fluent in two or more languages to serve as interpreters and translators. That, however, is awkward, time-consuming, and expensive. Hence throughout history lingua francas emerge, Latin in the Classical and

TABLE 3.1
SPEAKERS OF MAJOR LANGUAGES
(Percentages of World Population*)

Year Language	1958	1970	1980	1992
Arabic	2.7	2.9	3.3	3.5
Bengali	2.7	2.9	3.2	3.2
English	9.8	9.1	8.7	7.6
Hindi	5.2	5.3	5.3	6.4
Mandarin	15.6	16.6	15.8	15.2
Russian	5.5	5.6	6.0	4.9
Spanish	5.0	5.2	5.5	6.1

* Total number of people speaking languages spoken by 1 million or more people

Source: Percentages calculated from data compiled by Professor Sidney S. Culbert, Department of Psychology, University of Washington, Seattle, on the number of people speaking languages spoken by 1 million people or more and reported annually in the *World Almanac and Book of Facts*. His estimates include both "mother-tongue" and "nonmother tongue" speakers and are derived from national censuses, sample surveys of the population, surveys of radio and television broadcasts, population growth data, secondary studies, and other sources.

TABLE 3.2
SPEAKERS OF PRINCIPAL CHINESE
AND WESTERN LANGUAGES

Language	1958		1992	
	No. of Speakers (in millions)	Percentage of World	No. of Speakers (in millions)	Percentage of World
Mandarin	444	15.6	907	15.2
Cantonese	43	1.5	65	1.1
Wu	39	1.4	64	1.1
Min	36	1.3	50	0.8
Hakka	19	0.7	33	0.6
Chinese Languages	581	20.5	1119	18.8
English	278	9.8	456	7.6
Spanish	142	5.0	362	6.1
Portuguese	74	2.6	177	3.0
German	120	4.2	119	2.0
French	70	2.5	123	2.1
Western Languages	684	24.1	1237	20.8
World Total	2845	44.5	5979	39.4

Source: Percentages calculated from language data compiled by Professor Sidney S. Culbert, Department of Psychology, University of Washington, Seattle, and reported in the *World Almanac and Book of Facts* for 1959 and 1993.

medieval worlds, French for several centuries in the West, Swahili in many parts of Africa, and English throughout much of the world in the latter half of the twentieth century. Diplomats, businessmen, scientists, tourists and the services catering to them, airline pilots and air traffic controllers, need some means of efficient communication with each other, and now do it largely in English.

In this sense, English is the world's way of communicating interculturally just as the Christian calendar is the world's way of tracking time, Arabic numbers are the world's way of counting, and the metric system is, for the most part, the world's way of measuring. The use of English in this way, however, is *intercultural* communication; it presupposes the existence of separate cultures. A lingua franca is a way of coping with linguistic and cultural differences, not a way of eliminating them. It is a tool for communication not a source of identity and community. Because a Japanese banker and an Indonesian businessman talk to each other in English does not mean that either one of them is being Anglofied or Westernized. The same can be said of German-and French-speaking Swiss who are as likely to communicate with each other in English as in either of their national languages. Similarly, the maintenance of English as an associate national language in India, despite Nehru's plans to the contrary, testifies to the intense desires of the non-Hindi-speaking peoples of India to preserve their own languages and cultures and the necessity of India remaining a multilingual society.

As the leading linguistic scholar Joshua Fishman has observed, a language is more likely to be accepted as a lingua franca or LWC if it is not identified with a particular ethnic group, religion, or ideology. In the past English had many of these identifications. More recently English has been "de-ethnicized (or minimally ethnicized)"as happened in the past with Akkadian, Aramaic, Greek, and Latin. "It is part of the relative good fortune of English as an additional language that neither its British nor its American fountainheads have been widely or deeply viewed in an ethnic or ideological context *for the past quarter century or so*" [Italics his].[12] The use of English for intercultural communication thus helps to maintain and, indeed, reinforces peoples' separate cultural identities. Precisely because people want to preserve their own culture they use English to communicate with peoples of other cultures.

The people who speak English throughout the world also increasingly speak different Englishes. English is indigenized and takes on local colorations which distinguish it from British or American English and which, at the extreme, make these Englishes almost unintelligible one to the other, as is also the case with varieties of Chinese. Nigerian Pidgin English, Indian English, and other forms of English are being incorporated into their respective host cultures and presumably will continue to differentiate themselves so as to become related but distinct languages, even as Romance languages evolved out of Latin. Unlike Italian, French, and Spanish, however, these English-derived languages will either be spoken by only a small portion of people in the society or they will be used primarily for communication between particular linguistic groups.

All these processes can be seen at work in India. Purportedly, for instance, there were 18 million English speakers in 1983 out of a population of 733 million and 20 million in 1991 out of a population of 867 million. The proportion of English speakers in the Indian population has thus remained relatively stable at about 2 to 4 percent.[13] Outside of a relatively narrow elite, English does not even serve as a lingua franca. "The ground reality," two professors of English at New Delhi University allege, "is that when one travels from Kashmir down to the southern-most tip at Kanyakumari, the communication link is best maintained through a form of Hindi rather than through English." In addition, Indian English is taking on many distinctive characteristics of its own: it is being Indianized, or rather it is being localized as differences develop among the various speakers of English with different local tongues.[14] English is being absorbed into Indian culture just as Sanskrit and Persian were earlier.

Throughout history the distribution of languages in the world has reflected the distribution of power in the world. The most widely spoken languages — English, Mandarin, Spanish, French, Arabic, Russian — are or were the languages of imperial states which actively promoted use of their languages by other peoples. Shifts in the distribution of power produce shifts in the use of languages. "[T]wo centuries of British and American colonial, commercial, industrial, scientific, and fiscal power have left a substantial legacy in higher education, government, trade, and technology" throughout the world.[15] Britain and France insisted on the use of their languages in their colonies. Following independence, however, most of the former colonies attempted in varying degrees and with varying success to replace the imperial language with indigenous ones. During the heyday of the Soviet Union, Russian was the lingua franca from Prague to Hanoi. The decline of Russian power is accompanied by a parallel decline in the use of Russian as a second language. As with other forms of culture, increasing power generates both linguistic assertiveness by native speakers and incentives to learn the language by others. In the heady days immediately after the Berlin Wall came down and it seemed as if the united Germany was the new behemoth, there was a noticeable tendency for Germans fluent in English to speak German at international meetings. Japanese economic power has stimulated the learning of Japanese by non-Japanese, and the economic development of China is producing a similar boom in Chinese. Chinese is rapidly displacing English as the predominant language in Hong Kong[16] and, given the role of the overseas Chinese in Southeast Asia, has become the language in which much of that area's international business is transacted. As the power of the West gradually declines relative to that of other civilizations, the use of English and other Western languages in other societies and for communications between societies will also slowly erode. If at some point in the distant future China displaces the West as the dominant civilization in the world, English will give way to Mandarin as the world's lingua franca.

As the former colonies moved toward independence and became independent, promotion or use of the indigenous languages and suppression of the languages of empire was one way for nationalist elites to distinguish themselves from the Western colonialists and to define their own identity. Following independence, however, the elites of these societies needed to distinguish themselves from the common people of their societies. Fluency in English, French, or another Western language did this. As a result, elites of non-Western societies are often better able to communicate with Westerners and each other than with the people of their own society (a situation like that in the West in the seventeenth and eighteenth centuries when aristocrats from different countries could easily communicate in French with each other but could not speak the vernacular of their own country). In non-Western societies two opposing trends appear to be underway. On the one hand, English is increasingly used at the university level to equip graduates to function effectively in the global competition for capital and customers. On the other hand, social and political pressures increasingly lead to the more general use of indigenous languages, Arabic displacing French in North Africa, Urdu supplanting English as the language of government and education in Pakistan, and indigenous language media replacing English media in India. This development was foreseen by the Indian

Education Commission in 1948, when it argued that "use of English . . . divides the people into two nations, the few who govern and the many who are governed, the one unable to talk the language of the other, and mutually uncomprehending." Forty years later the persistence of English as the elite language bore out this prediction and had created "an unnatural situation in a working democracy based on adult suffrage. . . . English-speaking India and politically-conscious India diverge more and more" stimulating "tensions between the minority at the top who know English, and the many millions — armed with the vote — who do not."[17] To the extent that non-Western societies establish democratic institutions and the people in those societies participate more extensively in government, the use of Western languages declines and indigenous languages become more prevalent.

The end of the Soviet empire and of the Cold War promoted the proliferation and rejuvenation of languages which had been suppressed or forgotten. Major efforts have been underway in most of the former Soviet republics to revive their traditional languages. Estonian, Latvian, Lithuanian, Ukrainian, Georgian, and Armenian are now the national languages of independent states. Among the Muslim republics similar linguistic assertion has occurred, and Azerbaijan, Kyrgyzstan, Turkmenistan, and Uzbekistan have shifted from the Cyrillic script of their former Russian masters to the Western script of their Turkish kinsmen, while Persian-speaking Tajikistan has adopted Arabic script. The Serbs, on the other hand, now call their language Serbian rather than Serbo-Croatian and have shifted from the Western script of their Catholic enemies to the Cyrillic script of their Russian kinsmen. In parallel moves, the Croats now call their language Croatian and are attempting to purge it of Turkish and other foreign words, while the same "Turkish and Arabic borrowings, linguistic sediment left by the Ottoman Empire's 450-year presence in the Balkans, have come back into vogue" in Bosnia.[18] Language is realigned and reconstructed to accord with the identities and contours of civilizations. As power diffuses Babelization spreads.

Religion. A universal religion is only slightly more likely to emerge than is a universal language. The late twentieth century has seen a global resurgence of religions around the world (see pp. 95–101). That resurgence has involved the intensification of religious consciousness and the rise of fundamentalist movements. It has thus reinforced the differences among religions. It has not necessarily involved significant shifts in the proportions of the world's population adhering to different religions. The data available on religious adherents are even more fragmentary and unreliable than the data available on language speakers. Table 3.3 sets out figures derived from one widely used source. These and other data suggest that the relative numerical strength of religions around the world has not changed dramatically in this century. The largest change recorded by this source was the increase in the proportion of people classified

TABLE 3.3
PROPORTION OF WORLD POPULATION ADHERING TO MAJOR RELIGIOUS TRADITIONS
(in percentages)

Year Religion	1900	1970	1980	1985 (est)	2000 (est)
Western Christian	26.9	30.6	30.0	29.7	29.9
Orthodox Christian	7.5	3.1	2.8	2.7	2.4
Muslim	12.4	15.3	16.5	17.1	19.2
Nonreligious	0.2	15.0	16.4	16.9	17.1
Hindu	12.5	12.8	13.3	13.5	13.7
Buddhist	7.8	6.4	6.3	6.2	5.7
Chinese folk	23.5	5.9	4.5	3.9	2.5
Tribal	6.6	2.4	2.1	1.9	1.6
Atheist	0.0	4.6	4.5	4.4	4.2

Source: David B. Barrett, ed., *World Christian Encyclopedia: A comparative study of churches and religions in the modern world A.D. 1900–2000* (Oxford: Oxford University Press, 1982).

as "nonreligious" and "atheist" from 0.2 percent in 1900 to 20.9 percent in 1980. Conceivably this could reflect a major shift away from religion, and in 1980 the religious resurgence was just gathering steam. Yet this 20.7 percent increase in nonbelievers is closely matched by a 19.0 percent decrease in those classified as adherents of "Chinese folk-religions" from 23.5 percent in 1900 to 4.5 percent in 1980. These virtually equal increases and decreases suggest that with the advent of communism the bulk of China's population was simply reclassified from folk-religionist to nonbelieving.

The data do show increases in the proportions of the world population adhering to the two major proselytizing religions, Islam and Christianity, over eighty years. Western Christians were estimated at 26.9 percent of the world's population in 1900 and 30 percent in 1980. Muslims increased more dramatically from 12.4 percent in 1900 to 16.5 percent or by other estimates 18 percent in 1980. During the last decades of the twentieth century both Islam and Christianity significantly expanded their numbers in Africa, and a major shift toward Christianity occurred in South Korea. In rapidly modernizing societies, if the traditional religion is unable to adapt to the requirements of modernization, the potential exists for the spread of Western Christianity and Islam. In these societies the most successful protagonists of Western culture are not neo-classical economists or crusading democrats or multinational corporation executives. They are and most likely will continue to be Christian missionaries. Neither Adam Smith nor Thomas Jefferson will meet the psychological, emotional, moral, and social needs of urban migrants and first-generation secondary school graduates. Jesus Christ may not meet them either, but He is likely to have a better chance.

In the long run, however, Mohammed wins out. Christianity spreads primarily by conversion, Islam by conversion and reproduction. The percentage of Christians in the world peaked at about 30 percent in the 1980s, leveled off, is now declining, and will probably approximate about 25 percent of the world's population by 2025. As a result of their extremely high rates of population growth (see chapter 5), the proportion of Muslims in the world will continue to increase dramatically, amounting to 20 percent of the world's population about the turn of the century, surpassing the number of Christians some years later, and probably accounting for about 30 percent of the world's population by 2025.[19]

UNIVERSAL CIVILIZATION: SOURCES

The concept of a universal civilization is a distinctive product of Western civilization. In the nineteenth century the idea of "the white man's burden" helped justify the extension of Western political and economic domination over non-Western societies. At the end of the twentieth century the concept of a universal civilization helps justify Western cultural dominance of other societies and the need for those societies to ape Western practices and institutions. Universalism is the ideology of the West for confrontations with non-Western cultures. As is often the case with marginals or converts, among the most enthusiastic proponents of the single civilization idea are intellectual migrants to the West, such as Naipaul and Fouad Ajami, for whom the concept provides a highly satisfying answer to the central question: Who am I? "White man's nigger," however, is the term one Arab intellectual applied to these migrants,[20] and the idea of a universal civilization finds little support in other civilizations. The non-Wests see as Western what the West sees as universal. What Westerners herald as benign global integration, such as the proliferation of worldwide media, non-Westerners denounce as nefarious Western imperialism. To the extent that non-Westerners see the world as one, they see it as a threat.

The arguments that some sort of universal civilization is emerging rest on one or more of three assumptions as to why this should be the case. First, there is the assumption, discussed in chapter 1, that the collapse of Soviet communism meant the end of history and the universal victory of liberal democracy throughout the world. This argument suffers from the single alternative fallacy. It is rooted in the Cold War perspective that the only alternative to communism is liberal democracy and that the demise of the first produces the universality of the second. Obviously, however, there are many forms of authoritarianism, nationalism, corporatism, and market communism (as in China) that are alive and well in today's world. More significantly, there are all the religious alternatives that lie outside the world of secular ideologies. In the modern world, religion is a central, perhaps *the* central, force that motivates and mobilizes people. It is sheer hubris to think that because Soviet communism has collapsed, the West has won the world for all time and that Muslims, Chinese, Indians, and others are going to rush to embrace Western liberalism as the only alternative. The Cold War division of humanity is over. The more fundamental divisions of humanity in terms of ethnicity, religions, and civilizations remain and spawn new conflicts.

Second, there is the assumption that increased interaction among peoples — trade, investment, tourism, media, electronic communication generally — is generating a common world culture. Improvements in transportation and communications technology have indeed made it easier and cheaper to move money, goods, people, knowledge, ideas, and images around the world. No doubt exists as to the increased international traffic in these items. Much doubt exists, however, as to the impact of this increased traffic. Does trade increase or decrease the likelihood of conflict? The assumption that it reduces the probability of war between nations is, at a minimum, not proven, and much evidence exists to the contrary. International trade expanded significantly in the 1960s and 1970s and in the following decade the Cold War came to an end. In 1913, however, international trade was at record highs and in the next few years nations slaughtered each other in unprecedented numbers.[21] If international commerce at that level could not prevent war, when can it? The evidence simply does not support the liberal, internationalist assumption that commerce promotes peace. Analyses done in the 1990s throw that assumption further into question. One study concludes that "increasing levels of trade may be a highly divisive force . . . for international politics" and that "increasing trade in the international system is, by itself, unlikely to ease international tensions or promote greater international stability."[22] Another study argues that high levels of economic interdependence "can be either peace-inducing *or* war-inducing, depending on the expectations of future trade." Economic interdependence fosters peace only "when states expect that high trade levels will continue into the foreseeable future." If states do not expect high levels of interdependence to continue, war is likely to result.[23]

The failure of trade and communications to produce peace or common feeling is consonant with the findings of social science. In social psychology, distinctiveness theory holds that people define themselves by what makes them different from others in a particular context: "one perceives oneself in terms of characteristics that distinguish oneself from other humans, especially from people in one's usual social milieu . . . a woman psychologist in the company of a dozen women who work at other occupations thinks of herself as a psychologist; when with a dozen male psychologists, she thinks of herself as a woman."[24] People define their identity by what they are not. As increased communications, trade, and travel multiply the interactions among civilizations, people increasingly accord greater relevance to their civilizational identity. Two Europeans, one German and one French, interacting with each other will identify each other as German and French. Two Europeans, one German and one French, interacting with two Arabs, one Saudi and one Egyptian, will define themselves as Europeans and Arabs. North African immigration to France generates hostility among the French and at the same time increased receptivity to immigration by European Catholic Poles. Americans react far more negatively to Japanese investment than to larger investments from Canada and European countries. Similarly, as Donald Horowitz has pointed out, "An Ibo may be . . . an Owerri Ibo or an Onitsha Ibo in what was the Eastern region of Nigeria. In Lagos, he is simply an Ibo. In London, he is Nigerian. In New York, he is an African."[25] From sociology, globalization theory produces a similar conclusion: "in an increasingly globalized world — characterized by historically exceptional degrees of civilizational, societal and other modes of interdependence and widespread consciousness thereof — there is an *exacerbation* of civilizational, societal and ethnic self-consciousness." The global religious revival, "the return to the sacred," is a response to people's perception of the world as "a single place."[26]

THE WEST AND MODERNIZATION

The third and most general argument for the emergence of a universal civilization sees it as the result of the broad processes of modernization that have been going on since the eighteenth century. Modernization involves industrialization, urbanization, increasing levels of literacy, education, wealth, and social mobilization, and more complex and diversified occupational structures. It is a product of the tremendous expansion of scientific and engineering knowledge beginning in the eighteenth century that made it possible for humans to control and shape their environment in totally unprecedented ways. Modernization is a revolutionary process comparable only to the shift from primitive to civilized societies, that is, the emergence of civilization in the singular, which began in the valleys of the Tigris and Euphrates, the Nile, and the Indus about 5000 B.C.[27] The attitudes, values, knowledge, and culture of people in a modern society differ greatly from those in a traditional society. As the first civilization to modernize, the West leads in the acquisition of the culture of modernity. As other societies acquire similar patterns of education, work, wealth, and class structure, the argument runs, this modern Western culture will become the universal culture of the world.

That significant differences exist between modern and traditional cultures is beyond dispute. It does not necessarily follow, however, that societies with modern cultures resemble each other more than do societies with traditional cultures. Obviously a world in which some societies are highly modern and others still traditional will be less homogeneous than a world in which all societies are at comparable high levels of modernity. But what about a world in which all societies were traditional? This world existed a few hundred years ago. Was it any less homogeneous than a future world of universal modernity is likely to be? Possibly not. "Ming China . . . was assuredly closer to the France of the Valois," Braudel argues, "than the China of Mao Tse-tung is to the France of the Fifth Republic."[28]

Yet modern societies could resemble each other more than do traditional societies for two reasons. First, the increased interaction among modern societies may not generate a common culture but it does facilitate the transfer of techniques, inventions, and practices from one society to another with a speed and to a degree that were impossible in the traditional world. Second, traditional society was based on agriculture; modern society is based on industry, which may evolve from handicrafts to classic heavy industry to knowledge-based industry. Patterns of agriculture and the social structure which goes with them are much more dependent on the natural environment than are patterns of industry. They vary with soil and climate and thus may give rise to different forms of land ownership, social structure, and government. Whatever the overall merits of Wittfogel's hydraulic civilization thesis, agriculture dependent on the construction and operation of massive irrigation systems does foster the emergence of centralized and bureaucratic political authorities. It could hardly be otherwise. Rich soil and good climate are likely to encourage development of large-scale plantation agriculture and a consequent social structure involving a small class of wealthy landowners and a large class of peasants, slaves, or serfs who work the plantations. Conditions inhospitable to large-scale agriculture may encourage emergence of a society of independent farmers. In agricultural societies, in short, social structure is shaped by geography. Industry, in contrast, is much less dependent on the local natural environment. Differences in industrial organization are likely to derive from differences in culture and social structure rather than geography, and the former conceivably can converge while the latter cannot.

Modern societies thus have much in common. But do they necessarily merge into homogeneity? The argument that they do rests on the assumption that modern society must approximate a single type, the Western type, that modern civilization is Western civilization and that Western civilization is modern civilization. This, however, is a totally false identification. Western civilization emerged in the eighth and ninth centuries and developed its distinctive characteristics in the following centuries. It did not begin to modernize until the seventeenth and eighteenth centuries. The West was the West long before it was modern. The central characteristics of the West, those which distinguish it from other civilizations, antedate the modernization of the West.

What were these distinguishing characteristics of Western society during the hundreds of years before it modernized? Various scholars have produced answers to this question which differ in some specifics but agree on the key institutions, practices, and beliefs that may legitimately be identified as the core of Western civilization. These include the following.[29]

The Classical legacy. As a third generation civilization, the West inherited much from previous civilizations, including most notably Classical civilization. The legacies of the West from Classical civilization are many, including Greek philosophy and rationalism, Roman law, Latin, and Christianity. Islamic and

Orthodox civilizations also inherited from Classical civilization but nowhere near to the same degree the West did.

Catholicism and Protestantism. Western Christianity, first Catholicism and then Catholicism and Protestantism, is historically the single most important characteristic of Western civilization. During most of its first millennium, indeed, what is now known as Western civilization was called Western Christendom; there existed a well-developed sense of community among Western Christian peoples that they were distinct from Turks, Moors, Byzantines, and others; and it was for God as well as gold that Westerners went out to conquer the world in the sixteenth century. The Reformation and Counter-Reformation and the division of Western Christendom into a Protestant north and a Catholic south are also distinctive features of Western history, totally absent from Eastern Orthodoxy and largely removed from the Latin American experience.

European languages. Language is second only to religion as a factor distinguishing people of one culture from those of another. The West differs from most other civilizations in its multiplicity of languages. Japanese, Hindi, Mandarin, Russian, and even Arabic are recognized as the core languages of their civilizations. The West inherited Latin, but a variety of nations emerged and with them national languages grouped loosely into the broad categories of Romance and Germanic. By the sixteenth century these languages had generally assumed their contemporary form.

Separation of spiritual and temporal authority. Throughout Western history first the Church and then many churches existed apart from the state. God and Caesar, church and state, spiritual authority and temporal authority, have been a prevailing dualism in Western culture. Only in Hindu civilization were religion and politics also so distinctly separated. In Islam, God is Caesar; in China and Japan, Caesar is God; in Orthodoxy, God is Caesar's junior partner. The separation and recurring clashes between church and state that typify Western civilization have existed in no other civilization. This division of authority contributed immeasurably to the development of freedom in the West.

Rule of law. The concept of the centrality of law to civilized existence was inherited from the Romans. Medieval thinkers elaborated the idea of natural law according to which monarchs were supposed to exercise their power, and a common law tradition developed in England. During the phase of absolutism in the sixteenth and seventeenth centuries the rule of law was observed more in the breach than in reality, but the idea persisted of the subordination of human power to some external restraint: *"Non sub homine sed sub Deo et lege."* The tradition of the rule of law laid the basis for constitutionalism and the protection of human rights, including property rights, against the exercise of arbitrary power. In most other civilizations law was a much less important factor in shaping thought and behavior.

Social pluralism. Historically Western society has been highly pluralistic. As Deutsch notes, what is distinctive about the West "is the rise and persistence of diverse autonomous groups not based on blood relationship or marriage."[30] Beginning in the sixth and seventh centuries, these groups initially included monasteries, monastic orders, and guilds, but then expanded to include in many areas of Europe a variety of other associations and societies.[31] Associational pluralism was supplemented by class pluralism. Most Western European societies included a relatively strong and autonomous aristocracy, a substantial peasantry, and a small but significant class of merchants and traders. The strength of the feudal aristocracy was particularly significant in limiting the extent to which absolutism was able to take firm root in most European nations. This European pluralism contrasts sharply with the poverty of civil society, the weakness of the aristocracy, and the strength of the centralized bureaucratic empires which simultaneously existed in Russia, China, the Ottoman lands, and other non-Western societies.

Representative bodies. Social pluralism early gave rise to estates, parliaments, and other institutions to represent the interests of the aristocracy, clergy, merchants, and other groups. These bodies provided forms of representation which in the course of modernization evolved into the institutions of modern democracy. In some instances these bodies were abolished or their powers were greatly limited during the period of absolutism. Even when that happened, however, they could, as in France, be resurrected to provide a vehicle for expanded political participation. No other contemporary civilization has a comparable heritage of representative bodies stretching back for a millennium. At the local level also, beginning about the ninth century, movements for self-government developed in the Italian cities and then spread northward "forcing bishops, local barons and other great nobles to share power with the burghers, and in the end often yield to them altogether."[32] Representation at the national level was thus supplemented by a measure of autonomy at the local level not duplicated in other regions of the world.

Individualism. Many of the above features of Western civilization contributed to the emergence of a sense of individualism and a tradition of individual rights and liberties unique among civilized societies. Individualism developed in the fourteenth and fifteenth centuries and acceptance of the right of individual choice — what Deutsch terms "the Romeo and Juliet revolution" — prevailed in the West by the seventeenth century. Even claims for *equal* rights for all individuals — "the poorest he in England has a life to live as much as the richest he" — were articulated if not universally accepted. Individualism remains a distinguishing mark of the West among twentieth-century civilizations. In one analysis involving similar samples from fifty countries, the top twenty countries scoring highest on the individualism index included all the Western countries except Portugal plus Israel.[33] The author of another cross-cultural survey of individualism and collectivism similarly highlighted the dominance of individualism in the West compared to the prevalence of collectivism elsewhere and concluded that "the values that are most important in the West are least important worldwide." Again and again both Westerners and non-Westerners point to individualism as the central distinguishing mark of the West.[34]

The above list is not meant to be an exhaustive enumeration of the distinctive characteristics of Western civilization. Nor is it meant to imply that those characteristics were always and universally present in Western society. Obviously they were not: the many despots in Western history regularly ignored the rule of law and suspended representative bodies. Nor is it meant to suggest that none of these characteristics appeared in other civilizations. Obviously they do: the Koran and the *shari'a* constitute basic law for Islamic societies; Japan and India had class systems paralleling that of the West (and perhaps as a result are the only two major non-Western societies to sustain democratic governments for any length of time). Individually almost none of these factors was unique to the West. The combination of them was, however, and this is what gave the West its distinctive quality. These concepts, practices, and institutions simply have been more prevalent in the West than in other civilizations. They form at least part of the essential continuing core of Western civilization. They are what is Western but not modern about the West. They are also in large part the factors which enabled the West to take the lead in modernizing itself and the world.

RESPONSES TO THE WEST AND MODERNIZATION

The expansion of the West has promoted both the modernization and the Westernization of non-Western societies. The political and intellectual leaders of these societies have responded to the Western impact in one or more of three ways: rejecting both modernization and Westernization; embracing both; embracing the first and rejecting the second.[35]

Rejectionism. Japan followed a substantially rejectionist course from its first contacts with the West in 1542 until the mid-nineteenth century. Only limited forms of modernization were permitted, such as the acquisition of firearms, and the import of Western culture, including most notably Christianity, was highly restricted. Westerners were totally expelled in the mid-seventeenth century. This rejectionist stance came to an end with the forcible opening of Japan by Commodore Perry in 1854 and the dramatic efforts to learn from the West following the Meiji Restoration in 1868. For several centuries China also attempted to bar any significant modernization or Westernization. Although Christian emissaries were allowed into China in 1601 they were then effectively excluded in 1722. Unlike Japan, China's rejectionist policy was in large part rooted in the Chinese image of itself as the Middle Kingdom and the firm belief in the superiority of Chinese culture to those of all other peoples. Chinese isolation, like Japanese isolation, was brought to an end by Western arms, applied to China by the British in the Opium War of 1839–1842. As these cases suggest, during the nineteenth century Western power made it increasingly difficult and eventually impossible for non-Western societies to adhere to purely exclusionist strategies.

In the twentieth century improvements in transportation and communication and global interdependence increased tremendously the costs of exclusion. Except for small, isolated, rural communities willing to exist at a subsistence level, the total rejection of modernization as well as Westernization is hardly possible in a world becoming overwhelmingly modern and highly interconnected. "Only the very most extreme fundamentalists," Daniel Pipes writes concerning Islam, "reject modernization as well as Westernization. They throw television sets into rivers, ban wrist watches, and reject the internal combustion engine. The impracticality of their program severely limits the appeal of such groups, however; and in several cases — such as the Yen Izala of Kano, Sadat's assassins, the Mecca mosque attackers, and some Malaysian *dakwah* groups — their defeats in violent encounters with the authorities caused them then to disappear with few traces."[36] Disappearance with few traces summarizes generally the fate of purely rejectionist policies by the end of the twentieth century. Zealotry, to use Toynbee's term, is simply not a viable option.

Kemalism. A second possible response to the West is Toynbee's Herodianism, to embrace both modernization and Westernization. This response is based on the assumptions that modernization is desirable and necessary, that the indigenous culture is incompatible with modernization and must be abandoned or abolished, and that society must fully Westernize in order to successfully modernize. Modernization and Westernization reinforce each other and have to go together. This approach was epitomized in the arguments of some late nineteenth century Japanese and Chinese intellectuals that in order to modernize, their societies should abandon their historic languages and adopt English as their national language. This view, not surprisingly, has been even more popular among Westerners than among non-Western elites. Its message is: "To be successful, you must be like us; our way is the only way." The argument is that "the religious values, moral assumptions, and social structures of these [non-Western] societies are at best alien, and sometime hostile, to the values and practices of industrialism." Hence economic development will "require a radical and destructive remaking of life and society, and, often, a reinterpretation of the meaning of existence itself as it has been understood by the people who live in these civilizations."[37] Pipes makes the same point with explicit reference to Islam:

> To escape anomy, Muslims have but one choice, for modernization requires Westernization. . . . Islam does not offer an alternative way to modernize. . . . Secularism cannot be avoided. Modern science and technology require an absorption of the thought processes which accompany them; so too with political institutions. Because content must be emulated no less than form, the predominance of Western civilization must be acknowledged so as to be

able to learn from it. European languages and Western educational institutions cannot be avoided, even if the latter do encourage freethinking and easy living. Only when Muslims explicitly accept the Western model will they be in a position to technicalize and then to develop.[38]

Sixty years before these words were written Mustafa Kemal Ataturk had come to similar conclusions, had created a new Turkey out of the ruins of the Ottoman empire, and had launched a massive effort both to Westernize it and to modernize it. In embarking on this course, and rejecting the Islamic past, Ataturk made Turkey a "torn country," a society which was Muslim in its religion, heritage, customs, and institutions but with a ruling elite determined to make it modern, Western, and at one with the West. In the late twentieth century several countries are pursuing the Kemalist option and trying to substitute a Western for a non-Western identity. Their efforts are analyzed in chapter 6.

Reformism. Rejection involves the hopeless task of isolating a society from the shrinking modern world. Kemalism involves the difficult and traumatic task of destroying a culture that has existed for centuries and putting in its place a totally new culture imported from another civilization. A third choice is to attempt to combine modernization with the preservation of the central values, practices, and institutions of the society's indigenous culture. This choice has understandably been the most popular one among non-Western elites. In China in the last stages of the Ch'ing dynasty, the slogan was *Ti-Yong*, "Chinese learning for the fundamental principles, Western learning for practical use." In Japan it was *Wakon, Yōsei*, "Japanese spirit, Western technique." In Egypt in the 1830s Muhammad Ali "attempted technical modernization without excessive cultural Westernization." This effort failed, however, when the British forced him to abandon most of his modernizing reforms. As a result, Ali Mazrui observes, "Egypt's destiny was not a Japanese fate of technical modernization *without* cultural Westernization, nor was it an Ataturk fate of technical modernization *through* cultural Westernization."[39] In the latter part of the nineteenth century, however, Jamal al-Din al-Afghani, Muhammad 'Abduh, and other reformers attempted a new reconciliation of Islam and modernity, arguing "the compatibility of Islam with modern science and the best of Western thought" and providing an "Islamic rationale for accepting modern ideas and institutions, whether scientific, technological, or political (constitutionalism and representative government)."[40] This was a broad-gauged reformism, tending toward Kemalism, which accepted not only modernity but also some Western institutions. Reformism of this type was the dominant response to the West on the part of Muslim elites for fifty years from the 1870s to the 1920s, when it was challenged by the rise first of Kemalism and then of a much purer reformism in the shape of fundamentalism.

Rejectionism, Kemalism, and reformism are based on different assumptions as to what is possible and what is desirable. For rejectionism both modernization and Westernization are undesirable and it is possible to reject both. For Kemalism both modernization and Westernization are desirable, the latter because it is indispensable to achieving the former, and both are possible. For reformism, modernization is desirable and possible without substantial Westernization, which is undesirable. Conflicts thus exist between rejectionism and Kemalism on the desirability of modernization and Westernization and between Kemalism and reformism as to whether modernization can occur without Westernization.

Figure 3.1 diagrams these three courses of action. The rejectionist would remain at Point A; the Kemalist would move along the diagonal to Point B; the reformer would move horizontally toward Point C. Along what path, however, have societies actually moved? Obviously each non-Western society has followed its own course, which may differ substantially from these three prototypical paths. Mazrui even argues that Egypt and Africa have moved toward Point D through a "painful process of cultural Westernization *without* technical modernization." To the extent that any general pattern of modernization and Westernization exists in the responses of non-Western societies to the West, it would appear to be along the curve A–E. Initially, Westernization and modernization are closely linked, with the non-Western society absorbing substantial elements of Western culture and making slow progress toward modernization. As the pace of modernization increases, however, the rate of Westernization

FIGURE 3.1
ALTERNATIVE RESPONSES TO THE IMPACT OF THE WEST

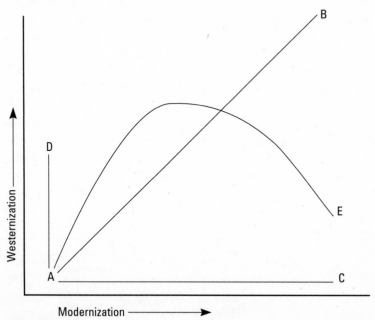

declines and the indigenous culture goes through a revival. Further modernization then alters the civilizational balance of power between the West and the non-Western society and strengthens commitment to the indigenous culture.

In the early phases of change, Westernization thus promotes modernization. In the later phases, modernization promotes de-Westernization and the resurgence of indigenous culture in two ways. At the societal level, modernization enhances the economic, military, and political power of the society as a whole and encourages the people of that society to have confidence in their culture and to become culturally assertive. At the individual level, modernization generates feelings of alienation and anomie as traditional bonds and social relations are broken and leads to crises of identity to which religion provides an answer. This causal flow is set forth in simple form in Figure 3.2.

This hypothetical general model is congruent with both social science theory and historical experience. Reviewing at length the available evidence concerning "the invariance hypothesis," Rainer Baum concludes that "the continuing quest of man's search for meaningful authority and meaningful personal autonomy occurs in culturally distinct fashions. In these matters there is no convergence toward a cross-culturally homogenizing world. Instead, there seems to be invariance in the patterns that were developed in distinct forms during the historical and early modern stages of development."[41] Borrowing theory, as elaborated by Frobenius, Spengler, and Bozeman among others, stresses the extent to which recipient civilizations selectively borrow items from other civilizations and adapt, transform, and assimilate them so as to strengthen and insure the survival of the core values or "paideuma" of their culture.[42] Almost all of the non-Western civilizations in the world have existed for at least one millennium and in some cases for several. They have a demonstrated record of borrowing from other civilizations in ways to enhance their own survival. China's absorption of Buddhism from India, scholars agree, failed to produce the "Indianization" of China. The Chinese adapted Buddhism to Chinese purposes and needs. Chinese culture remained Chinese. The Chinese have to date consistently defeated intense Western efforts to Christianize them. If, at some point, they do import Christianity, it is to be expected that it will be absorbed and adapted in such a manner as to be compatible with the central elements of Chinese culture. Similarly, Muslim Arabs received, valued, and made use of their "Hellenic inheritance for essentially utilitarian reasons. Being mostly

Figure 3.2
Modernization and Cultural Resurgence

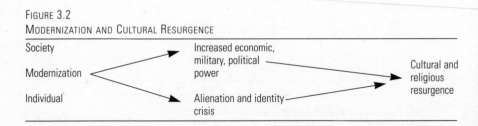

interested in borrowing certain external forms or technical aspects, they knew how to disregard all elements in the Greek body of thought that would conflict with 'the truth' as established in their fundamental Koranic norms and precepts."[43] Japan followed the same pattern. In the seventh century Japan imported Chinese culture and made the "transformation on its own initiative, free from economic and military pressures" to high civilization. "During the centuries that followed, periods of relative isolation from continental influences during which previous borrowings were sorted out and the useful ones assimilated would alternate with periods of renewed contact and cultural borrowing."[44] Through all these phases, Japanese culture maintained its distinctive character.

The moderate form of the Kemalist argument that non-Western societies *may* modernize by Westernizing remains unproven. The extreme Kemalist argument that non-Western societies *must* Westernize in order to modernize does not stand as a universal proposition. It does, however, raise the question: Are there some non-Western societies in which the obstacles the indigenous culture poses to modernization are so great that the culture must be substantially replaced by Western culture if modernization is to occur? In theory this should be more probable with consummatory than with instrumental cultures. Instrumental cultures are "characterized by a large sector of intermediate ends separate from and independent of ultimate ends." These systems "innovate easily by spreading the blanket of tradition upon change itself. . . . Such systems can innovate without appearing to alter their social institutions fundamentally. Rather, innovation is made to serve immemoriality." Consummatory systems, in contrast, "are characterized by a close relationship between intermediate and ultimate ends. . . . society, the state, authority, and the like are all part of an elaborately sustained, high-solidarity system in which religion as a cognitive guide is pervasive. Such systems have been hostile to innovation."[45] Apter uses these categories to analyze change in African tribes. Eisenstadt applies a parallel analysis to the great Asian civilizations and comes to a similar conclusion. Internal transformation is "greatly facilitated by autonomy of social, cultural, and political institutions."[46] For this reason, the more instrumental Japanese and Hindu societies moved earlier and more easily into modernization than Confucian and Islamic societies. They were better able to import the modern technology and use it to bolster their existing culture. Does this mean that Chinese and Islamic societies must either forgo both modernization and Westernization or embrace both? The choices do not appear that limited. In addition to Japan, Singapore, Taiwan, Saudi Arabia, and, to a lesser degree, Iran have become modern societies without becoming Western. Indeed, the effort by the Shah to follow a Kemalist course and do both generated an intense anti-Western but not antimodern reaction. China is clearly embarked on a reformist path.

Islamic societies have had difficulty with modernization, and Pipes supports his claim that Westernization is a prerequisite by pointing to the conflicts between Islam and modernity in economic matters such as interest, fasting, inheritance laws, and female participation in the work force. Yet even he approvingly quotes Maxine Rodinson to the effect that "there is nothing to indicate in a compelling way that the Muslim religion prevented the Muslim world from developing along the road to modern capitalism" and argues that in most matters other than economic

> Islam and modernization do not clash. Pious Muslims can cultivate the sciences, work efficiently in factories, or utilize advanced weapons. Modernization requires no one political ideology or set of institutions: elections, national boundaries, civic associations, and the other hallmarks of Western life are not necessary to economic growth. As a creed, Islam satisfies management consultants as well as peasants. The Shari'a has nothing to say about the changes that accompany modernization, such as the shift from agriculture to industry, from countryside to city, or from social stability to social flux; nor does it impinge on such matters as mass education, rapid communications, new forms of transportation, or health care.[47]

Similiarly, even extreme proponents of anti-Westernism and the revitalization of indigenous cultures do not hesitate to use modern techniques of e-mail, cassettes, and television to promote their cause.

Modernization, in short, does not necessarily mean Westernization. Non-Western societies can modernize and have modernized without abandoning their own cultures and adopting wholesale Western values, institutions, and practices. The latter, indeed, may be almost impossible: whatever obstacles non-Western cultures pose to modernization pale before those they pose to Westernization. It would, as Braudel observes, almost "be childish" to think that modernization or the "triumph of *civilization* in the singular" would lead to the end of the plurality of historic cultures embodied for centuries in the world's great civilizations.[48] Modernization, instead, strengthens those cultures and reduces the relative power of the West. In fundamental ways, the world is becoming more modern and less Western.

II

·

The

Shifting Balance

of

Civilizations

Chapter 4

•

The Fading of the West: Power, Culture, and Indigenization

WESTERN POWER: DOMINANCE AND DECLINE

Two pictures exist of the power of the West in relation to other civilizations. The first is of overwhelming, triumphant, almost total Western dominance. The disintegration of the Soviet Union removed the only serious challenger to the West and as a result the world is and will be shaped by the goals, priorities, and interests of the principal Western nations, with perhaps an occasional assist from Japan. As the one remaining superpower, the United States together with Britain and France make the crucial decisions on political and security issues; the United States together with Germany and Japan make the crucial decisions on economic issues. The West is the only civilization which has substantial interests in every other civilization or region and has the ability to affect the politics, economics, and security of every other civilization or region. Societies from other civilizations usually need Western help to achieve their goals and protect their interests. Western nations, as one author summarized it:

- Own and operate the international banking system
- Control all hard currencies
- Are the world's principal customer
- Provide the majority of the world's finished goods
- Dominate international capital markets
- Exert considerable moral leadership within many societies
- Are capable of massive military intervention
- Control the sea lanes

- Conduct most advanced technical research and development
- Control leading edge technical education
- Dominate access to space
- Dominate the aerospace industry
- Dominate international communications
- Dominate the high-tech weapons industry[1]

The second picture of the West is very different. It is of a civilization in decline, its share of world political, economic, and military power going down relative to that of other civilizations. The West's victory in the Cold War has produced not triumph but exhaustion. The West is increasingly concerned with its internal problems and needs, as it confronts slow economic growth, stagnating populations, unemployment, huge government deficits, a declining work ethic, low savings rates, and in many countries including the United States social disintegration, drugs, and crime. Economic power is rapidly shifting to East Asia, and military power and political influence are starting to follow. India is on the verge of economic takeoff and the Islamic world is increasingly hostile toward the West. The willingness of other societies to accept the West's dictates or abide its sermons is rapidly evaporating, and so are the West's self-confidence and will to dominate. The late 1980s witnessed much debate about the declinist thesis concerning the United States. In the mid-1990s, a balanced analysis came to a somewhat similar conclusion:

[I]n many important respects, its [the United States'] relative power will decline at an accelerating pace. In terms of its raw economic capabilities, the position of the United States in relation to Japan and eventually China is likely to erode still further. In the military realm, the balance of effective capabilities between the United States and a number of growing regional powers (including, perhaps, Iran, India, and China) will shift from the center toward the periphery. Some of America's structural power will flow to other nations; some (and some of its soft power as well) will find its way into the hands of nonstate actors like multinational corporations.[2]

Which of these two contrasting pictures of the place of the West in the world describes reality? The answer, of course, is: they both do. The West is overwhelmingly dominant now and will remain number one in terms of power and influence well into the twenty-first century. Gradual, inexorable, and fundamental changes, however, are also occurring in the balances of power among civilizations, and the power of the West relative to that of other civilizations will continue to decline. As the West's primacy erodes, much of its power will simply evaporate and the rest will be diffused on a regional basis among the several major civilizations and their core states. The most significant increases in power are accruing and will accrue to Asian civilizations, with China gradu-

ally emerging as the society most likely to challenge the West for global influence. These shifts in power among civilizations are leading and will lead to the
revival and increased cultural assertiveness of non-Western societies and to their
increasing rejection of Western culture.

The decline of the West has three major characteristics.

First, it is a slow process. The rise of Western power took four hundred years.
Its recession could take as long. In the 1980s the distinguished British scholar
Hedley Bull argued that "European or Western dominance of the universal
international society may be said to have reached its apogee about the year
1900."[3] Spengler's first volume appeared in 1918 and the "decline of the West"
has been a central theme in twentieth-century history. The process itself has
stretched out through most of the century. Conceivably, however, it could
accelerate. Economic growth and other increases in a country's capabilities
often proceed along an S curve: a slow start then rapid acceleration followed
by reduced rates of expansion and leveling off. The decline of countries may
also occur along a reverse S curve, as it did with the Soviet Union: moderate
at first then rapidly accelerating before bottoming out. The decline of the West
is still in the slow first phase, but at some point it might speed up dramatically.

Second, decline does not proceed in a straight line. It is highly irregular with
pauses, reversals, and reassertions of Western power following manifestations of
Western weakness. The open democratic societies of the West have great capacities for renewal. In addition, unlike many civilizations, the West has had two
major centers of power. The decline which Bull saw starting about 1900 was
essentially the decline of the European component of Western civilization.
From 1910 to 1945 Europe was divided against itself and preoccupied with its
internal economic, social, and political problems. In the 1940s, however, the
American phase of Western domination began, and in 1945 the United States
briefly dominated the world to an extent almost comparable to the combined
Allied Powers in 1918. Postwar decolonization further reduced European influence but not that of the United States, which substituted a new transnational
imperialism for the traditional territorial empire. During the Cold War, however, American military power was matched by that of the Soviets and American economic power declined relative to that of Japan. Yet periodic efforts at
military and economic renewal did occur. In 1991, indeed, another distinguished British scholar, Barry Buzan, argued that "The deeper reality is that
the centre is now more dominant, and the periphery more subordinate, than at
any time since decolonization began."[4] The accuracy of that perception, however, fades as the military victory that gave rise to it also fades into history.

Third, power is the ability of one person or group to change the behavior of
another person or group. Behavior may be changed through inducement,
coercion, or exhortation, which require the power-wielder to have economic,
military, institutional, demographic, political, technological, social, or other
resources. The power of a state or group is hence normally estimated by

measuring the resources it has at its disposal against those of the other states or groups it is trying to influence. The West's share of most, but not all, of the important power resources peaked early in the twentieth century and then began to decline relative to those of other civilizations.

Territory and Population. In 1490 Western societies controlled most of the European peninsula outside the Balkans or perhaps 1.5 million square miles out of a global land area (apart from Antarctica) of 52.5 million square miles. At the peak of its territorial expansion in 1920, the West directly ruled about 25.5 million square miles or close to half the earth's earth. By 1993 this territorial control had been cut in half to about 12.7 million square miles. The West was back to its original European core plus its spacious settler-populated lands in North America, Australia, and New Zealand. The territory of independent Islamic societies, in contrast, rose from 1.8 million square miles in 1920 to over 11 million square miles in 1993. Similar changes occurred in the control of population. In 1900 Westerners composed roughly 30 percent of the world's population and Western governments ruled almost 45 percent of that population then and 48 percent in 1920. In 1993, except for a few small imperial remnants like Hong Kong, Western governments ruled no one but Westerners. Westerners amounted to slightly over 13 percent of humanity and are due to drop to about 11 percent early in the next century and to 10 percent by 2025.[5] In terms of total population, in 1993 the West ranked fourth behind Sinic, Islamic, and Hindu civilizations.

Quantitatively Westerners thus constitute a steadily decreasing minority of

TABLE 4.1

TERRITORY UNDER THE POLITICAL CONTROL OF CIVILIZATIONS, 1900–1993

AGGREGATE TERRITORY ESTIMATES OF CIVILIZATIONS IN THOUSANDS OF SQUARE MILES								
Year	Western	African	Sinic	Hindu	Islamic	Japanese	Latin American	Orthodox	Other
1900	20,290	164	4,317	54	3,592	161	7,721	8,733	7,468
1920	25,447	400	3,913	54	1,811	261	8,098	10,258	2,258
1971	12,806	4,636	3,936	1,316	9,183	142	7,833	10,346	2,302
1993	12,711	5,682	3,923	1,279	11,054	145	7,819	7,169	2,718
WORLD TERRITORY ESTIMATES IN PERCENTAGES*									
1900	38.7	0.3	8.2	0.1	6.8	0.3	14.7	16.6	14.3
1920	48.5	0.8	7.5	0.1	3.5	0.5	15.4	19.5	4.3
1971	24.4	8.8	7.5	2.5	17.5	0.3	14.9	19.7	4.4
1993	24.2	10.8	7.5	2.4	21.1	0.3	14.9	13.7	5.2

Note: *Relative world territorial shares based on prevailing state borders as of indicated year.*

* World territory estimate of 52.5 million square miles does not include Antarctica.

Sources: *Statesman's Year-Book* (New York: St. Martin's Press, 1901–1927); *World Book Atlas* (Chicago: Field Enterprises Educational Corp., 1970); *Britannica Book of the Year* (Chicago: Encyclopaedia Britannica, Inc., 1992–1994).

TABLE 4.2
POPULATIONS OF COUNTRIES BELONGING TO THE WORLD'S MAJOR CIVILIZATIONS, 1993 (in thousands)

Sinic	1,340,900	Latin American	507,500
Islamic	927,600	African	392,100
Hindu	915,800	Orthodox	261,300
Western	805,400	Japanese	124,700

Source: Calculated from figures in *Encyclopedia Britannica, 1994 Book of the Year* (Chicago: Encyclopedia Britannica, 1994), pp. 764–69.

the world's population. Qualitatively the balance between the West and other populations is also changing. Non-Western peoples are becoming healthier, more urban, more literate, better educated. By the early 1990s infant mortality rates in Latin America, Africa, the Middle East, South Asia, East Asia, and Southeast Asia were one-third to one-half what they had been thirty years earlier. Life expectancy in these regions had increased significantly, with gains varying from eleven years in Africa to twenty-three years in East Asia. In the early 1960s in most of the Third World less than one-third of the adult population was literate. In the early 1990s, in very few countries apart from Africa was less than one-half the population literate. About fifty percent of Indians and 75 percent of Chinese could read and write. Literacy rates in developing countries in 1970 averaged 41 percent of those in developed countries; in 1992 they averaged 71 percent. By the early 1990s in every region except Africa virtually the entire age group was enrolled in primary education. Most significantly, in the early 1960s in Asia, Latin America, the Middle East, and Africa less than

TABLE 4.3
SHARES OF WORLD POPULATION UNDER THE POLITICAL CONTROL OF CIVILIZATIONS,
1900–2025 (in percentages)

Year [World total]*	Western	African	Sinic	Hindu	Islamic	Japanese	Latin American	Orthodox	Other
1900 [1.6]	44.3	0.4	19.3	0.3	4.2	3.5	3.2	8.5	16.3
1920 [1.9]	48.1	0.7	17.3	0.3	2.4	4.1	4.6	13.9	8.6
1971 [3.7]	14.4	5.6	22.8	15.2	13.0	2.8	8.4	10.0	5.5
1990 [5.3]	14.7	8.2	24.3	16.3	13.4	2.3	9.2	6.5	5.1
1995 [5.8]	13.1	9.5	24.0	16.4	15.9†	2.2	9.3	6.1‡	3.5
2010 [7.2]	11.5	11.7	22.3	17.1	17.9†	1.8	10.3	5.4‡	2.0
2025 [8.5]	10.1	14.4	21.0	16.9	19.2†	1.5	9.2	4.9‡	2.8

Notes: Relative world population estimates based on prevailing state borders as of indicated year. Population estimates for 1995 to 2025 assume 1994 borders.

*World population estimate in billions.

† Estimates do not include members of the Commonwealth of Independent States or Bosnia.

‡ Estimates include the Commonwealth of Independent States, Georgia, and the former Yugoslavia.

Sources: United Nations, Population Division, Department for Economic and Social Information and Policy Analysis, *World Population Prospects, The 1992 Revision* (New York: United Nations, 1993); *Statesman's Year-Book* (New York: St. Martin's Press, 1901–1927); *World Almanac and Book of Facts* (New York: Press Pub. Co., 1970–1993).

one-third of the appropriate age group was enrolled in secondary education; by the early 1990s one-half of the age group was enrolled except in Africa. In 1960 urban residents made up less than one-quarter of the population of the less developed world. Between 1960 and 1992, however, the urban percentage of the population rose from 49 percent to 73 percent in Latin America, 34 percent to 55 percent in Arab countries, 14 percent to 29 percent in Africa, 18 percent to 27 percent in China, and 19 percent to 26 percent in India.[6]

These shifts in literacy, education, and urbanization created socially mobilized populations with enhanced capabilities and higher expectations who could be activated for political purposes in ways in which illiterate peasants could not. Socially mobilized societies are more powerful societies. In 1953, when less than 15 percent of Iranians were literate and less than 17 percent urban, Kermit Roosevelt and a few CIA operatives rather easily suppressed an insurgency and restored the Shah to his throne. In 1979, when 50 percent of Iranians were literate and 47 percent lived in cities, no amount of U.S. military power could have kept the Shah on his throne. A significant gap still separates Chinese, Indians, Arabs, and Africans from Westerners, Japanese, and Russians. Yet the gap is narrowing rapidly. At the same time, a different gap is opening. The average ages of Westerners, Japanese, and Russians are increasingly steadily, and the larger proportion of the population that no longer works imposes a mounting burden on those still productively employed. Other civilizations are burdened by large numbers of children, but children are future workers and soldiers.

Economic Product. The Western share of the global economic product also may have peaked in the 1920s and has clearly been declining since World War II. In 1750 China accounted for almost one-third, India for almost one-quarter, and the West for less than a fifth of the world's manufacturing output. By 1830 the West had pulled slightly ahead of China. In the following decades, as Paul

TABLE 4.4

SHARES OF WORLD MANUFACTURING OUTPUT BY CIVILIZATION OR COUNTRY, 1750–1980 (in percentages, World = 100%)

Country	1750	1800	1830	1860	1880	1900	1913	1928	1938	1953	1963	1973	1980
West	18.2	23.3	31.1	53.7	68.8	77.4	81.6	84.2	78.6	74.6	65.4	61.2	57.8
China	32.8	33.3	29.8	19.7	12.5	6.2	3.6	3.4	3.1	2.3	3.5	3.9	5.0
Japan	3.8	3.5	2.8	2.6	2.4	2.4	2.7	3.3	5.2	2.9	5.1	8.8	9.1
India/Pakistan	24.5	19.7	17.6	8.6	2.8	1.7	1.4	1.9	2.4	1.7	1.8	2.1	2.3
Russia/USSR*	5.0	5.6	5.6	7.0	7.6	8.8	8.2	5.3	9.0	16.0	20.9	20.1	21.1
Brazil & Mexico	—	—	—	0.8	0.6	0.7	0.8	0.8	0.8	0.9	1.2	1.6	2.2
Others	15.7	14.6	13.1	7.6	5.3	2.8	1.7	1.1	0.9	1.6	2.1	2.3	2.5

* Includes Warsaw Pact countries during the Cold War years.

Source: Paul Bairoch, "International Industrialization Levels from 1750 to 1980," *Journal of European Economic History,* 11 (Fall 1982), 269–334.

Bairoch points out, the industrialization of the West led to the deindustrialization of the rest of the world. In 1913 the manufacturing output of non-Western countries was roughly two-thirds what it had been in 1800. Beginning in the mid-nineteenth century the Western share rose dramatically, peaking in 1928 at 84.2 percent of world manufacturing output. Thereafter the West's share declined as its rate of growth remained modest and as less industrialized countries expanded their output rapidly after World War II. By 1980 the West accounted for 57.8 percent of global manufacturing output, roughly the share it had 120 years earlier in the 1860s.[7]

Reliable data on gross economic product are not available for the pre–World War II period. In 1950, however, the West accounted for roughly 64 percent of the gross world product; by the 1980s this proportion had dropped to 49 percent. (See Table 4.5.) By 2013, according to one estimate, the West will account for only 30% of the world product. In 1991, according to another estimate, four of the world's seven largest economies belonged to non-Western nations: Japan (in second place), China (third), Russia (sixth), and India (seventh). In 1992 the United States had the largest economy in the world, and the top ten economies included those of five Western countries plus the leading states of five other civilizations: China, Japan, India, Russia, and Brazil. In 2020 plausible projections indicate that the top five economies will be in five different civilizations, and the top ten economies will include only three Western countries. This relative decline of the West is, of course, in large part a function of the rapid rise of East Asia.[8]

Gross figures on economic output partially obscure the West's qualitative advantage. The West and Japan almost totally dominate advanced technology industries. Technologies are being disseminated, however, and if the West wishes to maintain its superiority it will do what it can to minimize that dissemination. Thanks to the interconnected world which the West has created,

TABLE 4.5
CIVILIZATION SHARES OF WORLD GROSS ECONOMIC PRODUCT, 1950–1992
(in percentages)

Year	Western	African	Sinic	Hindu	Islamic	Japanese	Latin American	Orthodox*	Other†
1950	64.1	0.2	3.3	3.8	2.9	3.1	5.6	16.0	1.0
1970	53.4	1.7	4.8	3.0	4.6	7.8	6.2	17.4	1.1
1980	48.6	2.0	6.4	2.7	6.3	8.5	7.7	16.4	1.4
1992	48.9	2.1	10.0	3.5	11.0	8.0	8.3	6.2	2.0

* Orthodox estimate for 1992 includes the former USSR and the former Yugoslavia.

† "Other" includes other civilizations and rounding error.

Sources: 1950, 1970, 1980 percentages calculated from constant dollar data by Herbert Block, *The Planetary Product in 1980: A Creative Pause?* (Washington, D.C.: Bureau of Public Affairs, U.S. Dept. of State, 1981), pp. 30–45. 1992 percentages are calculated from World Bank purchasing power parity estimates in table 30 of *World Development Report 1994* (New York: Oxford University Press, 1994).

however, slowing the diffusion of technology to other civilizations is increasingly difficult. It is made all the more so in the absence of a single, overpowering, agreed-upon threat such as existed during the Cold War and gave measures of technology control some modest effectiveness.

It appears probable that for most of history China had the world's largest economy. The diffusion of technology and the economic development of non-Western societies in the second half of the twentieth century are now producing a return to the historical pattern. This will be a slow process, but by the middle of the twenty-first century, if not before, the distribution of economic product and manufacturing output among the leading civilizations is likely to resemble that of 1800. The two-hundred-year Western "blip" on the world economy will be over.

Military Capability. Military power has four dimensions: quantitative — the numbers of men, weapons, equipment, and resources; technological — the effectiveness and sophistication of weapons and equipment; organizational — the coherence, discipline, training, and morale of the troops and the effectiveness of command and control relationships; and societal — the ability and willingness of the society to apply military force effectively. In the 1920s the West was far ahead of everyone else in all these dimensions. In the years since, the military power of the West has declined relative to that of other civilizations, a decline reflected in the shifting balance in military personnel, one measure, although clearly not the most important one, of military capability. Modernization and economic development generate the resources and desire for states to develop their military capabilities, and few states fail to do so. In the 1930s Japan and the Soviet Union created very powerful military forces, as they demonstrated in World War II. During the Cold War the Soviet Union had one of the world's two most powerful military forces. Currently the West mo-

TABLE 4.6
CIVILIZATION SHARES OF TOTAL WORLD MILITARY MANPOWER
(in percentages)

Year [World total]	Western	African	Sinic	Hindu	Islamic	Japanese	Latin American	Orthodox	Other
1900 [10,086]	43.7	1.6	10.0	0.4	16.7	1.8	9.4	16.6	0.1
1920 [8,645]	48.5	3.8	17.4	0.4	3.6	2.9	10.2	12.8*	0.5
1970 [23,991]	26.8	2.1	24.7	6.6	10.4	0.3	4.0	25.1	2.3
1991 [25,797]	21.1	3.4	25.7	4.8	20.0	1.0	6.3	14.3	3.5

Notes: Estimates based on prevailing state borders as of the year indicated.
    World total (active duty) armed forces estimate for each selected year displayed in thousands.

* USSR component of figure is an estimate for the year 1924 by J. M. Mackintosh in B. H. Liddell-Hart, *The Red Army: The Red Army—1918 to 1945, The Soviet Army—1946 to present* (New York: Harcourt, Brace, 1956).

Sources: U.S. Arms Control and Disarmament Agency, *World Military Expenditures and Arms Transfers* (Washington, D.C.: The Agency, 1971–1994); *Statesman's Year-Book* (New York: St. Martin's Press, 1901–1927).

nopolizes the ability to deploy substantial conventional military forces any-
where in the world. Whether it will continue to maintain that capability is
uncertain. It seems reasonably certain, however, that no non-Western state or
group of states will create a comparable capability during the coming decades.

Overall, the years after the Cold War have been dominated by five major
trends in the evolution of global military capabilities.

First, the armed forces of the Soviet Union ceased to exist shortly after the
Soviet Union ceased to exist. Apart from Russia, only Ukraine inherited significant military capabilities. Russian forces were greatly reduced in size and were
withdrawn from Central Europe and the Baltic states. The Warsaw Pact ended.
The goal of challenging the U.S. Navy was abandoned. Military equipment
was either disposed of or allowed to deteriorate and become nonoperational.
Budget allocations for defense were drastically reduced. Demoralization pervaded the ranks of both officers and men. At the same time the Russian military
were redefining their missions and doctrine and restructuring themselves for
their new roles in protecting Russians and dealing with regional conflicts in
the near abroad.

Second, the precipitous reduction in Russian military capabilities stimulated
a slower but significant decline in Western military spending, forces, and capabilities. Under the plans of the Bush and Clinton administrations, U.S. military
spending was due to drop by 35 percent from $342.3 billion (1994 dollars) in
1990 to $222.3 in 1998. The force structure that year would be half to two-
thirds what it was at the end of the Cold War. Total military personnel would
go down from 2.1 million to 1.4 million. Many major weapons programs have
been and are being canceled. Between 1985 and 1995 annual purchases of
major weapons went down from 29 to 6 ships, 943 to 127 aircraft, 720 to 0
tanks, and 48 to 18 strategic missiles. Beginning in the late 1980s, Britain,
Germany, and, to a lesser degree, France went through similar reductions in
defense spending and military capabilities. In the mid-1990s, the German
armed forces were scheduled to decline from 370,000 to 340,000 and probably to 320,000; the French army was to drop from its strength of 290,000 in
1990 to 225,000 in 1997. British military personnel went down from 377,100
in 1985 to 274,800 in 1993. Continental members of NATO also shortened
terms of conscripted service and debated the possible abandonment of conscription.

Third, the trends in East Asia differed significantly from those in Russia and
the West. Increased military spending and force improvements were the order
of the day; China was the pacesetter. Stimulated by both their increasing
economic wealth and the Chinese buildup, other East Asian nations are modernizing and expanding their military forces. Japan has continued to improve
its highly sophisticated military capability. Taiwan, South Korea, Thailand,
Malaysia, Singapore, and Indonesia all are spending more on their military and
purchasing planes, tanks, and ships from Russia, the United States, Britain,

France, Germany, and other countries. While NATO defense expenditures declined by roughly 10 percent between 1985 and 1993 (from $539.6 billion to $485.0 billion) (constant 1993 dollars), expenditures in East Asia rose by 50 percent from $89.8 billion to $134.8 billion during the same period.[9]

Fourth, military capabilities including weapons of mass destruction are diffusing broadly across the world. As countries develop economically, they generate the capacity to produce weapons. Between the 1960s and 1980s, for instance, the number of Third World countries producing fighter aircraft increased from one to eight, tanks from one to six, helicopters from one to six, and tactical missiles from none to seven. The 1990s have seen a major trend toward the globalization of the defense industry, which is likely further to erode Western military advantages.[10] Many non-Western societies either have nuclear weapons (Russia, China, Israel, India, Pakistan, and possibly North Korea) or have been making strenuous efforts to acquire them (Iran, Iraq, Libya, and possibly Algeria) or are placing themselves in a position quickly to acquire them if they see the need to do so (Japan).

Finally, all those developments make regionalization the central trend in military strategy and power in the post–Cold War world. Regionalization provides the rationale for the reductions in Russian and Western military forces and for increases in the military forces of other states. Russia no longer has a global military capability but is focusing its strategy and forces on the near abroad. China has reoriented its strategy and forces to emphasize local power projection and the defense of Chinese interests in East Asia. European countries are similarly redirecting their forces, through both NATO and the Western European Union, to deal with instability on the periphery of Western Europe. The United States has explicitly shifted its military planning from deterring and fighting the Soviet Union on a global basis to preparing to deal simultaneously with regional contingencies in the Persian Gulf and Northeast Asia. The United States, however, is not likely to have the military capability to meet these goals. To defeat Iraq, the United States deployed in the Persian Gulf 75 percent of its active tactical aircraft, 42 percent of its modern battle tanks, 46 percent of its aircraft carriers, 37 percent of its army personnel, and 46 percent of its marine personnel. With significantly reduced forces in the future, the United States will be hard put to carry out one intervention, much less two, against substantial regional powers outside the Western Hemisphere. Military security throughout the world increasingly depends not on the global distribution of power and the actions of superpowers but on the distribution of power within each region of the world and the actions of the core states of civilizations.

In sum, overall the West will remain the most powerful civilization well into the early decades of the twenty-first century. Beyond then it will probably continue to have a substantial lead in scientific talent, research and development capabilities, and civilian and military technological innovation. Control over the other power resources, however, is becoming increasingly dispersed among the core states and leading countries of non-Western civilizations. The West's control of these resources peaked in the 1920s and has since been declining irregularly but significantly. In the 2020s, a hundred years after that peak, the West will probably control about 24 percent of the world's territory (down from a peak of 49 percent), 10 percent of the total world population (down from 48 percent) and perhaps 15–20 percent of the socially mobilized population, about 30 percent of the world's economic product (down from a peak of probably 70 percent), perhaps 25 percent of manufacturing output (down from a peak of 84 percent), and less than 10 percent of global military manpower (down from 45 percent).

In 1919 Woodrow Wilson, Lloyd George, and Georges Clemenceau together virtually controlled the world. Sitting in Paris, they determined what countries would exist and which would not, what new countries would be created, what their boundaries would be and who would rule them, and how the Middle East and other parts of the world would be divided up among the victorious powers. They also decided on military intervention in Russia and economic concessions to be extracted from China. A hundred years later, no small group of statesmen will be able to exercise comparable power; to the extent that any group does it will not consist of three Westerners but leaders of the core states of the world's seven or eight major civilizations. The successors to Reagan, Thatcher, Mitterrand, and Kohl will be rivaled by those of Deng Xiaoping, Nakasone, Indira Gandhi, Yeltsin, Khomeini, and Suharto. The age of Western dominance will be over. In the meantime the fading of the West and the rise of other power centers is promoting the global processes of indigenization and the resurgence of non-Western cultures.

INDIGENIZATION: THE RESURGENCE OF NON-WESTERN CULTURES

The distribution of cultures in the world reflects the distribution of power. Trade may or may not follow the flag, but culture almost always follows power. Throughout history the expansion of the power of a civilization has usually occurred simultaneously with the flowering of its culture and has almost always involved its using that power to extend its values, practices, and institutions to other societies. A universal civilization requires universal power. Roman power created a near-universal civilization within the limited confines of the Classical world. Western power in the form of European colonialism in the nineteenth century and American hegemony in the twentieth century extended Western culture throughout much of the contemporary world. European colonialism is over; American hegemony is receding. The erosion of Western culture follows, as indigenous, historically rooted mores, languages, beliefs, and institutions reassert themselves. The growing power of non-Western societies produced by modernization is generating the revival of non-Western cultures throughout the world.*

A distinction exists, Joseph Nye has argued, between "hard power," which is the power to command resting on economic and military strength, and "soft power," which is the ability of a state to get "other countries to *want* what it wants" through the appeal of its culture and ideology. As Nye recognizes, a broad diffusion of hard power is occurring in the world and the major nations "are less able to use their traditional power resources to achieve their purposes than in the past." Nye goes on to say that if a state's "culture and ideology are attractive, others will be more willing to follow" its leadership, and hence soft power is "just as important as hard command power." [11] What, however, makes culture and ideology attractive? They become attractive when they are seen as rooted in material success and influence. Soft power is power only when it rests on a foundation of hard power. Increases in hard economic and military power produce enhanced self-confidence, arrogance, and belief in the superiority of one's own culture or soft power compared to those of other peoples and greatly increase its attractiveness to other peoples. Decreases in economic and military power lead to self-doubt, crises of identity, and efforts to find in other cultures the keys to economic, military, and political success. As non-Western societies enhance their economic, military, and political capacity, they increasingly trumpet the virtues of their own values, institutions, and culture.

Communist ideology appealed to people throughout the world in the 1950s and 1960s when it was associated with the economic success and military force of the Soviet Union. That appeal evaporated when the Soviet economy stagnated and was unable to maintain Soviet military strength. Western values and institutions have appealed to people from other cultures because they were seen as the source of Western power and wealth. This process has been going on for centuries. Between 1000 and 1300, as William McNeill points out, Christianity, Roman law, and other elements of Western culture were adopted by Hungarians, Poles, and Lithuanians, and this "acceptance of Western civilization was stimulated by mingled fear and admiration of the military prowess of Western princes." [12] As Western power declines, the ability of the West to impose Western concepts of human rights, liberalism, and democracy on other civilizations also declines and so does the attractiveness of those values to other civilizations.

It already has. For several centuries non-Western peoples envied the eco-

---

* The link between power and culture is almost universally ignored by those who argue that a universal civilization is and should be emerging as well as by those who argue that Westernization is a prerequisite to modernization. They refuse to recognize that the logic of their argument requires them to support the expansion and consolidation of Western domination of the world, and that if other societies are left free to shape their own destinies they reinvigorate old creeds, habits, and practices which, according to the universalists, are inimical to progress. The people who argue the virtues of a universal civilization, however, do not usually argue the virtues of a universal empire.

nomic prosperity, technological sophistication, military power, and political cohesion of Western societies. They sought the secret of this success in Western values and institutions, and when they identified what they thought might be the key they attempted to apply it in their own societies. To become rich and powerful, they would have to become like the West. Now, however, these Kemalist attitudes have disappeared in East Asia. East Asians attribute their dramatic economic development not to their import of Western culture but rather to their adherence to their own culture. They are succeeding, they argue, because they are different from the West. Similarly, when non-Western societies felt weak in relation to the West, they invoked Western values of self-determination, liberalism, democracy, and independence to justify their opposition to Western domination. Now that they are no longer weak but increasingly powerful, they do not hesitate to attack those same values which they previously used to promote their interests. The revolt against the West was originally legitimated by asserting the universality of Western values; it is now legitimated by asserting the superiority of non-Western values.

The rise of these attitudes is a manifestation of what Ronald Dore has termed the "second-generation indigenization phenomenon." In both former Western colonies and independent countries like China and Japan, "The first 'modern-izer' or 'post-independence' generation has often received its training in foreign (Western) universities in a Western cosmopolitan language. Partly because they first go abroad as impressionable teenagers, their absorption of Western values and life-styles may well be profound." Most of the much larger second generation, in contrast, gets its education at home in universities created by the first generation, and the local rather than the colonial language is increasingly used for instruction. These universities "provide a much more diluted contact with metropolitan world culture" and "knowledge is indigenized by means of transla-tions — usually of limited range and of poor quality." The graduates of these universities resent the dominance of the earlier Western-trained generation and hence often "succumb to the appeals of nativist opposition movements."[13] As Western influence recedes, young aspiring leaders cannot look to the West to provide them with power and wealth. They have to find the means of success within their own society, and hence they have to accommodate to the values and culture of that society.

The process of indigenization need not wait for the second generation. Able, perceptive, and adaptive first generation leaders indigenize themselves. Three notable cases are Mohammad Ali Jinnah, Harry Lee, and Solomon Bandara-naike. They were brilliant graduates of Oxford, Cambridge, and Lincoln's Inn, respectively, superb lawyers, and thoroughly Westernized members of the elites of their societies. Jinnah was a committed secularist. Lee was, in the words of one British cabinet minister, "the best bloody Englishman east of Suez." Bandaranaike was raised a Christian. Yet to lead their nations to and after independence they had to indigenize. They reverted to their ancestral cultures, and in the process at times changed identities, names, dress, and beliefs. The

English lawyer M. A. Jinnah became Pakistan's Quaid-i-Azam, Harry Lee became Lee Kuan Yew. The secularist Jinnah became the fervent apostle of Islam as the basis for the Pakistani state. The Anglofied Lee learned Mandarin and became an articulate promoter of Confucianism. The Christian Bandaranaike converted to Buddhism and appealed to Sinhalese nationalism.

Indigenization has been the order of the day throughout the non-Western world in the 1980s and 1990s. The resurgence of Islam and "re-Islamization" are the central themes in Muslim societies. In India the prevailing trend is the rejection of Western forms and values and the "Hinduization" of politics and society. In East Asia, governments are promoting Confucianism, and political and intellectual leaders speak of the "Asianization" of their countries. In the mid-1980s Japan became obsessed with "*Nihonjinron* or the theory of Japan and the Japanese." Subsequently a leading Japanese intellectual argued that historically Japan has gone through "cycles of importation of external cultures" and " 'indigenization' of those cultures through replication and refinement, inevitable turmoil resulting from exhausting the imported and creative impulse, and eventual reopening to the outside world." At present Japan is "embarking on the second phase of this cycle."[14] With the end of the Cold War, Russia again became a "torn" country with the reemergence of the classic struggle between Westernizers and Slavophiles. For a decade, however, the trend was from the former to the latter, as the Westernized Gorbachev gave way to Yeltsin, Russian in style, Western in articulated beliefs, who, in turn, was threatened by nationalists epitomizing Russian Orthodox indigenization.

Indigenization is furthered by the democracy paradox: adoption by non-Western societies of Western democratic institutions encourages and gives access to power to nativist and anti-Western political movements. In the 1960s and 1970s Westernized and pro-Western governments in developing countries were threatened by coups and revolutions; in the 1980s and 1990s they are increasingly in danger of being ousted by elections. Democratization conflicts with Westernization, and democracy is inherently a parochializing not a cosmopolitanizing process. Politicians in non-Western societies do not win elections by demonstrating how Western they are. Electoral competition instead stimulates them to fashion what they believe will be the most popular appeals, and those are usually ethnic, nationalist, and religious in character.

The result is popular mobilization against Western-educated and Western-oriented elites. Islamic fundamentalist groups have done well in the few elections that have occurred in Muslim countries and would have come to national power in Algeria if the military had not canceled the 1992 election. In India competition for electoral support has arguably encouraged communal appeals and communal violence.[15] Democracy in Sri Lanka enabled the Sri Lanka Freedom Party to throw out the Western-oriented, elitist United National Party in 1956 and provided opportunity for the rise of the Pathika Chintanaya Sinhalese nationalist movement in the 1980s. Prior to 1949 both South African and Western elites viewed South Africa as a Western state. After the apartheid regime took shape, Western elites gradually read South Africa out of the Western camp, while white South Africans continued to think of themselves as Westerners. In order to resume their place in the Western international order, however, they had to introduce Western democratic institutions, which resulted in the coming to power of a highly Westernized black elite. If the second generation indigenization factor operates, however, their successors will be much more Xhosa, Zulu, and African in outlook and South Africa will increasingly define itself as an African state.

At various times before the nineteenth century, Byzantines, Arabs, Chinese, Ottomans, Moguls, and Russians were highly confident of their strength and achievements compared to those of the West. At these times they also were contemptuous of the cultural inferiority, institutional backwardness, corruption, and decadence of the West. As the success of the West fades relatively, such attitudes reappear. People feel "they don't have to take it anymore." Iran is an extreme case, but, as one observer noted, "Western values are rejected in different ways, but no less firmly, in Malaysia, Indonesia, Singapore, China, and Japan."[16] We are witnessing "the end of the progressive era" dominated by Western ideologies and are moving into an era in which multiple and diverse civilizations will interact, compete, coexist, and accommodate each other.[17] This global process of indigenization is manifest broadly in the revivals of religion occurring in so many parts of the world and most notably in the cultural resurgence in Asian and Islamic countries generated in large part by their economic and demographic dynamism.

LA REVANCHE DE DIEU

In the first half of the twentieth century intellectual elites generally assumed that economic and social modernization was leading to the withering away of religion as a significant element in human existence. This assumption was shared by both those who welcomed and those who deplored this trend. Modernizing secularists hailed the extent to which science, rationalism, and pragmatism were eliminating the superstitions, myths, irrationalities, and rituals that formed the core of existing religions. The emerging society would be tolerant, rational, pragmatic, progressive, humanistic, and secular. Worried conservatives, on the other hand, warned of the dire consequences of the disappearance of religious beliefs, religious institutions, and the moral guidance religion provided for individual and collective human behavior. The end result would be anarchy, depravity, the undermining of civilized life. "If you will not have God (and He is a jealous God)," T. S. Eliot said, "you should pay your respects to Hitler or Stalin."[18]

The second half of the twentieth century proved these hopes and fears unfounded. Economic and social modernization became global in scope, and at the same time a global revival of religion occurred. This revival, *la revanche de Dieu*, Gilles Kepel termed it, has pervaded every continent, every civilization, and virtually every country. In the mid-1970s, as Kepel observes, the trend to secularization and toward the accommodation of religion with secularism "went into reverse. A new religious approach took shape, aimed no longer at adapting to secular values but at recovering a sacred foundation for the organization of society—by changing society if necessary. Expressed in a multitude of ways, this approach advocated moving on from a modernism that had failed, attributing its setbacks and dead ends to separation from God. The theme was no longer *aggiornamento* but a 'second evangelization of Europe,' the aim was no longer to modernize Islam but to 'Islamize modernity.' " [19]

This religious revival has in part involved expansion by some religions, which gained new recruits in societies where they had previously not had them. To a much larger extent, however, the religious resurgence involved people returning to, reinvigorating, and giving new meaning to the traditional religions of their communities. Christianity, Islam, Judaism, Hinduism, Buddhism, Orthodoxy, all experienced new surges in commitment, relevance, and practice by erstwhile casual believers. In all of them fundamentalist movements arose committed to the militant purification of religious doctrines and institutions and the reshaping of personal, social, and public behavior in accordance with religious tenets. The fundamentalist movements are dramatic and can have significant political impact. They are, however, only the surface waves of the much broader and more fundamental religious tide that is giving a different cast to human life at the end of the twentieth century. The renewal of religion throughout the world far transcends the activities of fundamentalist extremists. In society after society it manifests itself in the daily lives and work of people and the concerns and projects of governments. The cultural resurgence in the secular Confucian culture takes the form of the affirmation of Asian values but in the rest of the world manifests itself in the affirmation of religious values. The "unsecularization of the world," as George Weigel remarked "is one of the dominant social facts in the late twentieth century." [20]

The ubiquity and relevance of religion has been dramatically evident in former communist states. Filling the vacuum left by the collapse of ideology, religious revivals have swept through these countries from Albania to Vietnam. In Russia, Orthodoxy has gone through a major resurgence. In 1994, 30 percent of Russians below the age of twenty-five said they had switched from atheism to a belief in God. The number of active churches in the Moscow area grew from 50 in 1988 to 250 in 1993. Political leaders became uniformly respectful of religion and the government supportive of it. In Russian cities, as one acute observer reported in 1993, "The sound of church bells once again fills the air. Newly gilded cupolas gleam in the sun. Churches only recently in ruins reverberate again with magnificent song. Churches are the busiest place in town." [21] Simultaneously with the revival of Orthodoxy in the Slavic republics, an Islamic revival swept through Central Asia. In 1989, 160 functioning mosques and one *medressah* (Islamic seminary) existed in Central Asia; by early 1993 there were about 10,000 mosques and ten *medressahs*. While this revival involved some fundamentalist political movements and was encouraged from the outside by Saudi Arabia, Iran, and Pakistan, it was basically an extremely broad-based, mainstream, cultural movement.[22]

How can this global religious resurgence be explained? Particular causes obviously operated in individual countries and civilizations. Yet it is too much to expect that a large number of different causes would have produced simultaneous and similar developments in most parts of the world. A global phenomenon demands a global explanation. However much events in particular countries may have been influenced by unique factors, some general causes must have been at work. What were they?

The most obvious, most salient, and most powerful cause of the global religious resurgence is precisely what was supposed to cause the death of religion: the processes of social, economic, and cultural modernization that swept across the world in the second half of the twentieth century. Long-standing sources of identity and systems of authority are disrupted. People move from the countryside into the city, become separated from their roots, and take new jobs or no job. They interact with large numbers of strangers and are exposed to new sets of relationships. They need new sources of identity, new forms of stable community, and new sets of moral precepts to provide them with a sense of meaning and purpose. Religion, both mainstream and fundamentalist, meets these needs. As Lee Kuan Yew explained for East Asia:

> We are agricultural societies that have industrialized within one or two generations. What happened in the West over 200 years or more is happening here in about 50 years or less. It is all crammed and crushed into a very tight time frame, so there are bound to be dislocations and malfunctions. If you look at the fast-growing countries — Korea, Thailand, Hong Kong, and Singapore — there's been one remarkable phenomenon: the rise of religion. . . . The old customs and religions — ancestor worship, shamanism — no longer completely satisfy. There is a quest for some higher explanations about man's purpose, about why we are here. This is associated with periods of great stress in society.[23]

People do not live by reason alone. They cannot calculate and act rationally in pursuit of their self-interest until they define their self. Interest politics presupposes identity. In times of rapid social change established identities dissolve, the self must be redefined, and new identities created. For people facing the need to determine Who am I? Where do I belong? religion provides compelling answers, and religious groups provide small social communities to replace those lost through urbanization. All religions, as Hassan al-Turabi said, furnish "people with a sense of identity and a direction in life." In this process, people rediscover or create new historical identities. Whatever universalist goals they may have, religions give people identity by positing a basic distinction between believers and nonbelievers, between a superior in-group and a different and inferior out-group.[24]

In the Muslim world, Bernard Lewis argues, there has been "a recurring tendency, in times of emergency, for Muslims to find their basic identity and loyalty in the religious community — that is to say, in an entity defined by Islam rather than by ethnic or territorial criteria." Gilles Kepel similarly highlights the centrality of the search for identity: "Re-Islamization 'from below' is first and foremost a way of rebuilding an identity in a world that has lost its meaning and become amorphous and alienating." [25] In India, "a new Hindu identity is under construction" as a response to tensions and alienation generated by modernization. [26] In Russia the religious revival is the result "of a passionate desire for identity which only the Orthodox church, the sole unbroken link with the Russians' 1000-year past, can provide," while in the Islamic republics the revival similarly stems "from the Central Asians' most powerful aspiration: to assert the identities that Moscow suppressed for decades." [27] Fundamentalist movements, in particular, are "a way of coping with the experience of chaos, the loss of identity, meaning and secure social structures created by the rapid introduction of modern social and political patterns, secularism, scientific culture and economic development." The fundamentalist "movements that matter," agrees William H. McNeill, ". . . are those that recruit from society at large and spread because they answer, or seem to answer, newly felt human needs. . . . It is no accident that these movements are all based in countries where population pressure on the land is making continuation of old village ways impossible for a majority of the population, and where urban-based mass communications, by penetrating the villages, have begun to erode an age-old framework of peasant life." [28]

More broadly, the religious resurgence throughout the world is a reaction against secularism, moral relativism, and self-indulgence, and a reaffirmation of the values of order, discipline, work, mutual help, and human solidarity. Religious groups meet social needs left untended by state bureaucracies. These include the provision of medical and hospital services, kindergartens and schools, care for the elderly, prompt relief after natural and other catastrophes, and welfare and social support during periods of economic deprivation. The breakdown of order and of civil society creates vacuums which are filled by religious, often fundamentalist, groups. [29]

If traditionally dominant religions do not meet the emotional and social needs of the uprooted, other religious groups move in to do so and in the process greatly expand their memberships and the saliency of religion in social and political life. South Korea historically was an overwhelmingly Buddhist country, with Christians numbering in 1950 perhaps 1 percent to 3 percent of the population. As South Korea took off into rapid economic development, with massive urbanization and occupational differentiation, Buddhism was found wanting. "For the millions who poured into the cities and for many who stayed behind in the altered countryside, the quiescent Buddhism of Korea's agrarian age lost its appeal. Christianity with its message of personal salvation and individual destiny offered a surer comfort in a time of confusion and change."[30] By the 1980s Christians, largely Presbyterians and Catholics, were at least 30 percent of South Korea's population.

A similar and parallel shift occurred in Latin America. The number of Protestants in Latin America increased from roughly 7 million in 1960 to about 50 million in 1990. The reasons for this success, the Latin American Catholic bishops recognized in 1989, included the Catholic Church's "slowness in coming to terms with the technicalities of urban life" and "its structure that occasionally makes it incapable of responding to the psychological needs of present-day people." Unlike the Catholic Church, one Brazilian priest observed, the Protestant churches meet "the basic needs of the person — human warmth, healing, a deep spiritual experience." The spread of Protestantism among the poor in Latin America is not primarily the replacement of one religion by another but rather a major net increase in religious commitment and participation as nominal and passive Catholics become active and devout Evangelicals. In Brazil in the early 1990s, for instance, 20 percent of the population identified themselves as Protestant and 73 percent as Catholic, yet on Sundays 20 million people were in Protestant churches and about 12 million were in Catholic ones.[31] Like the other world religions, Christianity is going through a resurgence connected to modernization, and in Latin America it has taken a Protestant rather than a Catholic form.

These changes in South Korea and Latin America reflect the inability of Buddhism and established Catholicism to meet the psychological, emotional, and social needs of people caught in the traumas of modernization. Whether additional significant shifts in religious adherence occur elsewhere depends on the extent to which the prevailing religion is able to meet these needs. Given its emotional aridity, Confucianism appears particularly vulnerable. In Confucian countries, Protestantism and Catholicism could have an appeal similar to those of evangelical Protestantism to Latin Americans, Christianity to South Koreans, and fundamentalism to Muslims and Hindus. In China in the late 1980s, as economic growth was in full swing, Christianity also spread "particularly among young people." Perhaps 50 million Chinese are Christian. The government has attempted to prevent their increase by jailing ministers, missionaries, and evangelists, prohibiting and suppressing religious ceremonies and activities, and in 1994 passing a law that prohibits foreigners from proselytizing or setting up religious schools or other religious organizations and prohibits religious groups from engaging in independent or overseas-financed activities. In Singapore, as in China, about 5 percent of the population is Christian. In the late 1980s and early 1990s government ministers warned evangelists against upsetting the country's "delicate religious balance," detained religious workers including officials of Catholic organizations, and harassed in various ways Christian groups and individuals.[32] With the end of the Cold War and the political openings that followed, Western churches also moved into the Orthodox former Soviet republics, competing with the revived Orthodox churches. Here too, as in China, an effort was made to curb their proselytizing. In 1993, at the urging of the Orthodox Church, the Russian parliament passed legislation requiring foreign religious groups to be accredited by the state or to be affiliated with a Russian religious organization if they were going to engage in missionary or educational work. President Yeltsin, however, refused to sign this bill into law.[33] Overall, the record suggests that where they conflict, *la revanche de Dieu* trumps indigenization: if the religious needs of modernization cannot be met by their traditional faiths people turn to emotionally satisfying religious imports.

In addition to the psychological, emotional, and social traumas of modernization, other stimulants to religious revival included the retreat of the West and the end of the Cold War. Beginning in the nineteenth century, the responses of non-Western civilizations to the West generally moved through a progression of ideologies imported from the West. In the nineteenth century non-Western elites imbibed Western liberal values, and their first expressions of opposition to the West took the form of liberal nationalism. In the twentieth century Russian, Asian, Arab, African, and Latin American elites imported socialist and Marxist ideologies and combined them with nationalism in opposition to Western capitalism and Western imperialism. The collapse of communism in the Soviet Union, its severe modification in China, and the failure of socialist economies to achieve sustained development have now created an ideological vacuum. Western governments, groups, and international institutions, such as the IMF and World Bank, have attempted to fill this vacuum with the doctrines of neo-orthodox economics and democratic politics. The extent to which these doctrines will have a lasting impact in non-Western cultures is uncertain. Meanwhile, however, people see communism as only the latest secular god to have failed, and in the absence of compelling new secular deities they turn with relief and passion to the real thing. Religion takes over from ideology, and religious nationalism replaces secular nationalism.[34]

The movements for religious revival are antisecular, antiuniversal, and, except in their Christian manifestations, anti-Western. They also are opposed to the relativism, egotism, and consumerism associated with what Bruce B. Lawrence has termed "modernism" as distinct from "modernity." By and large they do not reject urbanization, industrialization, development, capitalism, science, and technology, and what these imply for the organization of society. In this sense, they are not antimodern. They accept modernization, as Lee Kuan Yew observes, and "the inevitability of science and technology and the change in the life-styles they bring," but they are "unreceptive to the idea that they be Westernized." Neither nationalism nor socialism, al-Turabi argues, produced development in the Islamic world. "Religion is the motor of development," and a purified Islam will play a role in the contemporary era comparable to that of the Protestant ethic in the history of the West. Nor is religion incompatible with the development of a modern state.[35] Islamic fundamentalist movements have been strong in the more advanced and seemingly more secular Muslim societies, such as Algeria, Iran, Egypt, Lebanon, and Tunisia.[36] Religious movements, including particularly fundamentalist ones, are highly adept at using modern communications and organizational techniques to spread their message, illustrated most dramatically by the success of Protestant televangelism in Central America.

Participants in the religious resurgence come from all walks of life but overwhelmingly from two constituencies, both urban and both mobile. Recent migrants to the cities generally need emotional, social, and material support and guidance, which religious groups provide more than any other source. Religion for them, as Régis Debray put it, is not "the opium of the people, but the vitamin of the weak."[37] The other principal constituency is the new middle class embodying Dore's "second-generation indigenization phenomenon." The activists in Islamic fundamentalist groups are not, as Kepel points out, "aging conservatives or illiterate peasants." With Muslims as with others, the religious revival is an urban phenomenon and appeals to people who are modern-oriented, well-educated, and pursue careers in the professions, government, and commerce.[38] Among Muslims, the young are religious, their parents secular. Much the same is the case with Hinduism, where the leaders of revivalist movements again come from the indigenized second generation and are often "successful businessmen and administrators" labeled in the Indian press "Scuppies" — saffron-clad yuppies. Their supporters in the early 1990s were increasingly from "India's solid middle class Hindus — its merchants and accountants, its lawyers and engineers" and from its "senior civil servants, intellectuals, and journalists."[39] In South Korea, the same types of people increasingly filled Catholic and Presbyterian churches during the 1960s and 1970s.

Religion, indigenous or imported, provides meaning and direction for the rising elites in modernizing societies. "The attribution of value to a traditional religion," Ronald Dore noted, "is a claim to parity of respect asserted against 'dominant other' nations, and often, simultaneously and more proximately, against a local ruling class which has embraced the values and life-styles of those dominant other nations." "More than anything else," William McNeill observes, "reaffirmation of Islam, whatever its specific sectarian form, means the repudiation of European and American influence upon local society, politics, and morals."[40] In this sense, the revival of non-Western religions is the most powerful manifestation of anti-Westernism in non-Western societies. That revival is not a rejection of modernity; it is a rejection of the West and of the secular, relativistic, degenerate culture associated with the West. It is a rejection of what has been termed the "Westoxification" of non-Western societies. It is a declaration of cultural independence from the West, a proud statement that: "We will be modern but we won't be you."

Chapter 5

•

Economics, Demography, and the Challenger Civilizations

Indigenization and the revival of religion are global phenomena. They have been most evident, however, in the cultural assertiveness and challenges to the West that have come from Asia and from Islam. These have been the dynamic civilizations of the last quarter of the twentieth century. The Islamic challenge is manifest in the pervasive cultural, social, and political resurgence of Islam in the Muslim world and the accompanying rejection of Western values and institutions. The Asian challenge is manifest in all the East Asian civilizations — Sinic, Japanese, Buddhist, and Muslim — and emphasizes their cultural differences from the West and, at times, the commonalities they share, often identified with Confucianism. Both Asians and Muslims stress the superiority of their cultures to Western culture. In contrast, people in other non-Western civilizations — Hindu, Orthodox, Latin American, African — may affirm the distinctive character of their cultures, but as of the mid-1990s had been hesitant about proclaiming their superiority to Western culture. Asia and Islam stand alone, and at times together, in their increasingly confident assertiveness with respect to the West.

Related but different causes lie behind these challenges. Asian assertiveness is rooted in economic growth; Muslim assertiveness stems in considerable measure from social mobilization and population growth. Each of these challenges is having and will continue to have into the twenty-first century a highly destabilizing impact on global politics. The nature of those impacts, however, differs significantly. The economic development of China and other Asian societies provides their governments with both the incentives and the resources to become more demanding in their dealing with other countries. Population growth in Muslim countries, and particularly the expansion of the fifteen- to twenty-four-year-old age cohort, provides recruits for fundamentalism, terrorism, insurgency, and migration. Economic growth strengthens Asian governments; demographic growth threatens Muslim governments and non-Muslim societies.

THE ASIAN AFFIRMATION

The economic development of East Asia has been one of the most significant developments in the world in the second half of the twentieth century. This process began in Japan in the 1950s, and for a while Japan was thought to be the great exception: a non-Western country that had successfully modernized and become economically developed. The process of economic development, however, spread to the Four Tigers (Hong Kong, Taiwan, South Korea, Singapore) and then to China, Malaysia, Thailand, and Indonesia, and is taking hold in the Philippines, India, and Vietnam. These countries have often sustained for a decade or more average annual growth rates of 8–10 percent or more. An equally dramatic expansion of trade has occurred first between Asia and the world and then within Asia. This Asian economic performance contrasts dramatically with the modest growth of the European and American economies and the stagnation that has pervaded much of the rest of the world.

The exception is thus no longer just Japan, it is increasingly all of Asia. The identity of wealth with the West and underdevelopment with the non-West will not outlast the twentieth century. The speed of this transformation has been overwhelming. As Kishore Mahbubani has pointed out, it took Britain and the United States fifty-eight years and forty-seven years, respectively, to double their per capita output, but Japan did it in thirty-three years, Indonesia in seventeen, South Korea in eleven, and China in ten. The Chinese economy grew at annual rates averaging 8 percent during the 1980s and the first half of the 1990s, and the Tigers were close behind (see Figure 5.1). The "Chinese Economic Area," the World Bank declared in 1993, had become the world's "fourth growth pole," along with the United States, Japan, and Germany. According to most estimates, the Chinese economy will become the world's largest early in the twenty-first century. With the second and third largest economies in the world in the 1990s, Asia is likely to have four of the five largest and seven of the ten largest economies by 2020. By that date Asian societies are likely to account for over 40 percent of the global economic product. Most of the more competitive economies will also probably be Asian.[1] Even if Asian economic growth levels off sooner and more precipitously than expected, the consequences of the growth that has already occurred for Asia and the world are still enormous.

East Asian economic development is altering the balance of power between

FIGURE 5.1
The Economic Challenge: Asia and the West

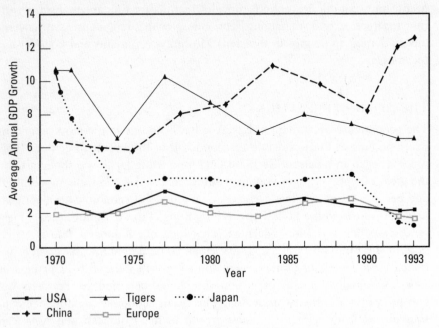

Source: World Bank, *World Tables 1995, 1991* (Baltimore: Johns Hopkins University Press, 1995, 1991);
Directorate-General of Budget, Accounting and Statistics, R. O. C., *Statistical Abstract of National
Income, Taiwan Area, Republic of China, 1951–1995* (1995). Note: Data representations are chain-
weighted three-year averages.

Asia and the West, specifically the United States. Successful economic development generates self-confidence and assertiveness on the part of those who
produce it and benefit from it. Wealth, like power, is assumed to be proof of
virtue, a demonstration of moral and cultural superiority. As they have become
more successful economically, East Asians have not hesitated to emphasize the
distinctiveness of their culture and to trumpet the superiority of their values
and way of life compared to those of the West and other societies. Asian
societies are decreasingly responsive to U.S. demands and interests and increasingly able to resist pressure from the United States or other Western countries.

A "cultural renaissance," Ambassador Tommy Koh noted in 1993, "is sweeping across" Asia. It involves a "growing self-confidence," which means Asians
"no longer regard everything Western or American as necessarily the best."[2]
This renaissance manifests itself in increasing emphasis on both the distinctive cultural identities of individual Asian countries and the commonalities of
Asian cultures which distinguish them from Western culture. The significance
of this cultural revival is written in the changing interaction of East Asia's two
major societies with Western culture.

When the West forced itself on China and Japan in the mid-nineteenth century, after a momentary infatuation with Kemalism, the prevailing elites opted for a reformist strategy. With the Meiji Restoration a dynamic group of reformers came to power in Japan, studied and borrowed Western techniques, practices, and institutions, and started the process of Japanese modernization. They did this in such a way, however, as to preserve the essentials of traditional Japanese culture, which in many respects contributed to modernization and which made it possible for Japan to invoke, reformulate, and build on the elements of that culture to arouse support for and justify its imperialism in the 1930s and 1940s. In China, on the other hand, the decaying Ch'ing dynasty was unable to adapt successfully to the impact of the West. China was defeated, exploited, and humiliated by Japan and the European powers. The collapse of the dynasty in 1910 was followed by division, civil war, and invocation of competing Western concepts by competing Chinese intellectual and political leaders: Sun Yat Sen's three principles of "Nationalism, Democracy, and the People's Livelihood"; Liang Ch'i-ch'ao's liberalism; Mao Tse-tung's Marxist-Leninism. At the end of the 1940s the import from the Soviet Union won out over those from the West — nationalism, liberalism, democracy, Christianity — and China was defined as a socialist society.

In Japan total defeat in World War II produced total cultural discombobulation. "It is very difficult now," one Westerner deeply involved in Japan commented in 1994, "for us to appreciate the extent to which everything — religion, culture, every single aspect of this country's mental existence — was drawn into the service of that war. The loss of the war was a complete shock to the system. In their minds the whole thing became worthless and was thrown out."[3] In its place, everything connected with the West and particularly the victorious United States came to be seen as good and desirable. Japan thus attempted to emulate the United States even as China emulated the Soviet Union.

By the late 1970s the failure of communism to produce economic development and the success of capitalism in Japan and increasingly in other Asian societies led new Chinese leadership to move away from the Soviet model. The collapse of the Soviet Union a decade later further underlined the failures of this import. The Chinese thus faced the issue of whether to turn Westward or to turn inward. Many intellectuals and some others advocated wholesale Westernization, a trend that reached its cultural and popular culminations in the television series *River Elegy* and the Goddess of Democracy erected in Tiananmen Square. This Western orientation, however, commanded the support of neither the few hundred people who counted in Beijing nor the 800 million peasants who lived in the countryside. Total Westernization was no more practical at the end of the twentieth century than it had been at the end of the nineteenth century. The leadership instead chose a new version of *Ti-Yong*: capitalism and involvement in the world economy, on the one hand, combined with political authoritarianism and recommitment to traditional Chinese culture, on the other. In place of the revolutionary legitimacy of

Marxist-Leninism, the regime substituted performance legitimacy provided by surging economic development and nationalist legitimacy provided by invocation of the distinctive characteristics of Chinese culture. "The post-Tiananmen regime," one commentator observed, "has eagerly embraced Chinese nationalism as a new fount of legitimacy" and has consciously aroused anti-Americanism to justify its power and its behavior.[4] A Chinese cultural nationalism is thus emerging, epitomized in the words of one Hong Kong leader in 1994: "We Chinese feel nationalist which we never felt before. We are Chinese and feel proud in that." In China itself in the early 1990s there developed a "popular desire to return to what is authentically Chinese, which often is patriarchal, nativistic, and authoritarian. Democracy, in this historical reemergence, is discredited, as is Leninism, as just another foreign imposition."[5]

In the early twentieth century Chinese intellectuals, independently paralleling Weber, identified Confucianism as the source of Chinese backwardness. In the late twentieth century, Chinese political leaders, paralleling Western social scientists, celebrate Confucianism as the source of Chinese progress. In the 1980s the Chinese government began to promote interest in Confucianism, with party leaders declaring it "the mainstream" of Chinese culture.[6] Confucianism also, of course, become an enthusiasm of Lee Kuan Yew, who saw it as a source of Singapore's success and became a missionary of Confucian values to the rest of the world. In the 1990s the Taiwanese government declared itself to be "the inheritor of Confucian thought" and President Lee Teng-hui identified of roots of Taiwan's democratization in its Chinese "cultural heritage" stretching back to Kao Yao (twenty-first century B.C.), Confucius (fifth century B.C.), and Mencius (third century B.C.).[7] Whether they wish to justify authoritarianism or democracy, Chinese leaders look for legitimation in their common Chinese culture not in imported Western concepts.

The nationalism promoted by the regime is Han nationalism, which helps to suppress the linguistic, regional, and economic differences among 90 percent of the Chinese population. At the same time, it also underlines the differences with the non-Chinese ethnic minorities that constitute less than 10 percent of China's population but occupy 60 percent of its territory. It also provides a basis for the regime's opposition to Christianity, Christian organizations, and Christian proselytizing, which offer an alternative Western faith to fill the void left by the collapse of Maoist-Leninism.

Meanwhile in Japan in the 1980s successful economic development contrasted with the perceived failures and "decline" of the American economy and social system led Japanese to become increasingly disenchanted with Western models and increasingly convinced that the sources of their success must lie within their own culture. The Japanese culture which produced military disaster in 1945 and hence had to be rejected had produced economic triumph by 1985 and hence could be embraced. The increased familiarity of Japanese with Western society led them to "realize that being Western is not magically wonderful in and of itself. They get that out of their system." While the Japanese of the Meiji Restoration adopted a policy of "disengaging from Asia and joining Europe," the Japanese of the late twentieth century cultural revival endorsed a policy of "distancing from America and engaging Asia."[8] This trend involved, first, a reidentification with Japanese cultural traditions and renewed assertion of the values of those traditions, and second and more problematical, an effort to "Asianize" Japan and identify Japan, despite its distinctive civilization, with a general Asian culture. Given the extent to which after World War II Japan in contrast to China identified itself with the West and given the extent to which the West, whatever its failings, did not collapse totally as the Soviet Union did, the incentives for Japan to reject the West totally have been nowhere near as great as those for China to distance itself from both the Soviet and Western models. On the other hand, the uniqueness of Japanese civilization, the memories in other countries of Japanese imperialism, and the economic centrality of Chinese in most other Asian countries also mean that it will be easier for Japan to distance itself from the West than it will be for it to blend itself with Asia.[9] By reasserting its own cultural identity, Japan emphasizes its uniqueness and its differences from both Western and other Asian cultures.

While Chinese and Japanese found new value in their own cultures, they also shared in a broader reassertion of the value of Asian culture generally compared to that of the West. Industrialization and the growth that accompanied it produced in the 1980s and 1990s articulation by East Asians of what may be appropriately termed the Asian affirmation. This complex of attitudes has four major components.

First, Asians believe that East Asia will sustain its rapid economic development, will soon surpass the West in economic product, and hence will be increasingly powerful in world affairs compared to the West. Economic growth stimulates among Asian societies a sense of power and an affirmation of their ability to stand up to the West. "The days when the United States sneezed and Asia caught cold are over," declared a leading Japanese journalist in 1993, and a Malaysian official added to the medical metaphor that "even a high fever in America will not make Asia cough." Asians, another Asian leader said, are "at the end of the era of awe and the beginning of the era of talking back" in their relations with the United States. "Asia's increasing prosperity," Malaysia's deputy prime minister asserted, "means that it is now in a position to offer serious alternatives to the dominant global political, social and economic arrangements."[10] It also means, East Asians argue, that the West is rapidly losing its ability to make Asian societies conform to Western standards concerning human rights and other values.

Second, Asians believe this economic success is largely a product of Asian culture, which is superior to that of the West, which is culturally and socially decadent. During the heady days of the 1980s when the Japanese economy, exports, trade balance, and foreign exchange reserves were booming, the Japanese, like the Saudis before them, boasted of their new economic power, spoke contemptuously of the decline of the West, and attributed their success and

Western failings to the superiority of their culture and the decadence of Western culture. In the early 1990s Asian triumphalism was articulated anew in what can only be described as the "Singaporean cultural offensive." From Lee Kuan Yew on down, Singaporean leaders trumpeted the rise of Asia in relation to the West and contrasted the virtues of Asian, basically Confucian, culture responsible for this success — order, discipline, family responsibility, hard work, collectivism, abstemiousness — to the self-indulgence, sloth, individualism, crime, inferior education, disrespect for authority, and "mental ossification" responsible for the decline of the West. To compete with the East, it was argued, the United states "needs to question its fundamental assumptions about its social and political arrangements and, in the process, learn a thing or two from East Asian societies." [11]

For East Asians, East Asian success is particularly the result of the East Asian cultural stress on the collectivity rather than the individual. "[T]he more communitarian values and practices of the East Asians — the Japanese, Koreans, Taiwanese, Hong Kongers, and the Singaporeans — have proved to be clear assets in the catching up process," argued Lee Kuan Yew. "The values that East Asian culture upholds, such as the primacy of group interests over individual interests, support the total group effort necessary to develop rapidly." "The work ethic of the Japanese and Koreans, consisting of discipline, loyalty, and diligence," Malaysia's prime minister agreed, "has served as the motive force for their respective countries' economic and social development. This work ethic is born out of the philosophy that the group and the country are more important than the individual." [12]

Third, while recognizing the differences among Asian societies and civilizations, East Asians argue that there are also significant commonalities. Central among these, one Chinese dissident observed, is "the value system of Confucianism — honored by history and shared by most of the countries in the region," particularly its emphasis on thrift, family, work, and discipline. Equally important is the shared rejection of individualism and the prevalence of "soft" authoritarianism or very limited forms of democracy. Asian societies have common interests vis-à-vis the West in defending these distinctive values and promoting their own economic interests. Asians argue that this requires the development of new forms of intra-Asian cooperation such as the expansion of the Association of Southeast Asian Nations and the creation of the East Asian Economic Caucus. While the immediate economic interest of East Asian societies is to maintain access to Western markets, in the longer term economic regionalism is likely to prevail and hence East Asia must increasingly promote intra-Asian trade and investment. [13] In particular, it is necessary for Japan, as the leader in Asian development, to move away from its historic "policy of de-Asianization and pro-Westernization" and to pursue "a path of re-Asianization" or, more broadly, to promote "the Asianization of Asia," a path endorsed by Singaporean officials. [14]

Fourth, East Asians argue that Asian development and Asian values are models which other non-Western societies should emulate in their efforts to catch up with the West and which the West should adopt in order to renew itself. The "Anglo-Saxon developmental model, so revered over the past four decades as the best means of modernizing the economies of developing nations and of building a viable political system, isn't working," East Asians allege. The East Asian model is taking its place, as countries from Mexico and Chile to Iran and Turkey and the former Soviet republics now attempt to learn from its success, even as previous generations attempted to learn from Western success. Asia must "transmit to the rest of the world those Asian values that are of universal worth. . . . the transmission of this ideal means the export of the social system of Asia, East Asia in particular." It is necessary for Japan and other Asian countries to promote "Pacific globalism," to "globalize Asia," and hence to "decisively shape the character of the new world order." [15]

Powerful societies are universalistic; weak societies are particularistic. The mounting self-confidence of East Asia has given rise to an emerging Asian universalism comparable to that which has been characteristic of the West. "Asian values are universal values. European values are European values," declaimed Prime Minister Mahathir to the heads of European governments in 1996.[16] Along with this also comes an Asian "Occidentalism" portraying the West in much the same uniform and negative way which Western Orientalism allegedly once portrayed the East. To the East Asians economic prosperity is proof of moral superiority. If at some point India supplants East Asia as the world's economically most rapidly developing area, the world should be prepared for extended disquisitions on the superiority of Hindu culture, the contributions of the caste system to economic development, and how by returning to its roots and overcoming the deadening Western legacy left by British imperialism, India finally achieved its proper place in the top rank of civilizations. Cultural assertion follows material success; hard power generates soft power.

THE ISLAMIC RESURGENCE

While Asians became increasingly assertive as a result of economic development, Muslims in massive numbers were simultaneously turning toward Islam as a source of identity, meaning, stability, legitimacy, development, power, and hope, hope epitomized in the slogan "Islam is the solution." This Islamic Resurgence * in its extent and profundity is the latest phase in the adjustment

---

* Some readers may wonder why "Resurgence" in "Islamic Resurgence" is capitalized. The reason is that it refers to an extremely important historical event affecting one-fifth or more of humanity, that it is at least as significant as the American Revolution, French Revolution, or Russian Revolution, whose "r's" are usually capitalized, and that it is similar to and comparable to the Protestant Reformation in Western society, whose "R" is almost invariably capitalized.

of Islamic civilization to the West, an effort to find the "solution" not in Western ideologies but in Islam. It embodies acceptance of modernity, rejection of Western culture, and recommitment to Islam as the guide to life in the modern world. As a top Saudi official explained in 1994, " 'Foreign imports' are nice as shiny or high-tech 'things.' But intangible social and political institutions imported from elsewhere can be deadly—ask the Shah of Iran. . . . Islam for us is not just a religion but a way of life. We Saudis want to modernize, but not necessarily Westernize." [17]

The Islamic Resurgence is the effort by Muslims to achieve this goal. It is a broad intellectual, cultural, social, and political movement prevalent throughout the Islamic world. Islamic "fundamentalism," commonly conceived as political Islam, is only one component in the much more extensive revival of Islamic ideas, practices, and rhetoric and the rededication to Islam by Muslim populations. The Resurgence is mainstream not extremist, pervasive not isolated.

The Resurgence has affected Muslims in every country and most aspects of society and politics in most Muslim countries. "The indices of an Islamic awakening in personal life," John L. Esposito has written,

> are many: increased attention to religious observances (mosque attendance, prayer, fasting), proliferation of religious programming and publications, more emphasis on Islamic dress and values, the revitalization of Sufism (mysticism). This broader-based renewal has also been accompanied by Islam's reassertion in public life: an increase in Islamically oriented governments, organizations, laws, banks, social welfare services, and educational institutions. Both governments and opposition movements have turned to Islam to enhance their authority and muster popular support. . . . Most rulers and governments, including more secular states such as Turkey and Tunisia, becoming aware of the potential strength of Islam, have shown increased sensitivity to and anxiety about Islamic issues.

In similar terms, another distinguished scholar of Islam, Ali E. Hillal Dessouki, sees the Resurgence as involving efforts to reinstitute Islamic law in place of Western law, the increased use of religious language and symbolism, expansion of Islamic education (manifested in the multiplication of Islamic schools and Islamization of the curricula in regular state schools), increased adherence to Islamic codes of social behavior (e.g., female covering, abstinence from alcohol), and increased participation in religious observances, domination of the opposition to secular governments in Muslim societies by Islamic groups, and expanding efforts to develop international solidarity among Islamic states and societies.[18] *La revanche de Dieu* is a global phenomenon, but God, or rather Allah, has made His revenge most pervasive and fulfilling in the *ummah*, the community of Islam.

In its political manifestations, the Islamic Resurgence bears some resemblance to Marxism, with scriptural texts, a vision of the perfect society, commitment to fundamental change, rejection of the powers that be and the nation state, and doctrinal diversity ranging from moderate reformist to violent revolutionary. A more useful analogy, however, is the Protestant Reformation. Both are reactions to the stagnation and corruption of existing institutions; advocate a return to a purer and more demanding form of their religion; preach work, order, and discipline; and appeal to emerging, dynamic, middle-class people. Both are also complex movements, with diverse strands, but two major ones, Lutheranism and Calvinism, Shi'ite and Sunni fundamentalism, and even parallels between John Calvin and the Ayatollah Khomeini and the monastic discipline they tried to impose on their societies. The central spirit of both the Reformation and the Resurgence is fundamental reform. "Reformation must be universal," one Puritan minister declared, " . . . reform all places, all persons and callings; reform the benches of judgment, the inferior magistrates. . . . Reform the universities, reform the cities, reform the countries, reform inferior schools of learning, reform the Sabbath, reform the ordinances, the worship of God." In similar terms, al-Turabi asserts, "this awakening is comprehensive — it is not just about individual piety; it is not just intellectual and cultural, nor is it just political. It is all of these, a comprehensive reconstruction of society from top to bottom."[19] To ignore the impact of the Islamic Resurgence on Eastern Hemisphere politics in the late twentieth century is equivalent to ignoring the impact of the Protestant Reformation on European politics in the late sixteenth century.

The Resurgence differs from the Reformation in one key aspect. The latter's impact was largely limited to northern Europe; it made little progress in Spain, Italy, eastern Europe, and the Hapsburg lands generally. The Resurgence, in contrast, has touched almost every Muslim society. Beginning in the 1970s, Islamic symbols, beliefs, practices, institutions, policies, and organizations won increasing commitment and support throughout the world of 1 billion Muslims stretching from Morocco to Indonesia and from Nigeria to Kazakhstan. Islamization tended to occur first in the cultural realm and then to move on to the social and political spheres. Intellectual and political leaders, whether they favored it or not, could neither ignore it nor avoid adapting to it in one way or another. Sweeping generalizations are always dangerous and often wrong. One, however, does seem justified. In 1995 every country with a predominantly Muslim population, except Iran, was more Islamic and Islamist culturally, socially, and politically than it was fifteen years earlier.[20]

In most countries a central element of Islamization was the development of Islamic social organizations and the capture of previously existing organizations by Islamic groups. Islamists paid particular attention both to establishing Islamic schools and to expanding Islamic influence in state schools. In effect Islamic groups brought into existence in Islamic "civil society" which paralleled, surpassed, and often supplanted in scope and activity the frequently frail institutions of secular civil society. In Egypt by the early 1990s Islamic organizations had developed an extensive network of organizations which, filling a vacuum left by the government, provided health, welfare, educational, and other services to a large number of Egypt's poor. After the 1992 earthquake in Cairo, these organizations "were on the streets within hours, handing out food and blankets while the Government's relief efforts lagged." In Jordan the Muslim Brotherhood consciously pursued a policy of developing the social and cultural "infrastructure of an Islamic republic" and by the early 1990s, in this small country of 4 million people, was operating a large hospital, twenty clinics, forty Islamic schools, and 120 Koranic study centers. Next door in the West Bank and Gaza, Islamic organizations established and operated "student unions, youth organizations, and religious, social, and educational associations," including schools ranging from kindergartens to an Islamic university, clinics, orphanages, a retirement home, and a system of Islamic judges and arbitrators. Islamic organizations spread throughout Indonesia in the 1970s and 1980s. By the early 1980s, the largest, the *Muhhammadijah*, had 6 million members, constituted a "religious-welfare-state-within-the-secular-state," and provided "cradle-to-grave" services for the entire country through an elaborate network of schools, clinics, hospitals, and university-level institutions. In these and other Muslim societies, Islamist organizations, banned from political activity, were providing social services comparable to those of the political machines in the United States in the early twentieth century.[21]

The political manifestations of the Resurgence have been less pervasive than its social and cultural manifestations, but they still are the single most important political development in Muslim societies in the last quarter of the twentieth century. The extent and makeup of the political support for Islamist movements has varied from country to country. Yet certain broad tendencies exist. By and large those movements do not get much support from rural elites, peasants, and the elderly. Like fundamentalists in other religions, Islamists are overwhelmingly participants in and products of the processes of modernization. They are mobile and modern-oriented younger people drawn in large part from three groups.

As with most revolutionary movements, the core element has consisted of students and intellectuals. In most countries fundamentalists winning control of student unions and similar organizations was the first phase in the process of political Islamization, with the Islamist "breakthrough" in universities occurring in the 1970s in Egypt, Pakistan, and Afghanistan, and then moving on to other Muslim countries. The Islamist appeal was particularly strong among students in technical institutes, engineering faculties, and scientific departments. In the 1990s, in Saudi Arabia, Algeria, and elsewhere, "second generation indigenization" was manifesting itself with increasing proportions of university students being educated in their home languages and hence increasingly exposed to Islamist influences.[22] Islamists also often developed a substantial appeal to women, and Turkey witnessed a clear demarcation between the older generation of secularist women and their Islamist-oriented daughters and granddaughters.[23] One study of the militant leaders of Egyptian Islamist groups found they had five major characteristics, which appear to be typical of Islamists in other countries. They were young, overwhelmingly in their twenties and thirties. Eighty percent were university students or university graduates. Over half came from elite colleges or from the intellectually most demanding fields of technical specialization such as medicine and engineering. Over 70 percent were from lower middle-class, "modest, but not poor backgrounds," and were the first generation in their family to get higher education. They spent their childhoods in small towns or rural areas but had become residents of large cities.[24]

While students and intellectuals formed the militant cadres and shock troops of Islamist movements, urban middle-class people made up the bulk of the active membership. In some degree these came from what are often termed "traditional" middle-class groups: merchants, traders, small business proprietors, *bazaaris*. These played a crucial role in the Iranian Revolution and provided significant support to fundamentalist movements in Algeria, Turkey, and Indonesia. To an even greater extent, however, fundamentalists belonged to the more "modern" sectors of the middle class. Islamist activists "probably include a disproportionately large number of the best-educated and most intelligent young people in their respective populations," including doctors, lawyers, engineers, scientists, teachers, civil servants.[25]

The third key element in the Islamist constituency was recent migrants to the cities. Throughout the Islamic world in the 1970s and 1980s urban populations grew at dramatic rates. Crowded into decaying and often primitive slum areas, the urban migrants needed and were the beneficiaries of the social services provided by Islamist organizations. In addition, Ernest Gellner points out, Islam offered "a dignified identity" to these "newly uprooted masses." In Istanbul and Ankara, Cairo and Asyut, Algiers and Fes, and on the Gaza strip, Islamist parties successfully organized and appealed to "the downtrodden and dispossessed." "The mass of revolutionary Islam," Oliver Roy said, is "a product of modern society . . . the new urban arrivals, the millions of peasants who have tripled the populations of the great Muslim metropolises."[26]

By the mid-1990s explicitly Islamist governments had come to power only in Iran and Sudan. A small number of Muslim countries, such as Turkey and Pakistan, had regimes with some claim to democratic legitimacy. The governments in the two score other Muslim countries were overwhelmingly nondemocratic: monarchies, one-party systems, military regimes, personal dictatorships, or some combination of these, usually resting on a limited family, clan, or tribal base and in some cases highly dependent on foreign support. Two regimes, in Morocco and Saudi Arabia, attempted to invoke some form of Islamic legitimacy. Most of these governments, however, lacked any basis for justifying their rule in terms of Islamic, democratic, or nationalist values. They were "bunker regimes," to use Clement Henry Moore's phrase, repressive, corrupt, divorced from the needs and aspirations of their societies. Such regimes may sustain themselves for long periods of time; they need not fail. In the modern world, however, the probability that they will change or collapse is high. In the mid-1990s, consequently, a central issue concerned the likely alternatives: Who or what would be their successors? In almost every country in the mid-1990s the most likely successor regime was an Islamist one.

During the 1970s and 1980s a wave of democratization swept across the world, encompassing several dozen countries. This wave had an impact on Muslim societies, but it was a limited one. While democratic movements were gaining strength and coming to power in southern Europe, Latin America, the East Asian periphery, and central Europe, Islamist movements were simultaneously gaining strength in Muslim countries. Islamism was the functional substitute for the democratic opposition to authoritarianism in Christian societies, and it was in large part the product of similar causes: social mobilization, loss of performance legitimacy by authoritarian regimes, and a changing international environment, including oil price increases, which in the Muslim world encouraged Islamist rather than democratic trends. Priests, ministers, and lay religious groups played major roles in opposing authoritarian regimes in Christian societies, and *ulema*, mosque-based groups, and Islamists played comparable opposition roles in Muslim countries. The Pope was central to ending the communist regime in Poland, the ayatollah to bringing down the Shah's regime in Iran.

In the 1980s and 1990s Islamist movements dominated and often monopolized the opposition to governments in Muslim countries. Their strength was in part a function of the weakness of alternative sources of opposition. Leftist and communist movements had been discredited and then seriously undermined by the collapse of the Soviet Union and international communism. Liberal, democratic opposition groups had existed in most Muslim societies but were usually confined to limited numbers of intellectuals and others with Western roots or connections. With only occasional exceptions, liberal democrats were unable to achieve sustained popular support in Muslim societies, and even Islamic liberalism failed to establish roots. "In one Muslim society after another," Fouad Ajami observes, "to write of liberalism and of a national bourgeois tradition is to write obituaries of men who took on impossible odds and then failed."[27] The general failure of liberal democracy to take hold in Muslim societies is a continuing and repeated phenomenon for an entire century beginning in the late 1800s. This failure has its source at least in part in the inhospitable nature of Islamic culture and society to Western liberal concepts.

The success of Islamist movements in dominating the opposition and establishing themselves as the only viable alternative to incumbent regimes was also greatly helped by the policies of those regimes. At one time or another during the Cold War many governments, including those of Algeria, Turkey, Jordan, Egypt, and Israel, encouraged and supported Islamists as a counter to communist or hostile nationalist movements. At least until the Gulf War, Saudi Arabia and other Gulf states provided massive funding to the Muslim Brotherhood and Islamist groups in a variety of countries. The ability of Islamist groups to dominate the opposition was also enhanced by government suppression of secular oppositions. Fundamentalist strength generally varied inversely with that of secular democratic or nationalist parties and was weaker in countries, such as Morocco and Turkey, that allowed some degree of multiparty competition than it was in countries that suppressed all opposition.[28] Secular opposition, however, is more vulnerable to repression than religious opposition. The latter can operate within and behind a network of mosques, welfare organizations, foundations, and other Muslim institutions which the government feels it cannot suppress. Liberal democrats have no such cover and hence are more easily controlled or eliminated by the government.

In an effort to preempt the growth of Islamist tendencies, governments expanded religious education in state-controlled schools, which often came to be dominated by Islamist teachers and ideas, and expanded their support for religion and religious educational institutions. These actions were in part evidence of the government's commitment to Islam, and, through funding, they extended governmental control over Islamic institutions and education. They also, however, led to the education of large numbers of students and people in Islamic values, making them more open to Islamist appeals, and graduated militants who went forth to work on behalf of Islamist goals.

The strength of the Resurgence and the appeal of Islamist movements induced governments to promote Islamic institutions and practices and to incorporate Islamic symbols and practices into their regime. At the broadest level this meant affirming or reaffirming the Islamic character of their state and society. In the 1970s and 1980s political leaders rushed to identify their regimes and themselves with Islam. King Hussein of Jordan, convinced that secular governments had little future in the Arab world, spoke of the need to create "Islamic democracy" and a "modernizing Islam." King Hassan of Morocco emphasized his descent from the Prophet and his role as "Commander of the Faithful." The sultan of Brunei, not previously noted for Islamic practices, became "increasingly devout" and defined his regime as a "Malay Muslim monarchy." Ben Ali in Tunisia began regularly to invoke Allah in his speeches and "wrapped himself in the mantle of Islam" to check the growing appeal of Islamic groups.[29] In the early 1990s Suharto explicitly adopted a policy of becoming "more Muslim." In Bangladesh the principle of "secularism" was dropped from the constitution in the mid 1970s, and by the early 1990s the secular, Kemalist identity of Turkey was, for the first time, coming under serious challenge.[30] To underline their Islamic commitment, governmental leaders — Özal, Suharto, Karimov — hastened to their *hajh.*

Governments in Muslim countries also acted to Islamicize law. In Indonesia

Islamic legal concepts and practices were incorporated into the secular legal system. Reflecting its substantial non-Muslim population, Malaysia, in contrast, moved toward the development of two separate legal systems, one Islamic and one secular.[31] In Pakistan during the regime of General Zia ul-Haq, extensive efforts were made to Islamicize the law and economy. Islamic penalties were introduced, a system of *shari'a* courts established, and the *shari'a* declared the supreme law of the land.

Like other manifestations of the global religious revival, the Islamic Resurgence is both a product of and an effort to come to grips with modernization. Its underlying causes are those generally responsible for indigenization trends in non-Western societies: urbanization, social mobilization, higher levels of literacy and education, intensified communication and media consumption, and expanded interaction with Western and other cultures. These developments undermine traditional village and clan ties and create alienation and an identity crisis. Islamist symbols, commitments, and beliefs meet these psychological needs, and Islamist welfare organizations, the social, cultural, and economic needs of Muslims caught in the process of modernization. Muslims feel the need to return to Islamic ideas, practices, and institutions to provide the compass and the motor of modernization.[32]

The Islamic revival, it has been argued, was also "a product of the West's declining power and prestige. . . . As the West relinquished total ascendance, its ideals and institutions lost luster." More specifically, the Resurgence was stimulated and fueled by the oil boom of the 1970s, which greatly increased the wealth and power of many Muslim nations and enabled them to reverse the relations of domination and subordination that had existed with the West. As John B. Kelly observed at the time, "For the Saudis, there is undoubtedly a double satisfaction to be gained from the infliction of humiliating punishments upon Westerners; for not only are they an expression of the power and independence of Saudi Arabia but they also demonstrate, as they are intended to demonstrate, contempt for Christianity and the pre-eminence of Islam." The actions of the oil-rich Muslim states "if placed in their historical, religious, racial and cultural setting, amount to nothing less than a bold attempt to lay the Christian West under tribute to the Muslim East."[33] The Saudi, Libyan, and other governments used their oil riches to stimulate and finance the Muslim revival, and Muslim wealth led Muslims to swing from fascination with Western culture to deep involvement in their own and willingness to assert the place and importance of Islam in non-Islamic societies. Just as Western wealth had previously been seen as the evidence of the superiority of Western culture, oil wealth was seen as evidence of the superiority of Islam.

The impetus provided by the oil prices hikes faded in the 1980s, but population growth was a continuing motor force. While the rise of East Asia has been fueled by spectacular rates of economic growth, the Resurgence of Islam has been fueled by equally spectacular rates of population growth. Population expansion in Islamic countries, particularly in the Balkans, North Africa, and Central Asia, has been significantly greater than that in the neighboring countries and in the world generally. Between 1965 and 1990 the total number of people on earth rose from 3.3 billion to 5.3 billion, an annual growth rate of 1.85 percent. In Muslim societies growth rates almost always were over 2.0 percent, often exceeded 2.5 percent, and at times were over 3.0 percent. Between 1965 and 1990, for instance, the Maghreb population increased at a rate of 2.65 percent a year, from 29.8 million to 59 million, with Algerians multiplying at a 3.0 percent annual rate. During these same years, the number of Egyptians rose at a 2.3 percent rate from 29.4 million to 52.4 million. In Central Asia, between 1970 and 1993, populations grew at rates of 2.9 percent in Tajikstan, 2.6 percent in Uzbekistan, 2.5 percent in Turkmenistan, 1.9 percent in Kyrgyzstan, but only 1.1 percent in Kazakhstan, whose population is almost half Russian. Pakistan and Bangladesh had population growth rates exceeding 2.5 percent a year, while Indonesia's was over 2.0 percent a year. Overall Muslims, as we mentioned, constituted perhaps 18 percent of the world's population in 1980 and are likely to be over 20 percent in 2000 and 30 percent in 2025.[34]

The rates of population increase in the Maghreb and elsewhere have peaked and are beginning to decline, but growth in absolute numbers will continue to be large, and the impact of that growth will be felt throughout the first part of the twenty-first century. For years to come Muslim populations will be disproportionately young populations, with a notable demographic bulge of teenagers and people in their twenties (Figure 5.2). In addition, the people in this age cohort will be overwhelmingly urban and have at least a secondary education. This combination of size and social mobilization has three significant political consequences.

First, young people are the protagonists of protest, instability, reform, and revolution. Historically, the existence of large cohorts of young people has tended to coincide with such movements. "The Protestant Reformation," it has been said, "is an example of one of the outstanding youth movements in history." Demographic growth, Jack Goldstone has persuasively argued, was a central factor in the two waves of revolution that occurred in Eurasia in the mid-seventeenth and late eighteenth centuries.[35] A notable expansion of the proportion of youth in Western countries coincided with the "Age of the Democratic Revolution" in the last decades of the eighteenth century. In the nineteenth century successful industrialization and emigration reduced the political impact of young populations in European societies. The proportions of youth rose again in the 1920s, however, providing recruits to fascist and other extremist movements.[36] Four decades later the post–World War II baby boom generation made its mark politically in the demonstrations and protests of the 1960s.

The youth of Islam have been making their mark in the Islamic Resurgence. As the Resurgence got under way in the 1970s and picked up steam in the

FIGURE 5.2
THE DEMOGRAPHIC CHALLENGE: ISLAM, RUSSIA, AND THE WEST

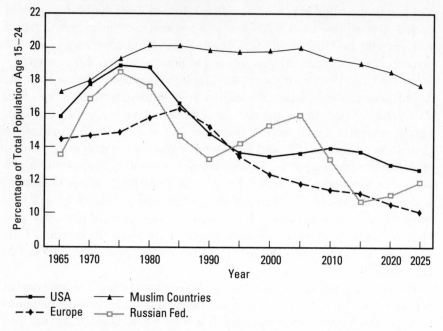

Source: United Nations, Population Division, Department for Economic and Social Information and Policy Analysis, World Population Prospects, *The 1994 Revision* (New York: United Nations, 1995); United Nations, Population Division, Department for Economic and Social Information and Policy Analysis, *Sex and Age Distribution of the World Populations, The 1994 Revision* (New York: United Nations, 1994);

1980s, the proportion of youth (that is, those fifteen to twenty-four years of age) in major Muslim countries rose significantly and began to exceed 20 percent of the total population. In many Muslim countries the youth bulge peaked in the 1970s and 1980s; in others it will peak early in the next century (Table 5.1). The actual or projected peaks in all these countries, with one exception, are above 20 percent; the estimated Saudi Arabian peak in the first decade of the twenty-first century falls just short of that. These youth provide the recruits for Islamist organizations and political movements. It is not perhaps entirely coincidental that the proportion of youth in the Iranian population rose dramatically in the 1970s, reaching 20 percent in the last half of that decade, and that the Iranian Revolution occurred in 1979 or that this benchmark was reached in Algeria in the early 1990s just as the Islamist FIS was winning popular support and scoring electoral victories. Potentially significant regional variations also occur in the Muslim youth bulge (Figure 5.3). While the data must be treated with caution, the projections suggest that the Bosnian and Albanian youth proportions will decline precipitously at the turn of the century. The youth bulge will, on the other hand, remain high in the Gulf states. In 1988

TABLE 5.1
YOUTH BULGE IN MUSLIM COUNTRIES

1970s	1980s	1990s	2000s	2010s
Bosnia	Syria	Algeria	Tajikistan	Kyrgyzstan
Bahrain	Albania	Iraq	Turkmenistan	Malaysia
UAE	Yemen	Jordan	Egypt	Pakistan
Iran	Turkey	Morocco	Iran	Syria
Egypt	Tunisia	Bangladesh	Saudi Arabia	Yeman
Kazakhstan	Pakistan	Indonesia	Kuwait	Jordan
	Malaysia		Sudan	Iraq
	Kyrgyzstan			Oman
	Tajikistan			Libya
	Turkmenistan			Afghanistan
	Azerbaijan			

Decades in which 15–24-year-olds have peaked or are expected to peak as proportion of total population (almost always greater than 20%). In some countries this proportion peaks twice.

Source: See Figure 5.2

Crown Prince Abdullah of Saudi Arabia said that the greatest threat to his country was the rise of Islamic fundamentalism among its youth.[37] According to these projections, that threat will persist well into the twenty-first century.

In major Arab countries (Algeria, Egypt, Morocco, Syria, Tunisia) the number of people in their early twenties seeking jobs will expand until about 2010. As compared to 1990, entrants into the job market will increase by 30 percent in Tunisia, by about 50 percent in Algeria, Egypt, and Morocco, and by over 100 percent in Syria. The rapid expansion of literacy in Arab societies also creates a gap between a literate younger generation and a largely illiterate older generation and thus a "dissociation between knowledge and power" likely "to put a strain on political systems."[38]

Larger populations need more resources, and hence people from societies with dense and/or rapidly growing populations tend to push outward, occupy territory, and exert pressure on other less demographically dynamic peoples. Islamic population growth is thus a major contributing factor to the conflicts along the borders of the Islamic world between Muslims and other peoples. Population pressure combined with economic stagnation promotes Muslim migration to Western and other non-Muslim societies, elevating immigration as an issue in those societies. The juxtaposition of a rapidly growing people of one culture and a slowly growing or stagnant people of another culture generates pressures for economic and/or political adjustments in both societies. In the 1970s, for instance, the demographic balance in the former Soviet Union shifted drastically with Muslims increasing by 24 percent while Russians increased by 6.5 percent, causing great concern among Central Asian communist leaders.[39] Similarly, rapid growth in the numbers of Albanians does not reassure Serbs, Greeks, or Italians. Israelis are concerned about the high growth rates of Palestinians, and Spain, with a population growing at less than one-fifth of 1

FIGURE 5.3
Muslim Youth Bulge by Region

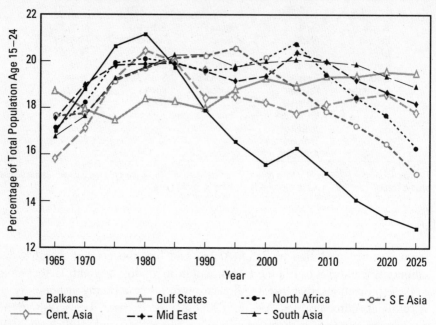

Source: United Nations, Population Division, Department for Economic and Social Information and Policy Analysis, World Population Prospects, *The 1994 Revision* (New York: United Nations, 1995); United Nations, Population Division, Department for Economic and Social Information and Policy Analysis, *Sex and Age Distribution of the World Populations, The 1994 Revision* (New York: United Nations, 1994);

percent a year, is uneasy confronted by Maghreb neighbors with populations growing more than ten times as fast and per capita GNP's about one-tenth its own.

CHANGING CHALLENGES

No society can sustain double digit economic growth indefinitely, and the Asian economic boom will level off sometime in the early twenty-first century. The rates of Japanese economic growth dropped substantially in the mid-1970s and afterwards were not significantly higher than those of the United States and European countries. One by one other Asian "economic miracle" states will see their growth rates decline and approximate the "normal" levels maintained in complex economies. Similarly, no religious revival or cultural movement lasts indefinitely, and at some point the Islamic Resurgence will subside and fade into history. That is most likely to happen when the demographic impulse powering it weakens in the second and third decades of the twenty-first century. At that time, the ranks of militants, warriors, and migrants will diminish, and the high levels of conflict within Islam and between Muslims and others (see chapter 10) are likely to decline. The relations between Islam and the West will not become close but they will become less conflictual, and quasi war (see chapter 9) is likely to give way to cold war or perhaps even cold peace.

Economic development in Asia will leave a legacy of wealthier, more complex economies, with substantial international involvements, prosperous bourgeoisies, and well-off middle classes. These are likely to lead towards more pluralistic and possibly more democratic politics, which will not necessarily, however, be more pro-Western. Enhanced power will instead promote continued Asian assertiveness in international affairs and efforts to direct global trends in ways uncongenial to the West and to reshape international institutions away from Western models and norms. The Islamic Resurgence, like comparable movements including the Reformation, will also leave important legacies. Muslims will have a much greater awareness of what they have in common and what distinguishes them from non-Muslims. The new generation of leaders that take over as the youth bulge ages will not necessarily be fundamentalist but will be much more committed to Islam than their predecessors. Indigenization will be reinforced. The Resurgence will leave a network of Islamist social, cultural, economic, and political organizations within societies and transcending societies. The Resurgence will also have shown that "Islam is the solution" to the problems of morality, identity, meaning, and faith, but not to the problems of social injustice, political repression, economic backwardness, and military weakness. These failures could generate widespread disillusionment with political Islam, a reaction against it, and a search for alternative "solutions" to these problems. Conceivably even more intensely anti-Western nationalisms could emerge, blaming the West for the failures of Islam. Alternatively, if Malaysia and Indonesia continue their economic progress, they might provide an "Islamic model" for development to compete with the Western and Asian models.

In any event, during the coming decades Asian economic growth will have deeply destabilizing effects on the Western-dominated established international order, with the development of China, if it continues, producing a massive shift in power among civilizations. In addition, India could move into rapid economic development and emerge as a major contender for influence in world affairs. Meanwhile Muslim population growth will be a destabilizing force for both Muslim societies and their neighbors. The large numbers of young people with secondary educations will continue to power the Islamic Resurgence and promote Muslim militancy, militarism, and migration. As a result, the early years of the twenty-first century are likely to see an ongoing resurgence of non-Western power and culture and the clash of the peoples of non-Western civilizations with the West and with each other.

III

·

The

Emerging Order

of

Civilizations

Chapter 6

•

The Cultural Reconfiguration of Global Politics

GROPING FOR GROUPINGS: THE POLITICS OF IDENTITY

Spurred by modernization, global politics is being reconfigured along cultural lines. Peoples and countries with similar cultures are coming together. Peoples and countries with different cultures are coming apart. Alignments defined by ideology and superpower relations are giving way to alignments defined by culture and civilization. Political boundaries increasingly are redrawn to coincide with cultural ones: ethnic, religious, and civilizational. Cultural communities are replacing Cold War blocs, and the fault lines between civilizations are becoming the central lines of conflict in global politics.

During the Cold War a country could be nonaligned, as many were, or it could, as some did, change its alignment from one side to another. The leaders of a country could make these choices in terms of their perceptions of their security interests, their calculations of the balance of power, and their ideological preferences. In the new world, however, cultural identity is the central factor shaping a country's associations and antagonisms. While a country could avoid Cold War alignment, it cannot lack an identity. The question, "Which side are you on?" has been replaced by the much more fundamental one, "Who are you?" Every state has to have an answer. That answer, its cultural identity, defines the state's place in world politics, its friends, and its enemies.

The 1990s have seen the eruption of a global identity crisis. Almost everywhere one looks, people have been asking, "Who are we?" "Where do we belong?" and "Who is not us?" These questions are central not only to peoples attempting to forge new nation states, as in the former Yugoslavia, but also much more generally. In the mid-1990s the countries where questions of national identity were actively debated included, among others: Algeria, Canada, China, Germany, Great Britain, India, Iran, Japan, Mexico, Morocco, Russia, South Africa, Syria, Tunisia, Turkey, Ukraine, and the United States. Identity issues are, of course, particularly intense in cleft countries that have sizable groups of people from different civilizations.

In coping with identity crisis, what counts for people are blood and belief, faith and family. People rally to those with similar ancestry, religion, language, values, and institutions and distance themselves from those with different ones. In Europe, Austria, Finland, and Sweden, culturally part of the West, had to be divorced from the West and neutral during the Cold War; they are now able to join their cultural kin in the European Union. The Catholic and Protestant countries in the former Warsaw Pact, Poland, Hungary, the Czech Republic, and Slovakia, are moving toward membership in the Union and in NATO, and the Baltic states are in line behind them. The European powers make it clear that they do not want a Muslim state, Turkey, in the European Union and are not happy about having a second Muslim state, Bosnia, on the European continent. In the north, the end of the Soviet Union stimulates the emergence of new (and old) patterns of association among the Baltic republics and between them, Sweden, and Finland. Sweden's prime minister pointedly reminds Russia that the Baltic republics are part of Sweden's "near abroad" and that Sweden could not be neutral in the event of Russian aggression against them.

Similar realignments occur in the Balkans. During the Cold War, Greece and Turkey were in NATO, Bulgaria and Romania were in the Warsaw Pact, Yugoslavia was nonaligned, and Albania was an isolated sometime associate of communist China. Now these Cold War alignments are giving way to civilizational ones rooted in Islam and Orthodoxy. Balkan leaders talk of crystallizing a Greek-Serb-Bulgarian Orthodox alliance. The "Balkan wars," Greece's prime minister alleges, ". . . have brought to the surface the resonance of Orthodox ties. . . . this is a bond. It was dormant, but with the developments in the Balkans, it is taking on some real substance. In a very fluid world, people are seeking identity and security. People are looking for roots and connections to defend themselves against the unknown." These views were echoed by the leader of the principal opposition party in Serbia: "The situation in southeastern Europe will soon require the formation of a new Balkan alliance of Orthodox countries, including Serbia, Bulgaria, and Greece, in order to resist the encroachment of Islam." Looking northward, Orthodox Serbia and Romania cooperate closely in dealing with their common problems with Catholic Hungary. With the disappearance of the Soviet threat, the "unnatural" alliance between Greece and Turkey becomes essentially meaningless, as conflicts intensify between them over the Aegean Sea, Cyprus, their military balance, their roles in NATO and the European Union, and their relations with the United States. Turkey reasserts its role as the protector of Balkan Muslims and provides support to Bosnia. In the former Yugoslavia, Russia backs Orthodox Serbia, Germany promotes Catholic Croatia, Muslim countries rally to the support of the Bosnian government, and the Serbs fight Croatians, Bosnian Muslims, and Albanian Muslims. Overall, the Balkans have once again been Balkanized along the religious lines. "Two axes are emerging," as Misha Glenny observed, "one dressed in the garb of Eastern Orthodoxy, one veiled in Islamic raiment" and the possibility exists of "an ever-greater struggle for influence between the Belgrade/Athens axis and the Albanian/Turkish alliance."[1]

Meanwhile in the former Soviet Union, Orthodox Belarus, Moldova, and Ukraine gravitate toward Russia, and Armenians and Azeris fight each other while their Russian and Turkish kin attempt both to support them and to contain the conflict. The Russian army fights Muslim fundamentalists in Tajikistan and Muslim nationalists in Chechnya. The Muslim former Soviet republics work to develop various forms of economic and political association among themselves and to expand their ties with their Muslim neighbors, while Turkey, Iran, and Saudi Arabia devote great effort to cultivating relations with these new states. In the Subcontinent, India and Pakistan remain at loggerheads over Kashmir and the military balance between them, fighting in Kashmir intensifies, and within India, new conflicts arise between Muslim and Hindu fundamentalists.

In East Asia, home to people of six different civilizations, arms buildups gain momentum and territorial disputes come to the fore. The three lesser Chinas, Taiwan, Hong Kong, and Singapore, and the overseas Chinese communities in Southeast Asia become increasingly oriented toward, involved in, and dependent on the mainland. The two Koreas move hesitatingly but meaningfully toward unification. The relations in Southeast Asian states between Muslims, on the one hand, and Chinese and Christians, on the other, become increasingly tense and at times violent.

In Latin America, economic associations — Mercosur, the Andean Pact, the tripartite pact (Mexico, Colombia, Venezuela), the Central American Common Market — take on a new life, reaffirming the point demonstrated most graphically by the European Union that economic integration proceeds faster and further when it is based on cultural commonality. At the same time, the United States and Canada attempt to absorb Mexico into the North American Free Trade Area in a process whose long-term success depends largely on the ability of Mexico to redefine itself culturally from Latin American to North American.

With the end of the Cold War order, countries throughout the world began developing new and reinvigorating old antagonisms and affiliations. They have been groping for groupings, and they are finding those groupings with countries of similar culture and the same civilization. Politicians invoke and publics identify with "greater" cultural communities that transcend nation state boundaries, including "Greater Serbia," "Greater China," "Greater Turkey," "Greater

Hungary," "Greater Croatia," "Greater Azerbaijan," "Greater Russia," "Greater Albania," "Greater Iran," and "Greater Uzbekistan."

Will political and economic alignments always coincide with those of culture and civilization? Of course not. Balance of power considerations will at times lead to cross-civilizational alliances, as they did when Francis I joined with the Ottomans against the Hapsburgs. In addition, patterns of association formed to serve the purposes of states in one era will persist into a new era. They are, however, likely to become weaker and less meaningful and to be adapted to serve the purposes of the new age. Greece and Turkey will undoubtedly remain members of NATO but their ties to other NATO states are likely to attenuate. So also are the alliances of the United States with Japan and Korea, its de facto alliance with Israel, and its security ties with Pakistan. Multicivilizational international organizations like ASEAN could face increasing difficulty in maintaining their coherence. Countries such as India and Pakistan, partners of different superpowers during the Cold War, now redefine their interests and seek new associations reflecting the realities of cultural politics. African countries which were dependent on Western support designed to counter Soviet influence look increasingly to South Africa for leadership and succor.

Why should cultural commonality facilitate cooperation and cohesion among people and cultural differences promote cleavages and conflicts?

First, everyone has multiple identities which may compete with or reinforce each other: kinship, occupational, cultural, institutional, territorial, educational, partisan, ideological, and others. Identifications along one dimension may clash with those along a different dimension: in a classic case the German workers in 1914 had to choose between their class identification with the international proletariat and their national identification with the German people and empire. In the contemporary world, cultural identification is dramatically increasing in importance compared to other dimensions of identity.

Along any single dimension, identity is usually most meaningful at the immediate face-to-face level. Narrower identities, however, do not necessarily conflict with broader ones. A military officer can identify institutionally with his company, regiment, division, and service. Similarly, a person can identify culturally with his or her clan, ethnic group, nationality, religion, and civilization. The increased salience of cultural identity at lower levels may well reinforce its salience at higher levels. As Burke suggested: "The love to the whole is not extinguished by this subordinate partiality. . . . To be attached to the subdivision, to love the little platoon we belong to in society, is the first principle (the germ, as it were) of public affections." In a world where culture counts, the platoons are tribes and ethnic groups, the regiments are nations, and the armies are civilizations. The increased extent to which people throughout the world differentiate themselves along cultural lines means that conflicts between cultural groups are increasingly important; civilizations are the broadest cultural entities; hence conflicts between groups from different civilizations become central to global politics.

Second, the increased salience of cultural identity is in large part, as is argued in chapters 3 and 4, the result of social-economic modernization at the individual level, where dislocation and alienation create the need for more meaningful identities, and at the societal level, where the enhanced capabilities and power of non-Western societies stimulate the revitalization of indigenous identities and culture.

Third, identity at any level — personal, tribal, racial, civilizational — can only be defined in relation to an "other," a different person, tribe, race, or civilization. Historically relations between states or other entities of the same civilization have differed from relations between states or entities of different civilizations. Separate codes governed behavior toward those who are "like us" and the "barbarians" who are not. The rules of the nations of Christendom for dealing with each other were different from those for dealing with the Turks and other "heathens." Muslims acted differently toward those of *Dar al-Islam* and those of *Dar al-harb.* The Chinese treated Chinese foreigners and non-Chinese foreigners in separate ways. The civilizational "us" and the extracivilizational "them" is a constant in human history. These differences in intra- and extracivilizational behavior stem from:

1. feelings of superiority (and occasionally inferiority) toward people who are perceived as being very different;
2. fear of and lack of trust in such people;
3. difficulty of communication with them as a result of differences in language and what is considered civil behavior;
4. lack of familiarity with the assumptions, motivations, social relationships, and social practices of other people.

In today's world, improvements in transportation and communication have produced more frequent, more intense, more symmetrical, and more inclusive interactions among people of different civilizations. As a result their civilizational identities become increasingly salient. The French, Germans, Belgians, and Dutch increasingly think of themselves as European. Middle East Muslims identify with and rally to the support of Bosnians and Chechens. Chinese throughout East Asia identify their interests with those of the mainland. Russians identify with and provide support to Serbs and other Orthodox peoples. These broader levels of civilizational identity mean deeper consciousness of civilizational differences and of the need to protect what distinguishes "us" from "them."

Fourth, the sources of conflict between states and groups from different civilizations are, in large measure, those which have always generated conflict between groups: control of people, territory, wealth, and resources, and relative power, that is the ability to impose one's own values, culture, and institutions on another group as compared to that group's ability to do that to you. Conflict between cultural groups, however, may also involve cultural issues. Differences in secular ideology between Marxist-Leninism and liberal democracy can at least be debated if not resolved. Differences in material interest can be negotiated and often settled by compromise in a way cultural issues cannot. Hindus and Muslims are unlikely to resolve the issue of whether a temple or a mosque should be built at Ayodhya by building both, or neither, or a syncretic building that is both a mosque and a temple. Nor can what might seem to be a straightforward territorial question between Albanian Muslims and Orthodox Serbs concerning Kosovo or between Jews and Arabs concerning Jerusalem be easily settled, since each place has deep historical, cultural, and emotional meaning to both peoples. Similarly, neither French authorities nor Muslim parents are likely to accept a compromise which would allow schoolgirls to wear Muslim dress every other day during the school year. Cultural questions like these involve a yes or no, zero-sum choice.

Fifth and finally is the ubiquity of conflict. It is human to hate. For self-definition and motivation people need enemies: competitors in business, rivals in achievement, opponents in politics. They naturally distrust and see as threats those who are different and have the capability to harm them. The resolution of one conflict and the disappearance of one enemy generate personal, social, and political forces that give rise to new ones. "The 'us' versus 'them' tendency is," as Ali Mazrui said, "in the political arena, almost universal."[2] In the contemporary world the "them" is more and more likely to be people from a different civilization. The end of the Cold War has not ended conflict but has rather given rise to new identities rooted in culture and to new patterns of conflict among groups from different cultures which at the broadest level are civilizations. Simultaneously, common culture also encourages cooperation among states and groups which share that culture, which can be seen in the emerging patterns of regional association among countries, particularly in the economic area.

CULTURE AND ECONOMIC COOPERATION

The early 1990s heard much talk of regionalism and the regionalization of world politics. Regional conflicts replaced the global conflict on the world's security agenda. Major powers, such as Russia, China, and the United States, as well as secondary powers, such as Sweden and Turkey, redefined their security interests in explicitly regional terms. Trade within regions expanded faster than trade between regions, and many foresaw the emergence of regional economic blocs, European, North American, East Asian, and perhaps others.

The term "regionalism," however, does not adequately describe what was happening. Regions are geographical not political or cultural entities. As with the Balkans or the Middle East, they may be riven by inter- and intracivilization conflicts. Regions are a basis for cooperation among states only to the extent that geography coincides with culture. Divorced from culture, propinquity does not yield commonality and may foster just the reverse. Military alliances and economic associations require cooperation among their members, cooperation depends on trust, and trust most easily springs from common values and culture. As a result, while age and purpose also play a role, the overall effectiveness of regional organizations generally varies inversely with the civilizational diversity of their membership. By and large, single civilization organizations do more things and are more successful than multicivilizational organizations. This is true of both political and security organizations, on the one hand, and economic organizations, on the other.

The success of NATO has resulted in large part from its being the central security organization of Western countries with common values and philosophical assumptions. The Western European Union is the product of a common European culture. The Organization for Security and Cooperation in Europe, on the other hand, includes countries from at least three civilizations with quite different values and interests which pose major obstacles to its developing a significant institutional identity and a wide range of important activities. The single civilization Caribbean Community (CARICOM), composed of thirteen English-speaking former British colonies, has created an extensive variety of cooperative arrangements, with more intensive cooperation among some sub-groupings. Efforts to create broader Caribbean organizations bridging the Anglo-Hispanic fault line in the Caribbean have, however, consistently failed. Similarly, the South Asian Association for Regional Co-operation, formed in 1985 and including seven Hindu, Muslim, and Buddhist states has been almost totally ineffectual, even to the point of not being able to hold meetings.[3]

The relation of culture to regionalism is clearly evident with respect to economic integration. From least to most integrated, the four recognized levels of economic association among countries are:

1. free trade area;
2. customs union;
3. common market;
4. economic union.

The European Union has moved furthest down the integration road with a common market and many elements of an economic union. The relatively homogeneous Mercosur and the Andean Pact countries in 1994 were in the process of establishing customs unions. In Asia the multicivilizational ASEAN only in 1992 began to move toward development of a free trade area. Other multicivilizational economic organizations lagged even further behind. In 1995, with the marginal exception of NAFTA, no such organization had created a free trade area much less any more extensive form of economic integration.

In Western Europe and Latin America civilizational commonality fosters cooperation and regional organization. Western Europeans and Latin Americans know they have much in common. Five civilizations (six if Russia is included) exist in East Asia. East Asia, consequently, is the test case for developing meaningful organizations not rooted in common civilization. As of the early 1990s no security organization or multilateral military alliance, comparable to NATO, existed in East Asia. One multicivilizational regional organization, ASEAN, had been created in 1967 with one Sinic, one Buddhist, one Christian, and two Muslim member states, all of which confronted active challenges from communist insurgencies and potential ones from North Vietnam and China.

ASEAN is often cited as an example of an effective multicultural organization. It is, however, an example of the limits of such organizations. It is not a military alliance. While its members at times cooperate militarily on a bilateral basis, they are also all expanding their military budgets and engaged in military buildups, in striking contrast to the reductions West European and Latin American countries are making. On the economic front, ASEAN was from the beginning designed to achieve "economic cooperation rather than economic integration," and as a result regionalism has developed at a "modest pace," and even a free trade area is not contemplated until the twenty-first century.[4] In 1978 ASEAN created the Post Ministerial Conference in which its foreign ministers could meet with those from its "dialogue partners": the United States, Japan, Canada, Australia, New Zealand, South Korea, and the European Community. The PMC, however, has been primarily a forum for bilateral conversations and has been unable to deal with "any significant security issues."[5] In 1993 ASEAN spawned a still larger arena, the ASEAN Regional Forum, which included its members and dialogue partners, plus Russia, China, Vietnam, Laos, and Papua New Guinea. As its name implies, however, this organization was a place for collective talk not collective action. Members used its first meeting in July 1994 to "air their views on regional security issues," but controversial issues were avoided because, as one official commented, if they were raised, "the participants concerned would begin attacking each other."[6] ASEAN and its offspring evidence the limitations that inhere in multicivilizational regional organizations.

Meaningful East Asian regional organizations will emerge only if there is sufficient East Asian cultural commonality to sustain them. East Asian societies undoubtedly share some things in common which differentiate them from the West. Malaysia's prime minister, Mahathir Mohammad, argues that these commonalities provide a basis for association and has promoted formation of the East Asian Economic Caucus on these grounds. It would include the ASEAN countries, Myanmar, Taiwan, Hong Kong, South Korea, and, most important, China and Japan. Mahathir argues that the EAEC is rooted in a common culture. It should be thought of "not just as a geographical group, because it is in East Asia, but also as a cultural group. Although East Asians may be Japanese or Koreans or Indonesians, culturally they have certain similarities. . . . Europeans flock together and Americans flock together. We Asians should flock together as well." Its purpose, as one of his associates said, is to enhance "regional trade among countries with commonalities here in Asia."[7]

The underlying premise of the EAEC is thus that economics follows culture. Australia, New Zealand, and the United States are excluded from it because culturally they are not Asian. The success of the EAEC, however, depends overwhelmingly on participation by Japan and China. Mahathir has pleaded with the Japanese to join. "Japan is Asian. Japan is of East Asia," he told a Japanese audience. "You cannot turn from this geo-cultural fact. You belong here."[8] The Japanese government, however, was reluctant to enlist in the EAEC, in part for fear of offending the United States and in part because it was divided over whether it should identify itself with Asia. If Japan joins the EAEC, it would dominate it, which is likely to cause fear and uncertainty among the members as well as intense antagonism on the part of China. For several years there was much talk of Japan creating an Asian "yen bloc" to balance the European Union and the NAFTA. Japan, however, is a lone country with few cultural connections with its neighbors and as of 1995 no yen bloc had materialized.

While ASEAN moved slowly, the yen bloc remained a dream, Japan wavered, and the EAEC did not get off the ground, economic interaction in East Asia nonetheless increased dramatically. This expansion was rooted in the cultural ties among East Asian Chinese communities. These ties gave rise to "continuing informal integration" of a Chinese-based international economy, comparable in many respects to the Hanseatic League, and "perhaps leading to a de facto Chinese common market"[9] (see pp. 168–74). In East Asia, as elsewhere, cultural commonality has been the prerequisite to meaningful economic integration.

The end of the Cold War stimulated efforts to create new and to revive old regional economic organizations. The success of these efforts has depended overwhelmingly on the cultural homogeneity of the states involved. Shimon Peres' 1994 plan for a Middle East common market is likely to remain a "desert mirage" for some while to come: "The Arab world," one Arab official commented, "is not in need of an institution or a development bank in which Israel participates."[10] The Association of Caribbean States, created in 1994 to link CARICOM to Haiti and the Spanish-speaking countries of the region, shows little signs of overcoming the linguistic and cultural differences of its diverse membership and the insularity of the former British colonies and their overwhelming orientation toward the United States.[11] Efforts involving more culturally homogeneous organizations, on the other hand, were making progress. Although divided along subcivilizational lines, Pakistan, Iran, and Turkey in 1985 revived the moribund Regional Cooperation for Development which they had established in 1977, renaming it the Economic Cooperation Organization. Agreements were subsequently reached on tariff reductions and a variety of other measures, and in 1992 ECO membership was expanded to include Afghanistan and the six Muslim former Soviet republics. Meanwhile, the five Central Asian former Soviet republics in 1991 agreed in principle to create a common market, and in 1994 the two largest states, Uzbekistan and Kazakhstan signed an agreement to allow the "free circulation of goods, services and capital" and to coordinate their fiscal, monetary, and tariff policies. In 1991 Brazil, Argentina, Uruguay, and Paraguay joined together in Mercosur with the goal of leapfrogging the normal stages of economic integration, and by 1995 a partial customs union was in place. In 1990 the previously stagnant Central American Common Market established a free trade area, and in 1994 the formerly equally passive Andean Group created a custom union. In 1992 the Visegrad countries (Poland, Hungary, the Czech Republic, and Slovakia) agreed to establish a Central European Free Trade Area and in 1994 speeded up the timetable for its realization.[12]

Trade expansion follows economic integration, and during the 1980s and early 1990s intraregional trade became increasingly more important relative to interregional trade. Trade within the European Community constituted 50.6 percent of the community's total trade in 1980 and grew to 58.9 percent by 1989. Similar shifts toward regional trade occurred in North America and East Asia. In Latin America, the creation of Mercosur and the revival of the Andean Pact stimulated an upsurge in intra–Latin American trade in the early 1990s, with trade between Brazil and Argentina tripling and Colombia-Venezuela trade quadrupling between 1990 and 1993. In 1994 Brazil replaced the United States as Argentina's principal trading partner. The creation of NAFTA was similarly accompanied by a significant increase in Mexican-U.S. trade. Trade within East Asia also expanded more rapidly than extraregional trade, but its expansion was hampered by Japan's tendency to keep its markets closed. Trade among the countries of the Chinese cultural zone (ASEAN, Taiwan, Hong Kong, South Korea, and China), on the other hand, increased from less than 20 percent of their total in 1970 to almost 30 percent of their total in 1992, while Japan's share of their trade declined from 23 percent to 13 percent. In 1992 Chinese zone exports to other zone countries exceeded both their exports to the United States and their combined exports to Japan and the European Community.[13]

As a society and civilization unique to itself, Japan faces difficulties developing its economic ties with East Asia and dealing with its economic differences with the United States and Europe. However strong the trade and investment links Japan may forge with other East Asian countries, its cultural differences from those countries, and particularly from their largely Chinese economic elites, preclude it from creating a Japanese-led regional economic grouping comparable to NAFTA or the European Union. At the same time, its cultural differences with the West exacerbate misunderstanding and antagonism in its economic relations with the United States and Europe. If, as seems to be the case, economic integration depends on cultural commonality, Japan as a culturally lone country could have an economically lonely future.

In the past the patterns of trade among nations have followed and paralleled the patterns of alliance among nations.[14] In the emerging world, patterns of trade will be decisively influenced by the patterns of culture. Businessmen make deals with people they can understand and trust; states surrender sovereignty to international associations composed of like-minded states they understand and trust. The roots of economic cooperation are in cultural commonality.

THE STRUCTURE OF CIVILIZATIONS

In the Cold War, countries related to the two superpowers as allies, satellites, clients, neutrals, and nonaligned. In the post–Cold War world, countries relate to civilizations as member states, core states, lone countries, cleft countries, and torn countries. Like tribes and nations, civilizations have political structures. A *member state* is a country fully identified culturally with one civilization, as Egypt is with Arab-Islamic civilization and Italy is with European-Western civilization. A civilization may also include people who share in and identify with its culture, but who live in states dominated by members of another civilization. Civilizations usually have one or more places viewed by their members as the principal source or sources of the civilization's culture. These sources are often located within the *core state* or states of the civilization, that is, its most powerful and culturally central state or states.

The number and role of core states vary from civilization to civilization and may change over time. Japanese civilization is virtually identical with the single Japanese core state. Sinic, Orthodox, and Hindu civilizations each have one overwhelmingly dominant core state, other member states, and people affiliated with their civilization in states dominated by people of a different civilization (overseas Chinese, "near abroad" Russians, Sri Lankan Tamils). Historically the West has usually had several core states; it has now two cores, the United States and a Franco-German core in Europe, with Britain an additional center of power adrift between them. Islam, Latin America, and Africa lack core states. This is in part due to the imperialism of the Western powers, which divided among themselves Africa, the Middle East, and in earlier centuries and less decisively, Latin America.

The absence of an Islamic core state poses major problems for both Muslim and non-Muslim societies, which are discussed in chapter 7. With respect to Latin America, conceivably Spain could have become the core state of a Spanish-speaking or even Iberian civilization but its leaders consciously chose to become a member state in European civilization, while at the same time maintaining cultural links with its former colonies. Size, resources, population, military and economic capacity, qualify Brazil to be the leader of Latin America, and conceivably it could become that. Brazil, however, is to Latin America what Iran is to Islam. Otherwise well-qualified to be a core state, subcivilizational differences (religious with Iran, linguistic with Brazil) make it difficult for it to assume that role. Latin America thus has several states, Brazil, Mexico, Venezuela, and Argentina, which cooperate in and compete for leadership. The Latin American situation is also complicated by the fact that Mexico has attempted to redefine itself from a Latin American to a North American identity and Chile and other states may follow. In the end, Latin American civilization could merge into and become one subvariant of a three-pronged Western civilization.

The ability of any potential core state to provide leadership to sub-Saharan Africa is limited by its division into French-speaking and English-speaking countries. For a while Côte d'Ivoire was the core state of French-speaking Africa. In considerable measure, however, the core state of French Africa has been France, which after independence maintained intimate economic, military, and political connections with its former colonies. The two African countries that are most qualified to become core states are both English-speaking. Size, resources, and location make Nigeria a potential core state, but its intercivilizational disunity, massive corruption, political instability, repressive government, and economic problems have severely limited its ability to perform this role, although it has done so on occasion. South Africa's peaceful and negotiated transition from apartheid, its industrial strength, its higher level of economic development compared to other African countries, its military capability, its natural resources, and its sophisticated black and white political leadership all mark South Africa as clearly the leader of southern Africa, probably the leader of English Africa, and possibly the leader of all sub-Saharan Africa.

A *lone country* lacks cultural commonality with other societies. Ethiopia, for example, is culturally isolated by its predominant language, Amharic, written in the Ethiopic script; its predominant religion, Coptic Orthodoxy; its imperial history; and its religious differentiation from the largely Muslim surrounding peoples. While Haiti's elite has traditionally relished its cultural ties to France, Haiti's Creole language, Voodoo religion, revolutionary slave origins, and brutal history combine to make it a lone country. "Every nation is unique," Sidney Mintz observed, but "Haiti is in a class by itself." As a result, during the Haitian crisis of 1994, Latin American countries did not view Haiti as a Latin American problem and were unwilling to accept Haitian refugees although they took in Cuban ones. "[I]n Latin America," as Panama's president-elect put it, "Haiti is not recognized as a Latin American country. Haitians speak a different language. They have different ethnic roots, a different culture. They are very different altogether." Haiti is equally separate from the English-speaking black countries of the Caribbean. Haitians, one commentator observed, are "just as strange to someone from Grenada or Jamaica as they would be to someone from Iowa or Montana." Haiti, "the neighbor nobody wants," is truly a kinless country.[15]

The most important lone country is Japan. No other country shares its distinct culture, and Japanese migrants are either not numerically significant in other countries or have assimilated to the cultures of those countries (e.g., Japanese-Americans). Japan's loneliness is further enhanced by the fact that its culture is highly particularistic and does not involve a potentially universal religion (Christianity, Islam) or ideology (liberalism, communism) that could be exported to other societies and thus establish a cultural connection with people in those societies.

Almost all countries are heterogeneous in that they include two or more ethnic, racial, and religious groups. Many countries are divided in that the differences and conflicts among these groups play an important role in the politics of the country. The depth of this division usually varies over time. Deep divisions within a country can lead to massive violence or threaten the country's existence. This latter threat and movements for autonomy or separation are most likely to arise when cultural differences coincide with differences in geographic location. If culture and geography do not coincide, they may be made to coincide through either genocide or forced migration.

Countries with distinct cultural groupings belonging to the same civilization may become deeply divided with separation either occurring (Czechoslovakia) or becoming a possibility (Canada). Deep divisions are, however, much more likely to emerge within a *cleft country* where large groups belong to different civilizations. Such divisions and the tensions that go with them often develop when a majority group belonging to one civilization attempts to define the state as its political instrument and to make its language, religion, and symbols those of the state, as Hindus, Sinhalese, and Muslims have attempted to do in India, Sri Lanka, and Malaysia.

Cleft countries that territorially bestride the fault lines between civilizations face particular problems maintaining their unity. In Sudan, civil war has gone on for decades between the Muslim north and the largely Christian south. The same civilizational division has bedeviled Nigerian politics for a similar length of time and stimulated one major war of secession plus coups, rioting, and other violence. In Tanzania, the Christian animist mainland and Arab Muslim Zanzibar have drifted apart and in many respects become two separate countries, with Zanzibar in 1992 secretly joining the Organization of the Islamic Conference and then being induced by Tanzania to withdraw from it the following year.[16] The same Christian-Muslim division has generated tensions and conflicts in Kenya. On the horn of Africa, largely Christian Ethiopia and overwhelmingly Muslim Eritrea separated from each other in 1993. Ethiopia was left, however, with a substantial Muslim minority among its Oromo people. Other countries divided by civilizational fault lines include: India (Muslims and Hindus), Sri Lanka (Sinhalese Buddhists and Tamil Hindus), Malaysia and Singapore (Chinese and Malay Muslims), China (Han Chinese, Tibetan Buddhists, Turkic Muslims), Philippines (Christians and Muslims), and Indonesia (Muslims and Timorese Christians).

The divisive effect of civilizational fault lines has been most notable in those cleft countries held together during the Cold War by authoritarian communist regimes legitimated by Marxist-Leninist ideology. With the collapse of communism, culture replaced ideology as the magnet of attraction and repulsion, and Yugoslavia and the Soviet Union came apart and divided into new entities grouped along civilizational lines: Baltic (Protestant and Catholic), Orthodox, and Muslim republics in the former Soviet Union; Catholic Slovenia and Croatia; partially Muslim Bosnia-Herzegovina; and Orthodox Serbia-Montenegro and Macedonia in the former Yugoslavia. Where these successor entities still encompassed multicivilizational groups, second-stage divisions manifested themselves. Bosnia-Herzegovina was divided by war into Serbian, Muslim, and Croatian sections, and Serbs and Croats fought each other in Croatia. The sustained peaceful position of Albanian Muslim Kosovo within Slavic Orthodox Serbia is highly uncertain, and tensions rose between the Albanian Muslim minority and the Slavic Orthodox majority in Macedonia. Many former Soviet republics also bestride civilizational fault lines, in part because the Soviet government shaped boundaries so as to create divided republics, Russian Crimea going to Ukraine, Armenian Nagorno-Karabakh to Azerbaijan. Russia has several, relatively small, Muslim minorities, most notably in the North Caucasus and the Volga region. Estonia, Latvia, and Kazakhstan have substantial Russian minorities, also produced in considerable measure by Soviet policy. Ukraine is divided between the Uniate nationalist Ukrainian-speaking west and the Orthodox Russian-speaking east.

In a cleft country major groups from two or more civilizations say, in effect, "We are different peoples and belong in different places." The forces of repulsion drive them apart and they gravitate toward civilizational magnets in other societies. A *torn country*, in contrast, has a single predominant culture which places it in one civilization but its leaders want to shift it to another civilization. They say, in effect, "We are one people and belong together in one place but we want to change that place." Unlike the people of cleft countries, the people of torn countries agree on who they are but disagree on which civilization is properly their civilization. Typically, a significant portion of the leaders embrace a Kemalist strategy and decide their society should reject its non-Western culture and institutions, should join the West, and should both modernize and Westernize. Russia has been a torn country since Peter the Great, divided over the issue of whether it is part of Western civilization or is the core of a distinct Eurasian Orthodox civilization. Mustafa Kemal's country is, of course, the classic torn country which since the 1920s has been trying to modernize, to Westernize, and to become part of the West. After almost two centuries of

Mexico defining itself as a Latin American country in opposition to the United States, its leaders in the 1980s made their country a torn country by attempting to redefine it as a North American society. Australia's leaders in the 1990s, in contrast, are trying to delink their country from the West and make it a part of Asia, thereby creating a torn-country-in-reverse. Torn countries are identifiable by two phenomena. Their leaders refer to them as a "bridge" between two cultures, and observers describe them as Janus-faced. "Russia looks West—and East"; "Turkey: East, West, which is best?"; "Australian nationalism: Divided loyalties"; are typical headlines highlighting torn country identity problems.[17]

Torn Countries: The Failure of Civilization Shifting

For a torn country successfully to redefine its civilizational identity, at least three requirements must be met. First, the political and economic elite of the country has to be generally supportive of and enthusiastic about this move. Second, the public has to be at least willing to acquiesce in the redefinition of identity. Third, the dominant elements in the host civilization, in most cases the West, have to be willing to embrace the convert. The process of identity redefinition will be prolonged, interrupted, and painful, politically, socially, institutionally, and culturally. It also to date has failed.

Russia. In the 1990s Mexico had been a torn country for several years and Turkey for several decades. Russia, in contrast, has been a torn country for several centuries, and unlike Mexico or republican Turkey, it is also the core state of a major civilization. If Turkey or Mexico successfully redefined themselves as members of Western civilization, the effect on Islamic or Latin American civilization would be minor or moderate. If Russia became Western, Orthodox civilization ceases to exist. The collapse of the Soviet Union rekindled among Russians debate on the central issue of Russia and the West.

Russia's relations with Western civilization have evolved through four phases. In the first phase, which lasted down to the reign of Peter the Great (1689–1725), Kievan Rus and Muscovy existed separately from the West and had little contact with Western European societies. Russian civilization developed as an offspring of Byzantine civilization and then for two hundred years, from the mid-thirteenth to the mid-fifteenth centuries, Russia was under Mongol suzerainty. Russia had no or little exposure to the defining historical phenomena of Western civilization: Roman Catholicism, feudalism, the Renaissance, the Reformation, overseas expansion and colonization, the Enlightenment, and the emergence of the nation state. Seven of the eight previously identified distinctive features of Western civilization—religion, languages, separation of church and state, rule of law, social pluralism, representative bodies, individualism—were almost totally absent from the Russian experience. The only possible exception is the Classical legacy, which, however, came to Russia via Byzantium and hence was quite different from that which came to the West directly from Rome. Russian civilization was a product of its indigenous roots in Kievan Rus and Moscovy, substantial Byzantine impact, and prolonged Mongol rule. These influences shaped a society and a culture which had little resemblance to those developed in Western Europe under the influence of very different forces.

At the end of the seventeenth century Russia was not only different from Europe, it was also backward compared to Europe, as Peter the Great learned during his European tour in 1697–1698. He became determined both to modernize and to Westernize his country. To make his people look European, the first thing Peter did on returning to Moscow was to shave the beards of his nobles and ban their long gowns and conical hats. Although Peter did not abolish the Cyrillic alphabet he did reform and simplify it and introduce Western words and phrases. He gave top priority, however, to the development and modernization of Russia's military forces: creating a navy, introducing conscription, building defense industries, establishing technical schools, sending people to the West to study, and importing from the West the latest knowledge concerning weapons, ships and shipbuilding, navigation, bureaucratic administration, and other subjects essential to military effectiveness. To provide for these innovations, he drastically reformed and expanded the tax system and also, toward the end of his reign, reorganized the structure of government. Determined to make Russia not only a European power but also a power in Europe, he abandoned Moscow, created a new capital at St. Petersburg, and launched the Great Northern War against Sweden in order to establish Russia as the predominant force in the Baltic and to create a presence in Europe.

In attempting to make his country modern and Western, however, Peter also reinforced Russia's Asiatic characteristics by perfecting despotism and eliminating any potential source of social or political pluralism. Russian nobility had never been powerful. Peter reduced them still further, expanding the service nobility, and establishing a Table of Ranks based on merit, not birth or social position. Noblemen like peasants were conscripted into the service of the state, forming the "cringing aristocracy" that later infuriated Custine.[18] The autonomy of the serfs was further restricted as they were bound more firmly to both their land and their master. The Orthodox Church, which had always been under broad state control, was reorganized and placed under a synod directly appointed by the tsar. The tsar was also given power to appoint his successor without reference to the prevailing practices of inheritance. With these changes, Peter initiated and exemplified the close connection in Russia between modernization and Westernization, on the one hand, and despotism, on the other. Following this Petrine model, Lenin, Stalin, and to a lesser degree Catherine II and Alexander II, also tried in varying ways to modernize and Westernize Russia and strengthen autocratic power. At least until the 1980s, the democratizers in Russia were usually Westernizers, but the Westernizers were not democratizers. The lesson of Russian history is that the centralization of power is the prerequisite to social and economic reform. In the late 1980s associates of Gorbachev lamented their failure to appreciate this fact in decrying the obstacles which *glasnost* had created for economic liberalization.

Peter was more successful making Russia part of Europe than making Europe part of Russia. In contrast to the Ottoman Empire, the Russian Empire came to be accepted as a major and legitimate participant in the European international system. At home Peter's reforms brought some changes but his society remained hybrid: apart from a small elite, Asiatic and Byzantine ways, institutions, and beliefs predominated in Russian society and were perceived to do so by both Europeans and Russians. "Scratch a Russian," de Maistre observed, "and you wound a Tatar." Peter created a torn country, and during the nineteenth century Slavophiles and Westernizers jointly lamented this unhappy state and vigorously disagreed on whether to end it by becoming thoroughly Europeanized or by eliminating European influences and returning to the true soul of Russia. A Westernizer like Chaadayev argued that the "sun is the sun of the West" and Russia must use this light to illuminate and to change its inherited institutions. A Slavophile like Danilevskiy, in words that were also heard in the 1990s, denounced Europeanizing efforts as "distorting the people's life and replacing its forms with alien, foreign forms," "borrowing foreign institutions and transplanting them to Russian soil," and "regarding both domestic and foreign relations and questions of Russian life from a foreign, European viewpoint, viewing them, as it were, through a glass fashioned to a European angle of refraction."[19] In subsequent Russian history Peter became the hero of Westernizers and the satan of their opponents, represented at the extreme by the Eurasians of the 1920s who denounced him as a traitor and hailed the Bolsheviks for rejecting Westernization, challenging Europe, and moving the capital back to Moscow.

The Bolshevik Revolution initiated a third phase in the relationship between Russia and the West very different from the ambivalent one that had existed for two centuries. It created a political-economic system which could not exist in the West in the name of an ideology which was created in the West. The Slavophiles and Westernizers had debated whether Russia could be different from the West without being backward compared to the West. Communism brilliantly resolved this issue: Russia was different from and fundamentally opposed to the West because it was more advanced than the West. It was taking the lead in the proletarian revolution which would eventually sweep across the world. Russia embodied not a backward Asiatic past but a progressive Soviet future. In effect, the Revolution enabled Russia to leapfrog the West, differentiating itself not because "you are different and we won't become like you," as the Slavophiles had argued, but because "we are different and eventually you will become like us," as was the message of the Communist International.

Yet at the same time that communism enabled Soviet leaders to distinguish themselves from the West, it also created powerful ties to the West. Marx and Engels were German; most of the principal exponents of their views in the late nineteenth and early twentieth centuries were Western European; by 1910 many labor unions and social democratic and labor parties in Western societies were committed to their ideology and were becoming increasingly influential in European politics. After the Bolshevik Revolution, left-wing parties split into communist and socialist parties, and both were often powerful forces in European countries. Throughout much of the West, the Marxist perspective prevailed: communism and socialism were seen as the wave of the future and were widely embraced in one way or another by political and intellectual elites. The debate in Russia between Slavophiles and Westernizers over the future of Russia was thus replaced by a debate in Europe between left and right over the future of the West and whether or not the Soviet Union epitomized that future. After World War II the power of the Soviet Union reinforced the appeal of communism both in the West and, more significantly, in those non-Western civilizations which were now reacting against the West. Elites in Western-dominated non-Western societies who wished to seduce the West talked in terms of self-determination and democracy; those who wished to confront the West invoked revolution and national liberation.

By adopting Western ideology and using it to challenge the West, Russians in a sense became closer to and more intimately involved with the West than at any previous time in their history. Although the ideologies of liberal democracy and communism differed greatly, both parties were, in a sense, speaking the same language. The collapse of communism and of the Soviet Union ended this political-ideological interaction between the West and Russia. The West hoped and believed the result would be the triumph of liberal democracy throughout the former Soviet empire. That, however, was not foreordained. As of 1995 the future of liberal democracy in Russia and the other Orthodox republics was uncertain. In addition, as the Russians stopped behaving like Marxists and began behaving like Russians, the gap between Russia and the West broadened. The conflict between liberal democracy and Marxist-Leninism was between ideologies which, despite their major differences, were both modern and secular and ostensibly shared ultimate goals of freedom, equality, and material well-being. A Western democrat could carry on an intellectual debate with a Soviet Marxist. It would be impossible for him to do that with a Russian Orthodox nationalist.

During the Soviet years the struggle between Slavophiles and Westernizers was suspended as both Solzhenitsyns and Sakharovs challenged the communist synthesis. With the collapse of that synthesis, the debate over Russia's true identity reemerged in full vigor. Should Russia adopt Western values, institutions, and practices, and attempt to become part of the West? Or did Russia embody a distinct Orthodox and Eurasian civilization, different from the West's with a unique destiny to link Europe and Asia? Intellectual and political elites and the general public were seriously divided over these questions. On the one hand were the Westernizers, "cosmopolitans," or "Atlanticists," and on the other, the successors to the Slavophiles, variously referred to as "nationalists," "Eurasianists," or "*derzhavniki*" (strong state supporters).[20]

The principal differences between these groups were over foreign policy and to a lesser degree economic reform and state structure. Opinions were distributed over a continuum from one extreme to another. Grouped toward one end of the spectrum were those who articulated "the new thinking" espoused by Gorbachev and epitomized in his goal of a "common European home" and many of Yeltsin's top advisors, expressed in his desire that Russia become "a normal country" and be accepted as the eighth member of the G-7 club of major industrialized democracies. The more moderate nationalists such as Sergei Stankevich argued that Russia should reject the "Atlanticist" course and should give priority to the protection of Russians in other countries, emphasize its Turkic and Muslim connections, and promote "an appreciable redistribution of our resources, our options, our ties, and our interests in favor of Asia, or the eastern direction."[21] People of this persuasion criticized Yeltsin for subordinating Russia's interests to those of the West, for reducing Russian military strength, for failing to support traditional friends such as Serbia, and for pushing economic and political reform in ways injurious to the Russian people. Indicative of this trend was the new popularity of the ideas of Peter Savitsky, who in the 1920s argued that Russia was a unique Eurasian civilization.

The more extreme nationalists were divided between Russian nationalists, such as Solzhenitsyn, who advocated a Russia including all Russians plus closely linked Slavic Orthodox Byelorussians and Ukrainians but no one else, and the imperial nationalists, such as Vladimir Zhirinovsky, who wanted to recreate the Soviet empire and Russian military strength. People in the latter group at times were anti-Semitic as well as anti-Western and wanted to reorient Russian foreign policy to the East and South, either dominating the Muslim South (as Zhirinovsky urged) or cooperating with Muslim states and China against the West. The nationalists also backed more extensive support for the Serbs in their war with the Muslims. The differences between cosmopolitans and nationalists were reflected institutionally in the outlooks of the Foreign Ministry and the military. They were also reflected in the shifts in Yeltsin's foreign and security policies first in one direction and then in the other.

The Russian public was as divided as the Russian elites. A 1992 poll of a sample of 2069 European Russians found that 40 percent of the respondents were "open to the West," 36 percent "closed to the West," and 24 percent "undecided." In the December 1993 parliamentary elections reformist parties won 34.2 percent of the vote, antireform and nationalist parties 43.3 percent, and centrist parties 13.7 percent.[22] Similarly, in the June 1996 presidential election, the Russian public divided again with roughly 43 percent supporting the West's candidate, Yeltsin, and other reform candidates and 52 percent voting for nationalist and communist candidates. On the central issue of its identity, Russia in the 1990s clearly remained a torn country, with the Western-Slavophile duality "an inalienable trait of the . . . *national character.*"[23]

Turkey. Through a carefully calculated series of reforms in the 1920s and 1930s Mustafa Kemal Ataturk attempted to move his people away from their Ottoman and Muslim past. The basic principles or "six arrows" of Kemalism were populism, republicanism, nationalism, secularism, statism, and reformism. Rejecting the idea of a multinational empire, Kemal aimed to produce a homogeneous nation state, expelling and killing Armenians and Greeks in the process. He then deposed the sultan and established a Western type republican system of political authority. He abolished the caliphate, the central source of religious authority, ended the traditional education and religious ministries, abolished the separate religious schools and colleges, established a unified secular system of public education, and did away with the religious courts that applied Islamic law, replacing them with a new legal system based on the Swiss civil code. He also replaced the traditional calendar with the Gregorian calendar and formally disestablished Islam as the state religion. Emulating Peter the Great, he prohibited use of the fez because it was a symbol of religious traditionalism, encouraged people to wear hats, and decreed that Turkish would be written in Roman rather than Arabic script. This latter reform was of fundamental importance. "It made it virtually impossible for the new generations educated in the Roman script to acquire access to the vast bulk of traditional literature; it encouraged the learning of European languages; and it greatly eased the problem of increasing literacy."[24] Having redefined the national, political, religious, and cultural identity of the Turkish people, Kemal in the 1930s vigorously attempted to promote Turkish economic development. Westernization went hand-in-hand with and was to be the means of modernization.

Turkey remained neutral during the West's civil war between 1939 and 1945. Following that war, however, it quickly moved to identify itself still further with the West. Explicitly following Western models, it shifted from one-party rule to a competitive party system. It lobbied for and eventually achieved NATO membership in 1952, thus confirming itself as a member of the Free World. It became the recipient of billions of dollars of Western economic and security assistance; its military forces were trained and equipped by the West and integrated into the NATO command structure; it hosted American military bases. Turkey came to be viewed by the West as its eastern bulwark of containment, preventing the expansion of the Soviet Union toward the Mediterranean, the Middle East, and the Persian Gulf. This linkage with and self-identification with the West caused the Turks to be denounced by the non-Western, non-aligned countries at the 1955 Bandung Conference and to be attacked as blasphemous by Islamic countries.[25]

After the Cold War the Turkish elite remained overwhelmingly supportive of Turkey being Western and European. Sustained NATO membership is for them indispensable because it provides an intimate organizational tie with the West and is necessary to balance Greece. Turkey's involvement with the West, embodied in its NATO membership, was, however, a product of the Cold War. Its end removes the principal reason for that involvement and leads to a weakening and redefinition of that connection. Turkey is no longer useful to the West as a bulwark against the major threat from the north, but rather, as in the Gulf War, a possible partner in dealing with lesser threats from the south. In that war Turkey provided crucial help to the anti–Saddam Hussein coalition by shutting down the pipeline across its territory through which Iraqi oil reached the Mediterranean and by permitting American planes to operate against Iraq from bases in Turkey. These decisions by President Özal, however, stimulated substantial criticism in Turkey and prompted the resignation of the foreign minister, the defense minister, and the chief of the general staff, as well as large public demonstrations protesting Özal's close cooperation with the United States. Subsequently both President Demirel and Prime Minister Ciller urged early ending of U.N. sanctions against Iraq, which also imposed considerable economic burden on Turkey.[26] Turkey's willingness to work with the West in dealing with Islamic threats from the south is more uncertain than was its willingness to stand with the West against the Soviet threat. During the Gulf crisis, opposition by Germany, a traditional friend of Turkey's, to viewing an Iraqi missile attack on Turkey as an attack on NATO also showed that Turkey could not count on Western support against southern threats. Cold War confrontations with the Soviet Union did not raise the question of Turkey's civilization identity; post–Cold War relations with Arab countries do.

Beginning in the 1980s a primary, perhaps *the* primary, foreign policy goal of Turkey's Western-oriented elite has been to secure membership in the European Union. Turkey formally applied for membership in April 1987. In December 1989 Turkey was told that its application could not be considered before 1993. In 1994 the Union approved the applications of Austria, Finland, Sweden, and Norway, and it was widely anticipated that in the coming years favorable action would be taken on those of Poland, Hungary, and the Czech Republic, and later possibly on Slovenia, Slovakia, and the Baltic republics. The Turks were particularly disappointed that again Germany, the most influential member of the European Community, did not actively support their membership and instead gave priority to promoting membership for the Central European states.[27] Pressured by the United States, the Union did negotiate a customs union with Turkey; full membership, however, remains a distant and dubious possibility.

Why was Turkey passed over and why does it always seem to be at the end of the queue? In public, European officials referred to Turkey's low level of economic development and its less than Scandinavian respect for human rights. In private, both Europeans and Turks agreed that the real reasons were the intense opposition of the Greeks and, more importantly, the fact that Turkey is a Muslim country. European countries did not want to face the possibility of opening their borders to immigration from a country of 60 million Muslims and much unemployment. Even more significantly, they felt that culturally the Turks did not belong in Europe. Turkey's human rights record, as President Özal said in 1992, is a "made-up reason why Turkey should not join the EC. The real reason is that we are Muslim, and they are Christian," but he added, "they don't say that." European officials, in turn, agreed that the Union is "a Christian club" and that "Turkey is too poor, too populous, too Muslim, too harsh, too culturally different, too everything." The "private night-mare" of Europeans, one observer commented, is the historical memory of "Saracen raiders in Western Europe and the Turks at the gates of Vienna." These attitudes, in turn, generated the "common perception among Turks" that "the West sees no place for a Muslim Turkey within Europe."[28]

Having rejected Mecca, and being rejected by Brussels, Turkey seized the opportunity opened by the dissolution of the Soviet Union to turn toward Tashkent. President Özal and other Turkish leaders held out the vision of a community of Turkic peoples and made great efforts to develop links with the "external Turks" in Turkey's "near abroad" stretching "from the Adriatic to the borders of China." Particular attention was directed to Azerbaijan and the four Turkic-speaking Central Asian republics of Uzbekistan, Turkmenistan, Kazakhstan, and Kyrgyzstan. In 1991 and 1992 Turkey launched a wide range of activities designed to bolster its ties with and its influence in these new republics. These included $1.5 billion in long-term low-interest loans, $79 million in direct relief aid, satellite television (replacing a Russian language channel), telephone communications, airline service, thousands of scholarships for students to study in Turkey, and training in Turkey for Central Asian and Azeri bankers, businesspersons, diplomats, and hundreds of military officers. Teachers were sent to the new republics to teach Turkish, and about 2000 joint ventures were started. Cultural commonality smoothed these economic relationships. As one Turkish businessman commented, "The most important thing for success in Azerbaijan or Turkmenistan is finding the right partner. For Turkish people, it is not so difficult. We have the same culture, more or less the same language, and we eat from the same kitchen."[29]

Turkey's reorientation toward the Caucasus and Central Asia was fueled not only by the dream of being the leader of a Turkic community of nations but also by the desire to counter Iran and Saudi Arabia from expanding their influence and promoting Islamic fundamentalism in this region. The Turks saw themselves as offering the "Turkish model" or the "idea of Turkey" — a secular, democratic Muslim state with a market economy — as an alternative. In addition, Turkey hoped to contain the resurgence of Russian influence. By providing an alternative to Russia and Islam, Turkey also would bolster its claim for support from and eventual membership in the European Union.

Turkey's initial surge of activity with the Turkic republics became more restrained in 1993 due to the limits on its resources, the succession of Suleyman Demirel to the presidency following Özal's death, and the reassertion of Russia's influence in what it considered its "near abroad." When the Turkic former Soviet republics first became independent, their leaders rushed to Ankara to court Turkey. Subsequently, as Russia applied pressure and inducements, they swung back and generally stressed the need for "balanced" relationships between their cultural cousin and their former imperial master. The Turks, however, continued to attempt to use their cultural affiliations to expand their economic and political linkages and, in their most important coup, secured agreement of the relevant governments and oil companies to the construction of a pipeline to bring Central Asian and Azerbaijani oil through Turkey to the Mediterranean.[30]

While Turkey worked to develop its links with the Turkic former Soviet republics, its own Kemalist secular identity was under challenge at home. First, for Turkey, as for so many other counties, the end of the Cold War, together with the dislocations generated by social and economic development, raised major issues of "national identity and ethnic identification,"[31] and religion was there to provide an answer. The secular heritage of Ataturk and of the Turkish elite for two-thirds of a century came increasingly under fire. The experience of Turks abroad tended to stimulate Islamist sentiments at home. Turks coming back from West Germany "reacted to hostility there by falling back on what was familiar. And that was Islam." Mainstream opinion and practice became increasingly Islamist. In 1993 it was reported "that Islamic-style beards and veiled women have proliferated in Turkey, that mosques are drawing even larger crowds, and that some bookstores are overflowing with books and journals, cassettes, compact disks and videos glorifying Islamic history, precepts and way of life and exalting the Ottoman Empire's role in preserving the values of the Prophet Muhammad." Reportedly, "no fewer than 290 publishing houses and printing presses, 300 publications including four dailies, some hundred unlicensed radio stations and about 30 likewise unlicensed television channels were all propagating Islamic ideology."[32]

Confronted by rising Islamist sentiment, Turkey's rulers attempted to adopt fundamentalist practices and co-opt fundamentalist support. In the 1980s and 1990s the supposedly secular Turkish government maintained an Office of Religious Affairs with a budget larger than those of some ministries, financed the construction of mosques, required religious instruction in all public schools, and provided funding to Islamic schools, which quintupled in number during the 1980s, enrolling about 15 percent of secondary school children, and which preached Islamist doctrines and produced thousands of graduates, many of whom entered government service. In symbolic but dramatic contrast to France, the government in practice allowed schoolgirls to wear the traditional Muslim headscarf, seventy years after Ataturk banned the fez.[33] These government actions, in large part motivated by the desire to take the wind out of the sails of the Islamists, testify to how strong that wind was in the 1980s and early 1990s.

Second, the resurgence of Islam changed the character of Turkish politics. Political leaders, most notably Turgut Özal, quite explicitly identified themselves with Muslim symbols and policies. In Turkey, as elsewhere, democracy reinforced indigenization and the return to religion. "In their eagerness to curry favor with the public and gain votes, politicians — and even the military, the very bastion and guardian of secularism — had to take into account the religious aspirations of the population: not a few of the concessions they granted smacked of demagoguery." Popular movements were religiously inclined. While elite and bureaucratic groups, particularly the military, were secularly oriented, Islamist sentiments manifested themselves within the armed forces, and several hundred cadets were purged from military academies in 1987 because of suspected Islamist sentiments. The major political parties increasingly felt the need to seek electoral support from revived Muslim *tarikas*, or select societies, which Ataturk had banned.[34] In the March 1994 local elections, the fundamentalist Welfare Party, alone among the five major parties, increased its share of the vote, receiving roughly 19 percent of the votes as compared with 21 percent for Prime Minister Ciller's True Path Party and 20 percent for the late Özal's Motherland Party. The Welfare Party captured control of Turkey's two principal cities, Istanbul and Ankara, and ran extremely strong in the southeastern part of the country. In the December 1995 elections the Welfare Party won more votes and seats in parliament than any other party and six months later took over the government in coalition with one of the secular parties. As in other countries, support for the fundamentalists came from the young, returned migrants, the "downtrodden and dispossessed," and "new urban migrants, the 'sans culottes' of the big cities."[35]

Third, the resurgence of Islam affected Turkish foreign policy. Under President Özal's leadership, Turkey decisively sided with the West in the Gulf War, anticipating that this action would further its membership in the European Community. This consequence did not, however, materialize, and NATO hesitation over what response it would make if Turkey had been attacked by Iraq during that war did not reassure the Turks as to how NATO would respond to a non-Russian threat to their country.[36] Turkish leaders tried to expand their military connection with Israel, which provoked intense criticism from Turkish Islamists. More significantly, during the 1980s Turkey expanded its relations with Arab and other Muslim countries and in the 1990s actively promoted Islamic interests by providing significant support to the Bosnian Muslims as well as to Azerbaijan. With respect to the Balkans, Central Asia, or the Middle East, Turkish foreign policy was becoming increasingly Islamicized.

For many years Turkey met two of the three minimum requirements for a torn country to shift its civilizational identity. Turkey's elites overwhelmingly supported the move and its public was acquiescent. The elites of the recipient,

Western civilization, however, were not receptive. While the issue hung in the balance, the resurgence of Islam within Turkey activated anti-Western sentiments among the public and began to undermine the secularist, pro-Western orientation of Turkish elites. The obstacles to Turkey's becoming fully European, the limits on its ability to play a dominant role with respect to the Turkic former Soviet republics, and the rise of Islamic tendencies eroding the Ataturk inheritance, all seemed to insure that Turkey will remain a torn country.

Reflecting these conflicting pulls, Turkish leaders regularly described their country as a "bridge" between cultures. Turkey, Prime Minister Tansu Ciller argued in 1993, is both a "Western democracy" and "part of the Middle East" and "bridges two civilizations, physically and philosophically." Reflecting this ambivalence, in public in her own country Ciller often appeared as a Muslim, but when addressing NATO she argued that "the geographic and political fact is that Turkey is a European country." President Suleyman Demirel similarly called Turkey "a very significant bridge in a region extending from west to east, that is from Europe to China."[37] A bridge, however, is an artificial creation connecting two solid entities but is part of neither. When Turkey's leaders term their country a bridge, they euphemistically confirm that it is torn.

Mexico. Turkey became a torn country in the 1920s, Mexico not until the 1980s. Yet their historical relations with the West have certain similarities. Like Turkey, Mexico had a distinctly non-Western culture. Even in the twentieth century, as Octavio Paz put it, "the core of Mexico is Indian. It is non-European."[38] In the nineteenth century, Mexico, like the Ottoman empire, was dismembered by Western hands. In the second and third decades of the twentieth century, Mexico, like Turkey, went through a revolution which established a new basis of national identity and a new one-party political system. In Turkey, however, the revolution involved both a rejection of traditional Islamic and Ottoman culture and an effort to import Western culture and to join the West. In Mexico, as in Russia, the revolution involved incorporation and adaptation of elements of Western culture, which generated a new nationalism opposed to the capitalism and democracy of the West. Thus for sixty years Turkey tried to define itself as European, while Mexico tried to define itself in opposition to the United States. From the 1930s to the 1980s, Mexico's leaders pursued economic and foreign policies that challenged American interests.

In the 1980s this changed. President Miguel de la Madrid began and his successor President Carlos Salinas de Gortari carried forward a full-scale redefinition of Mexican purposes, practices, and identity, the most sweeping effort at change since the Revolution of 1910. Salinas became, in effect, the Mustafa Kemal of Mexico. Ataturk promoted secularism and nationalism, dominant themes in the West of his time; Salinas promoted economic liberalism, one of two dominant themes in the West of his time (the other, political democracy, he did not embrace). As with Ataturk, these views were broadly shared by political and economic elites, many of whom, like Salinas and de la Madrid, had been educated in the United States. Salinas dramatically reduced inflation, privatized large numbers of public enterprises, promoted foreign investment, reduced tariffs and subsidies, restructured the foreign debt, challenged the power of labor unions, increased productivity, and brought Mexico into the North American Free Trade Agreement with the United States and Canada. Just as Ataturk's reforms were designed to transform Turkey from a Muslim Middle Eastern country into a secular European country, Salinas's reforms were designed to change Mexico from a Latin American country into a North American country.

This was not an inevitable choice for Mexico. Conceivably Mexican elites could have continued to pursue the anti-U.S. Third World nationalist and protectionist path that their predecessors had followed for most of the century. Alternatively, as some Mexicans urged, they could have attempted to develop with Spain, Portugal, and South American countries an Iberian association of nations.

Will Mexico succeed in its North American quest? The overwhelming bulk of the political, economic, and intellectual elites favor that course. Also, unlike the situation with Turkey, the overwhelming bulk of the political, economic, and intellectual elites of the recipient civilization have favored Mexico's cultural realignment. The crucial intercivilizational issue of immigration highlights this difference. The fear of massive Turkish immigration generated resistance from both European elites and publics to bringing Turkey into Europe. In contrast, the fact of massive Mexican immigration, legal and illegal, into the United States was part of Salinas's argument for NAFTA: "Either you accept our goods or you accept our people." In addition, the cultural distance between Mexico and the United States is far less than that between Turkey and Europe. Mexico's religion is Catholicism, its language is Spanish, its elites were oriented historically to Europe (where they sent their children to be educated) and more recently to the United States (where they now send their children). The accommodation between Anglo-American North America and Spanish-Indian Mexico should be considerably easier than that between Christian Europe and Muslim Turkey. Despite these commonalities, after ratification of NAFTA, opposition to any closer involvement with Mexico developed in the Untied States with demands for restrictions on immigration, complaints about factories moving south, and questions about the ability of Mexico to adhere to North American concepts of liberty and the rule of law.[39]

The third prerequisite to the successful shift of identity by a torn country is general acquiescence, although not necessarily support, by its public. The importance of this factor depends, in some measure, on how important the views of the public are in the decision-making processes of the country. Mexico's pro-Western stance was, as of 1995, untested by democratization. The New Year's Day revolt of a few thousand well-organized and externally supported guerrillas in Chiapas was not, in itself, an indication of substantial resistance to North Americanization. The sympathetic response it engendered, however, among Mexican intellectuals, journalists, and other shapers of public opinion suggested that North Americanization in general and NAFTA in particular could encounter increasing resistance from Mexican elites and the public. President Salinas very consciously gave economic reform and Westernization priority over political reform and democratization. Both economic development and the increasing involvement with the United States, however, will strengthen forces promoting a real democratization of the Mexican political system. The key question for the future of Mexico is: To what extent will modernization and democratization stimulate de-Westernization, producing its withdrawal from or the drastic weakening of NAFTA and parallel changes in the policies imposed on Mexico by its Western-oriented elites of the 1980s and 1990s? Is Mexico's North Americanization compatible with its democratization?

Australia. In contrast to Russia, Turkey, and Mexico, Australia has, from its origins, been a Western society. Throughout the twentieth century it was closely allied with first Britain and then the United States; and during the Cold War it was not only a member of the West but also of the U.S.-U.K.-Canadian-Australian military and intelligence core of the West. In the early 1990s, however, Australia's political leaders decided, in effect, that Australia should defect from the West, redefine itself as an Asian society, and cultivate close ties with its geographical neighbors. Australia, Prime Minister Paul Keating declared, must cease being a "branch office of empire," become a republic, and aim for "enmeshment" in Asia. This was necessary, he argued, in order to establish Australia's identity as an independent country. "Australia cannot represent itself to the world as a multicultural society, engage in Asia, make that link and make it persuasively while in some way, at least in constitutional terms, remaining a derivative society." Australia, Keating declared, had suffered untold years of "anglophilia and torpor" and continued association with Britain would be "debilitating to our national culture, our economic future and our destiny in Asia and the Pacific." Foreign Minister Gareth Evans expressed similar sentiments.[40]

The case for redefining Australia as an Asian country was grounded on the assumption that economics overrides culture in shaping the destiny of nations. The central impetus was the dynamic growth of East Asian economies, which in turn spurred the rapid expansion of Australian trade with Asia. In 1971 East and Southeast Asia absorbed 39 percent of Australia's exports and provided 21 percent of Australia's imports. By 1994 East and Southeast Asia were taking 62 percent of Australia's exports and providing 41 percent of its imports. In contrast, in 1991 11.8 percent of Australian exports went to the European Community and 10.1 percent to the United States. This deepening economic tie with

Asia was reinforced in Australian minds by a belief that the world was moving in the direction of three major economic blocs and that Australia's place was in the East Asian bloc.

Despite these economic connections, the Australian Asian ploy appears unlikely to meet any of the requirements for success for a civilization shift by a torn country. First, in the mid-1990s Australian elites were far from overwhelmingly enthusiastic about this course. In some measure, this was a partisan issue with leaders of the Liberal Party ambivalent or opposed. The Labor government also came under substantial criticism from a variety of intellectuals and journalists. No clear elite consensus existed for the Asian choice, Second, public opinion was ambivalent. From 1987 to 1993, the proportion of the Australian public favoring the end of the monarchy rose from 21 percent to 46 percent. At that point, however, support began to waver and to erode. The proportion of the public supporting deletion of the Union Jack from the Australian flag dropped from 42 percent in May of 1992 to 35 percent in August 1993. As one Australian official observed in 1992, "It's hard for the public to stomach it. When I say periodically that Australia should be part of Asia, I can't tell you how many hate letters I get."[41]

Third and most important, the elites of Asian countries have been even less receptive to Australia's advances than European elites have been to Turkey's. They have made it clear that if Australia wants to be part of Asia it must become truly Asian, which they think unlikely if not impossible. "The success of Australia's integration with Asia," one Indonesian official said, "depends on one thing — how far Asian states welcome the Australian intention. Australia's acceptance in Asia depends on how well the government and people of Australia understand Asian culture and society." Asians see a gap between Australia's Asian rhetoric and its perversely Western reality. The Thais, according to one Australian diplomat, treat Australia's insistence it is Asian with "bemused tolerance."[42] "[C]ulturally Australia is still European," Prime Minister Mahathir of Malaysia declared in October 1994, " . . . we think it's European," and hence Australia should not be a member of the East Asian Economic Caucus. We Asians "are less prone to making outright criticism of other countries or passing judgment on them. But Australia, being European culturally, feels that it has a right to tell others what to do, what not to do, what is right, what is wrong. And then, of course, it is not compatible with the group. That is my reason [for opposing their membership in EAEC]. It is not the color of the skin, but the culture."[43] Asians, in short, are determined to exclude Australia from their club for the same reason that Europeans do Turkey: they are different from us. Prime Minister Keating liked to say that he was going to change Australia from "the odd man out to the odd man in" in Asia. That, however is an oxymoron: odd men don't get in.

As Mahathir stated, culture and values are the basic obstacle to Australia's joining Asia. Clashes regularly occur over the Australians' commitment to democracy, human rights, a free press, and its protests over the violations of those rights by the governments of virtually all its neighbors. "The real problem for Australia in the region," a senior Australian diplomat noted, "is not our flag, but the root social values. I suspect you won't find any Australians who are willing to surrender any of those values to be accepted in the region."[44] Differences in character, style, and behavior are also pronounced. As Mahathir suggested, Asians generally pursue their goals with others in ways which are subtle, indirect, modulated, devious, nonjudgmental, nonmoralistic, and non-confrontational. Australians, in contrast, are the most direct, blunt, outspoken, some would say insensitive, people in the English-speaking world. This clash of cultures was most dramatically evident in Paul Keating's own dealings with Asians. Keating embodied Australian national characteristics to an extreme. He has been described as "a pile driver of a politician" with a style that is "inherently provocative and pugnacious," and he did not hesitate to denounce his political opponents as "scumbags," "perfumed gigolos," and "brain-damaged looney crims."[45] While arguing that Australia must be Asian, Keating regularly irritated, shocked, and antagonized Asian leaders by his brutal frankness. The gap between cultures was so large that it blinded the proponent of cultural convergence to the extent his own behavior repelled those whom he claimed as cultural brethren.

The Keating-Evans choice could be viewed as the shortsighted result of overweighting economic factors and ignoring rather than renewing the country's culture, and as a tactical political ploy to distract attention from Australia's economic problems. Alternatively, it could be seen as a farsighted initiative designed to join Australia to and identify Australia with the rising centers of economic, political, and eventually military power in East Asia. In this respect, Australia could be the first of possibly many Western countries to attempt to defect from the West and bandwagon with rising non-Western civilizations. At the beginning of the twenty-second century, historians might look back on the Keating-Evans choice as a major marker in the decline of the West. If that choice is pursued, however, it will not eliminate Australia's Western heritage, and "the lucky country" will be a permanently torn country, both the "branch office of empire," which Paul Keating decried, and the "new white trash of Asia," which Lee Kuan Yew contemptuously termed it.[46]

This was not and is not an unavoidable fate for Australia. Accepting their desire to break with Britain, instead of defining Australia as an Asian power, Australia's leaders could define it as a Pacific country, as, indeed, Keating's predecessor as prime minister, Robert Hawke, attempted to do. If Australia wishes to make itself a republic separated from the British crown, it could align itself with the first country in the world to do that, a country which like Australia is of British origin, is an immigrant country, is of continental size, speaks English, has been an ally in three wars, and has an overwhelmingly European, if also like Australia increasingly Asian, population. Culturally, the values of the July 4th 1776 Declaration of Independence accord far more with Australian values than do those of any Asian country. Economically, instead of attempting to batter its way into a group of societies from which it is culturally alien and who for that reason reject it, Australia's leaders could propose expanding NAFTA into a North American–South Pacific (NASP) arrangement including the United States, Canada, Australia, and New Zealand. Such a grouping would reconcile culture and economics and provide a solid and enduring identity for Australia that will not come from futile efforts to make Australia Asian.

The Western Virus and Cultural Schizophrenia. While Australia's leaders embarked on a quest for Asia, those of other torn countries — Turkey, Mexico, Russia — attempted to incorporate the West into their societies and to incorporate their societies into the West. Their experience strongly demonstrates, however, the strength, resilience, and viscosity of indigenous cultures and their ability to renew themselves and to resist, contain, and adapt Western imports. While the rejectionist response to the West is impossible, the Kemalist response has been unsuccessful. If non-Western societies are to modernize, they must do it their own way not the Western way and, emulating Japan, build upon and employ their own traditions, institutions, and values.

Political leaders imbued with the hubris to think that they can fundamentally reshape the culture of their societies are destined to fail. While they can introduce elements of Western culture, they are unable permanently to suppress or to eliminate the core elements of their indigenous culture. Conversely, the Western virus, once it is lodged in another society, is difficult to expunge. The virus persists but is not fatal; the patient survives but is never whole. Political leaders can make history but they cannot escape history. They produce torn countries; they do not create Western societies. They infect their country with a cultural schizophrenia which becomes its continuing and defining characteristic.

Chapter 7

•

Core States,
Concentric Circles,
and Civilizational Order

CIVILIZATIONS AND ORDER

I n the emerging global politics, the core states of the major civilizations are supplanting the two Cold War superpowers as the principal poles of attraction and repulsion for other countries. These changes are most clearly visible with respect to Western, Orthodox, and Sinic civilizations. In these cases civilizational groupings are emerging involving core states, member states, culturally similar minority populations in adjoining states, and, more controversially, peoples of other cultures in neighboring states. States in these civilizational blocs often tend to be distributed in concentric circles around the core state or states, reflecting their degree of identification with and integration into that bloc. Lacking a recognized core state, Islam is intensifying its common consciousness but so far has developed only a rudimentary common political structure.

Countries tend to bandwagon with countries of similar culture and to balance against countries with which they lack cultural commonality. This is particularly true with respect to the core states. Their power attracts those who are culturally similar and repels those who are culturally different. For security reasons core states may attempt to incorporate or to dominate some peoples of other civilizations, who, in turn, attempt to resist or to escape such control (China vs. Tibetans and Uighurs; Russia vs. Tatars, Chechens, Central Asian Muslims). Historical relationships and balance of power considerations also lead some countries to resist the influence of their core state. Both Georgia and Russia are Orthodox countries, but the Georgians historically have resisted Russian domination and close association with Russia. Vietnam and China are both Confucian countries, yet a comparable pattern of historical enmity has existed between them. Over time, however, cultural commonality and development of a broader and stronger civilizational consciousness could bring these countries together, as Western European countries have come together.

During the Cold War, what order there was was the product of superpower dominance of their two blocs and superpower influence in the Third World. In the emerging world, global power is obsolete, global community a distant dream. No country, including the United States, has significant global security interests. The components of order in today's more complex and heterogeneous world are found within and between civilizations. The world will be ordered on the basis of civilizations or not at all. In this world the core states of civilizations are sources of order within civilizations and, through negotiations with other core states, between civilizations.

A world in which core states play a leading or dominating role is a spheres-of-influence world. But it is also a world in which the exercise of influence by the core state is tempered and moderated by the common culture it shares with member states of its civilization. Cultural commonality legitimates the leadership and order-imposing role of the core state for both member states and for the external powers and institutions. It is thus futile to do as U.N. Secretary General Boutros Boutros-Ghali did in 1994 and promulgate a rule of "sphere of influence keeping" that no more than one-third of the U.N. peacekeeping force should be provided by the dominant regional power. Such a requirement defies the geopolitical reality that in any given region where there is a dominant state peace can be achieved and maintained only through the leadership of that state. The United Nations is no alternative to regional power, and regional power becomes responsible and legitimate when exercised by core states in relation to other members of their civilization.

A core state can perform its ordering function because member states perceive it as cultural kin. A civilization is an extended family and, like older members of a family, core states provide their relatives with both support and discipline. In the absence of that kinship, the ability of a more powerful state to resolve conflicts in and impose order on its region is limited. Pakistan, Bangladesh, and even Sri Lanka will not accept India as the order provider in South Asia and no other East Asian state will accept Japan in that role in East Asia.

When civilizations lack core states the problems of creating order within civilizations or negotiating order between civilizations become more difficult. The absence of an Islamic core state which could legitimately and authoritatively relate to the Bosnians, as Russia did to the Serbs and Germany to the Croats, impelled the United States to attempt that role. Its ineffectiveness in doing so derived from the lack of American strategic interest in where state boundaries were drawn in the former Yugoslavia, the absence of any cultural connection between the United States and Bosnia, and European opposition to the creation of a Muslim state in Europe. The absence of core states in both Africa and the Arab world has greatly complicated efforts to resolve the ongoing civil war in Sudan. Where core states exist, on the other hand, they are the central elements of the new international order based on civilizations.

Bounding the West

During the Cold War the United States was at the center of a large, diverse, multicivilizational grouping of countries who shared the goal of preventing further expansion by the Soviet Union. This grouping, variously known as the "Free World," the "West," or the "Allies," included many but not all Western societies, Turkey, Greece, Japan, Korea, the Philippines, Israel, and, more loosely, other countries such as Taiwan, Thailand, and Pakistan. It was opposed by a grouping of countries only slightly less heterogeneous, which included all the Orthodox countries except Greece, several countries that were historically Western, Vietnam, Cuba, to a lesser degree India, and at times one or more African countries. With the end of the Cold War these multicivilizational, cross-cultural groupings fragmented. The dissolution of the Soviet system, particularly the Warsaw Pact, was dramatic. More slowly but similarly the multicivilizational "Free World" of the Cold War is being reconfigured into a new grouping more or less coextensive with Western civilization. A bounding process is underway involving the definition of the membership of Western international organizations.

The core states of the European Union, France and Germany, are circled first by an inner grouping of Belgium, Netherlands, and Luxembourg, all of which have agreed to eliminate all barriers to the transit of goods and persons; then other member countries such as Italy, Spain, Portugal, Denmark, Britain, Ireland, and Greece; states which became members in 1995 (Austria, Finland, Sweden); and those countries which as of that date were associate members (Poland, Hungary, Czech Republic, Slovakia, Bulgaria, and Romania). Reflecting this reality, in the fall of 1994 both the governing party in Germany and top French officials advanced proposals for a differentiated Union. The German plan proposed that the "hard core" consist of the original members minus Italy and that "Germany and France form the core of the hard core." The hard core countries would rapidly attempt to establish a monetary union and to integrate their foreign and defense policies. Almost simultaneously French Prime Minister Edouard Balladur suggested a three-tier Union with the five pro-integrationist states forming the core, the other current member states forming a second circle, and the new states on the way to becoming members constituting an outer circle. Subsequently French Foreign Minister Alain Juppé elaborated this concept proposing "an outer circle of 'partner' states, including Eastern and Central Europe; a middle circle of member states that would be required to accept common disciplines in certain fields (single market, customs union, etc.); and several inner circles of 'reinforced solidarities' incorporating those willing and able to move faster than others in such areas as defense, monetary integration, foreign policy and so on." [1] Other political leaders proposed other types of arrangements, all of which, however, involved an inner grouping of more closely associated states and then outer groupings of states less fully integrated with the core state until the line is reached separating members from nonmembers.

Establishing that line in Europe has been one of the principal challenges confronting the West in the post–Cold War world. During the Cold War Europe as a whole did not exist. With the collapse of communism, however, it became necessary to confront and answer the question: What is Europe? Europe's boundaries on the north, west, and south are delimited by substantial bodies of water, which to the south coincide with clear differences in culture. But where is Europe's eastern boundary? Who should be thought of as European and hence as potential members of the European Union, NATO, and comparable organizations?

The most compelling and pervasive answer to these questions is provided by the great historical line that has existed for centuries separating Western Christian peoples from Muslim and Orthodox peoples. This line dates back to the division of the Roman Empire in the fourth century and to the creation of the Holy Roman Empire in the tenth century. It has been in roughly its current place for at least five hundred years. Beginning in the north, it runs along what are now the borders between Finland and Russia and the Baltic states (Estonia, Latvia, Lithuania) and Russia, through western Belarus, through Ukraine separating the Uniate west from the Orthodox east, through Romania between Transylvania with its Catholic Hungarian population and the rest of the country, and through the former Yugoslavia along the border separating Slovenia and Croatia from the other republics. In the Balkans, of course, this line coincides with the historical division between the Austro-Hungarian and Ottoman empires. It is the cultural border of Europe, and in the post–Cold War world it is also the political and economic border of Europe and the West.

The civilizational paradigm thus provides a clear-cut and compelling answer to the question confronting West Europeans: Where does Europe end? Europe ends where Western Christianity ends and Islam and Orthodoxy begin. This is the answer which West Europeans want to hear, which they overwhelmingly support sotto voce, and which various intellectuals and political leaders have explicitly endorsed. It is necessary, as Michael Howard argued, to recognize the distinction, blurred during the Soviet years, between Central Europe or *Mitteleuropa* and Eastern Europe proper. Central Europe includes "those lands which once formed part of Western Christendom; the old lands of the Hapsburg Empire, Austria, Hungary and Czechoslovakia, together with Poland and the eastern marches of Germany. The term 'Eastern Europe' should be reserved for those regions which developed under the aegis of the Orthodox

*The Eastern
Boundary of
Western Civilization*

Church: the Black Sea communities of Bulgaria and Romania which only emerged from Ottoman domination in the nineteenth century, and the 'European' parts of the Soviet Union." Western Europe's first task, he argued, must "be to reabsorb the peoples of Central Europe into our cultural and economic community where they properly belong: to reknit the ties between London, Paris, Rome, Munich, and Leipzig, Warsaw, Prague and Budapest." A "new fault line" is emerging, Pierre Behar commented two years later, "a basically cultural divide between a Europe marked by western Christianity (Roman Catholic or Protestant), on the one hand, and a Europe marked by eastern Christianity and Islamic traditions, on the other." A leading Finn similarly saw the crucial division in Europe replacing the Iron Curtain as "the ancient cultural fault line between East and West" which places "the lands of the former Austro-Hungarian empire as well as Poland and the Baltic states" within the Europe of the West and the other East European and Balkan countries outside it. This was, a prominent Englishman agreed, the "great religious divide . . . between the Eastern and Western churches: broadly speaking, between those peoples who received their Christianity from Rome directly or through Celtic or German intermediaries, and those in the East and Southeast to whom it came through Constantinople (Byzantium)."[2]

People in Central Europe also emphasize the significance of this dividing line. The countries that have made significant progress in divesting themselves of the Communist legacies and moving toward democratic politics and market economies are separated from those which have not by "the line dividing Catholicism and Protestantism, on the one hand, from Orthodoxy, on the other." Centuries ago, the president of Lithuania argued, Lithuanians had to choose between "two civilizations" and "opted for the Latin world, converted to Roman Catholicism and chose a form of state organization founded on law." In similar terms, Poles say they have been part of the West since their choice in the tenth century of Latin Christianity against Byzantium.[3] People from Eastern European Orthodox countries, in contrast, view with ambivalence the new emphasis on this cultural fault line. Bulgarians and Romanians see the great advantages of being part of the West and being incorporated into its institutions; but they also identify with their own Orthodox tradition and, on the part of the Bulgarians, their historically close association with Russia and Byzantium.

The identification of Europe with Western Christendom provides a clear criterion for the admission of new members to Western organizations. The European Union is the West's primary entity in Europe and the expansion of its membership resumed in 1994 with the admission of culturally Western Austria, Finland, and Sweden. In the spring of 1994 the Union provisionally decided to exclude from membership all former Soviet republics except the Baltic states. It also signed "association agreements" with the four Central European states (Poland, Hungary, Czech Republic, and Slovakia) and two

Eastern European ones (Romania, Bulgaria). None of these states, however, is likely to become a full member of the EU until sometime in the twenty-first century, and the Central European states will undoubtedly achieve that status before Romania and Bulgaria, if, indeed, the latter ever do. Meanwhile eventual membership for the Baltic states and Slovenia looks promising, while the applications of Muslim Turkey, too-small Malta, and Orthodox Cyprus were still pending in 1995. In the expansion of EU membership, preference clearly goes to those states which are culturally Western and which also tend to be economically more developed. If this criterion were applied, the Visegrad states (Poland, Czech Republic, Slovakia, Hungary), the Baltic republics, Slovenia, Croatia, and Malta would eventually become EU members and the Union would be coextensive with Western civilization as it has historically existed in Europe.

The logic of civilizations dictates a similar outcome concerning the expansion of NATO. The Cold War began with the extension of Soviet political and military control into Central Europe. The United States and Western European countries formed NATO to deter and, if necessary, defeat further Soviet aggression. In the post–Cold War world, NATO is the security organization of Western civilization. With the Cold War over, NATO has one central and compelling purpose: to insure that it remains over by preventing the reimposition of Russian political and military control in Central Europe. As the West's security organization NATO is appropriately open to membership by Western countries which wish to join and which meet basic requirements in terms of military competence, political democracy, and civilian control of the military.

American policy toward post–Cold War European security arrangements initially embodied a more universalistic approach, embodied in the Partnership for Peace, which would be open generally to European and, indeed, Eurasian countries. This approach also emphasized the role of the Organization on Security and Cooperation in Europe. It was reflected in the remarks of President Clinton when he visited Europe in January 1994: "Freedom's boundaries now should be defined by new behavior, not by old history. I say to all . . . who would draw a new line in Europe: we should not foreclose the possibility of the best future for Europe — democracy everywhere, market economies everywhere, countries cooperating for mutual security everywhere. We must guard against a lesser outcome." A year later, however, the administration had come to recognize the significance of boundaries defined by "old history" and had come to accept a "lesser outcome" reflecting the realities of civilizational differences. The administration moved actively to develop the criteria and a schedule for the expansion of NATO membership, first to Poland, Hungary, the Czech Republic, and Slovakia, then to Slovenia, and later probably to the Baltic republics.

Russia vigorously opposed any NATO expansion, with those Russians who were presumably more liberal and pro-Western arguing that expansion would greatly strengthen nationalist and anti-Western political forces in Russia. NATO expansion limited to countries historically part of Western Christendom, however, also guarantees to Russia that it would exclude Serbia, Bulgaria, Romania, Moldova, Belarus, and Ukraine as long as Ukraine remained united. NATO expansion limited to Western states would also underline Russia's role as the core state of a separate, Orthodox civilization, and hence a country which should be responsible for order within and along the boundaries of Orthodoxy.

The usefulness of differentiating among countries in terms of civilization is manifest with respect to the Baltic republics. They are the only former Soviet republics which are clearly Western in terms of their history, culture, and religion, and their fate has consistently been a major concern of the West. The United States never formally recognized their incorporation into the Soviet Union, supported their move to independence as the Soviet Union was collapsing, and insisted that the Russians adhere to the agreed-on schedule for the removal of their troops from the republics. The message to the Russians has been that they must recognize that the Baltics are outside whatever sphere of influence they may wish to establish with respect to other former Soviet republics. This achievement by the Clinton administration was, as Sweden's prime minister said, "one of its most important contributions to European security and stability" and helped Russian democrats by establishing that any revanchist designs by extreme Russian nationalists were futile in the face of the explicit Western commitment to the republics.[4]

While much attention has been devoted to the expansion of the European Union and NATO, the cultural reconfiguration of these organizations also raises the issue of their possible contraction. One non-Western country, Greece, is a member of both organizations, and another, Turkey, is a member of NATO and an applicant for Union membership. These relationships were products of the Cold War. Do they have any place in the post–Cold War world of civilizations?

Turkey's full membership in the European Union is problematic and its membership in NATO has been attacked by the Welfare Party. Turkey is, however, likely to remain in NATO unless the Welfare Party scores a resounding electoral victory or Turkey otherwise consciously rejects its Ataturk heritage and redefines itself as a leader of Islam. This is conceivable and might be desirable for Turkey but also is unlikely in the near future. Whatever its role in NATO, Turkey will increasingly pursue its own distinctive interests with respect to the Balkans, the Arab world, and Central Asia.

Greece is not part of Western civilization, but it was the home of Classical civilization which was an important source of Western civilization. In their opposition to the Turks, Greeks historically have considered themselves spear-carriers of Christianity. Unlike Serbs, Romanians, or Bulgarians, their history has been intimately entwined with that of the West. Yet Greece is also an anomaly, the Orthodox outsider in Western organizations. It has never been an easy member of either the EU or NATO and has had difficulty adapting itself to the principles and mores of both. From the mid-1960s to the mid-1970s it was ruled by a military junta, and could not join the European Community until it shifted to democracy. Its leaders often seemed to go out of their way to deviate from Western norms and to antagonize Western governments. It was poorer than other Community and NATO members and often pursued economic policies that seemed to flout the standards prevailing in Brussels. Its behavior as president of the EU's Council in 1994 exasperated other members, and Western European officials privately label its membership a mistake.

In the post–Cold War world, Greece's policies have increasingly deviated from those of the West. Its blockade of Macedonia was strenuously opposed by Western governments and resulted in the European Commission seeking an injunction against Greece in the European Court of Justice. With respect to the conflicts in the former Yugoslavia, Greece separated itself from the policies pursued by the principal Western powers, actively supported the Serbs, and blatantly violated the U.N. sanctions levied against them. With the end of the Soviet Union and the communist threat, Greece has mutual interests with Russia in opposition to their common enemy, Turkey. It has permitted Russia to establish a significant presence in Greek Cyprus, and as a result of "their shared Eastern Orthodox religion," the Greek Cypriots have welcomed both Russians and Serbs to the island.[5] In 1995 some two thousand Russian-owned businesses were operating in Cyprus; Russian and Serbo-Croatian newspapers were published there; and the Greek Cypriot government was purchasing major supplies of arms from Russia. Greece also explored with Russia the possibility of bringing oil from the Caucasus and Central Asia to the Mediterranean through a Bulgarian-Greek pipeline bypassing Turkey and other Muslim countries. Overall Greek foreign policies have assumed a heavily Orthodox orientation. Greece will undoubtedly remain a formal member of NATO and the European Union. As the process of cultural reconfiguration intensifies, however, those memberships also undoubtedly will become more tenuous, less meaningful, and more difficult for the parties involved. The Cold War antagonist of the Soviet Union is evolving into the post–Cold War ally of Russia.

RUSSIA AND ITS NEAR ABROAD

The successor to the tsarist and communist empires is a civilizational bloc, paralleling in many respects that of the West in Europe. At the core, Russia, the equivalent of France and Germany, is closely linked to an inner circle including the two predominantly Slavic Orthodox republics of Belarus and Moldova, Kazakhstan, 40 percent of whose population is Russian, and Armenia, historically a close ally of Russia. In the mid-1990s all these countries had pro-Russian governments which had generally come to power through elections. Close but more tenuous relations exist between Russia and Georgia (overwhelmingly Orthodox) and Ukraine (in large part Orthodox); but both of which also have strong senses of national identity and past independence. In the Orthodox Balkans, Russia has close relations with Bulgaria, Greece, Serbia, and Cyprus, and somewhat less close ones with Romania. The Muslim republics of the former Soviet Union remain highly dependent on Russia both economically and in the security area. The Baltic republics, in contrast, responding to the gravitational pull of Europe effectively removed themselves from the Russian sphere of influence.

Overall Russia is creating a bloc with an Orthodox heartland under its leadership and a surrounding buffer of relatively weak Islamic states which it will in varying degrees dominate and from which it will attempt to exclude the influence of other powers. Russia also expects the world to accept and to approve this system. Foreign governments and international organizations, as Yeltsin said in February 1993, need to "grant Russia special powers as a guarantor of peace and stability in the former regions of the USSR." While the Soviet Union was a superpower with global interests, Russia is a major power with regional and civilizational interests.

The Orthodox countries of the former Soviet Union are central to the development of a coherent Russian bloc in Eurasian and world affairs. During the breakup of the Soviet Union, all five of these countries initially moved in a highly nationalist direction, emphasizing their new independence and distance from Moscow. Subsequently, recognition of economic, geopolitical, and cultural realities led the voters in four of them to elect pro-Russian governments and to back pro-Russian policies. The people in these countries look to Russia for support and protection. In the fifth, Georgia, Russian military intervention compelled a similar shift in the stance of the government.

Armenia has historically identified its interests with Russia and Russia has prided itself as Armenia's defender against its Muslim neighbors. This relationship has been reinvigorated in the post-Soviet years. The Armenians have been dependent upon Russian economic and military support and have backed Russia on issues concerning relations among the former Soviet republics. The two countries have converging strategic interests.

Unlike Armenia, Belarus has little sense of national identity. It is also even more dependent on Russian support. Many of its residents seem to identify as much with Russia as with their own country. In January 1994 the legislature replaced the centrist and moderate nationalist who was head of state with a conservative pro-Russian. In July 1994, 80 percent of the voters elected as president an extreme pro-Russian ally of Vladimir Zhirinovsky. Belarus early joined the Commonwealth of Independent States, was a charter member of the economic union created in 1993 with Russia and Ukraine, agreed to a monetary union with Russia, surrendered its nuclear weapons to Russia, and agreed to the stationing of Russian troops on its soil for the rest of this century. In 1995 Belarus was, in effect, part of Russia in all but name.

After Moldova became independent with the collapse of the Soviet Union, many looked forward to its eventual reintegration with Romania. The fear that this would happen, in turn, stimulated a secessionist movement in the Russified east, which had the tacit support of Moscow and the active support of the Russian 14th Army and led to the creation of the Trans-Dniester Republic. Moldovan sentiment for union with Romania, however, declined in response to the economic problems of both countries and Russian economic pressure. Moldova joined the CIS and trade with Russia expanded. In February 1994 pro-Russian parties were overwhelmingly successful in the parliamentary elections.

In these three states public opinion responding to some combination of strategic and economic interests produced governments favoring close alignment with Russia. A somewhat similar pattern eventually occurred in Ukraine. In Georgia the course of events was different. Georgia was an independent country until 1801 when its ruler, King George XIII, asked for Russian protection against the Turks. For three years after the Russian Revolution, 1918–1921, Georgia was again independent, but the Bolsheviks forcibly incorporated it into the Soviet Union. When the Soviet Union ended, Georgia once again declared independence. A nationalist coalition won the elections, but its leader engaged in self-destructive repression and was violently overthrown. Eduard A. Shevardnadze, who had been foreign minister of the Soviet Union, returned to lead the country and was confirmed in power by presidential elections in 1992 and 1995. He was, however, confronted by a separatist movement in Abkhazia, which became the recipient of substantial Russian support, and also by an insurrection led by the ousted Gamsakhurdia. Emulating King George, he concluded that "We do not have a great choice," and turned to Moscow for help. Russian troops intervened to support him at the price of Georgia joining the CIS. In 1994 the Georgians agreed to let the Russians keep three military bases in Georgia for an indefinite period of time. Russian military intervention first to weaken the Georgian government and then to sustain it thus brought independence-minded Georgia into the Russian camp.

Apart from Russia the most populous and most important former Soviet republic is Ukraine. At various times in history Ukraine has been independent. Yet during most of the modern era it has been part of a political entity governed from Moscow. The decisive event occurred in 1654 when Bohdan Khmelnytsky, Cossack leader of an uprising against Polish rule, agreed to swear allegiance to the tsar in return for help against the Poles. From then until 1991, except for a briefly independent republic between 1917 and 1920, what is now Ukraine was controlled politically from Moscow. Ukraine, however, is a cleft country with two distinct cultures. The civilizational fault line between the West and Orthodoxy runs through its heart and has done so for centuries. At times in the past, western Ukraine was part of Poland, Lithuania, and the Austro-Hungarian empire. A large portion of its population have been adherents of the Uniate Church which practices Orthodox rites but acknowledges the authority of the Pope. Historically, western Ukrainians have spoken Ukrainian and have been strongly nationalist in their outlook. The people of eastern Ukraine, on the other hand, have been overwhelmingly Orthodox and have in large part spoken Russian. In the early 1990s Russians made up 22 percent and native Russian speakers 31 percent of the total Ukrainian population. A majority of the elementary and secondary school students were taught in Russian.[6] The Crimea is overwhelmingly Russian and was part of the Russian Federation until 1954, when Khrushchev transferred it to Ukraine ostensibly in recognition of Khmelnytsky's decision 300 years earlier.

The differences between eastern and western Ukraine are manifest in the attitudes of their peoples. In late 1992, for instance, one-third of the Russians in western Ukraine as compared with only 10 percent in Kiev said they suffered from anti-Russian animosity.[7] The east-west split was dramatically evident in the July 1994 presidential elections. The incumbent, Leonid Kravchuk, who despite working closely with Russia's leaders identified himself as a nationalist, carried the thirteen provinces of the western Ukraine with majorities ranging up to over 90 percent. His opponent, Leonid Kuchma, who took Ukrainian speech lessons during the campaign, carried the thirteen eastern provinces by comparable majorities. Kuchma won with 52 percent of the vote. In effect, a slim majority of the Ukrainian public in 1994 confirmed Khmelnytsky's choice in 1654. The election, as one American expert observed, "reflected, even crystallized, the split between Europeanized Slavs in western Ukraine and the Russo-Slav vision of what Ukraine should be. It's not ethnic polarization so much as different cultures."[8]

Ukraine: A Cleft Country

As a result of this division, the relations between Ukraine and Russia could develop in one of three ways. In the early 1990s, critically important issues existed between the two countries concerning nuclear weapons, Crimea, the rights of Russians in Ukraine, the Black Sea fleet, and economic relations. Many people thought armed conflict was likely, which led some Western analysts to argue that the West should support Ukraine's having a nuclear arsenal to deter Russian aggression.[9] If civilization is what counts, however, violence between Ukrainians and Russians is unlikely. These are two Slavic, primarily Orthodox peoples who have had close relationships for centuries and between whom intermarriage is common. Despite highly contentious issues and the pressure of extreme nationalists on both sides, the leaders of both countries worked hard and largely successfully to moderate these disputes. The election of an explicitly Russian-oriented president in Ukraine in mid-1994 further reduced the probability of exacerbated conflict between the two countries. While serious fighting occurred between Muslims and Christians elsewhere in the former Soviet Union and much tension and some fighting between Russians and Baltic peoples, as of 1995 virtually no violence had occurred between Russians and Ukrainians.

A second and somewhat more likely possibility is that Ukraine could split along its fault line into two separate entities, the eastern of which would merge with Russia. The issue of secession first came up with respect to Crimea. The Crimean public, which is 70 percent Russian, substantially supported Ukrainian independence from the Soviet Union in a referendum in December 1991. In May 1992 the Crimean parliament also voted to declare independence from Ukraine and then, under Ukrainian pressure, rescinded that vote. The Russian parliament, however, voted to cancel the 1954 cession of Crimea to Ukraine. In January 1994 Crimeans elected a president who had campaigned on a platform of "unity with Russia." This stimulated some people to raise the question: "Will Crimea Be the Next Nagorno-Karabakh or Abkhazia?"[10] The answer was a resounding "No!" as the new Crimean president backed away from his commitment to hold a referendum on independence and instead negotiated with the Kiev government. In May 1994 the situation heated up again when the Crimean parliament voted to restore the 1992 constitution which made it virtually independent of Ukraine. Once again, however, the restraint of Russian and Ukrainian leaders prevented this issue from generating violence, and the election two months later of the pro-Russian Kuchma as Ukrainian president undermined the Crimean thrust for secession.

That election did, however, raise the possibility of the western part of the country seceding from a Ukraine that was drawing closer and closer to Russia. Some Russians might welcome this. As one Russian general put it, "Ukraine or rather Eastern Ukraine will come back in five, ten or fifteen years. Western Ukraine can go to hell!"[11] Such a rump Uniate and Western-oriented Ukraine, however, would only be viable if it had strong and effective Western support. Such support is, in turn, likely to be forthcoming only if relations between the West and Russia deteriorated seriously and came to resemble those of the Cold War.

The third and more likely scenario is that Ukraine will remain united, remain cleft, remain independent, and generally cooperate closely with Russia. Once the transition questions concerning nuclear weapons and military forces are resolved, the most serious longer term issues will be economic, the resolution of which will be facilitated by a partially shared culture and close personal ties. The Russian-Ukrainian relationship is to eastern Europe, John Morrison has pointed out, what the Franco-German relationship is to western Europe.[12] Just as the latter provides the core of the European Union, the former is the core essential to unity in the Orthodox world.

GREATER CHINA AND ITS CO-PROSPERITY SPHERE

China historically conceived itself as encompassing: a "Sinic Zone" including Korea, Vietnam, the Liu Chiu Islands, and at times Japan; an "Inner Asian Zone" of non-Chinese Manchus, Mongols, Uighurs, Turks, and Tibetans, who had to be controlled for security reasons; and then an "Outer Zone" of barbarians, who were nonetheless "expected to pay tribute and acknowledge China's superiority."[13] Contemporary Sinic civilization is becoming structured in a similar fashion: the central core of Han China, outlying provinces that are part of China but possess considerable autonomy, provinces legally part of China but heavily populated by non-Chinese people from other civilizations (Tibet, Xinjiang), Chinese societies which will or are likely to become part of Beijing-centered China on defined conditions (Hong Kong, Taiwan), one predominantly Chinese state increasingly oriented toward Beijing (Singapore), highly influential Chinese populations in Thailand, Vietnam, Malaysia, Indonesia, and the Philippines, and non-Chinese societies (North and South Korea, Vietnam) which nonetheless share much of China's Confucian culture.

During the 1950s China defined itself as an ally of the Soviet Union. Then, after the Sino-Soviet split, it saw itself as the leader of the Third World against both the superpowers, which produced substantial costs and few benefits. After the shift in U.S. policy in the Nixon administration, China sought to be the third party in a balance of power game with the two superpowers, aligning itself with the United States during the 1970s when the United States seemed weak and then shifting to a more equidistant position in the 1980s as U.S. military power increased and the Soviet Union declined economically and became bogged down in Afghanistan. With the end of the superpower competition, however, the "China card" lost all value, and China was compelled once more to redefine its role in world affairs. It set two goals: to become the champion of Chinese culture, the core state civilizational magnet toward which all other Chinese communities would orient themselves, and to resume its historical position, which it lost in the nineteenth century, as the hegemonic power in East Asia.

These emerging roles of China are seen in: first, the way in which China describes its position in world affairs; second, the extent to which overseas Chinese have become involved economically in China; and third, the increasing economic, political, and diplomatic connections with China of the three other principal Chinese entities, Hong Kong, Taiwan, and Singapore, as well as the enhanced orientation toward China of the Southeast Asian countries where Chinese have significant political influence.

The Chinese government sees mainland China as the core state of a Chinese civilization toward which all other Chinese communities should orient themselves. Having long since abandoned its efforts to promote its interests abroad through local communist parties, the government has sought "to position itself as the worldwide representative of Chineseness." [14] To the Chinese government, people of Chinese descent, even if citizens of another country, are members of the Chinese community and hence in some measure subject to the authority of the Chinese government. Chinese identity comes to be defined in racial terms. Chinese are those of the same "race, blood, and culture," as one PRC scholar put it. In the mid-1990s, this theme was increasingly heard from governmental and private Chinese sources. For Chinese and those of Chinese descent living in non-Chinese societies, the "mirror test" thus becomes the test of who they are: "Go look in the mirror," is the admonition of Beijing-oriented Chinese to those of Chinese descent trying to assimilate into foreign societies. Chinese of the diaspora, that is, *huaren* or people of Chinese origin, as distinguished from *zhongguoren* or people of the Chinese state, have increasingly articulated the concept of "cultural China" as a manifestation of their *gonshi* or common awareness. Chinese identity, subject to so many onslaughts from the West in the twentieth century, is now being reformulated in terms of the continuing elements of Chinese culture. [15]

Historically this identity has also been compatible with varying relationships to the central authorities of the Chinese state. This sense of cultural identity both facilitates and is reinforced by the expansion of the economic relationships among the several Chinas, which, in turn, have been a major element promoting rapid economic growth in mainland China and elsewhere, which, in turn, has provided the material and psychological impetus to enhance Chinese cultural identity.

"Greater China" is thus not simply an abstract concept. It is a rapidly growing cultural and economic reality and has begun to become a political one. Chinese were responsible for the dramatic economic development in the 1980s and 1990s: on the mainland, in the Tigers (three out of four of which are Chinese), and in Southeast Asia. The economy of East Asia is increasingly China-centered and Chinese-dominated. Chinese from Hong Kong, Taiwan, and Singapore have supplied much of the capital responsible for the growth of the mainland in the 1990s. Overseas Chinese elsewhere in Southeast Asia dominated the economies of their countries. In the early 1990s, Chinese made up 1 percent of the population of the Philippines but were responsible for 35 percent of the sales of domestically owned firms. In Indonesia in the mid 1980s, Chinese were 2–3 percent of the population, but owned roughly 70 percent of the private domestic capital. Seventeen of the twenty-five largest businesses were Chinese-controlled, and one Chinese conglomerate reportedly accounted for 5 percent of Indonesia's GNP. In the early 1990s Chinese were 10 percent of the population of Thailand but owned nine of the ten largest business groups and were responsible for 50 percent of its GNP. Chinese are about one-third of the population of Malaysia but almost totally dominate the economy.[16] Outside Japan and Korea the East Asian economy is basically a Chinese economy.

The emergence of the greater China co-prosperity sphere was greatly facilitated by a "bamboo network" of family and personal relationships and a common culture. Overseas Chinese are much more able than either Westerners or Japanese to do business in China. In China trust and commitment depend on personal contacts, not contracts or laws and other legal documents. Western businessmen find it easier to do business in India than in China where the sanctity of an agreement rests on the personal relationship between the parties. China, a leading Japanese observed with envy in 1993, benefited from "a borderless network of Chinese merchants in Hong Kong, Taiwan and Southeast Asia."[17] The overseas Chinese, an American businessman agreed, "have the entrepreneurial skills, they have the language, and they combine the bamboo network from family relations to contacts. That's an enormous advantage over someone who must report back to a board in Akron or Philadelphia." The advantages of nonmainland Chinese dealing with the mainland were also well stated by Lee Kuan Yew: "We are ethnic Chinese. We share certain characteristics through common ancestry and culture. . . . People feel a natural empathy for those who share their physical attributes. This sense of closeness is reinforced when they also share a basis for culture and language. It makes for easy rapport and trust, which is the foundation for all business relations."[18] In the late 1980s and 1990s, overseas ethnic Chinese were able "to demonstrate to a skeptical world that *quanxi* connections through the same language and culture can make up for a lack in the rule of law and transparency in rules and regulations." The roots of economic development in a common culture were highlighted in the Second World Chinese Entrepreneurs Conference in Hong Kong in November 1993, described as "a celebration of Chinese triumphalism attended by ethnic Chinese businessmen from around the world."[19] In the Sinic world as elsewhere cultural commonality promotes economic engagement.

The reduction in Western economic involvement in China after Tiananmen Square, following a decade of rapid Chinese economic growth, created the opportunity and incentive for overseas Chinese to capitalize on their common culture and personal contacts and to invest heavily in China. The result was a dramatic expansion of overall economic ties among the Chinese communities. In 1992, 80 percent of the foreign direct investment in China ($11.3 billion) came from overseas Chinese, primarily in Hong Kong (68.3 percent), but also in Taiwan (9.3 percent), Singapore, Macao, and elsewhere. In contrast, Japan provided 6.6 percent and the United States 4.6 percent of the total. Of total accumulated foreign investment of $50 billion, 67 percent was from Chinese sources. Trade growth was equally impressive. Taiwan's exports to China rose from almost nothing in 1986 to 8 percent of Taiwan's total exports in 1992, expanding that year at a rate of 35 percent. Singapore's exports to China increased 22 percent in 1992 compared with overall growth in its exports of less than 2 percent. As Murray Weidenbaum observed in 1993, "Despite the current Japanese dominance of the region, the Chinese-based economy of Asia is rapidly emerging as a new epicenter for industry, commerce, and finance. This strategic area contains substantial amounts of technology and manufacturing capability (Taiwan), outstanding entrepreneurial, marketing, and services acumen (Hong Kong), a fine communications network (Singapore), a tremendous pool of financial capital (all three), and very large endowments of land, resources, and labor (mainland China)."[20] In addition, of course, mainland China was the potentially biggest of all expanding markets, and by the mid-1990s investments in China were increasingly oriented to sales in that market as well as to exports from it.

Chinese in Southeast Asian countries assimilate in varying degrees with the local population, the latter often harboring anti-Chinese sentiments which, on occasion, as in the Medan riot in Indonesia in April 1994, erupt into violence. Some Malaysians and Indonesians criticized as "capital flight" the flow of Chinese investment to the mainland, and political leaders led by President Suharto had to reassure their publics that this would not damage their economies. Southeast Asian Chinese, in turn, insisted that their loyalties were strictly to their country of birth not that of their ancestors. In the early 1990s the outflow of Chinese capital from Southeast Asia to China was countered by the heavy flow of Taiwanese investment to the Philippines, Malaysia, and Vietnam.

The combination of growing economic power and shared Chinese culture led Hong Kong, Taiwan, and Singapore increasingly to involve themselves with the Chinese homeland. Accommodating themselves to the approaching transfer of power, Hong Kong Chinese began to adapt to rule from Beijing rather than London. Businessmen and other leaders became reluctant to criticize China or to do things that might offend China. When they did offend, the Chinese government did not hesitate to retaliate promptly. By 1994 hundreds of businessmen were cooperating with Beijing and serving as "Hong Kong Advisors" in what was in effect a shadow government. In the early 1990s Chinese economic influence in Hong Kong also expanded dramatically, with investment from the mainland by 1993 reportedly more than that from Japan and the United States combined.[21] By the mid-1990s the economic integration of Hong Kong and mainland China has become virtually complete, with political integration to be consummated in 1997.

Expansion of Taiwan's ties with the mainland lagged behind Hong Kong's.

Significant changes, nonetheless, began to occur in the 1980s. For three decades after 1949, the two Chinese republics refused to recognize each other's existence or legitimacy, had no communication with each other, and were in a virtual state of war, manifested from time to time in the exchange of gunfire at the offshore islands. After Deng Xiaoping consolidated his power and began the process of economic reform, however, the mainland government initiated a series of conciliatory moves. In 1981 the Taiwan government responded and started to shift away from its previous "three no's" policy of no contact, no negotiation, no compromise with the mainland. In May 1986 the first negotiations occurred between representatives of the two sides over the return of a Republic of China plane that had been hijacked to the mainland, and the following year the ROC dropped its ban on travel to the mainland.[22]

The rapid expansion of economic relations between Taiwan and the mainland that followed was greatly facilitated by their "shared Chineseness" and the mutual trust that resulted from it. The people of Taiwan and China, as Taiwan's principal negotiator observed, have a "blood-is-thicker-than-water kind of sentiment," and took pride in each other's accomplishments. By the end of 1993 there had been over 4.2 million visits of Taiwanese to the mainland and 40,000 visits of mainlanders to Taiwan; 40,000 letters and 13,000 phone calls were exchanged daily. Trade between the two Chinas reportedly reached $14.4 billion in 1993 and 20,000 Taiwan businesses had invested something between $15 billion and $30 billion in the mainland. Taiwan's attention was increasingly focused on and its success dependent on the mainland. "Before 1980, the most important market to Taiwan was America," one Taiwan official observed in 1993, "but for the 1990s we know the most critical factor in the success of Taiwan's economy is the mainland." The mainland's cheap labor was a main attraction for Taiwanese investors confronting a labor shortage at home. In 1994 a reverse process of rectifying the capital-labor imbalance between the two Chinas got under way with Taiwan fishing companies hiring 10,000 mainlanders to man their boats.[23]

Developing economic connections led to negotiations between the two governments. In 1991 Taiwan created the Straits Exchange Foundation, and the mainland the Association for Relations across the Taiwan Strait, for communication with each other. Their first meeting was held in Singapore in April 1993, with subsequent meetings occurring on the mainland and Taiwan. In August 1994 a "breakthrough" agreement was reached covering a number of key issues, and speculation began concerning a possible summit between top leaders of the two governments.

In the mid-1990s major issues still exist between Taipei and Beijing including the question of sovereignty, Taiwan's participation in international organizations, and the possibility that Taiwan might redefine itself as an independent state. The likelihood of the latter happening, however, became increasingly remote as the principal advocate of independence, the Democratic Progressive

Party, found that Taiwanese voters did not want to disrupt existing relations with the mainland and that its electoral prospects would be hurt by pressing the issue. DPP leaders hence emphasized that if they did win power, independence would not be an immediate item on their agenda. The two governments also shared a common interest in asserting Chinese sovereignty over the Spratly and other islands in the South China Sea and in assuring American most favored nation treatment in trade for the mainland. In the early 1990s, slowly but perceptively and ineluctably, the two Chinas were moving toward each other and developing common interests from their expanding economic relations and shared cultural identity.

This movement toward accommodation was abruptly suspended in 1995 as the Taiwanese government aggressively pushed for diplomatic recognition and admission to international organizations. President Lee Teng-hui made a "private" visit to the United States, and Taiwan held legislative elections in December 1995 followed by presidential elections in March 1996. In response, the Chinese government tested missiles in waters close to the major Taiwanese ports and engaged in military exercises near Taiwanese-controlled offshore islands. These developments raised two key issues. For the present, can Taiwan remain democratic without becoming formally independent? In the future could Taiwan be democratic without remaining actually independent?

In effect the relations of Taiwan to the mainland have gone through two phases and could enter a third. For decades the Nationalist government claimed to be the government of all of China; this claim obviously meant conflict with the government that was in fact the government of all of China except Taiwan. In the 1980s the Taiwanese government dropped this pretension and defined itself as the government of Taiwan, which provided the basis for accommodation with the mainland concept of "one country, two systems." Various individuals and groups in Taiwan, however, increasingly emphasized Taiwan's separate cultural identity, its relatively brief period under Chinese rule, and its local language incomprehensible to Mandarin speakers. In effect, they were attempting to define Taiwanese society as non-Chinese and hence legitimately independent of China. In addition, as the Taiwan government became more active internationally, it, too, seemed to be suggesting that it was a separate country not part of China. In short, the Taiwan government's self-definition appeared to evolve from government of all of China, to government of part of China, toward government of none of China. The latter position, formalizing its de facto independence, would be totally unacceptable to the Beijing government, which repeatedly affirmed its willingness to use force to prevent it from materializing. Chinese government leaders also stated that following incorporation into the PRC of Hong Kong in 1997 and Macao in 1999, they will move to reassociate Taiwan with the mainland. How this occurs depends, presumably, on the degree to which support for formal independence grows in Taiwan, the resolution of the succession struggle in Beijing which encourages political and military leaders to be strongly nationalist, and the development of Chinese military capabilities that would make feasible a block-ade or invasion of Taiwan. Early in the twenty-first century it seems likely that through coercion, accommodation, or most likely a mixture of both Taiwan will become more closely integrated with mainland China.

Until the late 1970s relations between staunchly anticommunist Singapore and the People's Republic were frosty, and Lee Kuan Yew and other Singa-porean leaders were contemptuous of Chinese backwardness. As Chinese eco-nomic development took off in the 1980s, however, Singapore began to reorient itself toward the mainland in classic bandwagoning fashion. By 1992 Singapore had invested $1.9 billion in China, and the following year plans were an-nounced to build an industrial township, "Singapore II," outside Shanghai, that would involve billions of dollars of investment. Lee became an enthusiastic booster of China's economic prospects and an admirer of its power. "China," he said in 1993, "is where the action is."[24] Singaporean foreign investment which had been heavily concentrated in Malaysia and Indonesia shifted to China. Half of the overseas projects helped by the Singaporean government in 1993 were in China. On his first visit to Beijing in the 1970s, Lee Kuan Yew reportedly insisted on speaking to Chinese leaders in English rather than Mandarin. It is unlikely he did that two decades later.

ISLAM: CONSCIOUSNESS WITHOUT COHESION

The structure of political loyalty among Arabs and among Muslims generally has been the opposite of that in the modern West. For the latter the nation state has been the apex of political loyalty. Narrower loyalties are subordinate to it and are subsumed into loyalty to the nation state. Groups transcending nation states — linguistic or religious communities, or civilizations — have com-manded less intense loyalty and commitment. Along a continuum of narrower to broader entities, Western loyalties thus tend to peak in the middle, the loyalty intensity curve forming in some measure an inverse U. In the Islamic world, the structure of loyalty has been almost exactly the reverse. Islam has had a hollow middle in its hierarchy of loyalties. The "two fundamental, original, and persisting structures," as Ira Lapidus has observed, have been the family, the clan, and the tribe, on the one hand, and the "unities of culture, religion, and empire on an ever-larger scale," on the other.[25] "Tribalism and Religion (Islam) played and still plays," one Libyan scholar similarly observed, "a signifi-cant and determining role in the social, economic, cultural, and political developments of Arab Societies and Political Systems. Indeed, they are inter-twined in such a way that they are considered the most important factors and variables which shape and determine Arab Political culture and [the] Arab Political Mind." Tribes have been central to politics in Arab states, many of which, as Tahsin Bashir put it, are simply "tribes with flags." The founder of

Saudi Arabia succeeded in large part as a result of his skill in creating a tribal coalition through marriage and other means, and Saudi politics has continued to be a largely tribal politics pitting Sudairis against Shammars and other tribes. At least eighteen major tribes have played significant roles in Libyan development, and some five hundred tribes are said to live in the Sudan, the largest of which encompasses 12 percent of the country's population.[26]

In Central Asia historically, national identities did not exist. "The loyalty was to the tribe, clan, and extended family, not to the state." At the other extreme, people did have "language, religion, culture, and life styles" in common, and "Islam was the strongest uniting force among people, more so than the emir's power." Some one hundred "mountainous" and seventy "plains" clans have existed among the Chechens and related North Caucasus peoples and controlled politics and the economy to such an extent that, in contrast to the Soviet planned economy, the Chechens were alleged to have a "clanned" economy.[27]

Throughout Islam the small group and the great faith, the tribe and the *ummah*, have been the principal foci of loyalty and commitment, and the nation state has been less significant. In the Arab world, existing states have legitimacy problems because they are for the most part the arbitrary, if not capricious, products of European imperialism, and their boundaries often did not even coincide with those of ethnic groups such as Berbers and Kurds. These states divided the Arab nation, but a Pan-Arab state, on the other hand, has never materialized. In addition, the idea of sovereign nation states is incompatible with belief in the sovereignty of Allah and the primacy of the *ummah*. As a revolutionary movement, Islamist fundamentalism rejects the nation state in favor of the unity of Islam just as Marxism rejected it in favor of the unity of the international proletariat. The weakness of the nation state in Islam is also reflected in the fact that while numerous conflicts occurred between Muslim *groups* during the years after World War II, major wars between Muslim *states* were rare, the most significant ones involving Iraq invading its neighbors.

In the 1970s and 1980s the same factors which gave rise to the Islamic Resurgence within countries also strengthened identification with the *ummah* or Islamic civilization as a whole. As one scholar observed in the mid-1980s:

A profound concern with Muslim identity and unity has been further stimulated by decolonization, demographic growth, industrialization, urbanization, and a changing international economic order associated with, among other things, the oil wealth beneath Muslim lands. . . . Modern communications have strengthened and elaborated the ties among Muslim peoples. There has been a steep growth in the numbers who make the pilgrimage to Mecca, creating a more intense sense of common identity among Muslims from as far afield as China and Senegal, Yemen and Bangladesh. Growing numbers of students from Indonesia, Malaysia, and the southern Philippines, and Africa are studying in Middle Eastern universities, spreading ideas and establishing personal contacts across national boundaries. There are regular and increasingly frequent conferences and consultations among Muslim intellectuals and *ulama* (religious scholars) held in such centers as Teheran, Mecca, and Kuala Lumpur. . . . Cassettes (sound, and now video) disseminate mosque sermons across international boundaries, so that influential preachers now reach audiences far beyond their local communities.[28]

The sense of Muslim unity has also been reflected in and encouraged by the actions of states and international organizations. In 1969 the leaders of Saudi Arabia, working with those of Pakistan, Morocco, Iran, Tunisia, and Turkey, organized the first Islamic summit at Rabat. Out of this emerged the Organization of the Islamic Conference, which was formally established with a headquarters in Jiddah in 1972. Virtually all states with substantial Muslim populations now belong to the Conference, which is the only interstate organization of its kind. Christian, Orthodox, Buddhist, Hindu governments do not have interstate organizations with memberships based on religion; Muslim governments do. In addition, the governments of Saudi Arabia, Pakistan, Iran, and Libya have sponsored and supported nongovernmental organizations such as the World Muslim Congress (a Pakistani creation) and the Muslim World League (a Saudi creation), as well as "numerous, often very distant, regimes, parties, movements, and causes that are believed to share their ideological orientations" and which are "enriching the flow of information and resources among Muslims."[29]

Movement from Islamic consciousness to Islamic cohesion, however, involves two paradoxes. First, Islam is divided among competing power centers each attempting to capitalize on Muslim identification with the *ummah* in order to promote Islamic cohesion under its leadership. This competition goes on between the established regimes and their organizations, on the one hand, and Islamist regimes and their organizations, on the other. Saudi Arabia took the lead in creating the OIC in part to have a counter to the Arab League, which at the time was dominated by Nasser. In 1991, after the Gulf War, the Sudanese leader Hassan al-Turabi created the Popular Arab and Islamic Conference (PAIC) as a counter to the Saudi dominated OIC. PAIC's third conference, in Khartoum in early 1995, was attended by several hundred delegates from Islamist organizations and movements in eighty countries.[30] In addition to these formal organizations, the Afghanistan war generated an extensive network of informal and underground groups of veterans who have shown up fighting for Muslim or Islamist causes in Algeria, Chechnya, Egypt, Tunisia, Bosnia, Palestine, the Philippines, and elsewhere. After the war their ranks were renewed with fighters trained at the University of Dawa and Jihad outside Peshawar and in camps sponsored by various factions and their foreign backers in Afghanistan. The common interests shared by radical regimes and movements have on occasion overcome more traditional antagonisms, and with

Iranian support linkages were created between Sunni and Shi'ite fundamentalist groups. Close military cooperation exists between Sudan and Iran, the Iranian air force and navy used Sudanese facilities, and the two governments cooperated in supporting fundamentalist groups in Algeria and elsewhere. Hassan al-Turabi and Saddam Hussein allegedly developed close ties in 1994, and Iran and Iraq moved toward reconciliation.[31]

Second, the concept of *ummah* presupposes the illegitimacy of the nation state and yet the *ummah* can be unified only through the actions of one or more strong core states which are currently lacking. The concept of Islam as a unified religious-political community has meant that cores states have usually materialized in the past only when religious and political leadership—the caliphate and the sultanate—have been combined in a single ruling institution. The rapid seventh-century Arab conquest of North Africa and the Middle East culminated in the Umayyad caliphate with its capital in Damascus. This was followed in the eighth century by the Baghdad-based, Persian-influenced, Abbasid caliphate, with secondary caliphates emerging in Cairo and Cordoba in the tenth century. Four hundred years later the Ottoman Turks swept across the Middle East, capturing Constantinople in 1453 and establishing a new caliphate in 1517. About the same time other Turkic peoples invaded India and founded the Mogul empire. The rise of the West undermined both the Ottoman and Mogul empires, and the end of the Ottoman empire left Islam without a core state. Its territories were, in considerable measure, divided among Western powers, which when they retreated left behind fragile states formed on a Western model alien to the traditions of Islam. Hence for most of the twentieth century no Muslim country has had both sufficient power and sufficient cultural and religious legitimacy to assume that role and be accepted as the leader of Islam by other Islamic states and non-Islamic countries.

The absence of an Islamic core state is a major contributor to the pervasive internal and external conflicts which characterize Islam. Consciousness without cohesion is a source of weakness to Islam and a source of threat to other civilizations. Is this condition likely to be sustained?

An Islamic core state has to possess the economic resources, military power, organizational competence, and Islamic identity and commitment to provide both political and religious leadership to the *ummah*. Six states are from time to time mentioned as possible leaders of Islam; at present, no one of them, however, has all the requisites to be an effective core state. Indonesia is the largest Muslim country and is growing rapidly economically, It is, however, located on the periphery of Islam far removed from its Arab center; its Islam is of the relaxed, Southeast Asian variety; and its people and culture are a mixture of indigenous, Muslim, Hindu, Chinese, and Christian influences. Egypt is an Arab country, with a large population, a central, strategically important geographical location in the Middle East, and the leading institution of Islamic learning, Al-Azhar University. It is also, however, a poor country, economically dependent on the United States, Western-controlled international institutions, and oil-rich Arab states.

Iran, Pakistan, and Saudi Arabia have all explicitly defined themselves as Muslim countries and have actively attempted to exercise influence in and provide leadership to the *ummah*. In so doing, they have competed with each other in sponsoring organizations, funding Islamic groups, providing support to the fighters in Afghanistan, and wooing the Muslim peoples of Central Asia. Iran has the size, central location, population, historical traditions, oil resources, and middle level of economic development which would qualify it to be an Islamic core state. Ninety percent of Muslims, however, are Sunni and Iran is Shi'ite; Persian is a distant second to Arabic as the language of Islam; and the relations between Persians and Arabs have historically been antagonistic.

Pakistan has size, population, and military prowess, and its leaders have fairly consistently tried to claim a role as the promoter of cooperation among Islamic states and the speaker for Islam to the rest of the world. Pakistan is, however, relatively poor and suffers serious internal ethnic and regional divisions, a record of political instability, and a fixation on the problem of its security vis-à-vis India, which accounts in large part for its interest in developing close relations with other Islamic countries, as well as non-Muslim powers like China and the United States.

Saudi Arabia was the original home of Islam; Islam's holiest shrines are there; its language is Islam's language; it has the world's largest oil reserves and the resulting financial influence; and its government has shaped Saudi society along strictly Islamic lines. During the 1970s and 1980s Saudi Arabia was the single most influential force in Islam. It spent billions of dollars supporting Muslim causes throughout the world, from mosques and textbooks to political parties, Islamist organizations, and terrorist movements, and was relatively indiscriminate in doing so. On the other hand, its relatively small population and geographical vulnerability make it dependent on the West for its security.

Finally, Turkey has the history, population, middle level of economic development, national coherence, and military tradition and competence to be the core state of Islam. In explicitly defining Turkey as a secular society, however, Ataturk prevented the Turkish republic from succeeding the Ottoman empire in that role. Turkey could not even become a charter member of the OIC because of the commitment to secularism in its constitution. So long as Turkey continues to define itself as a secular state, leadership of Islam is denied it.

What, however, if Turkey redefined itself? At some point, Turkey could be ready to give up its frustrating and humiliating role as a beggar pleading for membership in the West and to resume its much more impressive and elevated historical role as the principal Islamic interlocutor and antagonist of the West. Fundamentalism has been on the rise in Turkey; under Özal Turkey made extensive efforts to identify itself with the Arab world; it has capitalized on ethnic and linguistic ties to play a modest role in Central Asia; it has provided encouragement and support to the Bosnian Muslims. Among Muslim countries Turkey is unique in having extensive historical connections with Muslims in the Balkans, the Middle East, North Africa, and Central Asia. Conceivably, Turkey, in effect, could "do a South Africa": abandoning secularism as alien to its being as South Africa abandoned apartheid and thereby changing itself from a pariah state in its civilization to the leading state of that civilization. Having experienced the good and the bad of the West in Christianity and apartheid, South Africa is peculiarly qualified to lead Africa. Having experienced the bad and the good of the West in secularism and democracy, Turkey may be equally qualified to lead Islam. But to do so it would have to reject Ataturk's legacy more thoroughly than Russia has rejected Lenin's. It would also take a leader of Ataturk's caliber and one who combined religious and political legitimacy to remake Turkey from a torn country into a core state.

IV

·

Clashes
of
Civilizations

Chapter 8

•

The West and the Rest:
Intercivilizational Issues

Western Universalism

I n the emerging world, the relations between states and groups from different civilizations will not be close and will often be antagonistic. Yet some
intercivilization relations are more conflict-prone than others. At the micro
level, the most violent fault lines are between Islam and its Orthodox,
Hindu, African, and Western Christian neighbors. At the macro level, the
dominant division is between "the West and the rest," with the most intense
conflicts occurring between Muslim and Asian societies on the one hand, and
the West on the other. The dangerous clashes of the future are likely to arise
from the interaction of Western arrogance, Islamic intolerance, and Sinic assertiveness.

Alone among civilizations the West has had a major and at times devastating
impact on every other civilization. The relation between the power and culture
of the West and the power and cultures of other civilizations is, as a result, the
most pervasive characteristic of the world of civilizations. As the relative power
of other civilizations increases, the appeal of Western culture fades and non-
Western peoples have increasing confidence in and commitment to their indigenous cultures. The central problem in the relations between the West and
the rest is, consequently, the discordance between the West's — particularly
America's — efforts to promote a universal Western culture and its declining
ability to do so.

The collapse of communism exacerbated this discordance by reinforcing in
the West the view that its ideology of democratic liberalism had triumphed
globally and hence was universally valid. The West, and especially the United

States, which has always been a missionary nation, believe that the non-Western peoples should commit themselves to the Western values of democracy, free markets, limited government, human rights, individualism, the rule of law, and should embody these values in their institutions. Minorities in other civilizations embrace and promote these values, but the dominant attitudes toward them in non-Western cultures range from widespread skepticism to intense opposition. What is universalism to the West is imperialism to the rest.

The West is attempting and will continue to attempt to sustain its preeminent position and defend its interests by defining those interests as the interests of the "world community." That phrase has become the euphemistic collective noun (replacing "the Free World") to give global legitimacy to actions reflecting the interests of the United States and other Western powers. The West is, for instance, attempting to integrate the economies of non-Western societies into a global economic system which it dominates. Through the IMF and other international economic institutions, the West promotes its economic interests and imposes on other nations the economic policies it thinks appropriate. In any poll of non-Western peoples, however, the IMF undoubtedly would win the support of finance ministers and a few others but get an overwhelmingly unfavorable rating from almost everyone else, who would agree with Georgi Arbatov's description of IMF officials as "neo-Bolsheviks who love expropriating other people's money, imposing undemocratic and alien rules of economic and political conduct and stifling economic freedom."[1]

Non-Westerners also do not hesitate to point to the gaps between Western principle and Western action. Hypocrisy, double standards, and "but nots" are the price of universalist pretensions. Democracy is promoted but not if it brings Islamic fundamentalists to power; nonproliferation is preached for Iran and Iraq but not for Israel; free trade is the elixir of economic growth but not for agriculture; human rights are an issue with China but not with Saudi Arabia; aggression against oil-owning Kuwaitis is massively repulsed but not against non-oil-owning Bosnians. Double standards in practice are the unavoidable price of universal standards of principle.

Having achieved political independence, non-Western societies wish to free themselves from Western economic, military, and cultural domination. East Asian societies are well on their way to equalling the West economically. Asian and Islamic countries are looking for shortcuts to balance the West militarily. The universal aspirations of Western civilization, the declining relative power of the West, and the increasing cultural assertiveness of other civilizations ensure generally difficult relations between the West and the rest. The nature of those relations and the extent to which they are antagonistic, however, vary considerably and fall into three categories. With the challenger civilizations, Islam and China, the West is likely to have consistently strained and often highly antagonistic relations. Its relations with Latin America and Africa, weaker civilizations which have in some measure been dependent on the West, will involve much lower levels of conflict, particularly with Latin America. The relations of Russia, Japan, and India to the West are likely to fall between those of the other two groups, involving elements of cooperation and conflict, as these three core states at times line up with the challenger civilizations and at times side with the West. They are the "swing" civilizations between the West, on the one hand, and Islamic and Sinic civilizations, on the other.

Islam and China embody great cultural traditions very different from and in their eyes infinitely superior to that of the West. The power and assertiveness of both in relation to the West are increasing, and the conflicts between their values and interests and those of the West are multiplying and becoming more intense. Because Islam lacks a core state, its relations with the West vary greatly from country to country. Since the 1970s, however, a fairly consistent anti-Western trend has existed, marked by the rise of fundamentalism, shifts in power within Muslim countries from more pro-Western to more anti-Western governments, the emergence of a quasi war between some Islamic groups and the West, and the weakening of the Cold War security ties that existed between some Muslim states and the United States. Underlying the differences on specific issues is the fundamental question of the role these civilizations will play relative to the West in shaping the future of the world. Will the global institutions, the distribution of power, and the politics and economies of nations in the twenty-first century primarily reflect Western values and interests or will they be shaped primarily by those of Islam and China?

The realist theory of international relations predicts that the core states of non-Western civilizations should coalesce together to balance the dominant power of the West. In some areas this has happened. A general anti-Western coalition, however, seems unlikely in the immediate future. Islamic and Sinic civilizations differ fundamentally in terms of religion, culture, social structure, traditions, politics, and basic assumptions at the root of their way of life. Inherently each probably has less in common with the other than it has in common with Western civilization. Yet in politics a common enemy creates a common interest. Islamic and Sinic societies which see the West as their antagonist thus have reason to cooperate with each other against the West, even as the Allies and Stalin did against Hitler. This cooperation occurs on a variety of issues, including human rights, economics, and most notably the efforts by societies in both civilizations to develop their military capabilities, particularly weapons of mass destruction and the missiles for delivering them, so as to counter the conventional military superiority of the West. By the early 1990s a "Confucian-Islamic connection" was in place between China and North Korea, on the one hand, and in varying degrees Pakistan, Iran, Iraq, Syria, Libya, and Algeria, on the other, to confront the West on these issues.

The issues that divide the West and these other societies are increasingly important on the international agenda. Three such issues involve the efforts of the West: (1) to maintain its military superiority through policies of nonproliferation and counterproliferation with respect to nuclear, biological, and chemical weapons and the means to deliver them; (2) to promote Western political values and institutions by pressing other societies to respect human rights as conceived in the West and to adopt democracy on Western lines; and (3) to protect the cultural, social, and ethnic integrity of Western societies by restricting the number of non-Westerners admitted as immigrants or refugees. In all three areas the West has had and is likely to continue to have difficulties defending its interests against those of non-Western societies.

WEAPONS PROLIFERATION

The diffusion of military capabilities is the consequence of global economic and social development. As they become richer economically, Japan, China, other Asian countries will become more powerful militarily, as Islamic societies eventually will also. So will Russia if it is successful in reforming its economy. The last decades of the twentieth century have seen many non-Western nations acquire sophisticated weapons through arms transfers from Western societies, Russia, Israel, and China, and also create indigenous arms production facilities for highly sophisticated weapons. These processes will continue and probably accelerate during the early years of the twenty-first century. Nonetheless, well into that century, the West, meaning primarily the United States with some supplements from Britain and France, will alone be able to intervene militarily in almost any part of the world. And only the United States will have the air power capable of bombing virtually any place in the world. These are the central elements of the military position of the United States as a global power and of the West as the dominant civilization in the world. For the immediate future the balance of conventional military power between the West and the rest will overwhelmingly favor the West.

The time, effort, and expense required to develop a first-class conventional military capability provide tremendous incentives for non-Western states to pursue other ways of countering Western conventional military power. The perceived shortcut is the acquisition of weapons of mass destruction and the means to deliver them. The core states of civilizations and countries which are or aspire to be regionally dominant powers have special incentives to acquire these weapons. Such weapons, first, enable those states to establish their dominance over other states in their civilization and region, and, second, provide them with the means to deter intervention in their civilization and region by the United States or other external powers. If Saddam Hussein had delayed his invasion of Kuwait for two or three years until Iraq had nuclear weapons, he very likely would be in possession of Kuwait and quite possibly the Saudi oil fields also. Non-Western states draw the obvious lessons from the Gulf War. For the North Korean military these were: "Don't let the Americans build up their forces; don't let them put in air power; don't let them take the initiative;

don't let them fight a war with low U.S. casualties." For a top Indian military official the lesson was even more explicit: "Don't fight the United States unless you have nuclear weapons."[2] That lesson has been taken to heart by political leaders and military chiefs throughout the non-Western world, as has a plausible corollary: "If you have nuclear weapons, the United States won't fight you."

"Rather than reinforce power politics as usual," Lawrence Freedman has observed, "nuclear weapons in fact confirm a tendency towards the fragmentation of the international system in which the erstwhile great powers play a reduced role." The role of nuclear weapons for the West in the post–Cold War world is thus the opposite of that during the Cold War. Then, as Secretary of Defense Les Aspin pointed out, nuclear weapons compensated for Western conventional inferiority vis-à-vis the Soviet Union. They were "the equalizer." In the post–Cold War world, however, the United States has "unmatched conventional military power, and it is our potential adversaries who may attain nuclear weapons. We're the ones who could wind up being the equalizee."[3]

It is thus not surprising that Russia has emphasized the role of nuclear weapons in its defense planning and in 1995 arranged to purchase additional intercontinental missiles and bombers from Ukraine. "We are now hearing what we used to say about Russians in 1950s," one U.S. weapons expert commented. "Now the Russians are saying: 'We need nuclear weapons to compensate for their conventional superiority.' " In a related reversal, during the Cold War the United States, for deterrent purposes, refused to renounce the first use of nuclear weapons. In keeping with the new deterrent function of nuclear weapons in the post–Cold War world, Russia in 1993 in effect renounced the previous Soviet commitment to no-first-use. Simultaneously China, in developing its post–Cold War nuclear strategy of limited deterrence, also began to question and to weaken its 1964 no-first-use commitment.[4] As they acquire nuclear and other mass destruction weapons, other core states and regional powers are likely to follow these examples so as to maximize the deterrent effect of their weapons on Western conventional military action against them.

Nuclear weapons also can threaten the West more directly. China and Russia have ballistic missiles that can reach Europe and North America with nuclear warheads. North Korea, Pakistan, and India are expanding the range of their missiles and at some point are also likely to have the capability of targeting the West. In addition, nuclear weapons can be delivered by other means. Military analysts set forth a spectrum of violence from very low intensity warfare, such as terrorism and sporadic guerrilla war, through limited wars to larger wars involving massive conventional forces to nuclear war. Terrorism historically is the weapon of the weak, that is, of those who do not possess conventional military power. Since World War II, nuclear weapons have also been the weapon by which the weak compensate for conventional inferiority. In the past, terrorists could do only limited violence, killing a few people here or destroying a facility there. Massive military forces were required to do massive violence. At some point, however, a few terrorists will be able to produce massive violence and massive destruction. Separately, terrorism and nuclear weapons are the weapons of the non-Western weak. If and when they are combined, the non-Western weak will be strong.

In the post–Cold War world efforts to develop weapons of mass destruction and the means of delivering them have been concentrated in Islamic and Confucian states. Pakistan and probably North Korea have a small number of nuclear weapons or at least the ability to assemble them rapidly and are also developing or acquiring longer range missiles capable of delivering them. Iraq had a significant chemical warfare capability and was making major efforts to acquire biological and nuclear weapons. Iran has an extensive program to develop nuclear weapons and has been expanding its capability for delivering them. In 1988 President Rafsanjani declared that Iranians "must fully equip ourselves both in the offensive and defensive use of chemical, bacteriological, and radiological weapons," and three years later his vice president told an Islamic conference, "Since Israel continues to possess nuclear weapons, we, the Muslims, must cooperate to produce an atom bomb, regardless of U.N. attempts to prevent proliferation." In 1992 and 1993 top U.S. intelligence officials said Iran was pursuing the acquisition of nuclear weapons, and in 1995 Secretary of State Warren Christopher bluntly stated, "Today Iran is engaged in a crash effort to develop nuclear weapons." Other Muslim states reportedly interested in developing nuclear weapons include Libya, Algeria, and Saudi Arabia. "The crescent," in Ali Mazrui's colorful phrase, is "over the mushroom cloud," and can threaten others in addition to the West. Islam could end up "playing nuclear Russian roulette with two other civilizations — with Hinduism in South Asia and with Zionism and politicized Judaism in the Middle East."[5]

Weapons proliferation is where the Confucian-Islamic connection has been most extensive and most concrete, with China playing the central role in the transfer of both conventional and nonconventional weapons to many Muslim states. These transfers include: construction of a secret, heavily defended nuclear reactor in the Algerian desert, ostensibly for research but widely believed by Western experts to be capable of producing plutonium; the sale of chemical weapons materials to Libya; the provision of CSS-2 medium-range missiles to Saudi Arabia; the supply of nuclear technology or materials to Iraq, Libya, Syria, and North Korea; and the transfer of large numbers of conventional weapons to Iraq. Supplementing China's transfers, in the early 1990s North Korea supplied Syria with Scud-C missiles, delivered via Iran, and then the mobile chassis from which to launch them.[6]

The central buckle in the Confucian-Islamic arms connection has been the relation between China and to a lesser extent North Korea, on the one hand, and Pakistan and Iran, on the other. Between 1980 and 1991 the two chief recipients of Chinese arms were Iran and Pakistan, with Iraq a runner-up.

Beginning in the 1970s China and Pakistan developed an extremely intimate military relationship. In 1989 the two countries signed a ten-year memorandum of understanding for military "cooperation in the fields of purchase, joint research and development, joint production, transfer of technology, as well as export to third countries through mutual agreement." A supplementary agreement providing Chinese credits for Pakistani arms purchases was signed in 1993. As a result, China became "Pakistan's most reliable and extensive supplier of military hardware, transferring military-related exports of virtually every description and destined for every branch of the Pakistani military." China also helped Pakistan create production facilities for jet aircraft, tanks, artillery, and missiles. Of much greater significance, China provided essential help to Pakistan in developing its nuclear weapons capability: allegedly furnishing Pakistan with uranium for enrichment, advising on bomb design, and possibly allowing Pakistan to explode a nuclear device at a Chinese test site. China then supplied Pakistan with M-11, 300-kilometer range ballistic missiles that could deliver nuclear weapons, in the process violating a commitment to the United States. In return, China has secured midair refueling technology and Stinger missiles from Pakistan.[7]

By the 1990s the weapons connections between China and Iran also had become intensive. During the Iran-Iraq War in the 1980s, China supplied Iran with 22 percent of its arms and in 1989 became its single largest arms supplier. China also actively collaborated in Iran's openly declared efforts to acquire nuclear weapons. After signing "an initial Sino-Iranian cooperation agreement," the two countries then agreed in January 1990 to a ten-year understanding on scientific cooperation and military technology transfers. In September 1992 President Rafsanjani accompanied by Iranian nuclear experts visited Pakistan and then went on to China where he signed another agreement for nuclear cooperation, and in February 1993 China agreed to build two 300-MW nuclear reactors in Iran. In keeping with these agreements, China transferred nuclear technology and information to Iran, trained Iranian scientists and engi-

TABLE 8.1
SELECTED CHINESE ARMS TRANSFERS, 1980–1991

	Iran	Pakistan	Iraq
Main battle tanks	540	1,100	1,300
Armored personnel carriers	300	—	650
Antitank guided missiles	7,500	100	—
Artillery pieces/rocket launchers	1,200*	50	720
Fighter aircraft	140	212	—
Antishipping missiles	332	32	—
Surface-to-air missiles	788*	222*	—

* Indicates deliveries not all confirmed.

Source: Karl W. Eikenberry, *Explaining and Influencing Chinese Arms Transfers* (Washington: National Defense University, Institute for National Strategic Studies, McNair Paper No. 36, February, 1995), p. 12.

neers, and provided Iran with a calutron enriching device. In 1995, after sustained U.S. pressure, China agreed to "cancel," according to the United States, or to "suspend," according to China, the sale of the two 300-MW reactors. China was also a major supplier of missiles and missile technology to Iran, including in the late 1980s Silkworm missiles delivered through North Korea and "dozens, perhaps hundreds, of missile guidance systems and computerized machine tools" in 1994–1995. China also licensed production in Iran of Chinese surface-to-surface missiles. North Korea supplemented this assistance by shipping Scuds to Iran, aiding Iran to develop its own production facilities, and then agreeing in 1993 to supply Iran with its 600-mile-range Nodong I missile. On the third leg of the triangle, Iran and Pakistan also developed extensive cooperation in the nuclear area, with Pakistan training Iranian scientists, and Pakistan, Iran, and China agreeing in November 1992 to work together on nuclear projects.[8] The extensive Chinese help to Pakistan and Iran in developing weapons of mass destruction evidences an extraordinary level of commitment and cooperation between these countries.

As a result of these developments and the potential threats they pose to Western interests, the proliferation of weapons of mass destruction has moved to the top of the West's security agenda. In 1990, for instance, 59 percent of the American public thought that preventing the spread of nuclear weapons was an important foreign policy goal. In 1994, 82 percent of the public and 90 percent of foreign policy leaders identified it as such. President Clinton highlighted the priority of nonproliferation in September 1993, and in the fall of 1994 declared a "national emergency" to deal with the "unusual and extraordinary threat to the national security, foreign policy, and economy of the United States" by "the proliferation of nuclear, biological, and chemical weapons, and the means of delivering such weapons." In 1991 the CIA created a Nonproliferation Center with a 100-person staff and in December 1993, Secretary of Defense Aspin announced a new Defense Counterproliferation Initiative and the creation of a new position of assistant secretary for nuclear security and counterproliferation.[9]

During the Cold War the United States and the Soviet Union engaged in a classic arms race, developing more and more technologically sophisticated nuclear weapons and delivery vehicles for them. It was a case of buildup versus buildup. In the post–Cold War world the central arms competition is of a different sort. The West's antagonists are attempting to acquire weapons of mass destruction and the West is attempting to prevent them from doing so. It is not a case of buildup versus buildup but rather of buildup versus hold-down. The size and capabilities of the West's nuclear arsenal are not, apart from rhetoric, part of the competition. The outcome of an arms race of buildup versus buildup depends on the resources, commitment, and technological competence of the two sides. It is not foreordained. The outcome of a race between buildup and hold-down is more predictable. The hold-down efforts of the West may slow the weapons buildup of other societies, but they will not stop it. The economic and social development of non-Western societies, the commercial incentives for all societies Western and non-Western to make money through the sale of weapons, technology, and expertise, and the political motives of core states and regional powers to protect their local hegemonies, all work to subvert Western hold-down efforts.

The West promotes nonproliferation as reflecting the interests of all nations in international order and stability. Other nations, however, see nonproliferation as serving the interests of Western hegemony. That such is the case is reflected in the differences in concern over proliferation between the West and most particularly the United States, on the one hand, and regional powers whose security would be affected by proliferation, on the other. This was notable with respect to Korea. In 1993 and 1994 the United States worked itself up into a crisis state of mind over the prospect of North Korean nuclear weapons. In November 1993 President Clinton flatly stated, "North Korea cannot be allowed to develop a nuclear bomb. We have to be very firm about it." Senators, Representatives, and former officials of the Bush administration discussed the possible need for a preemptive attack on North Korean nuclear facilities, U.S. concern over the North Korean program was rooted in considerable measure in its concern with global proliferation; not only would such capability constrain and complicate possible U.S. actions in East Asia, but if North Korea sold its technology and/or weapons it could have comparable effects for the United States in South Asia and the Middle East.

South Korea, on the other hand, viewed the bomb in relation to its regional interests. Many South Koreans saw a North Korean bomb as a *Korean* bomb, one which would never be used against other Koreans but could be used to defend Korean independence and interests against Japan and other potential threats. South Korean civilian officials and military officers explicitly looked forward to a united Korea having that capability. South Korean interests were well served: North Korea would suffer the expense and international obloquy of developing the bomb; South Korea would eventually inherit it; the combination of northern nuclear weapons and southern industrial prowess would enable a unified Korea to assume its appropriate role as a major actor on the East Asian scene. As a result, marked differences existed in the extent to which Washington saw a major crisis existing on the Korean peninsula in 1994 and the absence of any significant sense of crisis in Seoul, creating a "panic gap" between the two capitals. One of the "oddities of the North Korean nuclear standoff, from its start several years ago," one journalist observed at the height of the "crisis" in June 1994, "is that the sense of crisis increases the farther one is from Korea." A similar gap between American security interests and those of regional powers occurred in South Asia with the United States being more concerned with nuclear proliferation there than the inhabitants of the region. India and Pakistan each found the other's nuclear threat easier to accept than American proposals to cap, reduce, or eliminate both threats.[10]

The efforts by the United States and other Western countries to prevent the proliferation of "equalizer" weapons of mass destruction have met with and are likely to continue to meet with limited success. A month after President Clinton said that North Korea could not be allowed to have a nuclear weapon, U.S. intelligence agencies informed him that it probably had one or two.[11] U.S. policy consequently shifted to offering the North Koreans carrots to induce them not to expand their nuclear arsenal. The United States was also unable to reverse or to stop nuclear weapons development by India and Pakistan and it has been unable to halt Iran's nuclear progress.

At the April 1995 conference on the Nuclear Nonproliferation Treaty the key issue was whether it should be renewed for an indefinite period or for twenty-five years. The United States led the effort for permanent extension. A wide range of other countries, however, objected to such an extension unless it was accompanied by much more drastic reduction in nuclear arms by the five recognized nuclear powers. In addition, Egypt opposed extension unless Israel signed the treaty and accepted safeguard inspections. In the end, the United States won an overwhelming consensus on indefinite extension through a highly successful strategy of arm twisting, bribes, and threats. Neither Egypt nor Mexico, for instance, both of whom had been against indefinite extension, could maintain its position in the face of their economic dependence on the United States. While the treaty was extended by consensus, the representatives of seven Muslim nations (Syria, Jordan, Iran, Iraq, Libya, Egypt, and Malaysia) and one African nation (Nigeria) expressed dissenting views in the final debate.[12]

In 1993 the primary goals of the West, as defined in American policy, shifted from nonproliferation to counterproliferation. This change was a realistic recognition of the extent to which some nuclear proliferation could not be avoided. In due course, U.S. policy will shift from countering proliferation to accommodating proliferation and, if the government can escape from its Cold War mind-set, to how promoting proliferation can serve U.S. and Western interests. As of 1995, however, the United States and the West remained committed to a hold-down policy which, in the end, is bound to fail. The proliferation of nuclear and other weapons of mass destruction is a central phenomenon of the slow but ineluctable diffusion of power in a multicivilizational world.

HUMAN RIGHTS AND DEMOCRACY

During the 1970s and 1980s over thirty countries shifted from authoritarian to democratic political systems. Several causes were responsible for this wave of transitions. Economic development was undoubtedly the major underlying factor generating these political changes. In addition, however, the policies and action of the United States, the major Western European powers, and international institutions helped to bring democracy to Spain and Portugal, many Latin American countries, the Philippines, South Korea, and Eastern

Europe. Democratization was most successful in countries where Christian and Western influences were strong. New democratic regimes appeared most likely to stabilize in the Southern and Central European countries that were predominantly Catholic or Protestant and, less certainly, in Latin American countries. In East Asia, the Catholic and heavily American influenced Philippines returned to democracy in the 1980s, while Christian leaders promoted movement toward democracy in South Korea and Taiwan. As has been pointed out previously, in the former Soviet Union, the Baltic republics appear to be successfully stabilizing democracy; the degree and stability of democracy in the Orthodox republics vary considerably and are uncertain; democratic prospects in the Muslim republics are bleak. By the 1990s, except for Cuba, democratic transitions had occurred in most of the countries, outside Africa, whose peoples espoused Western Christianity or where major Christian influences existed.

These transitions and the collapse of the Soviet Union generated in the West, particularly in the United States, the belief that a global democratic revolution was underway and that in short order Western concepts of human rights and Western forms of political democracy would prevail throughout the world. Promoting this spread of democracy hence became a high priority goal for Westerners. It was endorsed by the Bush administration with Secretary of State James Baker declaring in April 1990 that "Beyond containment lies democracy" and that for the post–Cold War world "President Bush has defined our new mission to be the promotion and consolidation of democracy." In his 1992 campaign Bill Clinton repeatedly said that the promotion of democracy would be a top priority of a Clinton administration, and democratization was the only foreign policy topic to which he devoted an entire major campaign speech. Once in office he recommended a two-thirds increase in funding for the National Endowment for Democracy; his assistant for national security defined the central theme of Clinton foreign policy as the "enlargement of democracy"; and his secretary of defense identified the promotion of democracy as one of four major goals and attempted to create a senior position in his department to promote that goal. To a lesser degree and in less obvious ways, the promotion of human rights and democracy also assumed a prominent role in the foreign policies of European states and in the criteria used by the Western-controlled international economic institutions for loans and grants to developing countries.

As of 1995 European and American efforts to achieve these goals had met with limited success. Almost all non-Western civilizations were resistant to this pressure from the West. These included Hindu, Orthodox, African, and in some measure even Latin American countries. The greatest resistance to Western democratization efforts, however, came from Islam and Asia. This resistance was rooted in the broader movements of cultural assertiveness embodied in the Islamic Resurgence and the Asian affirmation.

The failures of the United States with respect to Asia stemmed primarily from the increasing economic wealth and self-confidence of Asian governments. Asian publicists repeatedly reminded the West that the old age of dependence and subordination was past and that the West which produced half the world's economic product in the 1940s, dominated the United Nations, and wrote the Universal Declaration on Human Rights had disappeared into history. "[E]fforts to promote human rights in Asia," argued one Singaporean official, "must also reckon with the altered distribution of power in the post–Cold War world. . . . Western leverage over East and Southeast Asia has been greatly reduced." [13]

He is right. While the agreement on nuclear matters between the United States and North Korea might appropriately be termed a "negotiated surrender," the capitulation of the United States on human rights issues with China and other Asian powers was unconditional surrender. After threatening China with the denial of most favored nation treatment if it was not more forthcoming on human rights, the Clinton Administration first saw its secretary of state humiliated in Beijing, denied even a face-saving gesture, and then responded to this behavior by renouncing its previous policy and separating MFN status from human rights concerns. China, in turn, reacted to this show of weakness by continuing and intensifying the behavior to which the Clinton administration objected. The administration beat similar retreats in its dealings with Singapore over the caning of an American citizen and with Indonesia over its repressive violence in East Timor.

The ability of Asian regimes to resist Western human rights pressures was reinforced by several factors. American and European businesses were desperately anxious to expand their trade with and their investment in these rapidly growing countries and subjected their governments to intense pressure not to disrupt economic relations with them. In addition, Asian countries saw such pressure as an infringement on their sovereignty and rallied to each other's support when these issues arose. Taiwanese, Japanese, and Hong Kong businessmen who invested in China had a major interest in China's retaining its MFN privileges with the United States. The Japanese government generally distanced itself from American human rights policies: We will not let "abstract notions of human rights" affect our relations with China, Prime Minister Kiichi Miyazawa said not long after Tiananmen Square. The countries of ASEAN were unwilling to apply pressure to Myanmar and, indeed, in 1994 welcomed the military junta to their meeting while the European Union, as its spokesman said, had to recognize that its policy "had not been very successful" and that it would have to go along with the ASEAN approach to Myanmar. In addition, their growing economic power allowed states such as Malaysia and Indonesia to apply "reverse conditionalities" to countries and firms which criticize them or engage in other behavior they find objectionable. [14]

Overall the growing economic strength of the Asian countries renders them

increasingly immune to Western pressure concerning human rights and democracy. "Today China's economic power," Richard Nixon observed in 1994,
"makes U.S. lectures about human rights imprudent. Within a decade it will
make them irrelevant. Within two decades it will make them laughable."[15]
By that time, however, Chinese economic development could make Western
lectures unnecessary. Economic growth is strengthening Asian governments in
relation to Western governments. In the longer run it will also strengthen Asian
societies in relation to Asian governments. If democracy comes to additional
Asian countries it will come because the increasingly strong Asian bourgeoisies
and middle classes want it to come.

In contrast to agreement on the indefinite expansion of the nonproliferation
treaty, Western efforts to promote human rights and democracy in U.N. agencies generally came to naught. With a few exceptions, such as those condemning Iraq, human rights resolutions were almost always defeated in U.N. votes.
Apart from some Latin American countries, other governments were reluctant
to enlist in efforts to promote what many saw as "human rights imperialism."
In 1990, for instance, Sweden submitted on behalf of twenty Western nations
a resolution condemning the military regime in Myanmar, but opposition from
Asian and other countries killed it. Resolutions condemning Iran for human
rights abuses were also voted down, and for five straight years in the 1990s
China was able to mobilize Asian support to defeat Western-sponsored resolutions expressing concern over its human rights violations. In 1994 Pakistan
tabled a resolution in the U.N. Commission on Human Rights condemning
India's rights violations in Kashmir. Countries friendly to India rallied against
it, but so also did two of Pakistan's closest friends, China and Iran, who had
been the targets of similar measures, and who persuaded Pakistan to withdraw
the proposal. In failing to condemn Indian brutality in Kashmir, *The Economist*
observed, the U.N. Human Rights Commission "by default, sanctioned it.
Other countries, too, are getting away with murder: Turkey, Indonesia, Colombia, and Algeria have all escaped criticism. The commission is thus giving
succor to governments that practice butchery and torture, which is exactly the
opposite of what its creators intended."[16]

The differences over human rights between the West and other civilizations
and the limited ability of the West to achieve its goals were clearly revealed in
the U.N. World Conference on Human Rights in Vienna in June 1993. On
one side were the European and North American countries; on the other side
was a bloc of about fifty non-Western states, the fifteen most active members of
which included the governments of one Latin American country (Cuba), one
Buddhist country (Myanmar), four Confucian countries with widely varying
political ideologies, economic systems, and levels of development (Singapore,
Vietnam, North Korea, and China), and nine Muslim countries (Malaysia,
Indonesia, Pakistan, Iran, Iraq, Syria, Yemen, Sudan, and Libya). The leadership of this Asian-Islamic grouping came from China, Syria, and Iran. In

between these two groupings were the Latin American countries, apart from Cuba, which often supported the West, and African and Orthodox countries which sometimes supported but more often opposed Western positions.

The issues on which countries divided along civilizational lines included: universality vs. cultural relativism with respect to human rights; the relative priority of economic and social rights including the right to development versus political and civil rights; political conditionality with respect to economic assistance; the creation of a U.N. Commissioner for Human Rights; the extent to which the nongovernmental human rights organizations simultaneously meeting in Vienna should be allowed to participate in the governmental conference; the particular rights which should be endorsed by the conference; and more specific issues such as whether the Dalai Lama should be allowed to address the conference and whether human rights abuses in Bosnia should be explicitly condemned.

Major differences existed between the Western countries and the Asian-Islamic bloc on these issues. Two months before the Vienna conference the Asian countries met in Bangkok and endorsed a declaration which emphasized that human rights must be considered "in the context . . . of national and regional particularities and various historical religious and cultural backgrounds," that human rights monitoring violated state sovereignty, and that conditioning economic assistance on human rights performance was contrary to the right to development. The differences over these and other issues were so great that almost the entire document produced by the final pre-Vienna conference preparatory meeting in Geneva in early May was in brackets, indicating dissents by one or more countries.

The Western nations were ill prepared for Vienna, were outnumbered at the conference, and during its proceedings made more concessions than their opponents. As a result, apart from a strong endorsement of women's rights, the declaration approved by the conference was a minimal one. It was, one human rights supporter observed, "a flawed and contradictory" document, and represented a victory for the Asian-Islamic coalition and a defeat for the West.[17] The Vienna declaration contained no explicit endorsement of the rights to freedom of speech, the press, assembly, and religion, and was thus in many respects weaker than the Universal Declaration of Human Rights the U.N. had adopted in 1948. This shift reflected the decline in the power of the West. "The international human rights regime of 1945," an American human rights supporter remarked, "is no more. American hegemony has eroded. Europe, even with the events of 1992, is little more than a peninsula. The world is now as Arab, Asian, and African, as it is Western. Today the Universal Declaration of Human Rights and the International Covenants are less relevant to much of the planet than during the immediate post–World War II era." An Asian critic of the West had similar views: "For the first time since the Universal Declaration was adopted in 1948, countries not thoroughly steeped in the Judeo-Christian and natural law traditions are in the first rank. That unprecedented situation will define the new international politics of human rights. It will also multiply the occasions for conflict." [18]

"The big winner" at Vienna, another observer commented, "clearly, was China, at least if success is measured by telling other people to get out of the way. Beijing kept winning throughout the meeting simply by tossing its weight around." [19] Outvoted and outmaneuvered at Vienna, the West was nonetheless able a few months later to score a not-insignificant victory against China. Securing the 2000 summer Olympics for Beijing was a major goal of the Chinese government, which invested tremendous resources in trying to achieve it. In China there was immense publicity about the Olympic bid and public expectations were high; the government lobbied other governments to pressure their Olympic associations; Taiwan and Hong Kong joined in the campaign. On the other side, the United States Congress, the European Parliament, and human rights organizations all vigorously opposed selecting Beijing. Although voting in the International Olympic Committee is by secret ballot, it clearly was along civilizational lines. On the first ballot, Beijing, with reportedly wide-spread African support, was in first place with Sydney in second. On subsequent ballots, when Istanbul was eliminated, the Confucian-Islamic connection brought its votes overwhelmingly to Beijing; when Berlin and Manchester were eliminated, their votes went overwhelmingly to Sydney, giving it victory on the fourth ballot and imposing a humiliating defeat on China, which it blamed squarely on the United States.* "America and Britain," Lee Kuan Yew commented, "succeeded in cutting China down to size. . . . The apparent reason was 'human rights.' The real reason was political, to show Western political clout." [20] Undoubtedly many more people in the world are concerned with sports than with human rights, but given the defeats on human rights the West suffered at Vienna and elsewhere, this isolated demonstration of Western "clout" was also a reminder of Western weakness.

Not only is Western clout diminished, but the paradox of democracy also weakens Western will to promote democracy in the post-Cold War world. During the Cold War the West and the United States in particular confronted

* The voting on the four ballots was as follows:

	First	Second	Third	Fourth
Beijing	32	37	40	43
Sydney	30	30	37	45
Manchester	11	13	11	
Berlin	9	9		
Istanbul	7			
Abstain			1	1
Total	89	89	89	89

the "friendly tyrant" problem: the dilemmas of cooperating with military juntas and dictators who were anti-communist and hence useful partners in the Cold War. Such cooperation produced uneasiness and at times embarrassment when these regimes engaged in outrageous violations of human rights. Cooperation could, however, be justified as the lesser evil: these governments were usually less thoroughly repressive than communist regimes and could be expected to be less durable as well as more susceptible to American and other outside influences. Why not work with a less brutal friendly tyrant if the alternative was a more brutal unfriendly one? In the post-Cold War world the choice can be the more difficult one between a friendly tyrant and an unfriendly democracy. The West's easy assumption that democratically elected governments will be cooperative and pro-Western need not hold true in non-Western societies where electoral competition can bring anti-Western nationalists and fundamentalists to power. The West was relieved when the Algerian military intervened in 1992 and canceled the election which the fundamentalist FIS clearly was going to win. Western governments also were reassured when the fundamentalist Welfare Party in Turkey and the nationalist BJP in India were excluded from power after scoring electoral victories in 1995 and 1996. On the other hand, within the context of its revolution Iran in some respects has one of the more democratic regimes in the Islamic world, and competitive elections in many Arab countries including Saudi Arabia and Egypt would almost surely produce governments far less sympathetic to Western interests than their undemocratic predecessors. A popularly elected government in China could well be a highly nationalistic one. As Western leaders realize that democratic processes in non-Western societies often produce governments unfriendly to the West, they both attempt to influence those elections and also lose their enthusiasm for promoting democracy in those societies.

IMMIGRATION

If demography is destiny, population movements are the motor of history. In centuries past, differential growth rates, economic conditions, and governmental policies have produced massive migrations by Greeks, Jews, Germanic tribes, Norse, Turks, Russians, Chinese, and others. In some instances these movements were relatively peaceful, in others quite violent. Nineteenth-century Europeans were, however, the master race at demographic invasion. Between 1821 and 1924, approximately 55 million Europeans migrated overseas, 34 million of them to the United States. Westerners conquered and at times obliterated other peoples, explored and settled less densely populated lands. The export of people was perhaps the single most important dimension of the rise of the West between the sixteenth and twentieth centuries.

The late twentieth century has seen a different and even larger surge in migration. In 1990 legal international migrants numbered about 100 million, refugees about 19 million, and illegal migrants probably at least 10 million more. This new wave of migration was in part the product of decolonization, the establishment of new states, and state policies that encouraged or forced people to move. It was also, however, the result of modernization and technological development. Transportation improvements made migration easier, quicker, and cheaper; communications improvements enhanced the incentives to pursue economic opportunities and promoted relations between migrants and their home country families. In addition, as the economic growth of the West stimulated emigration in the nineteenth century, economic development in non-Western societies has stimulated emigration in the twentieth century. Migration becomes a self-reinforcing process. "If there is a single 'law' in migration," Myron Weiner argues, "it is that a migration flow, once begun, induces its own flow. Migrants enable their friends and relatives back home to migrate by providing them with information about how to migrate, resources to facilitate movement, and assistance in finding jobs and housing." The result is, in his phrase, a "global migration crisis."[21]

Westerners consistently and overwhelmingly have opposed nuclear proliferation and supported democracy and human rights. Their views on immigration, in contrast, have been ambivalent and changing with the balance shifting significantly in the last two decades of the twentieth century. Until the 1970s European countries generally were favorably disposed toward immigration and, in some cases, most notably Germany and Switzerland, encouraged it to remedy labor shortages. In 1965 the United States removed the European-oriented quotas dating from the 1920s and drastically revised its laws, making possible tremendous increases in and new sources of immigrants in the 1970s and 1980s. By the late 1980s, however, high unemployment rates, the increased numbers of immigrants, and their overwhelmingly "non-European" character produced sharp changes in European attitudes and policy. A few years later similar concerns led to a comparable shift in the United States.

A majority of late-twentieth-century migrants and refugees have moved from one non-Western society to another. The influx of migrants to Western societies, however, has approached in absolute numbers nineteenth-century Western emigration. In 1990 an estimated 20 million first generation immigrants were in the United States, 15.5 million in Europe, and 8 million in Australia and Canada. The proportion of immigrants to total population reached 7 percent to 8 percent in major European countries. In the United States immigrants constituted 8.7 percent of the population in 1994, twice that of 1970, and made up 25 percent of the people in California and 16 percent of those in New York. About 8.3 million people entered the United States in the 1980s and 4.5 million in the first four years of the 1990s.

The new immigrants came overwhelmingly from non-Western societies. In Germany, Turkish foreign residents numbered 1,675,000 in 1990, with Yugoslavia, Italy, and Greece providing the next largest contingents. In Italy the principal sources were Morocco, the United States (presumably largely Italian Americans going back), Tunisia, and the Philippines. By the mid-1990s, approximately 4 million Muslims lived in France and up to 13 million in Western Europe overall. In the 1950s two-thirds of the immigrants to the United States came from Europe and Canada; in the 1980s roughly 35 percent of the much larger number of immigrants came from Asia, 45 percent from Latin America, and less than 15 percent from Europe and Canada. Natural population growth is low in the United States and virtually zero in Europe. Migrants have high fertility rates and hence account for most future population growth in Western societies. As a result, Westerners increasingly fear "that they are now being invaded not by armies and tanks but by migrants who speak other languages, worship other gods, belong to other cultures, and, they fear, will take their jobs, occupy their land, live off the welfare system, and threaten their way of life."[22] These phobias, rooted in relative demographic decline, Stanley Hoffmann observes, "are based on genuine cultural clashes and worries about national identity."[23]

By the early 1990s two-thirds of the migrants in Europe were Muslim, and European concern with immigration is above all concern with Muslim immigration. The challenge is demographic — migrants account for 10 percent of the births in Western Europe, Arabs 50 percent of those in Brussels — and cultural. Muslim communities whether Turkish in Germany or Algerian in France have not been integrated into their host cultures and, to the concern of Europeans, show few signs of becoming so. There "is a fear growing all across Europe," Jean Marie Domenach said in 1991, "of a Muslim community that cuts across European lines, a sort of thirteenth nation of the European Community." With respect to immigrants, an American journalist commented,

> European hostility is curiously selective. Few in France worry about an on-slaught from the East — Poles, after all, are European and Catholic. And for the most part, non-Arab African immigrants are neither feared nor despised. The hostility is directed mostly at Muslims. The word "immigré" is virtually synonymous with Islam, now France's second largest religion, and reflects a cultural and ethnic racism deeply rooted in French history.[24]

The French, however, are more culturist than racist in any strict sense. They have accepted black Africans who speak perfect French in their legislature but they do not accept Muslim girls who wear headscarves in their schools. In 1990, 76 percent of the French public thought there were too many Arabs in France, 46 percent too many blacks, 40 percent too many Asians, and 24 percent too many Jews. In 1994, 47 percent of Germans said they would prefer not to have Arabs living in their neighborhoods, 39 percent did not want Poles, 36 percent Turks, and 22 percent Jews.[25] In Western Europe, anti-Semitism directed against Arabs has largely replaced anti-Semitism directed against Jews.

Public opposition to immigration and hostility toward immigrants manifested itself at the extreme in acts of violence against immigrant communities and individuals, which particularly became an issue in Germany in the early 1990s. More significant were increases in the votes for right-wing, nationalist, anti-immigration parties. These votes were, however, seldom large. The Republican Party in Germany got over 7 percent of the vote in the European elections in 1989, but only 2.1 percent in the national elections in 1990. In France the National Front vote, which had been negligible in 1981, went up to 9.6 percent in 1988 and thereafter stabilized between 12 percent and 15 percent in regional and parliamentary elections. In 1995 the two nationalist candidates for president captured 19.9 percent of the vote and the National Front elected mayors in several cities, including Toulon and Nice. In Italy the votes for the MSI/ National Alliance similarly rose from about 5 percent in the 1980s to between 10 percent and 15 percent in the early 1990s. In Belgium the Flemish Bloc/ National Front vote increased to 9 percent in 1994 local elections, with the Bloc getting 28 percent of the vote in Antwerp. In Austria the vote in the general elections for the Freedom Party increased from less than 10 percent in 1986 to over 15 percent in 1990 and almost 23 percent in 1994.[26]

These European parties opposing Muslim immigration were in large part the mirror image of Islamist parties in Muslim countries. Both were outsiders denouncing a corrupt establishment and its parties, exploiting economic grievances, particularly unemployment, making ethnic and religious appeals, and attacking foreign influences in their society. In both cases an extremist fringe engaged in acts of terrorism and violence. In most instances both Islamist and European nationalist parties tended to do better in local than in national elections. Muslim and European political establishments responded to these developments in similar fashion. In Muslim countries, as we have seen, governments universally became more Islamic in their orientations, symbols, policies, and practices. In Europe mainstream parties adopted the rhetoric and promoted the measures of the right-wing, anti-immigration parties. Where democratic politics was functioning effectively and two or more alternative parties existed to the Islamist or nationalist party, their vote hit a ceiling of about 20 percent. The protest parties broke through that ceiling only when no other effective alternative existed to the party or coalition in power, as was the case in Algeria, Austria, and, in considerable measure, Italy.

In the early 1990s European political leaders competed with each other to respond to anti-immigration sentiment. In France Jacques Chirac declared in 1990 that "Immigration must be totally stopped"; Interior Minister Charles Pasqua argued in 1993 for "zero immigration"; and Francois Mitterrand, Edith Cresson, Valery Giscard d'Estaing, and other mainstream politicians took anti-immigration stances. Immigration was a major issue in the parliamentary elections of 1993 and apparently contributed to the victory of the conservative parties. During the early 1990s French government policy was changed to make it more difficult for the children of foreigners to become citizens, for families of foreigners to immigrate, for foreigners to ask for the right of asylum, and for Algerians to get visas to come to France. Illegal immigrants were deported and the powers of the police and other government authorities dealing with immigration were strengthened.

In Germany Chancellor Helmut Kohl and other political leaders also expressed concerns about immigration, and in its most important move, the government amended Article XVI of the German constitution guaranteeing asylum to "people persecuted on political grounds" and cut benefits to asylum seekers. In 1992, 438,000 people came to Germany for asylum; in 1994 only 127,000 did. In 1980 Britain had drastically cut back its immigration to about 50,000 a year and hence the issue raised less intense emotions and opposition there than on the continent. Between 1992 and 1994, however, Britain reduced the number of asylum seekers permitted to stay from over 20,000 to less than 10,000. As barriers to movement within the European Union came down, British concerns were in large measure focused on the dangers of non-European migration from the continent. Overall in the mid-1990s Western European countries were moving inexorably toward reducing to a minimum if not totally eliminating immigration from non-European sources.

The immigration issue came to the fore somewhat later in the United States than it did in Europe and did not generate quite the same emotional intensity. The United States has always been a country of immigrants, has so conceived itself, and historically has developed highly successful processes for assimilating newcomers. In addition, in the 1980s and 1990s unemployment was considerably lower in the United States than in Europe, and fear of losing jobs was not a decisive factor shaping attitudes toward immigration. The sources of American immigration were also more varied than in Europe, and thus the fear of being swamped by a single foreign group was less nationally, although real in particular localities. The cultural distance of the two largest migrant groups from the host culture was also less than in Europe: Mexicans are Catholic and Spanish-speaking; Filipinos, Catholic and English-speaking.

Despite these factors, in the quarter century after passage of the 1965 act that permitted greatly increased Asian and Latin American immigration, American public opinion shifted decisively. In 1965 only 33 percent of the public wanted less immigration. In 1977, 42 percent did; in 1986, 49 percent did; and in 1990 and 1993, 61 percent did. Polls in the 1990s consistently show 60 percent or more of the public favoring reduced immigration.[27] While economic concerns and economic conditions affect attitudes toward immigration, the steadily rising opposition in good times and bad suggests that culture, crime, and way of life were more important in this change of opinion. "Many, perhaps most, Americans," one observer commented in 1994, "still see their nation as a European settled country, whose laws are an inheritance from England, whose language is (and should remain) English, whose institutions and public buildings find inspiration in Western classical norms, whose religion has Judeo-Christian roots, and whose greatness initially arose from the Protestant work ethic." Reflecting these concerns, 55 percent of a sample of the public said they thought immigration was a threat to American culture. While Europeans see the immigration threat as Muslim or Arab, Americans see it as both Latin American and Asian but primarily as Mexican. When asked in 1990 from which countries the United States was admitting too many immigrants, a sample of Americans identified Mexico twice as often as any other, followed in order by Cuba, the Orient (nonspecific), South America and Latin America (nonspecific), Japan, Vietnam, China, and Korea.[28]

Growing public opposition to immigration in the early 1990s prompted a political reaction comparable to that which occurred in Europe. Given the nature of the American political system, rightist and anti-immigration parties did not gain votes, but anti-immigration publicists and interest groups became more numerous, more active, and more vocal. Much of the resentment focused on the 3.5 million to 4 million illegal immigrants, and politicians responded. As in Europe, the strongest reaction was at the state and local levels, which bear most of the costs of the immigrants. As a result, in 1994 Florida, subsequently joined by six other states, sued the federal government for $884 million a year to cover the education, welfare, law enforcement, and other costs produced by illegal immigrants. In California, the state with the largest number of immigrants absolutely and proportionately, Governor Pete Wilson won public support by urging the denial of public education to children of illegal immigrants, refusing citizenship to U.S.-born children of illegal immigrants, and ending state payments for emergency medical care for illegal immigrants. In November 1994 Californians overwhelmingly approved Proposition 187, denying health, education, and welfare benefits to illegal aliens and their children.

Also in 1994 the Clinton administration, reversing its earlier stance, moved to toughen immigration controls, tighten rules governing political asylum, expand the Immigration and Naturalization Service, strengthen the Border Patrol, and construct physical barriers along the Mexican boundary. In 1995 the Commission on Immigration Reform, authorized by Congress in 1990, recommended reducing yearly legal immigration from over 800,000 to 550,000, giving preference to young children and spouses but not other relatives of current citizens and residents, a provision that "inflamed Asian-American and Hispanic families."[29] Legislation embodying many of the commission's recommendations and other measures restricting immigration was on its way through Congress in 1995–96. By the mid-1990s immigration had thus become a major political issue in the United States, and in 1996 Patrick Buchanan made opposition to immigration a central plank in his presidential campaign. The United States is following Europe in moving to cut back substantially the entry of non-Westerners into its society.

Can either Europe or the United States stem the migrant tide? France has experienced a significant strand of demographic pessimism, stretching from the searing novel of Jean Raspail in the 1970s to the scholarly analysis of Jean-Claude Chesnais in the 1990s and summed up in the 1991 comments of Pierre Lellouche: "History, proximity and poverty insure that France and Europe are destined to be overwhelmed by people from the failed societies of the south. Europe's past was white and Judeo-Christian. The future is not." * [30] The future, however, is not irrevocably determined; nor is any one future permanent. The issue is not whether Europe will be Islamicized or the United States Hispanicized. It is whether Europe and America will become cleft societies encompassing two distinct and largely separate communities from two different civilizations, which in turn depends on the numbers of immigrants and the extent to which they are assimilated into the Western cultures prevailing in Europe and America.

European societies generally either do not want to assimilate immigrants or have great difficulty doing so, and the degree to which Muslim immigrants and their children want to be assimilated is unclear. Hence sustained substantial immigration is likely to produce countries divided into Christian and Muslim communities. This outcome can be avoided to the extent that European governments and peoples are willing to bear the costs of restricting such immigration, which include the direct fiscal costs of anti-immigration measures, the social costs of further alienating existing immigrant communities, and the potential long-term economic costs of labor shortages and lower rates of growth.

The problem of Muslim demographic invasion is, however, likely to weaken as the population growth rates in North African and Middle Eastern societies peak, as they already have in some countries, and begin to decline.[31] Insofar as demographic pressure stimulates immigration, Muslim immigration could be much less by 2025. This is not true for sub-Saharan Africa. If economic development occurs and promotes social mobilization in West and Central Africa the incentives and capacities to migrate will increase, and the threat to Europe of "Islamization" will be succeeded by that of "Africanization." The extent to which this threat materializes will also be significantly influenced by the degree to which African populations are reduced by AIDS and other plagues and the degree to which South Africa attracts immigrants from elsewhere in Africa.

While Muslims pose the immediate problem to Europe, Mexicans pose the problem for the United States. Assuming continuation of current trends and policies, the American population will, as the figures in Table 8.2 show, change dramatically in the first half of the twenty-first century, becoming almost 50 percent white and 25 percent Hispanic. As in Europe, changes in immigration policy and effective enforcement of anti-immigration measures could change

---

* Raspail's *Le Camp des Saints* was first published in 1973 (Paris, Editions Robert Laffront) and was issued in a new edition in 1985 as concern over immigration intensified in France. The novel was dramatically called to the attention of Americans as concern intensified in the United States in 1994 by Matthew Connelly and Paul Kennedy, "Must It Be the Rest Against the West?" *Atlantic Monthly*, v. 274 (Dec. 1994), pp. 61ff., and Raspail's preface to the 1985 French edition was published in English in *The Social Contract*, v. 4 (Winter 1993–94), pp. 115–117.

THE UNITED STATES: A CLEFT COUNTRY?
PROJECTED PERCENT OF POPULATION THAT WILL BE BLACK, ASIAN, NATIVE AMERICAN, OR HISPANIC IN 2020, BY COUNTY

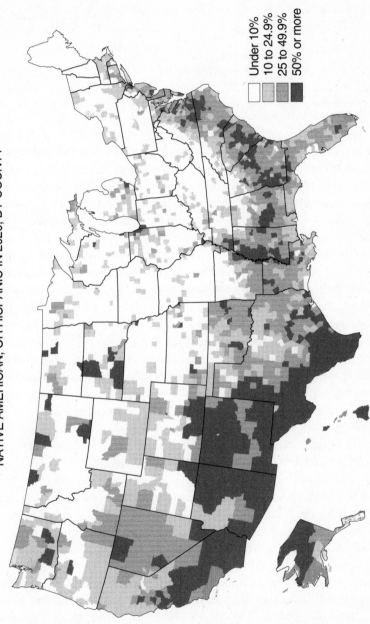

Under 10%
10 to 24.9%
25 to 49.9%
50% or more

Source: Based on data from U.S. Census Bureau.   Rodger Doyle Copyright 1995 for U.S. News & World Report.

TABLE 8.2
U.S. POPULATION BY RACE AND ETHNICITY
(in percentages)

	1995	2020 Est.	2050 Est.
Non-Hispanic White	74%	64%	53%
Hispanic	10	16	25
Black	12	13	14
Asian & Pacific Islander	3	6	8
American Indian & Alaskan Native	<1	<1	1
Total (Millions)	263	323	394

Source: U.S. Bureau of the Census. *Population Projections of the United States by Age, Sex, Race, and Hispanic Origin: 1995 to 2050* (Washington: U.S. Government Printing Office, 1996), pp. 12–13.

these projections. Even so, the central issue will remain the degree to which Hispanics are assimilated into American society as previous immigrant groups have been. Second and third generation Hispanics face a wide array of incentives and pressures to do so. Mexican immigration, on the other hand, differs in potentially important ways from other immigrations. First, immigrants from Europe or Asia cross oceans; Mexicans walk across a border or wade across a river. This plus the increasing ease of transportation and communication enables them to maintain close contacts and identity with their home communities. Second, Mexican immigrants are concentrated in the southwestern United States and form part of a continuous Mexican society stretching from Yucatan to Colorado (see Map 8.1). Third, some evidence suggests that resistance to assimilation is stronger among Mexican migrants than it was with other immigrant groups and that Mexicans tend to retain their Mexican identity, as was evident in the struggle over Proposition 187 in California in 1994. Fourth, the area settled by Mexican migrants was annexed by the United States after it defeated Mexico in the mid-nineteenth century. Mexican economic development will almost certainly generate Mexican revanchist sentiments. In due course, the results of American military expansion in the nineteenth century could be threatened and possibly reversed by Mexican demographic expansion in the twenty-first century.

The changing balance of power among civilizations makes it more and more difficult for the West to achieve its goals with respect to weapons proliferation, human rights, immigration, and other issues. To minimize its losses in this situation requires the West to wield skillfully its economic resources as carrots and sticks in dealing with other societies, to bolster its unity and coordinate its policies so as to make it more difficult for other societies to play one Western country off against another, and to promote and exploit differences among non-Western nations. The West's ability to pursue these strategies will be shaped by the the nature and intensity of its conflicts with the challenger civilizations, on the one hand, and the extent to which it can identify and develop common interests with the swing civilizations, on the other.

Chapter 9

•

The Global Politics of Civilizations

CORE STATE AND FAULT LINE CONFLICTS

Civilizations are the ultimate human tribes, and the clash of civilizations is tribal conflict on a global scale. In the emerging world, states and groups from two different civilizations may form limited, ad hoc, tactical connections and coalitions to advance their interests against entities from a third civilization or for other shared purposes. Relations between groups from different civilizations however will be almost never close, usually cool, and often hostile. Connections between states of different civilizations inherited from the past, such as Cold War military alliances, are likely to attenuate or evaporate. Hopes for close intercivilizational "partnerships," such as were once articulated by their leaders for Russia and America, will not be realized. Emerging intercivilizational relations will normally vary from distant to violent, with most falling somewhere in between. In many cases they are likely to approximate the "cold peace" that Boris Yeltsin warned could be the future of relations between Russia and the West. Other intercivilizational relations could approximate a condition of "cold war." The term *la guerra fria* was coined by thirteenth-century Spaniards to describe their "uneasy coexistence" with Muslims in the Mediterranean, and in the 1990s many saw a "civilizational cold war" again developing between Islam and the West.[1] In a world of civilizations, it will not be the only relationship characterized by that term. Cold peace, cold war, trade war, quasi war, uneasy peace, troubled relations, intense rivalry, competitive coexistence, arms races: these phrases are the most probable descriptions of relations between entities from different civilizations. Trust and friendship will be rare.

Intercivilizational conflict takes two forms. At the local or micro level, *fault line conflicts* occur between neighboring states from different civilizations, between groups from different civilizations within a state, and between groups which, as in the former Soviet Union and Yugoslavia, are attempting to create new states out of the wreckage of old. Fault line conflicts are particularly prevalent between Muslims and non-Muslims. The reasons for and the nature and dynamics of these conflicts are explored in chapters 10 and 11. At the global or macro level, *core state conflicts* occur among the major states of different civilizations. The issues in these conflicts are the classic ones of international politics, including:

1. relative influence in shaping global developments and the actions of global international organizations such as the U.N., IMF, and World Bank;
2. relative military power, which manifests itself in controversies over non-proliferation and arms control and in arms races;
3. economic power and welfare, manifested in disputes over trade, investment, and other issues;
4. people, involving efforts by a state from one civilization to protect kinsmen in another civilization, to discriminate against people from another civilization, or to exclude from its territory people from another civilization;
5. values and culture, conflicts over which arise when a state attempts to promote or to impose its values on the people of another civilization;
6. occasionally, territory, in which core states become front line participants in fault line conflicts.

These issues are, of course, the sources of conflict between humans throughout history. When states from different civilizations are involved, however, cultural differences sharpen the conflict. In their competition with each other, core states attempt to rally their civilizational cohorts, to get support from states of third civilizations, to promote division within and defections from opposing civilizations, and to use the appropriate mix of diplomatic, political, economic, and covert actions and propaganda inducements and coercions to achieve their objectives. Core states are, however, unlikely to use military force directly against each other, except in situations such as have existed in the Middle East and the Subcontinent where they adjoin each other on a civilizational fault line. Core state wars are otherwise likely to arise under only two circumstances. First, they could develop from the escalation of fault line conflicts between local groups as kin groups, including core states, rally to the support of the local combatants. This possibility, however, creates a major incentive for the core states in the opposing civilizations to contain or to resolve the fault line conflict.

Second, core state war could result from changes in the global balance of power among civilizations. Within Greek civilization, the increasing power of Athens, as Thucydides argued, led to the Peloponnesian War. Similarly the history of Western civilization is one of "hegemonic wars" between rising and falling powers. The extent to which similar factors encourage conflict between the rising and falling core states of different civilizations depends in part on whether balancing or bandwagoning is the preferred way in these civilizations for states to adjust to the rise of a new power. While bandwagoning may be more characteristic of Asian civilizations, the rise of Chinese power could generate balancing efforts from states in other civilizations, such as the United States, India, and Russia. The missing hegemonic war in Western history is that between Great Britain and the United States, and presumably the peaceful shift from the Pax Britannica to the Pax Americana was in large part due to the close cultural kinship of the two societies. The absence of such kinship in the shifting power balance between the West and China does not make armed conflict certain but does make it more probable. The dynamism of Islam is the ongoing source of many relatively small fault line wars; the rise of China is the potential source of a big intercivilizational war of core states.

ISLAM AND THE WEST

Some Westerners, including President Bill Clinton, have argued that the West does not have problems with Islam but only with violent Islamist extremists. Fourteen hundred years of history demonstrate otherwise. The relations between Islam and Christianity, both Orthodox and Western, have often been stormy. Each has been the other's Other. The twentieth-century conflict between liberal democracy and Marxist-Leninism is only a fleeting and superficial historical phenomenon compared to the continuing and deeply conflictual relation between Islam and Christianity. At times, peaceful coexistence has prevailed; more often the relation has been one of intense rivalry and of varying degrees of hot war. Their "historical dynamics," John Esposito comments, ". . . often found the two communities in competition, and locked at times in deadly combat, for power, land, and souls."[2] Across the centuries the fortunes of the two religions have risen and fallen in a sequence of momentous surges, pauses, and countersurges.

The initial Arab-Islamic sweep outward from the early seventh to the mid-eighth century established Muslim rule in North Africa, Iberia, the Middle East, Persia, and northern India. For two centuries or so the lines of division between Islam and Christianity stabilized. Then in the late eleventh century, Christians reasserted control of the western Mediterranean, conquered Sicily, and captured Toledo. In 1095 Christendom launched the Crusades and for a century and a half Christian potentates attempted, with decreasing success, to establish Christian rule in the Holy Land and adjoining areas in the Near East, losing Acre, their last foothold there, in 1291. Meanwhile the Ottoman Turks had appeared on the scene. They first weakened Byzantium and then conquered much of the Balkans as well as North Africa, captured Constantinople in 1453, and besieged Vienna in 1529. "For almost a thousand years," Bernard Lewis observes, "from the first Moorish landing in Spain to the second Turkish siege of Vienna, Europe was under constant threat from Islam."[3] Islam is the only civilization which has put the survival of the West in doubt, and it has done that at least twice.

By the fifteenth century, however, the tide had begun to turn. The Christians gradually recovered Iberia, completing the task at Granada in 1492. Meanwhile European innovations in ocean navigation enabled the Portuguese and then others to circumvent the Muslim heartland and penetrate into the Indian Ocean and beyond. Simultaneously the Russians brought to an end two centuries of Tatar rule. The Ottomans subsequently made one last push forward, besieging Vienna again in 1683. Their failure there marked the beginning of a long retreat, involving the struggle of Orthodox peoples in the Balkans to free themselves from Ottoman rule, the expansion of the Hapsburg Empire, and the dramatic advance of the Russians to the Black Sea and the Caucasus. In the course of a century or so "the scourge of Christendom" was transformed into "the sick man of Europe."[4] At the conclusion of World War I, Britain, France, and Italy administered the coup de grace and established their direct or indirect rule throughout the remaining Ottoman lands except for the territory of the Turkish Republic. By 1920 only four Muslim countries — Turkey, Saudi Arabia, Iran, and Afghanistan — remained independent of some form of non-Muslim rule.

The retreat of Western colonialism, in turn, began slowly in the 1920s and 1930s and accelerated dramatically in the aftermath of World War II. The collapse of the Soviet Union brought independence to additional Muslim societies. According to one count, some ninety-two acquisitions of Muslim territory by non-Muslim governments occurred between 1757 and 1919. By 1995, sixty-nine of these territories were once again under Muslim rule, and about forty-five independent states had overwhelmingly Muslim populations. The violent nature of these shifting relationships is reflected in the fact that 50 percent of wars involving pairs of states of different religions between 1820 and 1929 were wars between Muslims and Christians.[5]

The causes of this ongoing pattern of conflict lie not in transitory phenomena such as twelfth-century Christian passion or twentieth-century Muslim fundamentalism. They flow from the nature of the two religions and the civilizations based on them. Conflict was, on the one hand, a product of difference, particularly the Muslim concept of Islam as a way of life transcending and uniting religion and politics versus the Western Christian concept of the separate realms of God and Caesar. The conflict also stemmed, however, from their similarities. Both are monotheistic religions, which, unlike polytheistic ones, cannot easily assimilate additional deities, and which see the world in dualistic, us-and-them terms. Both are universalistic, claiming to be the one true faith to which all humans can adhere. Both are missionary religions believing that their adherents have an obligation to convert nonbelievers to that one true faith. From its origins Islam expanded by conquest and when the opportunity existed Christianity did also. The parallel concepts of "jihad" and "crusade" not only resemble each other but distinguish these two faiths from other major world religions. Islam and Christianity, along with Judaism, also have teleological views of history in contrast to the cyclical or static views prevalent in other civilizations.

The level of violent conflict between Islam and Christianity over time has been influenced by demographic growth and decline, economic developments, technological change, and intensity of religious commitment. The spread of Islam in the seventh century was accompanied by massive migrations of Arab peoples, "the scale and speed" of which were unprecedented, into the lands of the Byzantine and Sassanian empires. A few centuries later, the Crusades were in large part a product of economic growth, population expansion, and the "Clunaic revival" in eleventh-century Europe, which made it possible to mobilize large numbers of knights and peasants for the march to the Holy Land. When the First Crusade reached Constantinople, one Byzantine observer wrote, it seemed like "the entire West, including all the tribes of the barbarians living beyond the Adriatic Sea to the Pillars of Hercules, had started a mass migration and was on the march, bursting forth into Asia in a solid mass, with all its belongings."[6] In the nineteenth century spectacular population growth again produced a European eruption, generating the largest migration in history, which flowed into Muslim as well as other lands.

A comparable mix of factors has increased the conflict between Islam and the West in the late twentieth century. First, Muslim population growth has generated large numbers of unemployed and disaffected young people who become recruits to Islamist causes, exert pressure on neighboring societies, and migrate to the West. Second, the Islamic Resurgence has given Muslims renewed confidence in the distinctive character and worth of their civilization and values compared to those of the West. Third, the West's simultaneous efforts to universalize its values and institutions, to maintain its military and economic superiority, and to intervene in conflicts in the Muslim world generate intense resentment among Muslims. Fourth, the collapse of communism removed a common enemy of the West and Islam and left each the perceived major threat to the other. Fifth, the increasing contact between and intermingling of Muslims and Westerners stimulate in each a new sense of their own identity and how it differs from that of the other. Interaction and intermingling also exacerbate differences over the rights of the members of one civilization in a country dominated by members of the other civilization. Within both Muslim and Christian societies, tolerance for the other declined sharply in the 1980s and 1990s.

The causes of the renewed conflict between Islam and the West thus lie in fundamental questions of power and culture. *Kto? Kovo?* Who is to rule? Who is to be ruled? The central issue of politics defined by Lenin is the root of the contest between Islam and the West. There is, however, the additional conflict, which Lenin would have considered meaningless, between two different versions of what is right and what is wrong and, as a consequence, who is right and who is wrong. So long as Islam remains Islam (which it will) and the West remains the West (which is more dubious), this fundamental conflict between two great civilizations and ways of life will continue to define their relations in the future even as it has defined them for the past fourteen centuries.

These relations are further roiled by a number of substantive issues on which their positions differ or conflict. Historically one major issue was the control of territory, but that is now relatively insignificant. Nineteen of twenty-eight fault line conflicts in the mid-1990s between Muslims and non-Muslims were between Muslims and Christians. Eleven were with Orthodox Christians and seven with adherents of Western Christianity in Africa and Southeast Asia. Only one of these violent or potentially violent conflicts, that between Croats and Bosnians, occurred directly along the fault line between the West and Islam. The effective end of Western territorial imperialism and the absence so far of renewed Muslim territorial expansion have produced a geographical segregation so that only in a few places in the Balkans do Western and Muslim communities directly border on each other. Conflicts between the West and Islam thus focus less on territory than on broader intercivilizational issues such as weapons proliferation, human rights and democracy, control of oil, migration, Islamist terrorism, and Western intervention.

In the wake of the Cold War, the increasing intensity of this historical antagonism has been widely recognized by members of both communities. In 1991, for instance, Barry Buzan saw many reasons why a societal cold war was emerging "between the West and Islam, in which Europe would be on the front line."

This development is partly to do with secular versus religious values, partly to do with the historical rivalry between Christendom and Islam, partly to do with jealousy of Western power, partly to do with resentments over Western domination of the postcolonial political structuring of the Middle East, and partly to do with the bitterness and humiliation of the invidious comparison between the accomplishments of Islamic and Western civilizations in the last two centuries.

In addition, he noted a "societal Cold War with Islam would serve to strengthen the European identity all round at a crucial time for the process of European union." Hence, "there may well be a substantial community in the West prepared not only to support a societal Cold War with Islam, but to adopt policies that encourage it." In 1990 Bernard Lewis, a leading Western scholar of Islam, analyzed "The Roots of Muslim Rage," and concluded:

> It should now be clear that we are facing a mood and a movement far transcending the level of issues and policies and the governments that pursue them. This is no less than a clash of civilizations — that perhaps irrational but surely historic reaction of an ancient rival against our Judeo-Christian heritage, our secular present, and the worldwide expansion of both. It is crucially important that we on our side should not be provoked into an equally historic but also equally irrational reaction against that rival.[7]

Similar observations came from the Islamic community. "There are unmistakable signs," argued a leading Egyptian journalist, Mohammed Sid-Ahmed, in 1994, "of a growing clash between the Judeo-Christian Western ethic and the Islamic revival movement, which is now stretching from the Atlantic in the west to China in the east." A prominent Indian Muslim predicted in 1992 that the West's "next confrontation is definitely going to come from the Muslim world. It is in the sweep of the Islamic nations from the Maghreb to Pakistan that the struggle for a new world order will begin." For a leading Tunisian lawyer, the struggle was already underway: "Colonialism tried to deform all the cultural traditions of Islam. I am not an Islamist. I don't think there is a conflict between religions. There is a conflict between civilizations."[8]

In the 1980s and 1990s the overall trend in Islam has been in an anti-Western direction. In part, this is the natural consequence of the Islamic Resurgence and the reaction against the perceived *"gharbzadegi"* or Westoxication of Muslim societies. The "reaffirmation of Islam, whatever its specific sectarian form, means the repudiation of European and American influence upon local society, politics, and morals."[9] On occasion in the past, Muslim leaders did tell their people: "We must Westernize." If any Muslim leader has said that in the last quarter of the twentieth century, however, he is a lonely figure. Indeed, it is hard to find statements by any Muslims, whether politicians, officials, academics, businesspersons, or journalists, praising Western values and institutions. They instead stress the differences between their civilization and Western civilization, the superiority of their culture, and the need to maintain the integrity of that culture against Western onslaught. Muslims fear and resent Western power and the threat which this poses to their society and beliefs. They see Western culture as materialistic, corrupt, decadent, and immoral. They also see it as seductive, and hence stress all the more the need to resist its impact on their way of life. Increasingly, Muslims attack the West not for adhering to an imperfect, erroneous religion, which is nonetheless a "religion of the book," but for not adhering to any religion at all. In Muslim eyes Western secularism, irreligiosity, and hence immorality are worse evils than the Western Christianity that produced them. In the Cold War the West labeled its opponent "godless communism"; in the post–Cold War conflict of civilizations Muslims see their opponent as "the godless West."

These images of the West as arrogant, materialistic, repressive, brutal, and decadent are held not only by fundamentalist imams but also by those whom many in the West would consider their natural allies and supporters. Few books by Muslim authors published in the 1990s in the West received the praise given to Fatima Mernissi's *Islam and Democracy*, generally hailed by Westerners as the courageous statement of a modern, liberal, female Muslim.[10] The portrayal of the West in that volume, however, could hardly be less flattering. The West is "militaristic" and "imperialistic" and has "traumatized" other nations through "colonial terror" (pp. 3, 9). Individualism, the hallmark of Western culture, is "the source of all trouble" (p. 8). Western power is fearful. The West "alone decides if satellites will be used to educate Arabs or to drop bombs on them. . . . It crushes our potentialities and invades our lives with its imported products and televised movies that swamp the airwaves. . . . [It] is a power that crushes us, besieges our markets, and controls our merest resources, initiatives, and potentialities. That was how we perceived our situation, and the Gulf War turned our perception into certitude" (pp. 146–47). The West "creates its power through military research" and then sells the products of that research to underdeveloped countries who are its "passive consumers." To liberate themselves from this subservience, Islam must develop its own engineers and scientists, build its own weapons (whether nuclear or conventional, she does not specify), and "free itself from military dependence on the West" (pp. 43–44). These, to repeat, are not the views of a bearded, hooded ayatollah.

Whatever their political or religious opinions, Muslims agree that basic differences exist between their culture and Western culture. "The bottom line," as Sheik Ghanoushi put it, "is that our societies are based on values other than those of the West." Americans "come here," an Egyptian government official said, "and want us to be like them. They understand nothing of our values or our culture." "[W]e are different," an Egyptian journalist agreed. "We have a different background, a different history. Accordingly we have the right to different futures." Both popular and intellectually serious Muslim publications repeatedly describe what are alleged to be Western plots and designs to subordinate, humiliate, and undermine Islamic institutions and culture.[11]

The reaction against the West can be seen not only in the central intellectual thrust of the Islamic Resurgence but also in the shift in the attitudes toward the West of governments in Muslim countries. The immediate postcolonial governments were generally Western in their political and economic ideologies and policies and pro-Western in their foreign policies, with partial exceptions, like Algeria and Indonesia, where independence resulted from a nationalist revolution. One by one, however, pro-Western governments gave way to governments less identified with the West or explicitly anti-Western in Iraq, Libya, Yemen, Syria, Iran, Sudan, Lebanon, and Afghanistan. Less dramatic changes in the same direction occurred in the orientation and alignment of other states including Tunisia, Indonesia, and Malaysia. The two staunchest Cold War Muslim military allies of the United States, Turkey and Pakistan, are under Islamist political pressure internally and their ties with the West subject to increased strain.

In 1995 the only Muslim state which was clearly more pro-Western than it had been ten years previously was Kuwait. The West's close friends in the Muslim world are now either like Kuwait, Saudi Arabia, and the Gulf sheikdoms dependent on the West militarily or like Egypt and Algeria dependent on it economically. In the late 1980s the communist regimes of Eastern Europe collapsed when it became apparent that the Soviet Union no longer could or would provide them with economic and military support. If it became apparent that the West would no longer maintain its Muslim satellite regimes, they are likely to suffer a comparable fate.

Growing Muslim anti-Westernism has been paralleled by expanding Western concern with the "Islamic threat" posed particularly by Muslim extremism. Islam is seen as a source of nuclear proliferation, terrorism, and, in Europe, unwanted migrants. These concerns are shared by both publics and leaders. Asked in November 1994 whether the "Islamic revival" was a threat to U.S. interests in the Middle East, for instance, 61 percent of a sample of 35,000 Americans interested in foreign policy said yes and only 28 percent no. A year earlier, when asked what country posed the greatest danger to the United States, a random sample of the public picked Iran, China, and Iraq as the top three. Similarly, asked in 1994 to identify "critical threats" to the United States, 72 percent of the public and 61 percent of foreign policy leaders said nuclear proliferation and 69 percent of the public and 33 percent of leaders international terrorism — two issues widely associated with Islam. In addition, 33 percent of the public and 39 percent of the leaders saw a threat in the possible expansion of Islamic fundamentalism. Europeans have similar attitudes. In the spring of 1991, for instance, 51 percent of the French public said the principal threat to France was from the South with only 8 percent saying it would come from the East. The four countries which the French public most feared were all Muslim: Iraq, 52 percent; Iran, 35 percent; Libya, 26 percent; and Algeria, 22 percent.[12] Western political leaders, including the German chancellor and the French prime minister, expressed similar concerns, with the secretary general of NATO declaring in 1995 that Islamic fundamentalism was "at least as dangerous as communism" had been to the West, and a "very senior member" of the Clinton administration pointing to Islam as the global rival of the West.[13]

With the virtual disappearance of a military threat from the east, NATO's planning is increasingly directed toward potential threats from the south. "The Southern Tier," one U.S. Army analyst observed in 1992, is replacing the Central Front and "is rapidly becoming NATO's new front line." To meet these southern threats, NATO's southern members — Italy, France, Spain, and

Portugal — began joint military planning and operations and at the same time enlisted the Maghreb governments in consultations on ways of countering Islamist extremists. These perceived threats also provided a rational for continuing a substantial U.S. military presence in Europe. "While U.S. forces in Europe are not a panacea for the problems created by fundamentalist Islam," one former senior U.S. official observed, "those forces do cast a powerful shadow on military planning throughout the area. Remember the successful deployment of U.S., French and British forces from Europe in the Gulf War of 1990–1991? Those in the region do."[14] And, he might have added, they remember it with fear, resentment, and hate.

Given the prevailing perceptions Muslims and Westerners have of each other plus the rise of Islamist extremism, it is hardly surprising that following the 1979 Iranian Revolution, an intercivilizational quasi war developed between Islam and the West. It is a quasi war for three reasons. First, all of Islam has not been fighting all of the West. Two fundamentalist states (Iran, Sudan), three nonfundamentalist states (Iraq, Libya, Syria), plus a wide range of Islamist organizations, with financial support from other Muslim countries such as Saudi Arabia, have been fighting the United States and, at times, Britain, France, and other Western states and groups, as well as Israel and Jews generally. Second, it is a quasi war because, apart from the Gulf War of 1990–1991, it has been fought with limited means: terrorism on one side and air power, covert action, and economic sanctions on the other. Third, it is a quasi war because while the violence has been continuing, it has also not been continuous. It has involved intermittent actions by one side which provoke responses by the other. Yet a quasi war is still a war. Even excluding the tens of thousands of Iraqi soldiers and civilians killed by Western bombing in January-February 1991, the deaths and other casualties number well into the thousands, and they occurred in virtually every year after 1979. Many more Westerners have been killed in this quasi war than were killed in the "real" war in the Gulf.

Both sides have, moreover, recognized this conflict to be a war. Early on, Khomeini declared, quite accurately, that "Iran is effectively at war with America,"[15] and Qadhafi regularly proclaims holy war against the West. Muslim leaders of other extremist groups and states have spoken in similar terms. On the Western side, the United States has classified seven countries as "terrorist states," five of which are Muslim (Iran, Iraq, Syria, Libya, Sudan); Cuba and North Korea are the others. This, in effect, identifies them as enemies, because they are attacking the United States and its friends with the most effective weapon at their disposal, and thus recognizes the existence of a state of war with them. U.S. officials repeatedly refer to these states as "outlaw," "backlash," and "rogue" states — thereby placing them outside the civilized international order and making them legitimate targets for multilateral or unilateral countermeasures. The United States Government charged the World Trade Center bombers with intending "to levy a war of urban terrorism against the United

States" and argued that conspirators charged with planning further bombings in Manhattan were "soldiers" in a struggle "involving a war" against the United States. If Muslims allege that the West wars on Islam and if Westerners allege that Islamic groups war on the West, it seems reasonable to conclude that something very much like a war is underway.

In this quasi war, each side has capitalized on its own strengths and the other side's weaknesses. Militarily it has been largely a war of terrorism versus air power. Dedicated Islamic militants exploit the open societies of the West and plant car bombs at selected targets. Western military professionals exploit the open skies of Islam and drop smart bombs on selected targets. The Islamic participants plot the assassination of prominent Westerners; the United States plots the overthrow of extremist Islamic regimes. During the fifteen years between 1980 and 1995, according to the U.S. Defense Department, the United States engaged in seventeen military operations in the Middle East, all of them directed against Muslims. No comparable pattern of U.S. military operations occurred against the people of any other civilization.

To date, each side has, apart from the Gulf War, kept the intensity of the violence at reasonably low levels and refrained from labeling violent acts as acts of war requiring an all-out response. "If Libya ordered one of its submarines to sink an American liner," *The Economist* observed, "the United States would treat it as an act of war by a government, not seek the extradition of the submarine commander. In principle, the bombing of an airliner by Libya's secret service is no different." [16] Yet the participants in this war employ much more violent tactics against each other than the United States and Soviet Union directly employed against each other in the Cold War. With rare exceptions neither superpower purposefully killed civilians or even military belonging to the other. This, however, repeatedly happens in the quasi war.

American leaders allege that the Muslims involved in the quasi war are a small minority whose use of violence is rejected by the great majority of moderate Muslims. This may be true, but evidence to support it is lacking. Protests against anti-Western violence have been totally absent in Muslim countries. Muslim governments, even the bunker governments friendly to and dependent on the West, have been strikingly reticent when it comes to condemning terrorist acts against the West. On the other side, European governments and publics have largely supported and rarely criticized actions the United States has taken against its Muslim opponents, in striking contrast to the strenuous opposition they often expressed to American actions against the Soviet Union and communism during the Cold War. In civilizational conflicts, unlike ideological ones, kin stand by their kin.

The underlying problem for the West is not Islamic fundamentalism. It is Islam, a different civilization whose people are convinced of the superiority of their culture and are obsessed with the inferiority of their power. The problem for Islam is not the CIA or the U.S. Department of Defense. It is the West, a different civilization whose people are convinced of the universality of their culture and believe that their superior, if declining, power imposes on them the obligation to extend that culture throughout the world. These are the basic ingredients that fuel conflict between Islam and the West.

ASIA, CHINA, AND AMERICA

The Cauldron of Civilizations. The economic changes in Asia, particularly East Asia, are one of the most significant developments in the world in the second half of the twentieth century. By the 1990s this economic development had generated economic euphoria among many observers who saw East Asia and the entire Pacific Rim linked together in ever-expanding commercial networks that would insure peace and harmony among nations. This optimism was based on the highly dubious assumption that commercial interchange is invariably a force for peace. Such, however, is not the case. Economic growth creates political instability within countries and between countries, altering the balance of power among countries and regions. Economic exchange brings people into contact; it does not bring them into agreement. Historically it has often produced a deeper awareness of the differences between peoples and stimulated mutual fears. Trade between countries produces conflict as well as profit. If past experience holds, the Asia of economic sunshine will generate an Asia of political shadows, an Asia of instability and conflict.

The economic development of Asia and the growing self-confidence of Asian societies are disrupting international politics in at least three ways. First, economic development enables Asian states to expand their military capabilities, promotes uncertainty as to the future relationships among these countries, and brings to the fore issues and rivalries that had been suppressed during the Cold War, thus enhancing the probability of conflict and instability in the region. Second, economic development increases the intensity of conflicts between Asian societies and the West, primarily the United States, and strengthens the ability of Asian societies to prevail in those struggles. Third, the economic growth of Asia's largest power increases Chinese influence in the region and the likelihood of China reasserting its traditional hegemony in East Asia, thereby compelling other nations either to "bandwagon" and to accommodate themselves to this development or to "balance" and to attempt to contain Chinese influence.

During the several centuries of Western ascendancy the international relations that counted were a Western game played out among the major Western powers, supplemented in some degree first by Russia in the eighteenth century and then by Japan in the twentieth century. Europe was the principal arena of great power conflict and cooperation, and even during the Cold War the principal line of superpower confrontation was in the heart of Europe. Insofar as the international relations that count in the post–Cold War world have a primary turf, that turf is Asia and particularly East Asia. Asia is the cauldron of civilizations. East Asia alone contains societies belonging to six civilizations — Japanese, Sinic, Orthodox, Buddhist, Muslim, and Western — and South Asia adds Hinduism. The core states of four civilizations, Japan, China, Russia, and the United States, are major actors in East Asia; South Asia adds India; and Indonesia is a rising Muslim power. In addition, East Asia contains several middle-level powers with increasing economic clout, such as South Korea, Taiwan, and Malaysia, plus a potentially strong Vietnam. The result is a highly complex pattern of international relationships, comparable in many ways to those which existed in the eighteenth and nineteenth centuries in Europe, and fraught with all the fluidity and uncertainty that characterize multipolar situations.

The multipower, multicivilizational nature of East Asia distinguishes it from Western Europe, and economic and political differences reinforce this contrast. All the countries of Western Europe are stable democracies, have market econ- omies, and are at high levels of economic development. In the mid-1990s East Asia includes one stable democracy, several new and unstable democracies, four of the five communist dictatorships remaining in the world, plus military governments, personal dictatorships, and one-party-dominant authoritarian sys- tems. Levels of economic development varied from those of Japan and Singa- pore to those of Vietnam and North Korea. A general trend exists toward marketization and economic opening, but economic systems still run the gamut from the command economy of North Korea through various mixes of state control and private enterprise to the laissez-faire economy of Hong Kong.

Apart from the extent to which Chinese hegemony at times brought occa- sional order to the region, an international society (in the British sense of the term) has not existed in East Asia as it has in Western Europe.[17] In the late twentieth century Europe has been bound together by an extraordinarily dense complex of international institutions: the European Union, NATO, Western European Union, Council of Europe, Organization for Security and Coopera- tion in Europe, and others. East Asia has had nothing comparable except ASEAN, which does not include any major powers, has generally eschewed security matters, and is only beginning to move toward the most primitive forms of economic integration. In the 1990s the much broader organization, APEC, incorporating most of the Pacific Rim countries came into existence but it was an even weaker talking shop than ASEAN. No other major multilateral institutions bring together the principal Asian powers.

Again in contrast to Western Europe, the seeds for conflict among states are plentiful in East Asia. Two widely identified danger spots have involved the two Koreas and the two Chinas. These are, however, leftovers from the Cold War. Ideological differences are of declining significance and by 1995 relations had expanded significantly between the two Chinas and had begun to develop between the two Koreas. The probability of Koreans fighting Koreans exists but is low; the prospects of Chinese fighting Chinese are higher, but still limited, unless the Taiwanese should renounce their Chinese identity and formally constitute an independent Republic of Taiwan. As a Chinese military document approvingly quoted one general saying, "there should be limits to fights among family members."[18] While violence between the two Koreas or the two Chinas remains possible, cultural commonalities are likely to erode that possibility over time.

In East Asia conflicts inherited from the Cold War are being supplemented and supplanted by other possible conflicts reflecting old rivalries and new economic relationships. Analyses of East Asian security in the early 1990s regularly referred to East Asia as "a dangerous neighborhood," as "ripe for rivalry," as a region of "several cold wars," as "heading back to the future" in which war and instability would prevail.[19] In contrast to Western Europe, East Asia in the 1990s has unresolved territorial disputes, the most important of which include those between Russia and Japan over the northern islands and between China, Vietnam, the Philippines, and potentially other Southeast Asian states over the South China Sea. The differences over boundaries between China, on the one hand, and Russia and India, on the other, were reduced in the mid-1990s but could resurface, as could Chinese claims to Mongolia. Insurgencies or secessionist movements, in most cases supported from abroad, exist in Mindanao, East Timor, Tibet, southern Thailand, and eastern Myanmar. In addition, while interstate peace exists in East Asia in the mid-1990s, during the previous fifty years major wars have occurred in Korea and Vietnam, and the central power in Asia, China, has fought Americans plus almost all its neighbors including Koreans, Vietnamese, Nationalist Chinese, Indians, Tibetans, and Russians. In 1993 an analysis by the Chinese military identified eight regional hot spots that threatened China's military security, and the Chinese Central Military Commission concluded that generally the East Asian security outlook was "very grim." After centuries of strife, Western Europe is peaceful and war is unthinkable. In East Asia it is not, and, as Aaron Friedberg has suggested, Europe's past could be Asia's future.[20]

Economic dynamism, territorial disputes, resurrected rivalries, and political uncertainties fueled significant increases in East Asian military budgets and military capabilities in the 1980s and 1990s. Exploiting their new wealth and, in many cases, well-educated populations, East Asian governments have moved to replace large, poorly equipped, "peasant" armies with smaller, more professional, technologically sophisticated military forces. With doubt increasing concerning the extent of American commitment in East Asia, countries aim to become militarily self-reliant. While East Asian states continued to import substantial amounts of weapons from Europe, the United States, and the former Soviet Union, they gave preference to the import of technology which would enable them to produce at home sophisticated aircraft, missiles, and electronics equipment. Japan and the Sinic states — China, Taiwan, Singapore, and South Korea — have increasingly sophisticated arms industries. Given the littoral geography of East Asia, their emphasis has been on force projection and air and naval capabilities. As a result, nations that previously were not militarily capable of fighting each other are increasingly able to do so. These military buildups have involved little transparency and hence have fostered more suspicion and uncertainty.[21] In a situation of changing power relationships, every government necessarily and legitimately wonders: "Ten years from now who will be my enemy and who, if anyone, will be my friend?"

Asian-American Cold Wars. In the late 1980s and early 1990s relationships between the United States and Asian countries, apart from Vietnam, increasingly became antagonistic, and the ability of the United States to prevail in these controversies declined. These tendencies were particularly marked with respect to the major powers in East Asia, and American relations with China and Japan evolved along parallel paths. Americans, on the one hand, and Chinese and Japanese on the other, spoke of cold wars developing between their countries.[22] These simultaneous trends began in the Bush administration and accelerated in the Clinton administration. By the mid-1990s American relations with the two major Asian powers could at best be described as "strained" and there seemed to be little prospect for them to become less so.*

In the early 1990s Japanese-American relations became increasingly heated with controversies over a wide range of issues, including Japan's role in the Gulf War, the American military presence in Japan, Japanese attitudes toward American human rights policies with respect to China and other countries, Japanese participation in peacekeeping missions, and, most important, economic relations, especially trade. References to trade wars became commonplace.[23] American officials, particularly in the Clinton administration, demanded more and more concessions from Japan; Japanese officials resisted these demands more and more forcefully. Each Japanese-American trade con-

---

* It should be noted that, at least in the United States, terminological confusion exists with respect to relations between countries. "Good" relations are thought to be friendly, cooperative relations; "bad" relations are hostile, antagonistic relations. This usage conflates two very different dimensions: friendliness vs. hostility and desirability vs. undesirability. It reflects the peculiarly American assumption that harmony in international relations is always good and conflict always bad. The identification of good relations with friendly relations, however, is valid only if conflict is never desirable. Most Americans think it was "good" that the Bush administration made U.S. relations with Iraq "bad" by going to war over Kuwait. To avoid the confusion over whether "good" means desirable or harmonious and "bad" undesirable or hostile, I will use "good" and "bad" only to mean desirable and undesirable. Interestingly if perplexingly, Americans endorse competition in American society between opinions, groups, parties, branches of government, businesses. Why Americans believe that conflict is good within their own society and yet bad between societies is a fascinating question which, to the best of my knowledge, no one has seriously studied.

troversy was more acrimonious and more difficult to resolve than the previous one. In March 1994, for instance, President Clinton signed an order giving him authority to apply stricter trade sanctions on Japan, which brought protests not only from the Japanese but also from the head of GATT, the principal world trading organization. A short while later Japan responded with a "blistering attack" on U.S. policies, and shortly after that the United States "formally accused Japan" of discriminating against U.S. companies in awarding government contracts. In the spring of 1995 the Clinton administration threatened to impose 100 percent tariffs on Japanesse luxury cars, with an agreement averting this being reached just before the sanctions would have gone into effect. Something closely resembling a trade war was clearly underway between the two countries. By the mid-1990s the acrimony had reached the point where leading Japanese political figures began to question the U.S. military presence in Japan.

During these years the public in each country became steadily less favorably disposed toward the other country. In 1985, 87 percent of the American public said they had a generally friendly attitude toward Japan. By 1990 this had dropped to 67 percent, and by 1993 a bare 50 percent of Americans felt favorably disposed toward Japan and almost two-thirds said they tried to avoid buying Japanese products. In 1985, 73 percent of Japanese described U.S.-Japanese relations as friendly; by 1993, 64 percent said they were unfriendly. The year 1991 marked the crucial turning point in the shift of public opinion out of its Cold War mold. In that year each country displaced the Soviet Union in the perceptions of the other. For the first time Americans rated Japan ahead of the Soviet Union as a threat to American security, and for the first time Japanese rated the United States ahead of the Soviet Union as a threat to Japan's security.[24]

Changes in public attitudes were matched by changes in elite perceptions. In the United States a significant group of academic, intellectual, and political revisionists emerged who emphasized the cultural and structural differences between the two countries and the need for the United States to take a much tougher line in dealing with Japan on economic issues. The images of Japan in the media, nonfiction publications, and popular novels became increasingly derogatory. In parallel fashion in Japan a new generation of political leaders appeared who had not experienced American power in and benevolence after World War II, who took great pride in Japanese economic successes, and who were quite willing to resist American demands in ways their elders had not been. These Japanese "resisters" were the counterpart to the American "revisionists," and in both countries candidates found that advocating a tough line on issues affecting Japanese-American relations went over well with the voters.

During the late 1980s and early 1990s American relations with China also became increasingly antagonistic. The conflicts between the two countries, Deng Xiaoping said in September 1991, constituted "a new cold war," a phrase regularly repeated in the Chinese press. In August 1995 the government's press agency declared that "Sino-American relationships are at the lowest ebb since the two countries established diplomatic relations" in 1979. Chinese officials regularly denounced alleged interference in Chinese affairs. "We should point out," a 1992 Chinese government internal document argued, "that since becoming the sole superpower, the United States has been grasping wildly for a new hegemonism and power politics, and also that its strength is in relative decline and that there are limits to what it can do." "Western hostile forces," President Jiang Zemin said in August 1995, "have not for a moment abandoned their plot to Westernize and 'divide' our country." By 1995 a broad consensus reportedly existed among the Chinese leaders and scholars that the United States was trying to "divide China territorially, subvert it politically, contain it strategically and frustrate it economically." [25]

Evidence existed for all these charges. The United States allowed President Lee of Taiwan to come to the United States, sold 150 F-16s to Taiwan, designated Tibet an "occupied soverign territory," denounced China for its human rights abuses, denied Beijing the 2000 Olympics, normalized relations with Vietnam, accused China of exporting chemical weapons components to Iran, imposed trade sanctions on China for sales of missile equipment to Pakistan, and threatened China with additional sanctions over economic issues while at the same time barring China's admission to the World Trade Organization. Each side accused the other of bad faith: China, according to Americans, violated understandings on missile exports, intellectual property rights, and prison labor; the United States, according to the Chinese, violated agreements in letting President Lee come to the United States and selling advanced fighter aircraft to Taiwan.

The most important group in China with an antagonistic view toward the United States was the military, who, apparently, regularly pressured the government to take a tougher line with the United States. In June 1993, 100 Chinese generals reportedly sent a letter to Deng complaining of the government's "passive" policy toward the United States and its failure to resist U.S. efforts to "blackmail" China. In the fall of that year a confidential Chinese government document outlined the military's reasons for conflict with the United States: "Because China and the United States have longstanding conflicts over their different ideologies, social systems, and foreign policies, it will prove impossible to fundamentally improve Sino-U.S. relations." Since Americans believe that East Asia will become "the heart of the world economy . . . the United States cannot tolerate a powerful adversary in East Asia." [26] By the mid-1990s Chinese officials and agencies routinely portrayed the United States as a hostile power.

The growing antagonism between China and the United States was in part driven by domestic politics in both countries. As was the case with Japan, informed American opinion was divided. Many Establishment figures argued for constructive engagement with China, expanding economic relations, and drawing China into the so-called community of nations. Others emphasized the potential Chinese threat to American interests, argued that conciliatory moves toward China produced negative results, and urged a policy of firm containment. In 1993 the American public ranked China second only to Iran as the country that posed the greatest danger to the United States. American politics often operated so as to produce symbolic gestures, such as Lee's visit to Cornell and Clinton's meeting with the Dalai Lama, that outraged the Chinese, while at the same time leading the administration to sacrifice human rights considerations for economic interests, as in the extension of MFN treatment. On the Chinese side, the government needed a new enemy to bolster its appeals to Chinese nationalism and to legitimize its power. As the succession struggle lengthened, the political influence of the military rose, and President Jiang and other contestants for post-Deng power could not afford to be lax in promoting Chinese interests.

In the course of a decade American relations thus "deteriorated" with both Japan and China. This shift in Asian-American relations was so broad and encompassed so many different issue areas that it seems unlikely that its causes can be found in individual conflicts of interest over auto parts, camera sales, or military bases, on the one hand, or dissident jailings, weapons transfers, or intellectual piracy, on the other. In addition, it was clearly against American national interest to allow its relations simultaneously to become more conflictual with both major Asian powers. The elementary rules of diplomacy and power politics dictate that the United States should attempt to play one off against the other or at least to sweeten relations with one if they were becoming more conflictual with the other. Yet this did not happen. Broader factors were at work promoting conflict in Asian-American relations and making it more difficult to resolve the individual issues that came up in those relations. This general phenomenon had general causes.

First, increased interaction between Asian societies and the United States in the form of expanded communications, trade, investment, and knowledge of each other multiplied the issues and subjects where interests could, and did, clash. This increased interaction made threatening to each society practices and beliefs of the other which at a distance had seemed harmlessly exotic. Second, the Soviet threat in the 1950s led to the U.S.-Japan mutual security treaty. The growth of Soviet power in the 1970s led to the establishment of diplomatic relations between the United States and China in 1979 and ad hoc cooperation between the two countries to promote their common interest in neutralizing that threat. The end of the Cold War removed this overriding common interest of the United States and the Asian powers and left nothing in its place. Consequently, other issues where significant conflicts of interest existed came to the fore. Third, the economic development of the East Asian countries shifted the overall balance of power between them and the United States. Asians, as we have seen, increasingly affirmed the validity of their values and institutions and the superiority of their culture to Western culture. Americans, on the other hand, tended to assume, particularly after their Cold War victory, that their values and institutions were universally relevant and that they still had the power to shape the foreign and domestic policies of Asian societies.

This changing international environment brought to the fore the fundamental cultural differences between Asian and American civilizations. At the broadest level the Confucian ethos pervading many Asian societies stressed the values of authority, hierarchy, the subordination of individual rights and interests, the importance of consensus, the avoidance of confrontation, "saving face," and, in general, the supremacy of the state over society and of society over the individual. In addition, Asians tended to think of the evolution of their societies in terms of centuries and millennia and to give priority to maximizing long-term gains. These attitudes contrasted with the primacy in American beliefs of liberty, equality, democracy, and individualism, and the American propensity to distrust government, oppose authority, promote checks and balances, encourage competition, sanctify human rights, and to forget the past, ignore the future, and focus on maximizing immediate gains. The sources of conflict are in fundamental differences in society and culture.

These differences had particular consequences for the relations between the United States and the major Asian societies. Diplomats made great efforts to resolve American conflicts with Japan over economic issues, particularly Japan's trade surplus and the resistance of Japan to American products and investment. Japanese-American trade negotiations took on many of the characteristics of Cold War Soviet-American arms control negotiations. As of 1995 the former had produced even fewer results than the latter because these conflicts stem from the fundamental differences in the two economies, and particularly the unique nature of the Japanese economy among those of the major industrialized countries. Japan's imports of manufactured goods have amounted to about 3.1 percent of its GNP compared to an average of 7.4 percent for the other major industrialized powers. Foreign direct investment in Japan has been a minuscule 0.7 percent of GDP compared to 28.6 percent for the United States and 38.5 percent for Europe. Alone among the big industrial countries, Japan ran budget surpluses in the early 1990s.[27]

Overall the Japanese economy has not operated in the way the supposedly universal laws of Western economics dictate. The easy assumption by Western economists in the 1980s that devaluing the dollar would reduce the Japanese trade surplus proved false. While the Plaza agreement of 1985 rectified the American trade deficit with Europe, it had little effect on the deficit with Japan. As the yen appreciated to less than one hundred to the dollar, the Japanese trade surplus remained high and even increased. The Japanese were thus able to sustain both a strong currency and a trade surplus. Western economic thinking tends to posit a negative trade-off between unemployment and inflation, with an unemployment rate significantly less than 5 percent thought to trigger inflationary pressures. Yet for years Japan had unemployment averaging less than 3 percent and inflation averaging 1.5 percent. By the 1990s both American and Japanese economists had come to recognize and to conceptualize the basic differences in these two economic systems. Japan's uniquely low level of manufactured imports, one careful study concluded, "cannot be explained through standard economic factors." "The Japanese economy does not follow Western logic," another analyst argued, "whatever Western forecasters say, for the simple reason that it is not a Western free-market economy. The Japanese . . . have invented a type of economics that behaves in ways that confound the predictive powers of Western observers." [28]

What explains the distinctive character of the Japanese economy? Among major industrialized countries, the Japanese economy is unique because Japanese society is uniquely non-Western. Japanese society and culture differ from Western, and particularly American, society and culture. These differences have been highlighted in every serious comparative analysis of Japan and America. [29] Resolution of the economic issues between Japan and the United States depends on fundamental changes in the nature of one or both economies, which, in turn, depend upon basic changes in the society and culture of one or both countries. Such changes are not impossible. Societies and cultures do change. This may result from a major traumatic event: total defeat in World War II made two of the world's most militaristic countries into two of its most pacifist ones. It seems unlikely, however, that either the United States or Japan will impose an economic Hiroshima on the other. Economic development also can change a country's social structure and culture profoundly, as occurred in Spain between the early 1950s and the late 1970s, and perhaps economic wealth will make Japan into a more American-like consumption-oriented society. In the late 1980s people in both Japan and America argued that their country should become more like the other country. In a limited way the Japanese-American agreement on Structural Impediment Initiatives was designed to promote this convergence. The failure of this and similar efforts testifies to the extent to which economic differences are deeply rooted in the cultures of the two societies.

While the conflicts between the United States and Asia had their sources in cultural differences, the outcomes of their conflicts reflected the changing power relations between the United States and Asia. The United States scored some victories in these disputes, but the trend was in an Asian direction, and the shift in power further exacerbated the conflicts. The United States expected the Asian governments to accept it as the leader of "the international community" and to acquiesce in the application of Western principles and values to their societies. The Asians, on the other hand, as Assistant Secretary of State Winston Lord said, were "increasingly conscious and proud of their accomplishments," expected to be treated as equals, and tended to regard the United States as "an international nanny, if not bully." Deep imperatives within American culture, however, impel the United States to be at least a nanny if not a bully in international affairs, and as a result American expectations were increasingly at odds with Asian ones. Across a wide range of issues, Japanese and other Asian leaders learned to say no to their American counterparts, expressed at times in polite Asian versions of "buzz off." The symbolic turning point in Asian-American relations was perhaps what one senior Japanese official termed the "first big train wreck" in U.S.-Japanese relations, which occurred in February 1994, when Prime Minister Morihiro Hosokawa firmly rejected President Clinton's demand for numerical targets for Japanese imports of American manufactured goods. "We could not have imagined something like this happening even a year ago," commented another Japanese official. A year later Japan's foreign minister underlined this change stating that in an era of economic competition among nations and regions, Japan's national interest was more important than its "mere identity" as a member of the West.[30]

Gradual American accommodation to the changed balance of power was reflected in American policy toward Asia in the 1990s. First, in effect conceding that it lacked the will and/or the ability to pressure Asian societies, the United States separated issue areas where it might have leverage from issue areas where it had conflicts. Although Clinton had proclaimed human rights a top priority of American foreign policy toward China, in 1994 he responded to pressure from U.S. businesses, Taiwan, and other sources, delinked human rights from economic issues, and abandoned the effort to use extension of most favored nation status as a means of influencing Chinese behavior toward its political dissidents. In a parallel move, the administration explicitly separated security policy toward Japan, where presumably it could exert leverage, from trade and other economic issues, where its relations with Japan were most conflictual. The United States thus surrendered weapons it could have used to promote human rights in China and trade concessions from Japan.

Second, the United States repeatedly pursued a course of anticipated reciprocity with the Asian nations, making concessions with the expectation they would induce comparable ones from the Asians. This course was often justified by reference to the need to maintain "constructive engagement" or "dialogue" with the Asian country. More times than not, however, the Asian country interpreted the concession as a sign of American weakness and hence that it could go still further in rejecting American demands. This pattern was particularly noticeable with respect to China, which responded to the U.S. delinkage of MFN status by a new and intensive round of human rights violations. Because of the American penchant to identify "good" relations with "friendly" relations, the United States is at a considerable disadvantage in competing with Asian societies who identify "good" relations with ones that produce victories for them. To the Asians, American concessions are not to be reciprocated, they are to be exploited.

Third, a pattern developed in the recurring U.S.-Japan conflicts over trade issues in which the United States would make demands on Japan and threaten sanctions if they were not met. Prolonged negotiations would ensue and then at the last moment before the sanctions were to go into effect, agreement would be announced. The agreements were generally so ambiguously phrased that the United States could claim a victory in principle, and the Japanese could implement or not implement the agreement as they wished and everything would go on as before. In similar fashion, the Chinese would reluctantly agree to statements of broad principles concerning human rights, intellectual property, or proliferation, only to interpret them very differently from the United States and continue with their previous policies.

These differences in culture and the shifting power balance between Asia and America encouraged Asian societies to support each other in their conflicts with the United States. In 1994, for instance, virtually all Asian countries "from Australia to Malaysia to South Korea," rallied behind Japan in its resistance to the U.S. demand for numerical targets for imports. A similar rallying simultaneously took place in favor of MFN treatment for China, with Japan's Prime Minister Hosokawa in the lead arguing that Western human rights concepts could not be "blindly applied" to Asia, and Singapore's Lee Kuan Yew warning that if it pressured China "the United States will find itself all alone in the Pacific." [31] In another show of solidarity, Asians, Africans, and others rallied behind the Japanese in backing reelection of the Japanese incumbent as head of the World Health Organization against the opposition of the West, and Japan promoted a South Korean to head the World Trade Organization against the American candidate, former president of Mexico Carlos Salinas. The record shows indisputably that by the 1990s on trans-Pacific issues each country in East Asia felt that it had much more in common with other East Asian countries than it had in common with the United States.

The end of the Cold War, the increasing interaction between Asia and America, and the relative decline in American power thus brought to the surface the clash of cultures between the United States and Japan and other Asian societies and enabled the latter to resist American pressure. The rise of China posed a more fundamental challenge to the United States. U.S. conflicts with China covered a much broader range of issues than those with Japan, including economic questions, human rights, Tibet, Taiwan, the South China Sea, and weapons proliferation. On almost no major policy issue did the United States and China share common objectives. The differences go across the board. As with Japan, these conflicts were in large part rooted in the different cultures of the two societies. The conflicts between the United States and China, however, also involved fundamental issues of power. China is unwilling to accept American leadership or hegemony in the world; the United States is unwilling to accept Chinese leadership or hegemony in Asia. For over two hundred years the United States has attempted to prevent the emergence of an overwhelmingly dominant power in Europe. For almost a hundred years, beginning with its "Open Door" policy toward China, it has attempted to do the same in East Asia. To achieve these goals it has fought two world wars and a cold war against Imperial Germany, Nazi Germany, Imperial Japan, the Soviet Union, and Communist China. This American interest remains and was reaffirmed by Presidents Reagan and Bush. The emergence of China as the dominant regional power in East Asia, if it continues, challenges that central American interest. The underlying cause of conflict between America and China is their basic difference over what should be the future balance of power in East Asia.

Chinese Hegemony: Balancing and Bandwagoning. With six civilizations, eighteen countries, rapidly growing economies, and major political, economic and social differences among its societies, East Asia could develop any one of several patterns of international relations in the early twenty-first century. Conceivably an extremely complex set of cooperative and conflictual relations could emerge involving most of the major and middle-level powers of the region. Or a major power, multipolar international system could take shape with China, Japan, the United States, Russia, and possibly India balancing and competing with each other. Alternatively, East Asian politics could be dominated by a sustained bipolar rivalry between China and Japan or between China and the United States, with other countries aligning themselves with one side or the other or opting for nonalignment. Or conceivably East Asian politics could return to its traditional unipolar pattern with a hierarchy of power centered on Beijing. If China sustains its high levels of economic growth into the twenty-first century, maintains its unity in the post-Deng era, and is not hamstrung by succession struggles, it is likely to attempt to realize the last of these outcomes. Whether it succeeds depends upon the reactions of the other players in the East Asian power politics game.

China's history, culture, traditions, size, economic dynamism, and self-image all impel it to assume a hegemonic position in East Asia. This goal is a natural result of its rapid economic development. Every other major power, Britain and France, Germany and Japan, the United States and the Soviet Union, has engaged in outward expansion, assertion, and imperialism coincidental with or immediately following the years in which it went through rapid industrialization and economic growth. No reason exists to think that the acquisition of economic and military power will not have comparable effects in China. For two thousand years China was the preeminent power in East Asia. Chinese now increasingly assert their intention to resume that historic role and to bring to an end the overlong century of humiliation and subordination to the West and Japan that began with British imposition of the Treaty of Nanking in 1842.

In the late 1980s China began converting its growing economic resources into military power and political influence. If its economic development continues, this conversion process will assume major proportions. According to official figures, during most of the 1980s Chinese military spending declined. Between 1988 and 1993, however, military expenditures doubled in current amounts and increased by 50 percent in real terms. A 21 percent rise was planned for 1995. Estimates of Chinese military expenditures for 1993 range from roughly $22 billion to $37 billion at official exchange rates and up to $90 billion in terms of purchasing power parity. In the late 1980s China redrafted its military strategy, shifting from defense against invasion in a major war with the Soviet Union to a regional strategy emphasizing power projection. In accordance with this shift it began developing its naval capabilities, acquiring modernized, longer-range combat aircraft, developing an inflight refueling capability, and deciding to acquire an aircraft carrier. China also entered into a mutually beneficial arms purchasing relationship with Russia.

China is on its way to becoming the dominant power in East Asia. East Asian economic development is becoming more and more China-oriented, fueled by the rapid growth of the mainland and the three other Chinas plus the central role which ethnic Chinese have played in developing the economies of Thailand, Malaysia, Indonesia, and the Philippines. More threateningly, China is increasingly vigorous in asserting its claim to the South China Sea: developing its base in the Paracel Islands, fighting the Vietnamese over a handful of islands in 1988, establishing a military presence on Mischief Reef off the Philippines, and laying claim to the gas fields adjoining Indonesia's Natuna Island. China also ended its low-key support for a continued U.S. military presence in East Asia and began actively to oppose that deployment. Similarly, although during the Cold War China quietly urged Japan to strengthen its military power, in the post–Cold War years it has expressed increased concern over the Japanese military buildup. Acting in classic fashion as a regional hegemon, China is attempting to minimize obstacles to its achievement of regional military superiority.

With rare exceptions, such as possibly the South China Sea, Chinese hegemony in East Asia is unlikely to involve expansion of territorial control through the direct use of military force. It is likely to mean, however, that China will expect other East Asian countries, in varying degrees, to do some or all of the following:

- support Chinese territorial integrity, Chinese control of Tibet and Xinjiang, and the integration of Hong Kong and Taiwan into China;
- acquiesce in Chinese sovereignty over the South China Sea and possibly Mongolia;
- generally support China in conflicts with the West over economics, human rights, weapons proliferation, and other issues;
- accept Chinese military predominance in the region and refrain from acquiring nuclear weapons or conventional forces that could challenge that predominance;

• adopt trade and investment policies compatible with Chinese interests and conducive to Chinese economic development;

• defer to Chinese leadership in dealing with regional problems;

• be generally open to immigration from China;

• prohibit or suppress anti-China and anti-Chinese movements within their societies;

• respect the rights of Chinese within their societies, including their right to maintain close relations with their kin and provinces of origin in China;

• abstain from military alliances or anti-China coalitions with other powers;

• promote the use of Mandarin as a supplement to and eventually a replacement for English as the Language of Wider Communication in East Asia.

Analysts compare the emergence of China to the rise of Wilhelmine Germany as the dominant power in Europe in the late nineteenth century. The emergence of new great powers is always highly destabilizing, and if it occurs, China's emergence as a major power will dwarf any comparable phenomena during the last half of the second millennium. "The size of China's displacement of the world," Lee Kuan Yew observed in 1994, "is such that the world must find a new balance in 30 or 40 years. It's not possible to pretend that this is just another big player. This is the biggest player in the history of man." [32] If Chinese economic development continues for another decade, as seems possible, and if China maintains its unity during the succession period, as seems probable, East Asian countries and the world will have to respond to the increasingly assertive role of this biggest player in human history.

Broadly speaking, states can react in one or a combination of two ways to the rise of a new power. Alone or in coalition with other states they can attempt to insure their security by balancing against the emerging power, containing it, and, if necessary, going to war to defeat it. Alternatively, states can try to bandwagon with the emerging power, accommodating it, and assuming a secondary or subordinate position in relation to the emerging power with the expectation that their core interests will be protected. Or, conceivably, states could attempt some mixture of balancing and bandwagoning, although this runs the risk of both antagonizing the rising power and having no protection against it. According to Western international relations theory, balancing is usually a more desirable option and in fact has been more frequently resorted to than bandwagoning. As Stephen Walt has argued,

In general, calculations of intent should encourage states to balance. Bandwagoning is risky because it requires trust; one assists a dominant power in the hope that it will remain benevolent. It is safer to balance, in case the dominant power turns out to be aggressive. Furthermore, alignment with the weaker side enhances one's influence within the resulting coalition, because the weaker side has greater need of assistance. [33]

Walt's analysis of alliance formation in Southwest Asia showed that states almost always attempted to balance against external threats. It has also been generally assumed that balancing behavior was the norm throughout most modern European history, with the several powers shifting their alliances so as to balance and contain the threats they saw posed by Philip II, Louis XIV, Frederick the Great, Napoleon, the Kaiser, and Hitler. Walt concedes, however, that states may choose bandwagoning "under some conditions," and, as Randall Schweller argues, revisionist states are likely to bandwagon with a rising power because they are dissatisfied and hope to gain from changes in the status quo.[34] In addition, as Walt suggests, bandwagoning does require a degree of trust in the nonmalevolent intentions of the more powerful state.

In balancing power, states can play either primary or secondary roles. First, State A can attempt to balance power against State B, which it perceives to be a potential adversary, by making alliances with States C and D, by developing its own military and other power (which is likely to lead to an arms race), or by some combination of these means. In this situation States A and B are the *primary* balancers of each other. Second, State A may not perceive any other state as an immediate adversary but it may have an interest in promoting a balance of power between States B and C either of which if it became too powerful could pose a threat to State A. In this situation State A acts as a *secondary* balancer with respect to States B and C, which may be primary balancers of each other.

How will states react to China if it begins to emerge as the hegemonic power in East Asia? The responses will undoubtedly vary widely. Since China has defined the United States as its principal enemy, the predominant American inclination will be to act as a primary balancer and prevent Chinese hegemony. Assuming such a role would be in keeping with the traditional American concern with preventing the domination of either Europe or Asia by any single power. That goal is no longer relevant in Europe, but it could be in Asia. A loose federation in Western Europe closely linked to the United States culturally, politically, and economically will not threaten American security. A unified, powerful, and assertive China could. Is it in American interest to be ready to go to war if necessary to prevent Chinese hegemony in East Asia? If Chinese economic development continues, this could be the single most serious security issue American policymakers confront in the early twenty-first century. If the United States does want to stop Chinese domination of East Asia, it will need to redirect the Japanese alliance to that purpose, develop close military ties with other Asian nations, and enhance its military presence in Asia and the military power it can bring to bear in Asia. If the United States is not willing to fight against Chinese hegemony, it will need to foreswear its universalism, learn to live with that hegemony, and reconcile itself to a marked reduction in its ability to shape events on the far side of the Pacific. Either course involves major costs and risks. The greatest danger is that the United States will make no clear choice and stumble into a war with China without considering carefully whether that is in its national interest and without being prepared to wage such a war effectively.

Theoretically the United States could attempt to contain China by playing a secondary balancing role if some other major power acted as the primary balancer of China. The only conceivable possibility is Japan, and this would require major changes in Japanese policy: intensified Japanese rearmament, acquisition of nuclear weapons, and active competition with China for support among other Asian powers. While Japan might be willing to participate in a U.S.-led coalition to counter China, although that also is unsure, it is unlikely to become the primary balancer of China. In addition, the United States has not shown much interest or ability at playing a secondary balancing role. As a new small country, it attempted to do so during the Napoleonic era and ended up fighting wars with both Britain and France. During the first part of the twentieth century the United States made only minimum efforts to promote balances among European and Asian countries and as a result became engaged in world wars to restore balances that had been disrupted. During the Cold War the United States had no alternative to being the primary balancer of the Soviet Union. The United States has thus never been a secondary balancer as a great power. Becoming one means playing a subtle, flexible, ambiguous, and even disingenuous role. It could mean shifting support from one side to another, refusing to support or opposing a state that in terms of American values seems to be morally right, and supporting a state that is morally wrong. Even if Japan did emerge as the primary balancer of China in Asia, the ability of the United States to support that balance is open to question. The United States is far more able to mobilize directly against one existing threat than it is to balance off two potential threats. Finally, a bandwagoning propensity is likely to exist among Asian powers, which would preclude any U.S. effort at secondary balancing.

To the extent that bandwagoning depends on trust, three propositions follow. First, bandwagoning is more likely to occur between states belonging to the same civilization or otherwise sharing cultural commonalities than between states lacking any cultural commonality. Second, levels of trust are likely to vary with the context. A younger boy will bandwagon with his older brother when they confront other boys; he is less likely to trust his older brother when they are alone at home. Hence more frequent interactions between states of different civilizations will further encourage bandwagoning within civilizations. Third, bandwagoning and balancing propensities may vary between civilizations because the levels of trust among their members differ. The prevalence of balancing in the Middle East, for instance, may reflect the proverbial low levels of trust in Arab and other Middle Eastern cultures.

In addition to these influences, the propensity to bandwagon or balance will be shaped by expectations and preferences concerning the distribution of power. European societies went through a phase of absolutism but avoided the sustained bureaucratic empires or "oriental despotisms" that characterized Asia for much of history. Feudalism provided a basis for pluralism and the assumption that some dispersion of power was both natural and desirable. So also at the international level a balance of power was thought natural and desirable, and the responsibility of statesmen was to protect and sustain it. Hence when the equilibrium was threatened, balancing behavior was called for to restore it. The European model of international society, in short, reflected the European model of domestic society.

The Asian bureaucratic empires, in contrast, had little room for social or political pluralism and the division of power. Within China bandwagoning appears to have been far more important compared with balancing than was the case in Europe. During the 1920s, Lucian Pye notes, "the warlords first sought to learn what they could gain by identifying with strength, and only then would they explore the payoffs of allying with the weak. . . . for the Chinese warlords, autonomy was not the ultimate value, as it was in the traditional European balance-of-power calculations; rather they based their decisions upon associating with power." In a similar vein, Avery Goldstein argues that bandwagoning characterized politics in communist China while the authority structure was relatively clear from 1949 to 1966. When the Cultural Revolution then created conditions of near anarchy and uncertainty concerning authority and threatened the survival of political actors, balancing behavior began to prevail.[35] Presumably the restoration of a more clearly defined structure of authority after 1978 also restored bandwagoning as the prevailing pattern of political behavior.

Historically the Chinese did not draw a sharp distinction between domestic and external affairs. Their "image of world order was no more than a corollary of the Chinese internal order and thus an extended projection of the Chinese civilizational identity" which "was presumed to reproduce itself in a concentrically larger expandable circle as the correct cosmic order." Or, as Roderick MacFarquhar phrased it, "The traditional Chinese world view was a reflection of the Confucian vision of a carefully articulated hierarchical society. Foreign monarchs and states were assumed to be tributaries of the Middle Kingdom: 'There are not two suns in the sky, there cannot be two emperors on earth.' " As a result the Chinese have not been sympathetic to "multipolar or even multilateral concepts of security." Asians generally are willing to "accept hierarchy" in international relations, and European-type hegemonic wars have been absent from East Asian history. A functioning balance of power system that was typical of Europe historically was foreign to Asia. Until the arrival of the Western powers in the mid-nineteenth century, East Asian international relations were Sinocentric with other societies arranged in varying degrees of subordination to, cooperation with, or autonomy from Beijing.[36] The Confucian ideal of world order was, of course, never fully realized in practice. Nonetheless, the Asian hierarchy of power model of international politics contrasts dramatically with the European balance of power model.

As a consequence of this image of world order, the Chinese propensity toward bandwagoning in domestic politics also exists in international relations. The degree to which it shapes the foreign policies of individual states tends to vary with the extent they share in Confucian culture and with their historical relationships with China. Korea culturally has much in common with China and historically has tilted toward China. For Singapore communist China was an enemy during the Cold War. In the 1980s, however, Singapore began to shift its position and its leaders actively argued the need for the United States and other countries to come to terms with the realities of Chinese power. With its large Chinese population and the anti-Western proclivities of its leaders, Malaysia also strongly tilted in the Chinese direction. Thailand maintained its independence in the nineteenth and twentieth centuries by accommodating itself to European and Japanese imperialism and has shown every intention of doing the same with China, an inclination reinforced by the potential security threat it sees from Vietnam.

Indonesia and Vietnam are the two countries of Southeast Asia most inclined toward balancing and containing China. Indonesia is large, Muslim, and distant from China, but without the help of others it cannot prevent Chinese assertion of control over the South China Sea. In the fall of 1995 Indonesia and Australia joined in a security agreement that committed them to consult with each other in the event of "adverse challenges" to their security. Although both parties denied that this was an anti-China arrangement, they did identify China as the most likely source of adverse challenges.[37] Vietnam has a largely Confucian culture but historically has had highly antagonistic relations with China and in 1979 fought a brief war with China. Both Vietnam and China have claimed sovereignty over all the Spratly Islands, and their navies engaged each other on occasion in the 1970s and 1980s. In the early 1990s Vietnam's military capabilities declined in relation to those of China. More than any other East Asian state, Vietnam consequently has the motive to seek partners to balance China. Its admission into ASEAN and normalization of its relations with the United States in 1995 were two steps in this direction. The divisions within ASEAN and that association's reluctance to challenge China make it highly unlikely, however, that ASEAN will become an anti-China alliance or that it will provide much support to Vietnam in a confrontation with China. The United States would be a more willing container of China, but in the mid-1990s it is unclear how far it will go to contest an assertion of Chinese control over the South China Sea. In the end, for Vietnam "the least bad alternative" could be to accommodate China and accept Finlandization, which while it "would wound Vietnamese pride ... might guarantee survival."[38]

In the 1990s virtually all East Asian nations, other than China and North Korea, have expressed support for a continued U.S. military presence in the region. In practice, however, except for Vietnam, they tend to accommodate China. The Philippines ended the major U.S. air and naval bases there, and opposition has mounted in Okinawa to the extensive U.S. military forces on the island. In 1994 Thailand, Malaysia, and Indonesia rejected U.S. requests to moor six supply ships in their waters as a floating base to facilitate U.S. military intervention in either Southeast or Southwest Asia. In another manifestation of deference, at its first meeting the ASEAN Regional Forum acquiesced to China's demands that the Spratly Islands issues be kept off the agenda, and China's occupation of Mischief Reef off the Philippines in 1995 elicited protests from no other ASEAN countries. In 1995–1996 when China verbally and militarily threatened Taiwan, Asian governments again responded with a deafening silence. Their bandwagoning propensity was neatly summed up by Michael Oksenberg: "Asian leaders do worry that the balance of power could shift in China's favor but in anxious anticipation of the future, they do not want to confront Beijing now" and they "will not join the United States in an anti-China crusade."[39]

The rise of China will pose a major challenge to Japan, and the Japanese will be deeply divided as to which strategy Japan should pursue. Should it attempt to accommodate China, perhaps with some trade-off acknowledging China's political-military dominance in return for recognition of Japan's primacy in economic matters? Should it attempt to give new meaning and vigor to the U.S.-Japanese alliance as the core of a coalition to balance and contain China? Should it attempt to develop its own military power to defend its interests against any Chinese incursions? Japan will probably avoid as long as it can any clear-cut answer to these questions.

The core of any meaningful effort to balance and contain China would have to be the American-Japanese military alliance. Conceivably Japan might slowly acquiesce in redirecting the alliance to this purpose. Its doing so would depend upon Japan's having confidence in: (1) the overall American ability to sustain itself as the world's only superpower and to maintain its active leadership in world affairs; (2) the American commitment to maintain its presence in Asia and actively to combat China's efforts to expand its influence; and (3) the ability of the United States and Japan to contain China without high costs in terms of resources or high risks in terms of war.

In the absence of a major and improbable show of resolution by and commitment from the United States, Japan is likely to accommodate China. Except for the 1930s and 1940s when it pursued a unilateral policy of conquest in East Asia with disastrous consequences, Japan has historically sought security by allying itself with what it perceives to be the relevant dominant power. Even in the 1930s in joining the Axis, it was aligning itself with what appeared to be then the most dynamic military-ideological force in global politics. Earlier in the century it had quite consciously entered into the Anglo-Japanese alliance because Great Britain was the leading power in world affairs. In the 1950s

Japan similarly associated itself with the United States as the most powerful country in the world and the one that could insure Japan's security. Like the Chinese, the Japanese see international politics as hierarchical because their domestic politics are. As one leading Japanese scholar has observed:

When the Japanese think of their nation in international society, Japanese domestic models often offer analogies. The Japanese tend to see an international order as giving expression externally to cultural patterns that are manifested internally within Japanese society, which is characterized by the relevance of vertically organized structures. Such an image of international order has been influenced by Japan's long experience with pre-modern Sino-Japanese relations (a tribute system).

Hence, Japanese alliance behavior has been "basically bandwagoning, not balancing" and "alignment with the dominant power."[40] The Japanese, one long-time Western resident there agreed, "are quicker than most to bow to *force majeure* and cooperate with perceived moral superiors. . . . and quickest to resent abuse from a morally flabby, retreating hegemon." As the U.S. role in Asia subsides and China's becomes paramount, Japanese policy will adapt accordingly. Indeed, it has begun to do so. The key question in Sino-Japanese relations, Kishore Mahbubani has observed, is "who is number one?" And the answer is becoming clear. "There will be no explicit statements or understandings, but it was significant that the Japanese Emperor chose to visit China in 1992 at a time when Beijing was still relatively isolated internationally."[41]

Ideally, Japanese leaders and people would undoubtedly prefer the pattern of the past several decades and to remain under the sheltering arm of a predominant United States. As U.S. involvement in Asia declines, however, the forces in Japan urging that Japan "re-Asianize" will gain in strength and the Japanese will come to accept as inevitable the renewed dominance of China on the East Asia scene. When asked in 1994, for instance, which nation would have the greatest influence in Asia in the twenty-first century, 44 percent of the Japanese public said China, 30 percent said the United States, and only 16 percent said Japan.[42] Japan, as one high Japanese official predicted in 1995, will have the "discipline" to adapt to the rise of China. He then asked whether the United States would. His initial proposition is plausible; the answer to his subsequent question is uncertain.

Chinese hegemony will reduce instability and conflict in East Asia. It also will reduce American and Western influence there and compel the United States to accept what it has historically attempted to prevent: domination of a key region of the world by another power. The extent who which this hegemony threatens the interests of other Asian countries or the United States, however, depends in part on what happens in China. Economic growth generates military power and political influence, but it can also stimulate political development and movement toward a more open, pluralistic, and possibly democratic form of politics. Arguably it already has had that effect on South Korea and Taiwan. In both countries, however, the political leaders most active in pushing for democracy were Christians.

China's Confucian heritage, with its emphasis on authority, order, hierarchy, and the supremacy of the collectivity over the individual, creates obstacles to democratization. Yet economic growth is creating in south China increasingly high levels of wealth, a dynamic bourgeoisie, accumulations of economic power outside governmental control, and a rapidly expanding middle class. In addition, Chinese people are deeply involved in the outside world in terms of trade, investment, and education. All this creates a social basis for movement toward political pluralism.

The precondition for political opening usually is the coming to power of reform elements within the authoritarian system. Will this happen to China? Probably not in the first succession after Deng but possibly in the second. The new century could see the creation in south China of groups with political agendas, which in fact if not in name will be embryonic political parties, and which are likely to have close ties with and be supported by Chinese in Taiwan, Hong Kong, and Singapore. If such movements emerge in south China and if a reform faction took power in Beijing, some form of a political transition could occur. Democratization could encourage politicians to make nationalist appeals and increase the possibility of war, although in the long run a stable pluralistic system in China is likely to ease its relations with other powers.

Perhaps, as Friedberg suggested, Europe's past is Asia's future. More probably, Asia's past will be Asia's future. The choice for Asia is between power balanced at the price of conflict or peace secured at the price of hegemony. Western societies might go for conflict and balance. History, culture, and the realities of power strongly suggest that Asia will opt for peace and hegemony. The era that began with the Western intrusions of the 1840s and 1850s is ending, China is resuming its place as regional hegemon, and the East is coming into its own.

CIVILIZATIONS AND CORE STATES: EMERGING ALIGNMENTS

The post–Cold War, multipolar, multicivilizational world lacks an overwhelmingly dominant cleavage such as existed in the Cold War. So long as the Muslim demographic and Asian economic surges continue, however, the conflicts between the West and the challenger civilizations will be more central to global politics than other lines of cleavage. The governments of Muslim countries are likely to continue to become less friendly to the West, and intermittent low-intensity and at times perhaps high-intensity violence will occur between Islamic groups and Western societies. Relations between the United States, on the one hand, and China, Japan, and other Asian countries will be highly conflictual, and a major war could occur if the United States challenges China's rise as the hegemonic power in Asia.

Under these conditions, the Confucian-Islamic connection will continue and perhaps broaden and deepen. Central to this connection has been the cooperation of Muslim and Sinic societies opposing the West on weapons proliferation, human rights, and other issues. At its core have been the close relations among Pakistan, Iran, and China, which crystallized in the early 1990s with the visits of President Yang Shangkun to Iran and Pakistan and of President Rafsanjani to Pakistan and China. These "pointed to the emergence of an embryonic alliance between Pakistan, Iran, and China." On his way to China, Rafsanjani declared in Islamabad that "a strategic alliance" existed between Iran and Pakistan and that an attack on Pakistan would be considered an attack on Iran. Reinforcing this pattern, Benazir Bhutto visited Iran and China immediately after becoming prime minister in October 1993. The cooperation among the three countries has included regular exchanges among political, military, and bureaucratic officials and joint efforts in a variety of civil and military areas including defense production, in addition to the weapons transfers from China to the other states. The development of this relationship has been strongly supported by those in Pakistan belonging to the "independence" and "Muslim" schools of thought on foreign policy who looked forward to a "Tehran-Islamabad-Beijing axis," while in Tehran it was argued that the "distinctive nature of the contemporary world" required "close and consistent cooperation" among Iran, China, Pakistan, and Kazakhstan. By the mid-1990s something like a de facto alliance had come into existence among the three countries rooted in opposition to the West, security concerns over India, and the desire to counter Turkish and Russian influence in Central Asia.[43]

Are these three states likely to become the core of a broader grouping involving other Muslim and Asian countries? An informal "Confucian-Islamist alliance," Graham Fuller argues, "could materialize, not because Muhammad and Confucius are anti-West but because these cultures offer a vehicle for the expression of grievances for which the West is partly blamed — a West whose political, military, economic and cultural dominance increasingly rankles in a world where states feel 'they don't have to take it anymore.' " The most passionate call for such cooperation came from Mu'ammar al-Qadhafi, who in March 1994 declared:

The new world order means that Jews and Christians control Muslims and if they can, they will after that dominate Confucianism and other religions in India, China, and Japan. . . .

What the Christians and Jews are now saying: We were determined to crush Communism and the West must now crush Islam and Confucianism.

Now we hope to see a confrontation between China that heads the Confucianist camp and America that heads the Christian crusader camp. We have

no justifications but to be biased against the crusaders. We are standing with
Confucianism, and by allying ourselves with it and fighting alongside it in
one international front, we will eliminate our mutual opponent.

So, we as Muslims, will support China in its struggle against our mutual
enemy. . . .

We wish China victory. . . .[44]

Enthusiasm for a close anti-Western alliance of Confucian and Islamic states,
however, has been rather muted on the Chinese side, with President Jiang
Zemin declaring in 1995 that China would not establish an alliance with any
other country. This position presumably reflected the classical Chinese view
that as the Middle Kingdom, the central power, China did not need formal
allies, and other countries would find it in their interest to cooperate with
China. China's conflicts with the West, on the other hand, mean that it will
value partnership with other anti-Western states, of which Islam furnishes the
largest and most influential number. In addition, China's increasing needs for
oil are likely to impel it to expand its relations with Iran, Iraq, and Saudi Arabia
as well as Kazakhstan and Azerbaijan. Such an arms-for-oil axis, one energy
expert observed in 1994, "won't have to take orders from London, Paris or
Washington anymore."[45]

The relations of other civilizations and their core states to the West and its
challengers will vary widely. The Southern civilizations, Latin America and
Africa, lack core states, have been dependent on the West, and are relatively
weak militarily and economically (althouth that is changing rapidly for Latin
America). In their relations with the West, they probably will move in opposite directions. Latin America is culturally close to the West. During the
1980s and 1990s its political and economic systems came more and more to resemble Western ones. The two Latin American states that once pursued
nuclear weapons abandoned those attempts. With the lowest levels of overall
military effort of any civilization, Latin Americans may resent the military
dominance of the United States but show no intention of challenging it. The
rapid rise of Protestantism in many Latin American societies is both making
them more like the mixed Catholic-Protestant societies of the West and expanding Latin American–Western religious ties beyond those that go through
Rome. Conversely, the influx into the United States of Mexicans, Central
Americans, and Caribbeans and the resulting Hispanic impact on American
society also promotes cultural convergence. The principal conflictual issues
between Latin America and the West, which in practice means the United
States, are immigration, drugs and drug-related terrorism, and economic integration (i.e., admission of Latin American states to NAFTA vs. expansion of
Latin American groupings such as Mercosur and the Andean Pact). As the
problems that developed with respect to Mexico joining NAFTA indicate, the
marriage of Latin American and Western civilizations will not be easy, will

probably take shape slowly through much of the twenty-first century, and may never be consummated. Yet the differences between the West and Latin America remain small compared to those between the West and other civilizations.

The West's relations with Africa should involve only slightly higher levels of conflict primarily because Africa is so weak. Yet some significant issues exist. South Africa did not, like Brazil and Argentina, abandon a program to develop nuclear weapons; it destroyed nuclear weapons it had already built. These weapons were produced by a white government to deter foreign attacks on apartheid, and that government did not wish to bequeath them to a black government which might use them for other purposes. The ability to build nuclear weapons cannot be destroyed, however, and it is possible that a post-apartheid government could construct a new nuclear arsenal to insure its role as the core state of Africa and to deter the West from intervention in Africa. Human rights, immigration, economic issues, and terrorism are also on the agenda between Africa and the West. Despite France's efforts to maintain close ties with its former colonies, a long-term process of de-Westernization appears to be underway in Africa, the interest and influence of Western powers receding, indigenous culture reasserting itself, and South Africa over time subordinating the Afrikaner-English elements in its culture to African ones. While Latin America is becoming more Western, Africa is becoming less so. Both, however, remain in different ways dependent on the West and unable, apart from U.N. votes, to affect decisively the balance between the West and its challengers.

That is clearly not the case with the three "swing" civilizations. Their core states are major actors in world affairs and are likely to have mixed, ambivalent, and fluctuating relationships with the West and the challengers. They also will have varying relations with each other. Japan, as we have argued, over time and with great anguish and soul-searching is likely to shift away from the United States in the direction of China. Like other transcivilizational Cold War alliances, Japan's security ties to the United States will weaken although probably never be formally renounced. Its relations with Russia will remain difficult so long as Russia refuses to compromise on the Kurile islands it occupied in 1945. The moment at the end of the Cold War when this issue might have been resolved passed quickly with the rise of Russian nationalism, and no reason exists for the United States to back the Japanese claim in the future as it has in the past.

In the last decades of the Cold War, China effectively played the "China card" against the Soviet Union and the United States. In the post–Cold War world, Russia has a "Russia card" to play. Russia and China united would decisively tilt the Eurasian balance against the West and arouse all the concerns that existed about the Sino-Soviet relationship in the 1950s. A Russia working closely with the West would provide additional counterbalance to the Confucian-Islamic connection on global issues and reawaken in China its Cold War fears concerning an invasion from the north. Russia, however, also has problems with both these neighboring civilizations. With respect to the West, they tend to be more short term; a consequence of the end of the Cold War and the need for a redefinition of the balance between Russia and the West and agreement by both sides on their basic equality and their respective spheres of influence. In practice this would mean:

1. Russian acceptance of the expansion of the European Union and NATO to include the Western Christian states of Central and Eastern Europe, and Western commitment not to expand NATO further, unless Ukraine splits into two countries;
2. a partnership treaty between Russia and NATO pledging nonaggression, regular consultations on security issues, cooperative efforts to avoid arms competition, and negotiation of arms control agreements appropriate to their post–Cold War security needs;
3. Western recognition of Russia as primarily responsible for the maintenance of security among Orthodox countries and in areas where Orthodoxy predominates;
4. Western acknowledgment of the security problems, actual and potential, which Russia faces from Muslim peoples to its south and willingness to revise the CFE treaty and to be favorably disposed toward other steps Russia might need to take to deal with such threats;
5. agreement between Russia and the West to cooperate as equals in dealing with issues, such as Bosnia, involving both Western and Orthodox interests.

If an arrangement emerges along these or similar lines, neither Russia nor the West is likely to pose any longer-term security challenge to the other. Europe and Russia are demographically mature societies with low birth rates and aging populations; such societies do not have the youthful vigor to be expansionist and offensively oriented.

In the immediate post–Cold War period, Russian-Chinese relations became significantly more cooperative. Border disputes were resolved; military forces on both sides of the border were reduced; trade expanded; each stopped targeting the other with nuclear missiles; and their foreign ministers explored their common interests in combating fundamentalist Islam. Most importantly, Russia found in China an eager and substantial customer for military equipment and technology, including tanks, fighter aircraft, long-range bombers, and surface-to-air missiles.[46] From the Russian viewpoint, this warming of relations represented both a conscious decision to work with China as its Asian "partner," given the stagnant coolness of its relations with Japan, and a reaction to its conflicts with the West over NATO expansion, economic reform, arms control, economic assistance, and membership in Western international institutions. For its part, China was able to demonstrate to the West that it was not alone in the world and could acquire the military capabilities necessary to implement its power projection regional strategy. For both countries, a Russian-Chinese connection is, like the Confucian-Islamic connection, a means of countering Western power and universalism.

Whether that connection survives into the longer term depends largely on, first, the extent to which Russian relations with the West stabilize on a mutually satisfactory basis, and, second, the extent to which China's rise to hegemony in East Asia threatens Russian interests, economically, demographically, militarily. The economic dynamism of China has spilled over into Siberia, and Chinese, along with Korean and Japanese, businesspersons are exploring and exploiting opportunities there. Russians in Siberia increasingly see their economic future connected to East Asia rather than to European Russia. More threatening for Russia is Chinese immigration into Siberia, with illegal Chinese migrants there purportedly numbering in 1995 3 million to 5 million, compared to a Russian population in Eastern Siberia of about 7 million. "The Chinese," Russian Defense Minister Pavel Grachev warned, "are in the process of making a peaceful conquest of the Russian Far East." Russia's top immigration official echoed him, saying, "We must resist Chinese expansionism."[47] In addition, China's developing economic relations with the former Soviet republics of Central Asia may exacerbate relations with Russia. Chinese expansion could also become military if China decided that it should attempt to reclaim Mongolia, which the Russians detached from China after World War I and which was for decades a Soviet satellite. At some point the "yellow hordes" which have haunted Russian imagination since the Mongol invasions may again become a reality.

Russia's relations with Islam are shaped by the historical legacy of centuries of expansion through war against the Turks, North Caucasus peoples, and Central Asian emirates. Russia now collaborates with its Orthodox allies, Serbia and Greece, to counter Turkish influence in the Balkans, and with its Orthodox ally, Armenia, to restrict that influence in the Transcaucasus. It has actively attempted to maintain its political, economic, and military influence in the Central Asian republics, has enlisted them in the Commonwealth of Independent States, and deploys military forces in all of them. Central to Russian concerns are the Caspian Sea oil and gas reserves and the routes by which these resources will reach the West and East Asia. Russia has also been fighting one war in the North Caucasus against the Muslim people of Chechnya and a second war in Tajikistan supporting the government against an insurgency that includes Islamic fundamentalists. These security concerns provide a further incentive for cooperation with China in containing the "Islamic threat" in Central Asia and they also are a major motive for the Russian rapprochement with Iran. Russia has sold Iran submarines, sophisticated fighter aircraft, fighter bombers, surface-to-air missiles, and reconnaissance and electronic warfare equipment. In addition, Russia agreed to build lightwater nuclear reactors in Iran and to provide Iran with uranium-enrichment equipment. In return, Russia quite explicitly expects Iran to constrain the spread of fundamentalism in Central Asia and implicitly to cooperate in countering the spread of Turkish influence there and in the Caucasus. For the coming decades Russia's relations with Islam will be decisively shaped by its perceptions of the threats posed by the booming Muslim populations along its southern periphery.

During the Cold War, India, the third "swing" core state, was an ally of the Soviet Union and fought one war with China and several with Pakistan. Its relations with the West, particularly the United States, were distant when they were not acrimonious. In the post–Cold War world, India's relations with Pakistan are likely to remain highly conflictual over Kashmir, nuclear weapons, and the overall military balance on the Subcontinent. To the extent that Pakistan is able to win support from other Muslim countries, India's relations with Islam generally will be difficult. To counter this, India is likely to make special efforts, as it has in the past, to persuade individual Muslim countries to distance themselves from Pakistan. With the end of the Cold War, China's efforts to establish more friendly relations with its neighbors extended to India and tensions between the two lessened. This trend, however, is unlikely to continue for long. China has actively involved itself in South Asian politics and presumably will continue to do so: maintaining a close relation with Pakistan, strengthening Pakistan's nuclear and conventional military capabilities, and courting Myanmar with economic assistance, investment, and military aid, while possibly developing naval facilities there. Chinese power is expanding at the moment; India's power could grow substantially in the early twenty-first century. Conflict seems highly probable. "The underlying power rivalry between the two Asian giants, and their self-images as natural great powers and centers of civilization and culture," one analyst has observed, "will continue to drive them to support different countries and causes. India will strive to emerge, not only as an independent power center in the multipolar world, but as a counterweight to Chinese power and influence."[48]

Confronting at least a China-Pakistan alliance, if not a broader Confucian-Islamic connection, it clearly will be in India's interests to maintain its close relationship with Russia and to remain a major purchaser of Russian military equipment. In the mid-1990s India was acquiring from Russia almost every major type of weapon including an aircraft carrier and cryogenic rocket technology, which led to U.S. sanctions. In addition to weapons proliferation, other issues between India and the United States included human rights, Kashmir, and economic liberalization. Over time, however, the cooling of U.S.-Pakistan relations and their common interests in containing China are likely to bring India and the United States closer together. The expansion of Indian power in Southern Asia cannot harm U.S. interests and could serve them.

The relations between civilizations and their core states are complicated, often ambivalent, and they do change. Most countries in any one civilization will generally follow the lead of the core state in shaping their relations with countries in another civilization. But this will not always be the case, and obviously all the countries of one civilization do not have identical relations with all the countries in a second civilization. Common interests, usually a common enemy from a third civilization, can generate cooperation between countries of different civilizations. Conflicts also obviously occur within civili-

FIGURE 9.1
THE GLOBAL POLITICS OF CIVILIZATIONS: Emerging ALIGNMENTS

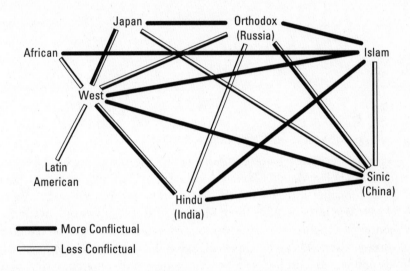

zations, particularly Islam. In addition, the relations between groups along fault lines may differ significantly from the relations between the core states of the same civilizations. Yet broad trends are evident and plausible generalizations can be made about what seem to be the emerging alignments and antagonisms among civilizations and core states. These are summarized in Figure 9.1 The relatively simple bipolarity of the Cold War is giving way to the much more complex relationships of a multipolar, multicivilizational world.

Chapter 10

•

From Transition Wars
to Fault Line Wars

Transition Wars: Afghanistan and the Gulf

"*L*a premiere guerre civilisationnelle*,*" the distinguished Moroccan scholar Mahdi Elmandjra called the Gulf War as it was being fought.[1] In fact it was the second. The first was the Soviet-Afghan War of 1979–1989. Both wars began as straightforward invasions of one country by another but were transformed into and in large part redefined as civilization wars. They were, in effect, transition wars to an era dominated by ethnic conflict and fault line wars between groups from different civilizations.

The Afghan War started as an effort by the Soviet Union to sustain a satellite regime. It became a Cold War war when the United States reacted vigorously and organized, funded, and equipped the Afghan insurgents resisting the Soviet forces. For Americans, Soviet defeat was vindication of the Reagan doctrine of promoting armed resistance to communist regimes and a reassuring humiliation of the Soviets comparable to that which the United States had suffered in Vietnam. It was also a defeat whose ramifications spread throughout Soviet society and its political establishment and contributed significantly to the disintegration of the Soviet empire. To Americans and to Westerners generally Afghanistan was the final, decisive victory, the Waterloo, of the Cold War.

For those who fought the Soviets, however, the Afghan War was something else. It was "the first successful resistance to a foreign power," one Western scholar observed,[2] "which was not based on either nationalist or socialist principles" but instead on Islamic principles, which was waged as a jihad, and which gave a tremendous boost to Islamic self-confidence and power. Its impact on the Islamic world was, in effect, comparable to the impact which the Japanese defeat of the Russians in 1905 had on the Oriental world. What the West sees as a victory for the Free World, Muslims see as a victory for Islam.

American dollars and missiles were indispensable to the defeat of the Soviets. Also indispensable, however, was the collective effort of Islam, in which a wide variety of governments and groups competed with each other in attempting to defeat the Soviets and to produce a victory that would serve their interests. Muslim financial support for the war came primarily from Saudi Arabia. Between 1984 and 1986 the Saudis gave $525 million to the resistance; in 1989 they agreed to supply 61 percent of a total of $715 million, or $436 million, with the remainder coming from the United States. In 1993 they provided $193 million to the Afghan government. The total amount they contributed during the course of the war was at least as much as and probably more than the $3 billion to $3.3 billion spent by the United States. During the war about 25,000 volunteers from other Islamic, primarily Arab, countries participated in the war. Recruited in large part in Jordan, these volunteers were trained by Pakistan's Inter-Service Intelligence agency. Pakistan also provided the indispensable external base for the resistance as well as logistical and other support. In addition, Pakistan was the agent and the conduit for the disbursement of American money, and it purposefully directed 75 percent of those funds to the more fundamentalist Islamist groups with 50 percent of the total going to the most extreme Sunni fundamentalist faction led by Gulbuddin Hekmatyar. Although fighting the Soviets, the Arab participants in the war were overwhelmingly anti-Western and denounced Western humanitarian aid agencies as immoral and subversive of Islam. In the end, the Soviets were defeated by three factors they could not effectively equal or counter: American technology, Saudi money, and Muslim demographics and zeal.[3]

The war left behind an uneasy coalition of Islamist organizations intent on promoting Islam against all non-Muslim forces. It also left a legacy of expert and experienced fighters, camps, training grounds, and logistical facilities, elaborate trans-Islam networks of personal and organizational relationships, a substantial amount of military equipment including 300 to 500 unaccounted-for Stinger missiles, and, most important, a heady sense of power and self-confidence over what had been achieved and a driving desire to move on to other victories. The "jihad credentials, religious and political," of the Afghan volunteers, one U.S. official said in 1994, "are impeccable. They beat one of the world's two superpowers and now they're working on the second."[4]

The Afghan War became a civilization war because Muslims everywhere saw it as such and rallied against the Soviet Union. The Gulf War became a civilization war because the West intervened militarily in a Muslim conflict, Westerners overwhelmingly supported that intervention, and Muslims throughout the world came to see that intervention as a war against them and rallied against what they saw as one more instance of Western imperialism.

Arab and Muslim governments were initially divided over the war. Saddam

Hussein violated the sanctity of borders and in August 1990 the Arab League voted by a substantial majority (fourteen in favor, two against, five abstaining or not voting) to condemn his action. Egypt and Syria agreed to contribute substantial numbers and Pakistan, Morocco, and Bangladesh lesser numbers of troops to the anti-Iraq coalition organized by the United States. Turkey closed the pipeline running through its territory from Iraq to the Mediterranean and allowed the coalition to use its air bases. In return for these actions, Turkey strengthened its claim to get into Europe; Pakistan and Morocco reaffirmed their close relationship with Saudi Arabia; Egypt got its debt canceled; and Syria got Lebanon. In contrast, the governments of Iran, Jordan, Libya, Mauritania, Yemen, Sudan, and Tunisia, as well as organizations such as the P.L.O., Hamas, and FIS, despite the financial support many had received from Saudi Arabia, supported Iraq and condemned Western intervention. Other Muslim governments, such as that of Indonesia, assumed compromise positions or tried to avoid taking any position.

While Muslim governments were initially divided, Arab and Muslim opinion was from the first overwhelmingly anti-West. The "Arab world," one American observer reported after visiting Yemen, Syria, Egypt, Jordan, and Saudi Arabia three weeks after the invasion of Kuwait, "is . . . seething with resentment against the U.S., barely able to contain its glee at the prospect of an Arab leader bold enough to defy the greatest power on earth."[5] Millions of Muslims from Morocco to China rallied behind Saddam Hussein and "acclaimed him a Muslim hero."[6] The paradox of democracy was "the great paradox of this conflict": support for Saddam Hussein was most "fervent and widespread" in those Arab countries where politics was more open and freedom of expression less restricted.[7] In Morocco, Pakistan, Jordan, Indonesia, and other countries massive demonstrations denounced the West and political leaders like King Hassan, Benazir Bhutto, and Suharto, who were seen as lackeys of the West. Opposition to the coalition even surfaced in Syria, where "a broad spectrum of citizens opposed the presence of foreign forces in the Gulf." Seventy-five percent of India's 100 million Muslims blamed the United States for the war, and Indonesia's 171 million Muslims were "almost universally" against U.S. military action in the Gulf. Arab intellectuals lined up in similar fashion and formulated intricate rationales for overlooking Saddam's brutality and denouncing Western intervention.[8]

Arabs and other Muslims generally agreed that Saddam Hussein might be a bloody tyrant, but, paralleling FDR's thinking, "he is our bloody tyrant." In their view, the invasion was a family affair to be settled within the family and those who intervened in the name of some grand theory of international justice were doing so to protect their own selfish interests and to maintain Arab subordination to the West. Arab intellectuals, one study reported, "despise the Iraqi regime and deplore its brutality and authoritarianism, but regard it as constituting a center of resistance to the great enemy of the Arab world, the

West." They "define the Arab world in opposition to the West." "What Saddam has done is wrong," a Palestinian professor said, "but we cannot condemn Iraq for standing up to Western military intervention." Muslims in the West and elsewhere denounced the presence of non-Muslim troops in Saudi Arabia and the resulting "desecration" of the Muslim holy sites.[9] The prevailing view, in short, was: Saddam was wrong to invade, the West was more wrong to intervene, hence Saddam is right to fight the West, and we are right to support him.

Saddam Hussein, like primary participants in other fault line wars, identified his previously secular regime with the cause that would have the broadest appeal: Islam. Given the U-shaped distribution of identities in the Muslim world, Saddam had no real alternative. This choice of Islam over either Arab nationalism or vague Third World anti-Westernism, one Egyptian commentator observed, "testifies to the value of Islam as a political ideology for mobilizing support."[10] Although Saudi Arabia is more strictly Muslim in its practices and institutions than other Muslim states, except possibly Iran and Sudan, and although it had funded Islamist groups throughout the world, no Islamist movement in any country supported the Western coalition against Iraq and virtually all opposed Western intervention.

For Muslims the war thus quickly became a war between civilizations, in which the inviolability of Islam was at stake. Islamist fundamentalist groups from Egypt, Syria, Jordan, Pakistan, Malaysia, Afghanistan, Sudan, and elsewhere denounced it as a war against "Islam and its civilization" by an alliance of "Crusaders and Zionists" and proclaimed their backing of Iraq in the face of "military and economic aggression against its people." In the fall of 1990 the dean of the Islamic College in Mecca, Safar al-Hawali, declared in a tape widely circulated in Saudi Arabia, that the war "is not the world against Iraq. It is the West against Islam." In similar terms, King Hussein of Jordan argued that it was "a war against all Arabs and all Muslims and not against Iraq alone." In addition, as Fatima Mernissi points out, President Bush's frequent rhetorical invocations of God on behalf of the United States reinforced Arab perception that it was "a religious war" with Bush's remarks reeking "of the calculating, mercenary attacks of the pre-Islamic hordes of the seventh century and the later Christian crusades." Arguments that the war was a crusade produced by Western and Zionist conspiracy, in turn, justified and even demanded mobilization of a jihad in response.[11]

Muslim definition of the war as the West vs. Islam facilitated reduction or suspension of antagonisms within the Muslim world. Old differences among Muslims shrank in importance compared to the overriding difference between Islam and the West. In the course of the war Muslim governments and groups consistently moved to distance themselves from the West. Like its Afghan predecessor, the Gulf War brought together Muslims who previously had often been at each other's throats: Arab secularists, nationalists, and fundamentalists; the Jordanian government and the Palestinians; the P.L.O. and Hamas; Iran and Iraq; opposition parties and governments generally. "Those Ba'athists of Iraq," as Safar al-Hawali put it, "are our enemies for a few hours, but Rome is our enemy until doomsday." [12] The war also started the process of reconciliation between Iraq and Iran. Iran's Shi'ite religious leaders denounced the Western intervention and called for a jihad against the West. The Iranian government distanced itself from measures directed against its former enemy, and the war was followed by a gradual improvement in relations between the two regimes.

An external enemy also reduces conflict within a country. In January 1991, for instance, Pakistan was reported to be "awash in anti-Western polemics" which brought that country, at least briefly, together. "Pakistan has never been so united. In the southern province of Sind, where native Sindhis and immigrants from India have been murdering each other for five years, people from either side demonstrate against the Americans arm in arm. In the ultraconservative tribal areas on the Northwest Frontier, even women are out in the streets protesting, often in places where people have never assembled for anything other than Friday prayers." [13]

As public opinion became more adamant against the war, the governments that had originally associated themselves with the coalition backtracked or became divided or developed elaborate rationalizations for their actions. Leaders like Hafiz al-Assad who contributed troops now argued these were necessary to balance and eventually to replace the Western forces in Saudi Arabia and that they would, in any event, be used purely for defensive purposes and the protection of the holy places. In Turkey and Pakistan top military leaders publicly denounced the alignment of their governments with the coalition. The Egyptian and Syrian governments, which contributed the most troops, had sufficient control of their societies to be able to suppress and ignore anti-Western pressure. The governments in somewhat more open Muslim countries were induced to move away from the West and adopt increasingly anti-Western positions. In the Maghreb "the explosion of support for Iraq" was "one of the biggest surprises of the war." Tunisian public opinion was strongly anti-West and President Ben Ali was quick to condemn Western intervention. The government of Morocco originally contributed 1500 troops to the coalition, but then as anti-Western groups mobilized also endorsed a general strike on behalf of Iraq. In Algeria a pro-Iraq demonstration of 400,000 people prompted President Bendjedid, who initially tilted toward the West, to shift his position, denounce the West, and declare that "Algeria will stand by the side of its brother Iraq." [14] In August 1990 the three Maghreb governments had voted in the Arab League to condemn Iraq. In the fall, reacting to the intense feelings of their people, they voted in favor of a motion to condemn the American intervention.

The Western military effort also drew little support from the people of non-Western, non-Muslim civilizations. In January 1991, 53 percent of Japanese polled opposed the war, while 25 percent supported it. Hindus split evenly in blaming Saddam Hussein and George Bush for the war, which *The Times of India* warned, could lead to "a far more sweeping confrontation between a strong and arrogant Judeo-Christian world and a weak Muslim world fired by religious zeal." The Gulf War thus began as a war between Iraq and Kuwait, then became a war between Iraq and the West, then one between Islam and the West, and eventually came to be viewed by many non-Westerners as a war of East versus West, "a white man's war, a new outbreak of old-fashioned imperialism." [15]

Apart from the Kuwaitis no Islamic people were enthusiastic about the war, and most overwhelmingly opposed Western intervention. When the war ended the victory parades in London and New York were not duplicated elsewhere. The "war's conclusion," Sohail H. Hashmi observed, "provided no grounds for rejoicing" among Arabs. Instead the prevailing atmosphere was one of intense disappointment, dismay, humiliation, and resentment. Once again the West had won. Once again the latest Saladin who had raised Arab hopes had gone down to defeat before massive Western power that had been forcefully intruded into the community of Islam. "What worse could happen to the Arabs than what the war produced," asked Fatima Mernissi, "the whole West with all its technology dropping bombs on us? It was the ultimate horror." [16]

Following the war, Arab opinion outside Kuwait became increasingly critical of a U.S. military presence in the Gulf. The liberation of Kuwait removed any rationale for opposing Saddam Hussein and left little rationale for a sustained American military presence in the Gulf. Hence even in countries like Egypt opinion became more and more sympathetic to Iraq. Arab governments which had joined the coalition shifted ground.[17] Egypt and Syria, as well as the others, opposed the imposition of a no-fly zone in southern Iraq in August 1992. Arab governments plus Turkey also objected to the air attacks on Iraq in January 1993. If Western air power could be used in response to attacks on Muslim Shi'ites and Kurds by Sunni Muslims, why was it not also used to respond to attacks on Bosnian Muslims by Orthodox Serbs? In June 1993 when President Clinton ordered a bombing of Baghdad in retaliation for the Iraqi effort to assassinate former President Bush, international reaction was strictly along civilizational lines. Israel and Western European governments strongly supported the raid; Russia accepted it as "justified" self-defense; China expressed "deep concern"; Saudi Arabia and the Gulf emirates said nothing; other Muslim governments, including that of Egypt, denounced it as another example of Western double standards, with Iran terming it "flagrant aggression" driven by American "neo-expansionism and egotism." [18] Repeatedly the question was raised: Why doesn't the United States and the "international community" (that is, the West) react in similar fashion to the outrageous behavior of Israel and its violations of U.N. resolutions?

The Gulf War was the first post–Cold War resource war between civilizations. At stake was whether the bulk of the world's largest oil reserves would be controlled by Saudi and emirate governments dependent on Western military power for their security or by independent anti-Western regimes which would be able and might be willing to use the oil weapon against the West. The West failed to unseat Saddam Hussein, but it scored a victory of sorts in dramatizing the security dependence of the Gulf states on the West and in achieving an expanded peacetime military presence in the Gulf. Before the war, Iran, Iraq, the Gulf Cooperation Council, and the United States jostled for influence over the Gulf. After the war the Persian Gulf was an American lake.

CHARACTERISTICS OF FAULT LINE WARS

Wars between clans, tribes, ethnic groups, religious communities, and nations have been prevalent in every era and in every civilization because they are rooted in the identities of people. These conflicts tend to be particularistic, in that they do not involve broader ideological or political issues of direct interest to nonparticipants, although they may arouse humanitarian concerns in outside groups. They also tend to be vicious and bloody, since fundamental issues of identity are at stake. In addition, they tend to be lengthy; they may be interrupted by truces or agreements but these tend to break down and the conflict is resumed. Decisive military victory by one side in an identity civil war, on the other hand, increases the likelihood of genocide.[19]

Fault line conflicts are communal conflicts between states or groups from different civilizations. Fault line wars are conflicts that have become violent. Such wars may occur between states, between nongovernmental groups, and between states and nongovernmental groups. Fault line conflicts within states may involve groups which are predominantly located in geographically distinct areas, in which case the group which does not control the government normally fights for independence and may or may not be willing to settle for something less than that. Within-state fault line conflicts may also involve groups which are geographically intermixed, in which case continually tense relations erupt into violence from time to time, as with Hindus and Muslims in India and Muslims and Chinese in Malaysia, or full-scale fighting may occur, particularly when new states and their boundaries are being determined, and produce brutal efforts to separate peoples by force.

Fault line conflicts sometimes are struggles for control over people. More frequently the issue is control of territory. The goal of at least one of the participants is to conquer territory and free it of other people by expelling them, killing them, or doing both, that is, by "ethnic cleansing." These conflicts tend to be violent and ugly, with both sides engaging in massacres, terrorism, rape, and torture. The territory at stake often is for one or both sides a highly charged symbol of their history and identity, sacred land to which they have an inviolable right: the West Bank, Kashmir, Nagorno-Karabakh, the Drina Valley, Kosovo.

Fault line wars share some but not all of the characteristics of communal wars generally. They are protracted conflicts. When they go on within states they have on the average lasted six times longer than interstate wars. Involving fundamental issues of group identity and power, they are difficult to resolve through negotiations and compromise. When agreements are reached, they often are not subscribed to by all parties on each side and usually do not last long. Fault line wars are off-again-on-again wars that can flame up into massive violence and then sputter down into low-intensity warfare or sullen hostility only to flame up once again. The fires of communal identity and hatred are rarely totally extinguished except through genocide. As a result of their protracted character, fault line wars, like other communal wars, tend to produce large numbers of deaths and refugees. Estimates of either have to be treated with caution, but commonly accepted figures for deaths in fault line wars underway in the early 1990s included: 50,000 in the Philippines, 50,000–100,000 in Sri Lanka, 20,000 in Kashmir, 500,000–1.5 million in Sudan, 100,000 in Tajikistan, 50,000 in Croatia, 50,000–200,000 in Bosnia, 30,000–50,000 in Chechnya, 100,000 in Tibet, 200,000 in East Timor.[20] Virtually all these conflicts generated much larger numbers of refugees.

Many of these contemporary wars are simply the latest round in a prolonged history of bloody conflicts, and the late-twentieth-century violence has resisted efforts to end it permanently. The fighting in Sudan, for instance, broke out in 1956, continued until 1972, when an agreement was reached providing some autonomy for southern Sudan, but resumed again in 1983. The Tamil rebellion in Sri Lanka began in 1983; peace negotiations to end it broke down in 1991 and were resumed in 1994 with an agreement reached on a cease-fire in January 1995. Four months later, however, the insurgent Tigers broke the truce and withdrew from the peace talks, and the war started up again with intensified violence. The Moro rebellion in the Philippines began in the early 1970s and slackened in 1976 after an agreement was reached providing autonomy for some areas of Mindanao. By 1993, however, renewed violence was occurring frequently and on an increasing scale, as dissident insurgent groups repudiated the peace efforts. Russian and Chechen leaders reached a demilitarization agreement in July 1995 designed to end the violence that had begun the previous December. The war eased off for a while but then was renewed with Chechen attacks on individual Russian or pro-Russian leaders, Russian retaliation, the Chechen incursion into Dagestan in January 1996, and the massive Russian offensive in early 1996.

While fault line wars share the prolonged duration, high levels of violence, and ideological ambivalence of other communal wars, they also differ from them in two ways. First, communal wars may occur between ethnic, religious, racial, or linguistic groups. Since religion, however, is the principal defining characteristic of civilizations, fault line wars are almost always between peoples of different religions. Some analysts downplay the significance of this factor.

They point, for instance, to the shared ethnicity and language, past peaceful coexistence, and extensive intermarriage of Serbs and Muslims in Bosnia, and dismiss the religious factor with references to Freud's "narcissism of small differences."[21] That judgment, however, is rooted in secular myopia. Millennia of human history have shown that religion is not a "small difference" but possibly the most profound difference that can exist between people. The frequency, intensity, and violence of fault line wars are greatly enhanced by beliefs in different gods.

Second, other communal wars tend to be particularistic, and hence are relatively unlikely to spread and involve additional participants. Fault line wars, in contrast, are by definition between groups which are part of larger cultural entities. In the usual communal conflict, Group A is fighting Group B, and Groups C, D, and E have no reason to become involved unless A or B directly attacks the interests of C, D, or E. In a fault line war, in contrast, Group A1 is fighting Group B1 and each will attempt to expand the war and mobilize support from civilization kin groups, A2, A3, A4, and B2, B3, and B4, and those groups will identify with their fighting kin. The expansion of transportation and communication in the modern world has facilitated the establishment of these connections and hence the "internationalization" of fault line conflicts. Migration has created diasporas in third civilizations. Communications make it easier for the contesting parties to appeal for help and for their kin groups to learn immediately the fate of those parties. The general shrinkage of the world thus enables kin groups to provide moral, diplomatic, financial, and material support to the contesting parties — and much harder not to do so. International networks develop to furnish such support, and the support in turn sustains the participants and prolongs the conflict. This "kin-country syndrome," in H.D.S. Greenway's phrase, is a central feature of late-twentieth-century fault line wars.[22] More generally, even small amounts of violence between people of different civilizations have ramifications and consequences which intracivilizational violence lacks. When Sunni gunmen killed eighteen Shi'ite worshippers in a mosque in Karachi in February 1995, they further disrupted the peace in the city and created a problem for Pakistan. When exactly a year earlier, a Jewish settler killed twenty-nine Muslims praying at the Cave of the Patriarchs in Hebron, he disrupted the Middle Eastern peace process and created a problem for the world.

INCIDENCE: ISLAM'S BLOODY BORDERS

Communal conflicts and fault line wars are the stuff of history, and by one count some thirty-two ethnic conflicts occurred during the Cold War, including fault line wars between Arabs and Israelis, Indians and Pakistanis, Sudanese Muslims and Christians, Sri Lankan Buddhists and Tamils, and Lebanese Shi'ites and Maronites. Identity wars constituted about half of all civil wars during the 1940s and 1950s but about three-quarters of civil wars during the following decades, and the intensity of rebellions involving ethnic groups tripled between the early 1950s and the late 1980s. Given the overreaching superpower rivalry, however, these conflicts, with some notable exceptions, attracted relatively little attention and were often viewed through the prism of the Cold War. As the Cold War wound down, communal conflicts became more prominent and, arguably, more prevalent than they had been previously. Something closely resembling an "upsurge" in ethnic conflict did in fact happen.[23]

These ethnic conflicts and fault line wars have not been evenly distributed among the world's civilizations. Major fault line fighting has occurred between Serbs and Croats in the former Yugoslavia and between Buddhists and Hindus in Sri Lanka, while less violent conflicts took place between non-Muslim groups in a few other places. The overwhelming majority of fault line conflicts, however, have taken place along the boundary looping across Eurasia and Africa that separates Muslims from non-Muslims. While at the macro or global level of world politics the primary clash of civilizations is between the West and the rest, at the micro or local level it is between Islam and the others.

Intense antagonisms and violent conflicts are pervasive between local Muslim and non-Muslim peoples. In Bosnia, Muslims have fought a bloody and disastrous war with Orthodox Serbs and have engaged in other violence with Catholic Croatians. In Kosovo, Albanian Muslims unhappily suffer Serbian rule and maintain their own underground parallel government, with high expectations of the probability of violence between the two groups. The Albanian and Greek governments are at loggerheads over the rights of their minorities in each other's countries. Turks and Greeks are historically at each others throats. On Cyprus, Muslim Turks and Orthodox Greeks maintain hostile adjoining states. In the Caucasus, Turkey and Armenia are historic enemies, and Azeris and Armenians have been at war over control of Nagorno-Karabakh. In the North Caucasus, for two hundred years Chechens, Ingush, and other Muslim peoples have fought on and off for their independence from Russia, a struggle bloodily resumed by Russia and Chechnya in 1994. Fighting also has occurred between the Ingush and the Orthodox Ossetians. In the Volga basin, the Muslim Tatars have fought the Russians in the past and in the early 1990s reached an uneasy compromise with Russia for limited sovereignty.

Throughout the nineteenth century Russia gradually extended by force its control over the Muslim peoples of Central Asia. During the 1980s Afghans and Russians fought a major war, and with the Russian retreat its sequel continued in Tajikistan between Russian forces supporting the existing government and largely Islamist insurgents. In Xinjiang, Uighurs and other Muslim groups struggle against Sinification and are developing relations with their ethnic and religious kin in the former Soviet republics. In the Subcontinent, Pakistan and India have fought three wars, a Muslim insurgency contests Indian rule in Kashmir, Muslim immigrants fight tribal peoples in Assam, and Muslims and Hindus engage in periodic riots and violence across India, these outbreaks fueled by the rise of fundamentalist movements in both religious communities. In Bangladesh, Buddhists protest discrimination against them by the majority Muslims, while in Myanmar Muslims protest discrimination by the Buddhist majority. In Malaysia and Indonesia, Muslims periodically riot against Chinese, protesting their domination of the economy. In southern Thailand, Muslim groups have been involved in an intermittent insurgency against a Buddhist government, while in the southern Philippines a Muslim insurgency fights for independence from a Catholic country and government. In Indonesia, on the other hand, Catholic East Timorians struggle against repression by a Muslim government.

In the Middle East, conflict between Arabs and Jews in Palestine goes back to the establishment of the Jewish homeland. Four wars have occurred between Israel and Arab states, and the Palestinians engaged in the *intifada* against Israeli rule. In Lebanon, Maronite Christians have fought a losing battle against Shi'ites and other Muslims. In Ethiopia, the Orthodox Amharas have historically suppressed Muslim ethnic groups and have confronted an insurgency from the Muslim Oromos. Across the bulge of Africa, a variety of conflicts have gone on between the Arab and Muslim peoples to the north and animist-Christian black peoples to the south. The bloodiest Muslim-Christian war has been in Sudan, which has gone on for decades and produced hundreds of thousands of casualties. Nigerian politics has been dominated by the conflict between the Muslim Fulani-Hausa in the north and Christian tribes in the south, with frequent riots and coups and one major war. In Chad, Kenya, and Tanzania, comparable struggles have occurred between Muslim and Christian groups.

In all these places, the relations between Muslims and peoples of other civilizations — Catholic, Protestant, Orthodox, Hindu, Chinese, Buddhist, Jewish — have been generally antagonistic; most of these relations have been violent at some point in the past; many have been violent in the 1990s. Wherever one looks along the perimeter of Islam, Muslims have problems living peaceably with their neighbors. The question naturally rises as to whether this pattern of late-twentieth-century conflict between Muslim and non-Muslim groups is equally true of relations between groups from other civilizations. In fact, it is not. Muslims make up about one-fifth of the world's population but in the 1990s they have been far more involved in intergroup violence than the people of any other civilization. The evidence is overwhelming.

1. Muslims were participants in twenty-six of fifty ethnopolitical conflicts in 1993–1994 analyzed in depth by Ted Robert Gurr (Table 10.1). Twenty of these conflicts were between groups from different civilizations, of which fifteen were between Muslims and non-Muslims. There were, in short, three times as many intercivilizational conflicts involving Muslims

as there were conflicts between all non-Muslim civilizations. The conflicts within Islam also were more numerous than those in any other
civilization, including tribal conflicts in Africa. In contrast to Islam, the
West was involved in only two intracivilizational and two intercivilizational conflicts. Conflicts involving Muslims also tended to be heavy in
casualties. Of the six wars in which Gurr estimates that 200,000 or more
people were killed, three (Sudan, Bosnia, East Timor) were between
Muslims and non-Muslims, two (Somalia, Iraq-Kurds) were between
Muslims, and only one (Angola) involved only non-Muslims.

2. The *New York Times* identified forty-eight locations in which some fifty-
nine ethnic conflicts were occurring in 1993. In half these places Muslims were clashing with other Muslims or with non-Muslims. Thirty-one
of the fifty-nine conflicts were between groups from different civilizations,
and, paralleling Gurr's data, two-thirds (twenty-one) of these intercivilizational conflicts were between Muslims and others (Table 10.2).

3. In yet another analysis, Ruth Leger Sivard identified twenty-nine wars
(defined as conflicts involving 1000 or more deaths in a year) under way
in 1992. Nine of twelve intercivilizational conflicts were between Muslims and non-Muslims, and Muslims were once again fighting more wars
than people from any other civilization.[24]

TABLE 10.1
ETHNOPOLITICAL CONFLICTS, 1993–1994

	Intracivilization	Intercivilization	Total
Islam	11	15	26
Others	19*	5	24
Total	30	20	50

* Of which 10 were tribal conflicts in Africa.

Source: Ted Robert Gurr, "Peoples Against States: Ethnopolitical Conflict and the Changing World System," *International Studies Quarterly*, Vol. 38 (September 1994), pp. 347–378. I have used Gurr's classification of conflicts except for shifting the Chinese-Tibetan conflict, which he classifies as noncivilizational into the intercivilizational category, since it clearly is a clash between Confucian Han Chinese and Lamaist Buddhist Tibetans.

TABLE 10.2
ETHNIC CONFLICTS, 1993

	Intracivilization	Intercivilization	Total
Islam	7	21	28
Others	21*	10	31
Total	28	31	59

* Of which 10 were tribal conflicts in Africa.

Source: *New York Times*, Feb. 7, 1993, pp. 1, 14.

Three different compilations of data thus yield the same conclusion: In the
early 1990s Muslims were engaged in more intergroup violence than were

non-Muslims, and two-thirds to three-quarters of intercivilizational wars were between Muslims and non-Muslims. Islam's borders *are* bloody, and so are its innards.*

The Muslim propensity toward violent conflict is also suggested by the degree to which Muslim societies are militarized. In the 1980s Muslim countries had military force ratios (that is, the number of military personnel per 1000 population) and military effort indices (force ratio adjusted for a country's wealth) significantly higher than those for other countries. Christian countries, in contrast, had force ratios and military effort indices significantly lower than those for other countries. The average force ratios and military effort ratios of Muslim countries were roughly twice those of Christian countries (Table 10.3). "Quite clearly," James Payne concludes, "there is a connection between Islam and militarism."[25]

TABLE 10.3
MILITARISM OF MUSLIM AND CHRISTIAN COUNTRIES

	Average force ratio	Average military effort
Muslim countries (n = 25)	11.8	17.7
Other countries (n = 112)	7.1	12.3
Christian countries (n = 57)	5.8	8.2
Other countries (n = 80)	9.5	16.9

Source: James L. Payne, *Why Nations Arm* (Oxford: Basil Blackwell, 1989), pp. 125, 138–139. Muslim and Christian countries are those in which more than 80 percent of the population adhere to the defining religion.

Muslim states also have had a high propensity to resort to violence in international crises, employing it to resolve 76 crises out of a total of 142 in which they were involved between 1928 and 1979. In 25 cases violence was the primary means of dealing with the crisis; in 51 crises Muslim states used violence in addition to other means. When they did use violence, Muslim states used high-intensity violence, resorting to full-scale war in 41 percent of the cases where violence was used and engaging in major clashes in another 38 percent of the cases. While Muslim states resorted to violence in 53.5 percent of their crises, violence was used by the United Kingdom in only 11.5 percent, by the United States in 17.9 percent, and by the Soviet Union in 28.5 percent of the crises in which they were involved. Among the major powers only China's violence propensity exceeded that of the Muslim states: it employed violence in 76.9 percent of its crises.[26] Muslim bellicosity and violence are late-twentieth-century facts which neither Muslims nor non-Muslims can deny.

* No single statement in my *Foreign Affairs* article attracted more critical comment than: "Islam has bloody borders." I made that judgment on the basis of a casual survey of intercivilizational conflicts. Quantitative evidence from every disinterested source conclusively demonstrates its validity.

CAUSES: HISTORY, DEMOGRAPHY, POLITICS

What was responsible for the late-twentieth-century upsurge in fault line wars and for the central role of Muslims in such conflicts? First, these wars had their roots in history. Intermittent fault line violence between different civilizational groups occurred in the past and existed in present memories of the past, which in turn generated fears and insecurities on both sides. Muslims and Hindus on the Subcontinent, Russians and Caucasians in the North Caucasus, Armenians and Turks in the Transcaucasus, Arabs and Jews in Palestine, Catholics, Muslims, and Orthodox in the Balkans, Russians and Turks from the Balkans to Central Asia, Sinhalese and Tamils in Sri Lanka, Arabs and blacks across Africa: these are all relationships which through the centuries have involved alternations between mistrustful coexistence and vicious violence. A historical legacy of conflict exists to be exploited and used by those who see reason to do so. In these relationships history is alive, well, and terrifying.

A history of off-again-on-again slaughter, however, does not itself explain why violence was on again in the late twentieth century. After all, as many pointed out, Serbs, Croats, and Muslims for decades lived very peacefully together in Yugoslavia. Muslims and Hindus did so in India. The many ethnic and religious groups in the Soviet Union coexisted, with a few notable exceptions produced by the Soviet government. Tamils and Sinhalese also lived quietly together on an island often described as a tropical paradise. History did not prevent these relatively peaceful relationships prevailing for substantial periods of time; hence history, by itself, cannot explain the breakdown of peace. Other factors must have intruded in the last decades of the twentieth century.

Changes in the demographic balance were one such factor. The numerical expansion of one group generates political, economic, and social pressures on other groups and induces countervailing responses. Even more important, it produces military pressures on less demographically dynamic groups. The collapse in the early 1970s of the thirty-year-old constitutional order in Lebanon was in large part a result of the dramatic increase in the Shi'ite population in relation to the Maronite Christians. In Sri Lanka, Gary Fuller has shown, the peaking of the Sinhalese nationalist insurgency in 1970 and of the Tamil insurgency in the late 1980s coincided exactly with the years when the fifteen-to-twenty-four-year-old "youth bulge" in those groups exceeded 20 percent of the total population of the group.[27] (See Figure 10.1.) The Sinhalese insurgents, one U.S. diplomat to Sri Lanka noted, were virtually all under twenty-four years of age, and the Tamil Tigers, it was reported, were "unique in their reliance on what amounts to a children's army," recruiting "boys and girls as young as eleven," with those killed in the fighting "not yet teenagers when they died, only a few older than eighteen." The Tigers, *The Economist* observed, were waging an "under-age war."[28] In similar fashion, the fault line wars between Russians and the Muslim peoples to their south were fueled by major

FIGURE 10.1
SRI LANKA: SINHALESE AND TAMIL YOUTH BULGES
Percentage of total population, age 15-24

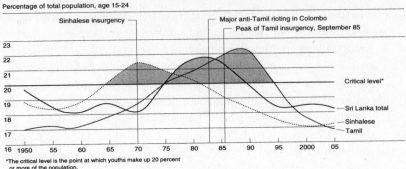

*The critical level is the point at which youths make up 20 percent
or more of the population.

differences in population growth. In the early 1990s the fertility rate of women in the Russian Federation was 1.5, while in the primarily Muslim Central Asian former Soviet republics the fertility rate was about 4.4 and the rate of net population increase (crude birth rate minus crude death rate) in the late 1980s in the latter was five to six times that in Russia. Chechens increased by 26 percent in the 1980s and Chechnya was one of the most densely populated places in Russia, its high birth rates producing migrants and fighters.[29] In similar fashion high Muslim birth rates and migration into Kashmir from Pakistan stimulated renewed resistance to Indian rule.

The complicated processes that led to intercivilizational wars in the former Yugoslavia had many causes and many starting points. Probably the single most important factor leading to these conflicts, however, was the demographic shift that took place in Kosovo. Kosovo was an autonomous province within the Serbian republic with the de facto powers of the six Yugoslav republics except the right to secede. In 1961 its population was 67 percent Albanian Muslim and 24 percent Orthodox Serb. The Albanian birth rate, however, was the highest in Europe, and Kosovo became the most densely populated area of Yugoslavia. By the 1980s close to 50 percent of the Albanians were less than twenty years old. Facing those numbers, Serbs emigrated from Kosovo in pursuit of economic opportunities in Belgrade and elsewhere. As a result, in 1991 Kosovo was 90 percent Muslim and 10 percent Serb.[30] Serbs, nonetheless, viewed Kosovo as their "holy land" or "Jerusalem," the site, among other things, of the great battle on June 28, 1389, when they were defeated by the Ottoman Turks and, as a result, suffered Ottoman rule for almost five centuries.

By the late 1980s the shifting demographic balance led the Albanians to demand that Kosovo be elevated to the status of a Yugoslav republic. The Serbs and the Yugoslav government resisted, afraid that once Kosovo had the right to secede it would do so and possibly merge with Albania. In March 1981 Albanian protests and riots erupted in support of their demands for republic status.

According to Serbs, discrimination, persecution, and violence against Serbs subsequently intensified. "In Kosovo from the late 1970s on," observed a Croatian Protestant, ". . . numerous violent incidents took place which included property damage, loss of jobs, harassment, rapes, fights, and killings." As a result, the "Serbs claimed that the threat to them was of genocidal proportions and that they could no longer tolerate it." The plight of the Kosovo Serbs resonated elsewhere within Serbia and in 1986 generated a declaration by 200 leading Serbian intellectuals, political figures, religious leaders, and military officers, including editors of the liberal opposition journal *Praxis*, demanding that the government take vigorous measures to end the genocide of Serbs in Kosovo. By any reasonable definition of genocide, this charge was greatly exaggerated, although according to one foreign observer sympathetic to the Albanians, "during the 1980s Albanian nationalists were responsible for a number of violent assaults on Serbs, and for the destruction of some Serb property."[31]

All this aroused Serbian nationalism and Slobodan Milosevic saw his opportunity. In 1987 he delivered a major speech at Kosovo appealing to Serbs to claim their own land and history. "Immediately a great number of Serbs — communist, noncommunist and even anticommunist — started to gather around him, determined not only to protect the Serbian minority in Kosovo, but to suppress the Albanians and turn them into second-class citizens. Milosevic was soon acknowledged as a national leader."[32] Two years later, on 28 June 1989, Milosevic returned to Kosovo together with 1 million to 2 million Serbs to mark the 600th anniversary of the great battle symbolizing their ongoing war with the Muslims.

The Serbian fears and nationalism provoked by the rising numbers and power of the Albanians were further heightened by the demographic changes in Bosnia. In 1961 Serbs constituted 43 percent and Muslims 26 percent of the population of Bosnia-Herzegovina. By 1991 the proportions were almost exactly reversed: Serbs had dropped to 31 percent and Muslims had risen to 44 percent. During these thirty years Croats went from 22 percent to 17 percent. Ethnic expansion by one group led to ethnic cleansing by the other. "Why do we kill children?" one Serb fighter asked in 1992 and answered, "Because someday they will grow up and we will have to kill them then." Less brutally Bosnian Croatian authorities acted to prevent their localities from being "demographically occupied" by the Muslims.[33]

Shifts in the demographic balances and youth bulges of 20 percent or more account for many of the intercivilizational conflicts of the late twentieth century. They do not, however, explain all of them. The fighting between Serbs and Croats, for instance, cannot be attributed to demography and, for that matter, only partially to history, since these two peoples lived relatively peacefully together until the Croat Ustashe slaughtered Serbs in World War II. Here and elsewhere politics was also a cause of strife. The collapse of the

Austro-Hungarian, Ottoman, and Russian empires at the end of World War I stimulated ethnic and civilizational conflicts among successor peoples and states. The end of the British, French, and Dutch empires produced similar results after World War II. The downfall of the communist regimes in the Soviet Union and Yugoslavia did the same at the end of the Cold War. People could no longer identify as communists, Soviet citizens, or Yugoslavs, and desperately needed to find new identities. They found them in the old standbys of ethnicity and religion. The repressive but peaceful order of states committed to the proposition that there is no god was replaced by the violence of peoples committed to different gods.

This process was exacerbated by the need for the emerging political entities to adopt the procedures of democracy. As the Soviet Union and Yugoslavia began to come apart, the elites in power did not organize national elections. If they had done so, political leaders would have competed for power at the center and might have attempted to develop multiethnic and multicivilizational appeals to the electorate and to put together similar majority coalitions in parliament. Instead, in both the Soviet Union and Yugoslavia elections were first organized on a republic basis, which created the irresistible incentive for political leaders to campaign against the center, to appeal to ethnic nationalism, and to promote the independence of their republics. Even within Bosnia the populace voted strictly along ethnic lines in the 1990 elections. The multiethnic Reformist Party and the former communist party each got less than 10 percent of the vote. The votes for the Muslim Party of Democratic Action (34 percent), the Serbian Democratic Party (30 percent), and the Croatian Democratic Union (18 percent) roughly approximated the proportions of Muslims, Serbs, and Croats in the population. The first fairly contested elections in almost every former Soviet and former Yugoslav republic were won by political leaders appealing to nationalist sentiments and promising vigorous action to defend their nationality against other ethnic groups. Electoral competition encourages nationalist appeals and thus promotes the intensification of fault line conflicts into fault line wars. When, in Bogdan Denitch's phrase, "ethnos becomes demos,"[34] the initial result is *polemos* or war.

The question remains as to why, as the twentieth century ends, Muslims are involved in far more intergroup violence than people of other civilizations. Has this always been the case? In the past Christians killed fellow Christians and other people in massive numbers. To evaluate the violence propensities of civilizations throughout history would require extensive research, which is impossible here. What can be done, however, is to identify possible causes of current Muslim group violence, both intra-Islam and extra-Islam, and distinguish between those causes which explain a greater propensity toward group conflict throughout history, if that exists, from those which only explain a propensity at the end of the twentieth century. Six possible causes suggest themselves. Three explain only violence between Muslims and non-Muslims

TABLE 10.4
POSSIBLE CAUSES OF MUSLIM CONFLICT PROPENSITY

	Extra-Muslim conflict	Intra- and Extra-conflict
Historical and contemporary conflict	Proximity Indigestibility	Militarism
Contemporary conflict	Victim status	Demographic bulge Core state absence

and three explain both that and intra-Islam violence. Three also explain only the contemporary Muslim propensity to violence, while three others explain that and a historical Muslim propensity, if it exists. If that historical propensity, however, does not exist, then its presumed causes that cannot explain a nonexistent historical propensity also presumably do not explain the demonstrated contemporary Muslim propensity to group violence. The latter then can be explained only by twentieth-century causes that did not exist in previous centuries (Table 10.4).

First, the argument is made that Islam has from the start been a religion of the sword and that it glorifies military virtues. Islam originated among "warring Bedouin nomadic tribes" and this "violent origin is stamped in the foundation of Islam. Muhammad himself is remembered as a hard fighter and a skillful military commander." [35] (No one would say this about Christ or Buddha.) The doctrines of Islam, it is argued, dictate war against unbelievers, and when the initial expansion of Islam tapered off, Muslim groups, quite contrary to doctrine, then fought among themselves. The ratio of *fitna* or internal conflicts to jihad shifted drastically in favor of the former. The Koran and other statements of Muslim beliefs contain few prohibitions on violence, and a concept of nonviolence is absent from Muslim doctrine and practice.

Second, from its origin in Arabia, the spread of Islam across northern Africa and much of the middle East and later to central Asia, the Subcontinent, and the Balkans brought Muslims into direct contact with many different peoples, who were conquered and converted, and the legacy of this process remains. In the wake of the Ottoman conquests in the Balkans urban South Slavs often converted to Islam while rural peasants did not, and thus was born the distinction between Muslim Bosnians and Orthodox Serbs. Conversely the expansion of the Russian Empire to the Black Sea, the Caucasus, and Central Asia brought it into continuing conflict for several centuries with a variety of Muslim peoples. The West's sponsorship, at the height of its power vis-à-vis Islam, of a Jewish homeland in the Middle East laid the basis for ongoing Arab-Israeli antagonism. Muslim and non-Muslim expansion by land thus resulted in Muslims and non-Muslims living in close physical proximity throughout Eurasia. In contrast, the expansion of the West by sea did not usually lead to Western peoples living in territorial proximity to non-Western peoples: these were either subjected to rule from Europe or, except in South Africa, were virtually decimated by Western settlers.

A third possible source of Muslim–non-Muslim conflict involves what one statesman, in reference to his own country, termed the "indigestibility" of Muslims. Indigestibility, however, works both ways: Muslim countries have problems with non-Muslim minorities comparable to those which non-Muslim countries have with Muslim minorities. Even more than Christianity, Islam is an absolutist faith. It merges religion and politics and draws a sharp line between those in the *Dar al-Islam* and those in the *Dar al-harb*. As a result, Confucians, Buddhists, Hindus, Western Christians, and Orthodox Christians have less difficulty adapting to and living with each other than any one of them has in adapting to and living with Muslims. Ethnic Chinese, for instance, are an economically dominant minority in most Southeast Asian countries. They have been successfully assimilated into the societies of Buddhist Thailand and the Catholic Philippines; there are virtually no significant instances of anti-Chinese violence by the majority groups in those countries. In contrast, anti-Chinese riots and/or violence have occurred in Muslim Indonesia and Muslim Malaysia, and the role of the Chinese in those societies remains a sensitive and potentially explosive issue in the way in which it is not in Thailand and the Philippines.

Militarism, indigestibility, and proximity to non-Muslim groups are continuing features of Islam and could explain Muslim conflict propensity throughout history, if that is the case. Three other temporally limited factors could contribute to this propensity in the late twentieth century. One explanation, advanced by Muslims, is that Western imperialism and the subjection of Muslim societies in the nineteenth and twentieth centuries produced an image of Muslim military and economic weakness and hence encourages non-Islamic groups to view Muslims as an attractive target. Muslims are, according to this argument, victims of a widespread anti-Muslim prejudice comparable to the anti-Semitism that historically pervaded Western societies. Muslim groups such as Palestinians, Bosnians, Kashmiris, and Chechens, Akbar Ahmed alleges, are like "Red Indians, depressed groups, shorn of dignity, trapped on reservations converted from their ancestral lands."[36] The Muslim as victim argument, however, does not explain conflicts between Muslim majorities and non-Muslim minorities in countries such as Sudan, Egypt, Iran, and Indonesia.

A more persuasive factor possibly explaining both intra- and extra-Islamic conflict is the absence of one or more core states in Islam. Defenders of Islam often allege that its Western critics believe there is a central, conspiratorial, directing force in Islam mobilizing it and coordinating its actions against the West and others. If the critics believe this, they are wrong. Islam is a source of instability in the world because it lacks a dominant center. States aspiring to be leaders of Islam, such as Saudi Arabia, Iran, Pakistan, Turkey, and potentially Indonesia, compete for influence in the Muslim world; no one of them is in a strong position to mediate conflicts within Islam; and no one of them is able to act authoritatively on behalf of Islam in dealing with conflicts between Muslim and non-Muslim groups.

Finally, and most important, the demographic explosion in Muslim societies and the availability of large numbers of often unemployed males between the ages of fifteen and thirty is a natural source of instability and violence both within Islam and against non-Muslims. Whatever other causes may be at work, this factor alone would go a long way to explaining Muslim violence in the 1980s and 1990s. The aging of this pig-in-the-python generation by the third decade of the twenty-first century and economic development in Muslim societies, if and as that occurs, could consequently lead to a significant reduction in Muslim violence propensities and hence to a general decline in the frequency and intensity of fault line wars.

Chapter 11

•

The Dynamics of
Fault Line Wars

IDENTITY: THE RISE OF CIVILIZATION CONSCIOUSNESS

Fault line wars go through processes of intensification, expansion, containment, interruption, and, rarely, resolution. These processes usually begin sequentially, but they also often overlap and may be repeated. Once started, fault line wars, like other communal conflicts, tend to take on a life of their own and to develop in an action-reaction pattern. Identities which had previously been multiple and casual become focused and hardened; communal conflicts are appropriately termed "identity wars."[1] As violence increases, the initial issues at stake tend to get redefined more exclusively as "us" against "them" and group cohesion and commitment are enhanced. Political leaders expand and deepen their appeals to ethnic and religious loyalties, and civilization consciousness strengthens in relation to other identities. A "hate dynamic" emerges, comparable to the "security dilemma" in international relations, in which mutual fears, distrust, and hatred feed on each other.[2] Each side dramatizes and magnifies the distinction between the forces of virtue and the forces of evil and eventually attempts to transform this distinction into the ultimate distinction between the quick and the dead.

As revolutions evolve, moderates, Girondins, and Mensheviks lose out to radicals, Jacobins, and Bolsheviks. A similar process tends to occur in fault line wars. Moderates with more limited goals, such as autonomy rather than independence, do not achieve these goals through negotiation, which almost always initially fails, and get supplemented or supplanted by radicals committed to achieving more extreme goals through violence. In the Moro-Philippine conflict, the principal insurgent group, the Moro National Liberation Front was first supplemented by the Moro Islamic Liberation Front, which had a more extreme position, and then by the Abu Sayyaf, which was still more extreme and rejected the cease-fires other groups negotiated with the Philippine government. In Sudan during the 1980s the government adopted increasingly extreme Islamist positions, and in the early 1990s the Christian insurgency split, with a new group, the Southern Sudan Independence Movement, advocating independence rather than simply autonomy. In the ongoing conflict between Israelis and Arabs, as the mainstream Palestine Liberation Organization moved toward negotiations with the Israeli government, the Muslim Brotherhood's Hamas challenged it for the loyalty of Palestinians. Simultaneously the engagement of the Israeli government in negotiations generated protests and violence from extremist religious groups in Israel. As the Chechen conflict with Russia intensified in 1992–93, the Dudayev government came to be dominated by "the most radical factions of the Chechen nationalists opposed to any accommodation with Moscow, with the more moderate forces pushed into opposition." In Tajikistan, a similar shift occurred. "As the conflict escalated during 1992, the Tajik nationalist-democratic groups gradually ceded influence to the Islamist groups who were more successful in mobilizing the rural poor and the disaffected urban youth. The Islamist message also became progressively more radicalized as younger leaders emerged to challenge the traditional and more pragmatic religious hierarchy." "I am shutting the dictionary of diplomacy," one Tajik leader said. "I am beginning to speak the language of the battlefield, which is the only appropriate language given the situation created by Russia in my homeland."[3] In Bosnia within the Muslim Party of Democratic Action (SDA), the more extreme nationalist faction led by Alija Izetbegovic became more influential than the more tolerant, multiculturally oriented faction led by Haris Silajdzic.[4]

The victory of the extremists is not necessarily permanent. Extremist violence is no more likely than moderate compromise to end a fault line war. As the costs in death and destruction escalate, with little to show for them, on each side moderates are likely to reappear, again pointing to the "senselessness" of it all and urging another attempt to end it through negotiations.

In the course of the war, multiple identities fade and the identity most meaningful in relation to the conflict comes to dominate. That identity almost always is defined by religion. Psychologically, religion provides the most reassuring and supportive justification for struggle against "godless" forces which are seen as threatening. Practically, its religious or civilizational community is the broadest community to which the local group involved in the conflict can appeal for support. If in a local war between two African tribes, one tribe can define itself as Muslim and the other as Christian, the former can hope to be bolstered by Saudi money, Afghan *mujahedeen*, and Iranian weapons and military advisers, while the latter can look for Western economic and humanitarian aid and political and diplomatic support from Western governments. Unless a group can do as the Bosnian Muslims did and convincingly portray itself as a victim of genocide and thereby arouse Western sympathy, it can only expect to receive significant assistance from its civilizational kin, and apart from the Bosnian Muslims, that has been the case. Fault line wars are by definition local wars between local groups with wider connections and hence promote civilizational identities among their participants.

The strengthening of civilizational identities has occurred among fault line war participants from other civilizations but was particularly prevalent among Muslims. A fault line war may have its origins in family, clan, or tribal conflicts, but because identities in the Muslim world tend to be U-shaped, as the struggle progresses the Muslim participants quickly seek to broaden their identity and appeal to all of Islam, as was the case even with an antifundamentalist secularist like Saddam Hussein. The Azerbaijan government similarly, one Westerner observed, played "the Islamic card." In Tajikistan, in a war which began as an intra-Tajikistan regional conflict, the insurgents increasingly defined their cause as the cause of Islam. In the nineteenth-century wars between the North Caucasus peoples and the Russians, the Muslim leader Shamil termed himself an Islamist and united dozens of ethnic and linguistic groups "on the basis of Islam and resistance to Russian conquest." In the 1990s Dudayev capitalized on the Islamic Resurgence that had taken place in the Caucasus in the 1980s to pursue a similar strategy. He was supported by Muslim clerics and Islamist parties, took his oath of office on the Koran (even as Yeltsin was blessed by the Orthodox patriarch), and in 1994 proposed that Chechnya become an Islamic state governed by *shari'a.* Chechen troops wore green scarves "emblazoned with the word 'Gavazat,' holy war in Chechen," and shouted "Allahu Akbar" as they went off to battle.[5] In similar fashion, the self-definition of Kashmir Muslims shifted from either a regional identity encompassing Muslims, Hindus, and Buddhists or an identification with Indian secularism to a third identity reflected in "the rise of Muslim nationalism in Kashmir and the spread of transnational Islamic fundamentalist values, which made Kashmiri Muslims feel a part of both Islamic Pakistan and the Islamic world." The 1989 insurgency against India was originally led by a "relatively secular" organization, supported by the Pakistan government. Pakistan's support then shifted to Islamic fundamentalist groups, which became dominant. These groups included "hardcore insurgents" who seemed "committed to continuing their *jihad* for its own sake whatever the hope and the outcome." Another observer reported, "Nationalist feelings have been heightened by religious differences; the global rise of Islamic militancy has given courage to Kashmiri insurgents and eroded Kashmir's tradition of Hindu-Muslim tolerance."[6]

A dramatic rise of civilizational identities occurred in Bosnia, particularly in its Muslim community. Historically, communal identities in Bosnia had not been strong; Serbs, Croats, and Muslims lived peacefully together as neighbors;

intergroup marriages were common; religious identifications were weak. Muslims, it was said, were Bosnians who did not go to the mosque, Croats were Bosnians who did not go to the cathedral, and Serbs were Bosnians who did not go to the Orthodox church. Once the broader Yugoslav identity collapsed, however, these casual religious identities assumed new relevance, and once fighting began they intensified. Multicommunalism evaporated and each group increasingly identified itself with its broader cultural community and defined itself in religious terms. Bosnian Serbs became extreme Serbian nationalists, identifying themselves with Greater Serbia, the Serbian Orthodox Church, and the more widespread Orthodox community. Bosnian Croats were the most fervent Croatian nationalists, considered themselves to be citizens of Croatia, emphasized their Catholicism, and together with the Croats of Croatia their identity with the Catholic West.

The Muslims' shift toward civilizational consciousness was even more marked. Until the war got underway Bosnian Muslims were highly secular in their outlook, viewed themselves as Europeans, and were the strongest supporters of a multicultural Bosnian society and state. This began to change, however, as Yugoslavia broke up. Like the Croats and Serbs, in the 1990 elections the Muslims rejected the multicommunal parties, voting overwhelmingly for the Muslim Party of the Democratic Action (SDA) led by Izetbegovic. He is a devout Muslim, was imprisoned for his Islamic activism by the communist government, and in a book, *The Islamic Declaration*, published in 1970, argues for "the incompatibility of Islam with non-Islamic systems. There can be neither peace nor coexistence between the Islamic religion and non-Islamic social and political institutions." When the Islamic movement is strong enough it must take power and create an Islamic republic. In this new state, it is particularly important that education and the media "should be in the hands of people whose Islamic moral and intellectual authority is indisputable."[7]

As Bosnia became independent Izetbegovic promoted a multiethnic state, in which the Muslims would be the dominant group although short of a majority. He was not, however, a person to resist the Islamization of his country produced by the war. His reluctance to repudiate publicly and explicitly *The Islamic Declaration*, generated fear among non-Muslims. As the war went on, Bosnian Serbs and Croats moved from areas controlled by the Bosnian government, and those who remained found themselves gradually excluded from desirable jobs and participation in social institutions. "Islam gained greater importance within the Muslim national community, and ... a strong Muslim national identity became a part of politics and religion." Muslim nationalism, as opposed to Bosnian multicultural nationalism, was increasingly expressed in the media. Religious teaching expanded in the schools, and new textbooks emphasized the benefits of Ottoman rule. The Bosnian language was promoted as distinct from Serbo-Croatian and more and more Turkish and Arabic words were incorporated into it. Government officials attacked mixed marriages and the broadcasting of "aggressor" or Serbian music. The government encouraged the Islamic religion and gave Muslims preference in hirings and promotions. Most important, the Bosnian army became Islamized, with Muslims constituting over 90 percent of its personnel by 1995. More and more army units identified themselves with Islam, engaged in Islamic practices, and made use of Muslim symbols, with the elite units being the most thoroughly Islamized ones and expanding in number. This trend led to a protest from five members (including two Croats and two Serbs) of the Bosnian presidency to Izetbegovic, which he rejected, and to the resignation in 1995 of the multicultural-oriented prime minister, Haris Silajdzic.[8]

Politically Izetbegovic's Muslim party, the SDA, extended its control over Bosnian state and society. By 1995 it dominated "the army, the civil service and public enterprises." "Muslims who do not belong to the party," it was reported, "let alone non-Muslims, find it hard to get decent jobs." The party, its critics charged, had "become a vehicle for an Islamic authoritarianism marked by the habits of Communist government."[9] Overall, another observer reported:

> Muslim nationalism is becoming more extreme. It now takes no account of other national sensibilities; it is the property, privilege, and political instrument of the newly predominant Muslim nation. . . .
>
> The main result of this new Muslim nationalism is a movement towards national homogenization. . . .
>
> Increasingly, Islamic religious fundamentalism is also gaining dominance in determining Muslim national interests.[10]

The intensification of religious identity produced by war and ethnic cleansing, the preferences of its leaders, and the support and pressure from other Muslim states were slowly but clearly transforming Bosnia from the Switzerland of the Balkans into the Iran of the Balkans.

In fault line wars, each side has incentives not only to emphasize it own civilizational identity but also that of the other side. In its local war, it sees itself not just fighting another local ethnic group but fighting another civilization. The threat is thus magnified and enhanced by the resources of a major civilization, and defeat has consequences not just for itself but for all of its own civilization. Hence the urgent need for its own civilization to rally behind it in the conflict. The local war becomes redefined as a war of religions, a clash of civilizations, fraught with consequences for huge segments of humankind. In the early 1990s as the Orthodox religion and the Orthodox Church again became central elements in Russian national identity, which "squeezed out other Russian confessions, of which Islam is the most important,"[11] the Russians found it in their interest to define the war between clans and regions in Tajikistan and the war with Chechnya as parts of a broader clash going back centuries between Orthodoxy and Islam, with its local opponents now committed to Islamic fundamentalism and jihad and the proxies for Islamabad, Tehran, Riyadh, and Ankara.

In the former Yugoslavia, Croats saw themselves as the gallant frontier guardians of the West against the onslaught of Orthodoxy and Islam. The Serbs defined their enemies not just as Bosnian Croats and Muslims but as "the Vatican" and as "Islamic fundamentalists" and "infamous Turks" who have been threatening Christianity for centuries. "Karadzic," one Western diplomat said of the Bosnian Serb leader, "sees this as the anti-imperialist war in Europe. He talks about having a mission to eradicate the last traces of the Ottoman Turkish empire in Europe."[12] The Bosnian Muslims, in turn, identified themselves as the victims of genocide, ignored by the West because of their religion, and hence deserving of support from the Muslim world. All the parties to, and most outside observers of, the Yugoslav wars thus came to see them as religious or ethnoreligious wars. The conflict, Misha Glenny pointed out, "increasingly assimilated the characteristics of a religious struggle, defined by three great European faiths — Roman Catholicism, Eastern Orthodoxy, and Islam, the confessional detritus of the empires whose frontiers collided in Bosnia."[13]

The perception of fault line wars as civilizational clashes also gave new life to the domino theory which had existed during the Cold War. Now, however, it was the major states of civilizations who saw the need to prevent defeat in a local conflict, which could trigger a sequence of escalating losses leading to disaster. The Indian government's tough stand on Kashmir derived in large part from the fear that its loss would stimulate other ethnic and religious minorities to push for independence and thus lead to the breakup of India. If Russia did not end the political violence in Tajikistan, Foreign Minister Kozyrev warned, it was likely to spread to Kyrgyzstan and Uzbekistan. This, it was argued, could then promote secessionist movements in the Muslim republics of the Russian Federation, with some people suggesting the ultimate result might be Islamic fundamentalism in Red Square. Hence the Afghan-Tajik border, Yeltsin said, is "in effect, Russia's." Europeans, in turn, expressed concern that the establishment of a Muslim state in the former Yugoslavia would create a base for the spread of Muslim immigrants and Islamic fundamentalism, reinforcing what the French press, interpreting Jacques Chirac, termed *"les odeurs d'Islam"* in Europe.[14] Croatia's border is, in effect, Europe's.

As a fault line war intensifies, each side demonizes its opponents, often portraying them as subhuman, and thereby legitimates killing them. "Mad dogs must be shot," said Yeltsin in reference to the Chechen guerrillas. "These ill-bred people have to be shot . . . and we will shoot them," said Indonesian General Try Sutrisno referring to the massacre of East Timorese in 1991. The devils of the past are resurrected in the present: Croats become "Ustashe"; Muslims, "Turks"; and Serbs, "Chetniks." Mass murder, torture, rape, and the brutal expulsion of civilians all are justifiable as communal hate feeds on communal hate. The central symbols and artifacts of the opposing culture

become targets. Serbs systematically destroyed mosques and Franciscan monasteries while Croats blew up Orthodox monasteries. As repositories of culture,
museums and libraries are vulnerable, with the Sinhalese security forces burn-
ing the Jaffna public library, destroying "irreplaceable literary and historical
documents" related to Tamil culture, and Serbian gunners shelling and destroying the National Library in Sarajevo. The Serbs cleanse the Bosnian town of
Zvornik of its 40,000 Muslims and plant a cross on the site of the Ottoman
tower they have just blown up which had replaced the Orthodox church razed
by the Turks in 1463.[15] In wars between cultures, culture loses.

CIVILIZATION RALLYING: KIN COUNTRIES AND DIASPORAS

For the forty years of the Cold War, conflict permeated downward as the
superpowers attempted to recruit allies and partners and to subvert, convert, or
neutralize the allies and partners of the other superpower. Competition was, of
course, most intense in the Third World, with new and weak states pressured
by the superpowers to join the great global contest. In the post–Cold War
world, multiple communal conflicts have superseded the single superpower
conflict. When these communal conflicts involve groups from different civilizations, they tend to expand and to escalate. As the conflict becomes more
intense, each side attempts to rally support from countries and groups belonging to its civilization. Support in one form or another, official or unofficial,
overt or covert, material, human, diplomatic, financial, symbolic, or military, is
always forthcoming from one or more kin countries or groups. The longer a
fault line conflict continues the more kin countries are likely to become involved in supporting, constraining, and mediating roles. As a result of this
"kin-country syndrome," fault line conflicts have a much higher potential for
escalation than do intracivilizational conflicts and usually require intercivilizational cooperation to contain and end them. In contrast to the Cold War,
conflict does not flow down from above, it bubbles up from below.

States and groups have different levels of involvement in fault line wars. At
the primary level are those parties actually fighting and killing each other.
These may be states, as in the wars between India and Pakistan and between
Israel and its neighbors, but they may also be local groups, which are not states
or are, at best, embryonic states, as was the case in Bosnia and with the
Nagorno-Karabakh Armenians. These conflicts may also involve secondary
level participants, usually states directly related to the primary parties, such as
the governments of Serbia and Croatia in the former Yugoslavia, and those of
Armenia and Azerbaijan in the Caucasus. Still more remotely connected with
the conflict are tertiary states, further removed from the actual fighting but
having civilizational ties with the participants, such as Germany, Russia, and
the Islamic states with respect to the former Yugoslavia; and Russia, Turkey,
and Iran in the case of the Armenian-Azeri dispute. These third level partici-

pants often are the core states of their civilizations. Where they exist, the diasporas of primary level participants also play a role in fault line wars. Given the small numbers of people and weapons usually involved at the primary level, relatively modest amounts of external aid, in the form of money, weapons, or volunteers, can often have a significant impact on the outcome of the war.

The stakes of the other parties to the conflict are not identical with those of primary level participants. The most devoted and wholehearted support for the primary level parties normally comes from diaspora communities who intensely identify with the cause of their kin and become "more Catholic than the Pope." The interests of second and third level governments are more complicated. They also usually provide support to first level participants, and even if they do not do so, they are suspected of doing so by opposing groups, which justifies the latter supporting their kin. In addition, however, second and third level governments have an interest in containing the fighting and not becoming directly involved themselves. Hence while supporting primary level participants, they also attempt to restrain those participants and to induce them to moderate their objectives. They also usually attempt to negotiate with their second and third level counterparts on the other side of the fault line and thus prevent a local war from escalating into a broader war involving core states. Figure 11.1 outlines the relationships of these potential parties to fault line wars. Not all such wars have had this full cast of characters, but several have, including those in the former Yugoslavia and the Transcaucasus, and almost any fault line war potentially could expand to involve all levels of participants.

In one way or another, diasporas and kin countries have been involved in every fault line war of the 1990s. Given the extensive primary role of Muslim groups in such wars, Muslim governments and associations are the most frequent secondary and tertiary participants. The most active have been the governments of Saudi Arabia, Pakistan, Iran, Turkey, and Libya, who together, at times with other Muslim states, have contributed varying degrees of support to Muslims fighting non-Muslims in Palestine, Lebanon, Bosnia, Chechnya, the Transcaucasus, Tajikistan, Kashmir, Sudan, and the Philippines. In addition to governmental support, many primary level Muslim groups have been bolstered by the floating Islamist international of fighters from the Afghanistan war, who have joined in conflicts ranging from the civil war in Algeria to Chechnya to the Philippines. This Islamist international was involved, one analyst noted, in the "dispatch of volunteers in order to establish Islamist rule in Afghanistan, Kashmir, and Bosnia; joint propaganda wars against governments opposing Islamists in one country or another; the establishment of Islamic centers in the diaspora that serve jointly as political headquarters for all of those parties."[16] The Arab League and the Organization of the Islamic Conference have also provided support for and attempted to coordinate the efforts of their members in reinforcing Muslim groups in intercivilizational conflicts.

The Soviet Union was a primary participant in the Afghanistan War, and in

FIGURE 11.1
THE STRUCTURE OF A COMPLEX FAULT LINE WAR

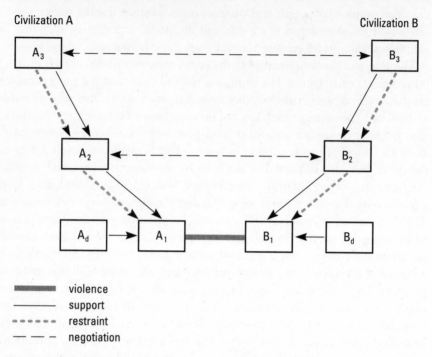

the post–Cold War years Russia has been a primary participant in the Chechen War, a secondary participant in the Tajikistan fighting, and a tertiary participant in the former Yugoslav wars. India has had a primary involvement in Kashmir and a secondary one in Sri Lanka. The principal Western states have been tertiary participants in the Yugoslav contests. Diasporas have played a major role on both sides of the prolonged struggles between Israelis and Palestinians, as well as in supporting Armenians, Croatians, and Chechens in their conflicts. Through television, faxes, and electronic mail, "the commitments of diasporas are reinvigorated and sometimes polarized by constant contact with their former homes; 'former' no longer means what it did." [17]

In the Kashmir war Pakistan provided explicit diplomatic and political support to the insurgents and, according to Pakistani military sources, substantial amounts of money and weapons, as well as training, logistical support, and a sanctuary. It also lobbied other Muslim governments on their behalf. By 1995 the insurgents had reportedly been reinforced by at least 1,200 *mujahedeen* fighters from Afghanistan, Tajikistan, and Sudan equipped with Stinger missiles and other weapons supplied by the Americans for their war against the Soviet Union." [18] The Moro insurgency in the Philippines benefited for a time from funds and equipment from Malaysia; Arab governments provided additional funds; several thousands insurgents were trained in Libya; and the extremist insurgent group, Abu Sayyaf, was organized by Pakistani and Afghan fundamentalists.[19] In Africa Sudan regularly helped the Muslim Eritrean rebels fighting Ethiopia, and in retaliation Ethiopia supplied "logistic and sanctuary support" to the "rebel Christians" fighting Sudan. The latter also received similar aid from Uganda, reflecting in part its "strong religious, racial, and ethnic ties to the Sudanese rebels." The Sudanese government, on the other hand, got $300 million in Chinese arms from Iran and training from Iranian military advisers, which enabled it to launch a major offensive against the rebels in 1992. A variety of Western Christian organizations provided food, medicine, supplies, and, according to the Sudanese government, arms to the Christian rebels.[20]

In the war between the Hindu Tamil insurgents and the Buddhist Sinhalese government in Sri Lanka, the Indian government originally provided substantial support to the insurgents, training them in southern India and giving them weapons and money. In 1987 when Sri Lankan government forces were on the verge of defeating the Tamil Tigers, Indian public opinion was aroused against this "genocide" and the Indian government airlifted food to the Tamils "in effect signaling [President] Jayewardene that India intended to prevent him from crushing the Tigers by force."[21] The Indian and Sri Lankan governments then reached an agreement that Sri Lanka would grant a considerable measure of autonomy to the Tamil areas and the insurgents would turn in their weapons to the Indian army. India deployed 50,000 troops to the island to enforce the agreement, but the Tigers refused to surrender their arms and the Indian military soon found themselves engaged in a war with the guerrilla forces they had previously supported. The Indian forces were withdrawn beginning in 1988. In 1991 the Indian prime minister, Rajiv Gandhi, was murdered, according to Indians by a supporter of the Tamil insurgents, and the Indian government's attitude toward the insurgency became increasingly hostile. Yet the government could not stop the sympathy and support for the insurgents among the 50 million Tamils in southern India. Reflecting this opinion, officials of the Tamil Nadu government, in defiance of New Delhi, allowed the Tamil Tigers to operate in their state with a "virtually free run" of their 500-mile coast and to send supplies and weapons across the narrow Palk Strait to the insurgents in Sri Lanka.[22]

Beginning in 1979 the Soviets and then the Russians became engaged in three major fault line wars with their Muslim neighbors to the south: the Afghan War of 1979–1989, its sequel the Tajikistan war that began in 1992, and the Chechen war that began in 1994. With the collapse of the Soviet Union a successor communist government came to power in Tajikistan. This government was challenged in the spring of 1922, by an opposition composed of rival regional and ethnic groups, including both secularists and Islamists. This opposition, bolstered by weapons from Afghanistan, drove the pro-Russian government out of the capital, Dushanbe, in September 1992. The Russian and Uzbekistan governments reacted vigorously, warning of the spread of Islamic fundamentalism. The Russian 201st Motorized Rifle Division, which had remained in Tajikistan, provided arms to the progovernment forces, and Russia dispatched additional troops to guard the border with Afghanistan. In November 1992 Russia, Uzbekistan, Kazakhstan, and Kyrgyzstan agreed on Russian and Uzbek military intervention ostensibly for peacekeeping but actually to participate in the war. With this support plus Russian arms and money, the forces of the former government were able to recapture Dushanbe and establish control over much of the country. A process of ethnic cleansing followed, and opposition refugees and troops retreated into Afghanistan.

Middle Eastern Muslim governments protested the Russian military intervention. Iran, Pakistan, and Afghanistan assisted the increasingly Islamist opposition with money, arms, and training. In 1993 reportedly many thousand fighters were being trained by the Afghan *mujahedeen*, and in the spring and summer of 1993, the Tajik insurgents launched several attacks across the border from Afghanistan killing a number of Russian border guards. Russia responded by deploying more troops to Tajikistan and delivering "a massive artillery and mortar" barrage and air attacks on targets in Afghanistan. Arab governments, however, supplied the insurgents with funds to purchase Stinger missiles to counter the aircraft. By 1995 Russia had about 25,000 troops deployed in Tajikistan and was providing well over half the funds necessary to support its government. The insurgents, on the other hand, were actively supported by the Afghanistan government and other Muslim states. As Barnett Rubin pointed out, the failure of international agencies or the West to provide significant aid to either Tajikistan or Afghanistan made the former totally dependent on the Russians and the latter dependent upon their Muslim civilizational kin. "Any Afghan commander who hopes for foreign aid today must either cater to the wishes of the Arab and Pakistani funders who wish to spread the *jihad* to Central Asia or join the drug trade."[23]

Russia's third anti-Muslim war, in the North Caucasus with the Chechens, had a prologue in the fighting in 1992–1993 between the neighboring Orthodox Ossetians and Muslim Ingush. The latter together with the Chechens and other Muslim peoples were deported to central Asia during World War II. The Ossetians remained and took over Ingush properties. In 1956–1957 the deported peoples were allowed to return and disputes commenced over the ownership of property and the control of territory. In November 1992 the Ingush launched attacks from their republic to regain the Prigorodny region, which the Soviet government had assigned to the Ossetians. The Russians responded with a massive intervention including Cossack units to support the Orthodox Ossetians. As one outside commentator described it: "In November 1992, Ingush villages in Ossetia were surrounded and shelled by Russian tanks. Those who survived the bombing were killed or taken away. The massacre was carried out by Ossetian OMON [special police] squads, but Russian troops sent to the region 'to keep the peace' provided their cover."[24] It was, *The Economist* reported, "hard to comprehend that so much destruction had taken place in less than a week." This was "the first ethnic-cleansing operation in the Russian federation." Russia then used this conflict to threaten the Chechen allies of the Ingush, which, in turn, "led to the immediate mobilization of Chechnya and the [overwhelmingly Muslim] Confederation of the Peoples of the Caucasus (KNK). The KNK threatened to send 500,000 volunteers against the Russian forces if they did not withdraw from Chechen territory. After a tense standoff, Moscow backed down to avoid the escalation of the North Ossetian–Ingush conflict into a regionwide conflagration."[25]

A more intense and extensive conflagration broke out in December 1994 when Russia launched a full-scale military attack on Chechnya. The leaders of two Orthodox republics, Georgia and Armenia, supported the Russian action, while the Ukrainian president was "diplomatically bland, merely calling for a peaceful settlement of the crisis." The Russian action was also endorsed by the Orthodox North Ossetian government and 55–60 percent of the North Ossetian people.[26] In contrast, Muslims within and without the Russian Federation overwhelmingly sided with the Chechens. The Islamist international immediately contributed fighters from Azerbaijan, Afghanistan, Pakistan, Sudan, and elsewhere. Muslim states endorsed the Chechen cause, and Turkey and Iran reportedly supplied material help, providing Russia with further incentives to attempt to conciliate Iran. A steady stream of arms for the Chechens began to enter the Russian Federation from Azerbaijan, causing Russia to close its border with that country, thereby also shutting off medical and other supplies to Chechnya.[27]

Muslims in the Russian Federation rallied behind the Chechens. While calls for a Caucasus-wide Muslim holy war against Russia did not produce that result, the leaders of the six Volga-Ural republics demanded Russia end its military action, and representatives of the Muslim Caucasus republics called for a civil disobedience campaign against Russian rule. The president of the Chuvash republic exempted Chuvash draftees from serving against their fellow Muslims. The "strongest protests against the war" occurred in Chechnya's two neighboring republics of Ingushetia and Dagestan. The Ingush attacked Russian troops on their way to Chechnya, leading the Russian defense minister to declare that the Ingush government "had virtually declared war on Russia," and attacks on Russian forces also occurred in Dagestan. The Russians responded by shelling Ingush and Dagestani villages.[28] The Russian leveling of the village of Pervomaiskoye after the Chechen raid into the city of Kizlyar in January 1996 further aroused Dagestani hostility to the Russians.

The Chechen cause was also helped by the Chechen diaspora, which had in large part been produced by the nineteenth-century Russian aggression against the Caucasus mountain peoples. The diaspora raised funds, procured weapons, and provided volunteers for the Chechen forces. It was particularly numerous in Jordan and Turkey, which led Jordan to take a strong stand against the Russians and reinforced Turkey's willingness to assist the Chechens. In January 1996 when the war spread to Turkey, Turkish public opinion sympathized with the seizure of a ferry and Russian hostages by members of the diaspora. With the help of Chechen leaders, the Turkish government negotiated resolution of the crisis in a way which further worsened the already strained relations between Turkey and Russia.

The Chechen incursion into Dagestan, the Russian response, and the ferry seizure at the start of 1996 highlighted the possible expansion of the conflict into a general conflict between the Russians and the mountain peoples, along the lines of the struggle that went on for decades in the nineteenth century. "The North Caucasus is a tinderbox," Fiona Hill warned in 1995, "where a conflict in one republic has the potential to spark a regional conflagration that will spread beyond its borders into the rest of the Russian Federation, and will invite involvement of Georgia, Azerbaijan, Turkey and Iran and their North Caucasian diasporas. As the war in Chechnya demonstrates, conflict in the region is not easily contained. . . . and the fighting has spilled into republics and territories adjacent to Chechnya." A Russian analyst agreed, arguing that "informal coalitions" were developing along civilizational lines. "Christian Georgia, Armenia, Nagorny-Karabakh and Northern Ossetia are lining up against Moslem Azerbaijan, Abkhazia, Chechnya and Ingushetia." Already fighting in Tajikistan, Russia was "running the risk of being drawn into a prolonged confrontation with the Moslem world."[29]

In another Orthodox-Muslim fault line war, the primary participants were the Armenians of the Nagorno-Karabakh enclave and the government and people of Azerbaijan, with the former fighting for independence from the latter. The government of Armenia was a secondary participant, and Russia, Turkey, and Iran had tertiary involvements. In addition, a major role was played by the substantial Armenian diaspora in Western Europe and North America. The fighting began in 1988 before the end of the Soviet Union, intensified during 1992–1993, and subsided after negotiation of a cease-fire in 1994. The Turks and other Muslims backed Azerbaijan, while Russia supported the Armenians but then used its influence with them also to contest Turkish influence in Azerbaijan. This war was the latest episode in both the struggle going back centuries to those between the Russian Empire and the Ottoman Empire for control of the Black Sea region and the Caucasus, and the intense antagonism between Armenians and Turks going back to the early-twentieth-century massacres of the former by the latter.

In this war, Turkey was a consistent supporter of Azerbaijan and opponent of the Armenians. The first recognition by any country of the independence of a non-Baltic Soviet republic was Turkey's recognition of Azerbaijan. Throughout the conflict Turkey provided financial and material support to Azerbaijan and trained Azerbaijani soldiers. As violence intensified in 1991–1992 and Armenians advanced into Azerbaijani territory, Turkish public opinion became aroused, and the Turkish government came under pressure to support its eth-nic-religious kinspeople. It also feared that this would highlight the Muslim-Christian divide, produce an outpouring of Western support for Armenia, and antagonize its NATO allies. Turkey thus faced the classic cross-pressures of a secondary participant in a fault line war. The Turkish government, however, found it in its interest to support Azerbaijan and confront Armenia. "[I]t's impossible not to be affected when your kin are killed," one Turkish official said, and another added, "We are under pressure. Our newspapers are full of the photos of atrocities. . . . Maybe we should show Armenia that there's a big Turkey in this region." President Turgut Özal agreed, saying that Turkey "should scare the Armenians a little bit." Turkey, along with Iran, warned the Armenians it would not countenance any change in borders. Özal blocked food and other supplies from getting to Armenia through Turkey, as a result of which the population of Armenia was on the verge of famine during the winter of 1992–1993. Also as a result, Russian Marshal Yevgeny Shaposhnikov warned that "If another side [i.e., Turkey] gets involved" in the war, "we will be on the edge of World War III." A year later Özal was still belligerent. "What can the Armenians do," he taunted, "if shots happened to be fired. . . . March into Turkey?" Turkey "will show its fangs."[30]

In the summer and fall of 1993 the Armenian offensive, which was ap-proaching the Iranian border, produced additional reactions from both Turkey and Iran, who were competing for influence within Azerbaijan and the Central Asian Muslim states. Turkey declared that the offensive threatened Turkey's security, demanded that the Armenian forces "immediately and uncondition-ally" withdraw from Azerbaijani territory, and sent reinforcements to its border with Armenia. Russian and Turkish troops reportedly exchanged gunfire across that border. Prime Minister Tansu Ciller of Turkey declared she would ask for a declaration of war if Armenian troops went into the Azerbaijani enclave of Nakhichevan close to Turkey. Iran also moved forces forward and into Azerbai-jan, allegedly to establish camps for the refugees from the Armenian offensives. The Iranian action reportedly led the Turks to believe they could take addi-tional measures without stimulating Russian countermoves and also gave them further incentive to compete with Iran in providing protection to Azerbaijan. The crisis was eventually eased by negotiations in Moscow by the leaders of Turkey, Armenia, and Azerbaijan, by American pressure on the Armenian government, and by Armenian government pressure on the Nagorno-Karabakh Armenians.[31]

Inhabiting a small, landlocked country with meager resources bordered by hostile Turkic peoples, Armenians have historically looked for protection to their Orthodox kin, Georgia and Russia. Russia, in particular, has been viewed as a big brother. As the Soviet Union was collapsing, however, and the Nagor-ono-Karabakh Armenians launched their drive for independence, the Gorba-chev regime rejected their demands and dispatched troops to the region to support what was viewed as a loyal communist government in Baku. After the end of the Soviet Union, these considerations gave way to more long-standing historical and cultural ones, with Azerbaijan accusing "the Russian government of turning 180 degrees" and actively supporting Christian Armenia. Russian military assistance to the Armenians actually had begun earlier in the Soviet army, in which Armenians were promoted to higher ranks and assigned to combat units much more frequently than Muslims. After the war began, the 366th Motorized Rifle Regiment of the Russian Army, based in Nagorno-Karabakh, played a leading role in the Armenian attack on the town of Khodjali, in which allegedly up to 1000 Azeris were massacred. Subsequently Russian *spetsnaz* troops also participated in the fighting. During the winter of 1992–1993, when Armenia suffered from the Turkish embargo, it was "rescued from total economic collapse by an infusion of billions of rubles in credits from Russia." That spring Russian troops joined regular Armenian forces to open a corridor connecting Armenia to Nagorno-Karabakh. A Russian armored force of forty tanks then reportedly participated in the Karabakh offensive in the summer of 1993.[32] Armenia, in turn, as Hill and Jewett observe, had "little option but to ally itself closely with Russia. It is dependent upon Russia for raw materials, energy and food supplies, and defense against historic enemies on its borders such as Azerbaijan and Turkey. Armenia has signed all of the CIS economic and military accords, permitted Russian troops to be stationed on its territory and relinquished all claims to former Soviet assets in Russia's favor."[33]

Russian support for the Armenians enhanced Russian influence with Azerbaijan. In June 1993 the Azerbaijani nationalist leader Abulfez Elchibey was ousted in a coup and replaced by the former communist and presumably pro-Russian Gaider Aliyev. Aliyev recognized the need to propitiate Russia in order to restrain Armenia. He reversed Azerbaijan's refusals to join the Commonwealth of Independent States and to allow Russian troops to be stationed on its territory. He also opened the way to Russian participation in an international consortium to develop Azerbaijan's oil. In return, Russia began to train Azerbaijani troops and pressured Armenia to end its support of the Karabakh forces and to induce them to withdraw from Azerbaijan territory. By shifting its weight from one side to the other, Russia was able also to produce results for Azerbaijan and counter Iranian and Turkish influence in that country. Russian support for Armenia thus not only strengthened its closest ally in the Caucasus but also weakened its principal Muslim rivals in that region.

Apart from Russia, Armenia's major source of support was its large, wealthy and influential diaspora in Western Europe and North America, including roughly 1 million Armenians in the United States and 450,000 in France. These provided money and supplies to help Armenia survive the Turkish blockade, officials for the Armenian government, and volunteers for the Armenian armed forces. Contributions to Armenian relief from the American community amounted to $50 million to $75 million a year in the mid-1990s. The diasporans also exercised considerable political influence with their host governments. The largest Armenian communities in the United States are in key states like California, Massachusetts, and New Jersey. As a result, Congress prohibited any foreign aid to Azerbaijan and made Armenia the third largest per capita recipient of U.S. assistance. This backing from abroad was essential to Armenia's survival and appropriately earned it the sobriquet of "the Israel of the Caucasus."[34] Just as the nineteenth-century Russian attacks on the North Caucasians generated the diaspora that helped the Chechens to resist the Russians, the early-twentieth-century Turkish massacres of Armenians produced a diaspora that enabled Armenia to resist Turkey and defeat Azerbaijan.

The former Yugoslavia was the site of the most complex, confused, and complete set of fault line wars of the early 1990s. At the primary level, in Croatia the Croatian government and Croats fought the Croatian Serbs, and in Bosnia-Herzegovina the Bosnian government fought the Bosnian Serbs and Bosnian Croats, who also fought each other. At the secondary level, the Serbian government promoted a "Greater Serbia" by helping Bosnian and Croatian Serbs, and the Croatian government aspired to a "Greater Croatia" and supported the Bosnian Croats. At the tertiary level, massive civilization rallying included: Germany, Austria, the Vatican, other European Catholic countries and groups and, later, the United States on behalf of Croatia; Russia, Greece, and other Orthodox countries and groups behind the Serbs; and Iran, Saudi Arabia, Turkey, Libya, the Islamist international, and Islamic countries generally on behalf of the Bosnian Muslims. The latter also received help from the United States, a noncivilization anomaly in the otherwise universal pattern of kin backing kin. The Croatian diaspora in Germany and the Bosnian diaspora in Turkey came to the support of their homelands. Churches and religious groups were active on all three sides. The actions of at least the German, Turkish, Russian, and American governments were significantly influenced by pressure groups and public opinion in their societies.

The support provided by secondary and tertiary parties was essential to the conduct of the war and the constraints they imposed essential to halting it. The Croatian and Serbian governments supplied weapons, supplies, funding, sanctuary, and at times military forces to their people fighting in other republics. Serbs, Croats, and Muslims all received substantial help from civilizational kin outside the former Yugoslavia in the form of money, weapons, supplies, volunteers, military training, and political and diplomatic support. The nongovernmental primary level Serbs and Croats were generally most extreme in their nationalism, unrelenting in their demands, and militant in pursuing their goals. The second level Croatian and Serbian governments initially vigorously supported their primary level kin but their own more diversified interests then led them to play more mediating and containing roles. In parallel fashion, the third level Russian, German, and American governments pushed the second level governments they had been backing toward restraint and compromise.

The breakup of Yugoslavia began in 1991 when Slovenia and Croatia moved toward independence and pleaded with Western European powers for support. The response of the West was defined by Germany, and the response of Germany was in large part defined by the Catholic connection. The Bonn government came under pressure to act from the German Catholic hierarchy, its coalition partner the Christian Social Union party in Bavaria, and the *Frankfurter Allgemeine Zeitung* and other media. The Bavarian media, in particular, played a crucial role in developing German public sentiment for recognition. "Bavarian TV," Flora Lewis noted, "much weighed upon by the very conservative Bavarian government and the strong, assertive Bavarian Catholic church which had close connections with the church in Croatia, provided the television reports for all of Germany when the war [with the Serbs] began in earnest. The coverage was very one-sided." The German government was hesitant about granting recognition, but given the pressures in German society it had little choice. "[S]upport for recognizing Croatia in Germany was opinion-pushed, not government-pulled." Germany pressured the European Union to recognize the independence of Slovenia and Croatia, and then, having secured that, pushed forward on its own to recognize them before the Union did in December 1991. "Throughout the conflict," one German scholar observed in 1995, "Bonn considered Croatia and its leader Franjo Tudjman as something of a German foreign-policy protege, whose erratic behavior was irritating but who could still rely on Germany's firm support."[35]

Austria and Italy promptly moved to recognize the two new states, and very quickly the other Western countries, including the United States, followed. The Vatican also played a central role. The Pope declared Croatia to be the "rampart of [Western] Christianity," and rushed to extend diplomatic recognition to the two states before the European Union did.[36] The Vatican thus became a partisan in the conflict, which had its consequences in 1994 when the Pope planned visits to the three republics. Opposition by the Serbian Orthodox Church prevented his going to Belgrade, and Serb unwillingness to guarantee his security led to the cancellation of his visit to Sarajevo. He did go to Zagreb, however, where he honored Cardinal Alojzieje Septinac, who was associated with the fascist Croatian regime in World War II that persecuted and slaughtered Serbs, Gypsies, and Jews.

Having secured recognition by the West of its independence, Croatia began to develop its military strength despite the U.N. arms embargo levied on all the former Yugoslav republics in September 1991. Arms flowed into Croatia from European Catholic countries such as Germany, Poland, and Hungary, as well as from Latin American countries such as Panama, Chile, and Bolivia. As the war escalated in 1991, Spanish arms exports, allegedly "in large part controlled by Opus Dei," increased sixfold in a short period of time, with most of these presumably finding their way to Ljubliana and Zagreb. In 1993 Croatia reportedly acquired several Mig-21s from Germany and Poland with the knowledge of their governments. The Croatian Defense Forces were joined by hundreds and perhaps thousands of volunteers "from Western Europe, the Croatian diaspora, and the Catholic countries of Eastern Europe" who were eager to fight in "a Christian crusade against both Serbian communism and Islamic fundamentalism." Military professionals from Western countries provided technical assistance. Thanks in part to this kin country help, the Croatians were able to strengthen their military forces and create a counter to the Serb-dominated Yugoslav army.[37]

Western support for Croatia also included overlooking the ethnic cleansing and the violations of human rights and the laws of war for which the Serbs were regularly denounced. The West was silent when in 1995 the revamped Croatian army launched an attack on the Serbs of Krajina, who had been there for centuries, and drove hundreds of thousands of them into exile in Bosnia and Serbia. Croatia also benefited from its sizable diaspora. Wealthy Croatians in Western Europe and North America contributed funds for arms and equipment. Associations of Croatians in the United States lobbied Congress and the President on their homeland's behalf. Particularly important and influential were the 600,000 Croatians in Germany. Supplying hundreds of volunteers for the Croatian army, "Croat communities in Canada, the United States, Australia, and Germany mobilized to defend their newly independent-homeland."[38]

In 1994 the United States joined in supporting the Croatian military buildup. Ignoring the massive Croatian violations of the U.N. arms embargo, the United States provided military training to the Croatians and authorized top-ranking retired U.S. generals to advise them. The U.S. and German governments gave the green light to the Croatian offensive into Krajina in 1995. American military advisers participated in planning this American-style attack, which according to the Croatians also benefited from intelligence supplied by American spy-satellites. Croatia has become "our de facto strategic ally," a State Department official declared. This development, it was argued, reflected "a long-term calculation that, ultimately, two local powers will dominate this part of the world—one in Zagreb, one in Belgrade; one tied to Washington, the other locked into a Slavic bloc extending to Moscow."[39]

The Yugoslav wars also produced a virtually unanimous rallying of the Orthodox world behind Serbia. Russian nationalists, military officers, parliamentarians, and Orthodox Church leaders were outspoken in their support for Serbia, their disparaging of the Bosnian "Turks," and their criticism of Western and NATO imperialism. Russian and Serbian nationalists worked together arousing opposition in both countries to the Western "new world order." In considerable measure these sentiments were shared by the Russian populace, with over 60 percent of Muscovites, for instance, opposing NATO air strikes in the summer of 1995. Russian nationalist groups successfully recruited young Russians in several major cities to join "the cause of Slavic brotherhood." Reportedly a thousand or more Russians, along with volunteers from Romania and Greece, enlisted in the Serbian forces to fight what they described as the "Catholic fascists" and "Islamic militants." In 1992 a Russian unit "in Cossack uniforms" was reported operating in Bosnia. In 1995 Russians were serving in elite Serbian military units, and, according to a U.N. report, Russian and Greek fighters participated in the Serbian attack on the U.N. safe area of Zepa.[40]

Despite the arms embargo, its Orthodox friends supplied Serbia with the weapons and equipment it needed. In early 1993 Russian military and intelligence organizations apparently sold $300 million worth of T-55 tanks, antimissile missiles, and antiaircraft missiles to the Serbs. Russian military technicians reportedly went to Serbia to operate this equipment and to train Serbs to do so. Serbia acquired arms from other Orthodox countries, with Romania and Bulgaria the "most active" suppliers and Ukraine also a source. In addition, Russian peacekeeping troops in Eastern Slavonia diverted U.N. supplies to the Serbs, facilitated Serbian military movements, and helped the Serbian forces acquire weapons.[41]

Despite economic sanctions, Serbia was able to sustain itself reasonably well off as a result of massive smuggling of fuel and other goods from Timisoara organized by Romanian government officials, and from Albania organized by first Italian and then Greek companies with the connivance of the Greek government. Shipments of food, chemicals, computers, and other goods from Greece went into Serbia through Macedonia, and comparable amounts of Serbian exports came out.[42] The combination of the lure of the dollar and sympathy for cultural kin made a mockery of U.N. economic sanctions against Serbia as they also did to the U.N. arms embargo against all the former Yugoslav republics.

Throughout the Yugoslav wars, the Greek government distanced itself from the measures endorsed by Western members of NATO, opposed NATO military action in Bosnia, supported the Serbs at the United Nations, and lobbied the U.S. government to lift the economic sanctions against Serbia. In 1994 the Greek prime minister, Andreas Papandreou, emphasizing the importance of the Orthodox connection with Serbia, publicly attacked the Vatican, Germany, and the European Union for their haste in extending diplomatic recognition to Slovenia and Croatia at the end of 1991.[43]

As the leader of a tertiary participant, Boris Yeltsin was cross-pressured by the desire, on the one hand, to maintain, expand, and benefit from good relations with the West and, on the other hand, to help the Serbs and to disarm his political opposition, which regularly accused him of caving into the West. Overall the latter concern won out, and Russian diplomatic support for the Serbs was frequent and consistent. In 1993 and 1995 the Russian government vigorously opposed imposing more stringent economic sanctions on Serbia, and the Russian parliament voted almost unanimously in favor of lifting the existing sanctions on the Serbs. Russia also pushed for the tightening of the arms embargo against the Muslims and for applying economic sanctions against Croatia. In December 1993 Russia urged weakening the economic sanctions so as to permit it to supply Serbia with natural gas for the winter, a proposal which was blocked by the United States and Great Britain. In 1994 and again in 1995 Russia staunchly opposed NATO air strikes against the Bosnian Serbs. In the latter year the Russian Duma denounced the bombing by an almost unanimous vote and demanded the resignation of Foreign Minister Andrei Kozyrev for his ineffectual defense of Russian national interests in the Balkans. Also in 1995 Russia accused NATO of "genocide" against the Serbs, and President Yeltsin warned that sustained bombing would drastically affect Russia's cooperation with the West including its participation in NATO's Partnership for Peace. "How can we conclude an agreement with NATO," he asked, "when NATO is bombing Serbs?" The West was clearly applying a double standard: "How is it, that when Muslims attack no action is taken against them? Or when the Croats attack?"[44] Russia also consistently opposed efforts to suspend the arms embargo against the former Yugoslav republics, which had its principal impact on the Bosnian Muslims, and regularly attempted to tighten that embargo.

In a variety of other ways Russia employed its position in the U.N. and elsewhere to defend Serbian interests. In December 1994 it vetoed a U.N. Security Council resolution, advanced by the Muslim countries, that would have prohibited the movement of fuel from Serbia to the Bosnian and Croatian Serbs. In April 1994 Russia blocked a U.N. resolution condemning the Serbs for ethnic cleansing. It also prevented appointment of anyone from a NATO country as U.N. war crimes prosecutor because of probable bias against the Serbs, objected to the indictment of Bosnian Serb military commander Ratko Mladic by the International War Crimes Tribunal, and offered Mladic asylum in Russia.[45] In September 1993 Russia held up renewal of U.N. authorization for the 22,000 U.N. peacekeepers in the former Yugoslavia. In the summer of 1995 Russia opposed but did not veto a Security Council resolution authorizing 12,000 more U.N. peacekeepers and attacked both the Croat offensive against the Krajina Serbs and the failure of Western governments to take action against that offensive.

The broadest and most effective civilization rallying was by the Muslim world on behalf of the Bosnian Muslims. The Bosnian cause was universally popular in Muslim countries; aid to the Bosnians came from a variety of sources, public and private; Muslim governments, most notably those of Iran and Saudi Arabia, competed with each other in providing support and in attempting to gain the influence that generated. Sunni and Shi'ite, fundamentalist and secular, Arab and non-Arab Muslim societies from Morocco to Malaysia all joined in. Manifestations of Muslim support for the Bosnians varied from humanitarian aid (including $90 million raised in 1995 in Saudi Arabia) through diplomatic support and massive military assistance to acts of violence, such as the killing of twelve Croatians in 1993 in Algeria by Islamist extremists "in response to the massacre of our Muslim co-religionists whose throats have been cut in Bosnia."[46] The rallying had a major impact on the course of the war. It was essential to the survival of the Bosnian state and its success in regaining territory after the initial sweeping victories of the Serbs. It greatly stimulated the Islamization of Bosnian society and identification of Bosnian Muslims with the global Islamic community. And it provided an incentive for the United States to be sympathetic to Bosnian needs.

Individually and collectively Muslim governments repeatedly expressed their solidarity with their Bosnian coreligionists. Iran took the lead in 1992, describing the war as a religious conflict with Christian Serbs engaging in genocide against Bosnian Muslims. In taking this lead, Fouad Ajami observed, Iran made "a down-payment on the gratitude of the Bosnian state" and set the model and provided the stimulus for other Muslim powers such as Turkey and Saudi Arabia to follow. At Iran's prodding the Organization of the Islamic Conference took up the issue and created a group to lobby for the Bosnian cause at the United Nations. In August 1992 Islamic representatives denounced the alleged genocide in the U.N. General Assembly, and on behalf of the OIC, Turkey introduced a resolution calling for military intervention under Article 7 of the U.N. charter. The Muslim countries set a deadline in early 1993 for the West to take action to protect the Bosnians after which they would feel free to provide Bosnia with arms. In May 1993 the OIC denounced the plan devised by the Western nations and Russia to provide safe havens for Muslims and to monitor the border with Serbia but to forswear any military intervention. It demanded the end of the arms embargo, the use of force against Serbian heavy weapons, aggressive patrolling of the Serbian border, and inclusion of troops from Muslim countries in the peacekeeping forces. The following month the OIC, over Western and Russian objections, got the U.N. Conference on Human Rights to approve a resolution denouncing Serb and Croat aggression and calling for an end to the arms embargo. In July 1993, somewhat to the embarrassment of the West, the OIC offered to provide 18,000 peacekeeping troops to the U.N., the soldiers to come from Iran, Turkey, Malaysia, Tunisia, Pakistan, and Bangladesh. The United States vetoed Iran, and the Serbs objected vigorously to Turkish troops. The latter nonetheless arrived in Bosnia in the summer of 1994, and by 1995 the U.N. Protection Force of 25,000 troops included 7000 from Turkey, Pakistan, Malaysia, Indonesia, and Bangladesh. In August 1993 an OIC delegation, led by the Turkish foreign minister, lobbied Boutros Boutros-Ghali and Warren Christopher to back immediate NATO air strikes to protect the Bosnians against Serb attacks. The failure of the West to take this action, it was reported, created serious strains between Turkey and its NATO allies.[47]

Subsequently the prime ministers of Turkey and Pakistan made a well-publicized visit to Sarajevo to dramatize Muslim concern, and the OIC again repeated its demands for military assistance to the Bosnians. In the summer of

1995 the failure of the West to defend the safe areas against Serb attacks led Turkey to approve military aid to Bosnia and to train Bosnian troops, Malaysia to commit itself to selling them arms in violation of the U.N. embargo, and the United Arab Emirates to agree to supply funds for military and humanitarian purposes. In August 1995 the foreign ministers of nine OIC countries declared the U.N. arms embargo invalid, and in September the fifty-two members of the OIC approved arms and economic assistance for the Bosnians.

While no other issue generated more unanimous support throughout Islam, the plight of the Bosnian Muslims had special resonance in Turkey. Bosnia had been part of the Ottoman Empire until 1878 in practice and 1908 in theory, and Bosnian immigrants and refugees make up roughly 5 percent of Turkey's population. Sympathy for the Bosnian cause and outrage at the perceived failure of the West to protect the Bosnians were pervasive among the Turkish people, and the opposition Islamist Welfare Party exploited this issue against the government. Government officials, in turn, emphasized Turkey's special responsibilities with respect to all Balkan Muslims, and the government regularly pushed for U.N. military intervention to safeguard the Bosnian Muslims.[48]

By far the most important help the *ummah* gave the Bosnian Muslims was military assistance: weapons, money to buy weapons, military training, and volunteers. Immediately after the war started the Bosnian government invited in the *mujahedeen*, and the total number of volunteers reportedly came to about 4000, more than the foreigners who fought for either the Serbs or the Croats. They included units from the Iranian Republican Guards and many who had fought in Afghanistan. Among them were natives of Pakistan, Turkey, Iran, Algeria, Saudi Arabia, Egypt, and Sudan, plus Albanian and Turkish guest workers from Germany, Austria, and Switzerland. Saudi religious organizations sponsored many volunteers; two dozen Saudis were killed in the very early months of the war in 1992; and the World Assembly of Muslim Youth flew wounded fighters back to Jiddah for medical care. In the fall of 1992 guerrillas from the Shi'ite Lebanese Hezbollah arrived to train the Bosnian army, training which was subsequently largely taken over by Iranian Republican Guards. In the spring of 1994 Western intelligence reported that an Iranian Republican Guard unit of 400 men was organizing extremist guerrilla and terrorist units. "The Iranians," a U.S. official said, "see this as a way to get at the soft underbelly of Europe." According to the United Nations, the *mujahedeen* trained 3000–5000 Bosnians for special Islamist brigades. The Bosnian government used the *mujahedeen* for "terrorist, illegal, and shocktroop activities," although these units often harassed the local population and caused other problems for the government. The Dayton agreements required all foreign combatants to leave Bosnia, but the Bosnian government helped some fighters stay by giving them Bosnian citizenship and enrolling the Iranian Republican Guards as relief workers. "The Bosnian Government owes these groups, and especially the Iranians, a lot," warned an American official in early 1996. "The Government has proved incapable of confronting them. In 12 months we will be gone, but the *mujahedeen* intend to remain."[49]

The wealthy states of the *ummah*, led by Saudi Arabia and Iran, contributed immense amounts of money to develop Bosnian military strength. In the early months of the war in 1992, Saudi government and private sources provided $150 million in aid to the Bosnians, ostensibly for humanitarian purposes but widely acknowledged to have been used largely for military ones. Reportedly the Bosnians got $160 million worth of weapons during the first two years of the war. During 1993–1995 the Bosnians received an additional $300 million for arms from the Saudis plus $500 million in purportedly humanitarian aid. Iran was also a major source of military assistance, and according to American officials, spent hundreds of millions of dollars a year on arms for the Bosnians. According to another report, 80 percent to 90 percent of a total of $2 billion worth of arms that went into Bosnia during the early years of the fighting went to the Muslims. As a result of this financial aid, the Bosnians were able to buy thousands of tons of weapons. Intercepted shipments included one of 4000 rifles and a million rounds of ammunition, a second of 11,000 rifles, 30 mortars, and 750,000 rounds of ammunition, and a third with surface-to-surface rockets, ammunition, jeeps, and pistols. All these shipments originated in Iran, which was the principal source of arms, but Turkey and Malaysia also were significant suppliers of weapons. Some weapons were flown directly to Bosnia, but most of them came through Croatia, either by air to Zagreb and then overland or by sea to Split or other Croatian ports and then overland. In return for permitting this, the Croatians appropriated a portion, reportedly one-third, of the weapons and, mindful that they could well be fighting Bosnia in the future, prohibited the transport of tanks and heavy artillery through their territory.[50]

The money, men, training, and weapons from Iran, Saudi Arabia, Turkey, and other Muslim countries enabled the Bosnians to convert what everyone called a "ragtag" army into a modestly well equipped, competent, military force. By the winter of 1994 outside observers reported dramatic increases in its organizational coherence and military effectiveness.[51] Putting their new military strength to work, the Bosnians broke a cease-fire and launched successful offensives first against Croatian militias and then later in the spring against the Serbs. In the fall of 1994 the Bosnian Fifth Corps moved out from the U.N. safe area of Bihac and drove back Serb forces, producing the biggest Bosnian victory up to that time and regaining substantial territory from the Serbs, who were hampered by President Milosevic's embargo on support for them. In March 1995 the Bosnian army again broke a truce and began a major advance near Tuzla, which was followed by an offensive in June around Sarajevo. The support of their Muslim kin was a necessary and decisive factor enabling the Bosnian government to make these changes in the military balance in Bosnia.

The war in Bosnia was a war of civilizations. The three primary participants came from different civilizations and adhered to different religions. With one partial exception, the participation of secondary and tertiary actors exactly followed the civilizational model. Muslim states and organizations universally rallied behind the Bosnian Muslims and opposed the Croats and Serbs. Orthodox countries and organizations universally backed the Serbs and opposed the Croats and Muslims. Western governments and elites backed the Croats, castigated the Serbs, and were generally indifferent to or fearful of the Muslims. As the war continued, the hatreds and cleavages among the groups deepened and their religious and civilizational identities intensified, most notably among the Muslims. Overall the lessons of the Bosnian war are, first, primary participants in fault line wars can count on receiving help, which may be substantial, from their civilizational kin; second, such help can significantly affect the course of the war; and third, governments and people of one civilization do not expend blood or treasure to help people of another civilization fight a fault line war.

The one partial exception to this civilizational pattern was the United States, whose leaders rhetorically favored the Muslims. In practice, however, American support was limited. The Clinton administration approved the use of American air power but not ground troops to protect U.N. safe areas and advocated the end of the arms embargo. It did not seriously pressure its allies to support the latter, but it did condone both Iranian shipments of arms to the Bosnians and Saudi funding of Bosnian arms purchases, and in 1994 it ceased enforcing the embargo.[52] By doing these things, the United States antagonized its allies and gave rise to what was widely perceived to be a major crisis in NATO. After the Dayton accords were signed, the United States agreed to cooperate with Saudi Arabia and other Muslim countries in training and equipping the Bosnian forces. The question thus is: Why during and after the war was the United States the only country to break the civilizational mold and become the single non-Muslim country promoting the interests of the Bosnian Muslims and working with Muslim countries on their behalf? What explains this American anomaly?

One possibility is that it really was not an anomaly, but rather carefully calculated civilizational realpolitik. By siding with the Bosnians and proposing, unsuccessfully, to end the embargo, the United States was attempting to reduce the influence of fundamentalist Muslim countries like Iran and Saudi Arabia with the previously secular and Europe-oriented Bosnians. If this was the motive, however, why did the United States acquiesce in Iranian and Saudi aid and why did it not push more vigorously to end the embargo which would have legitimized Western aid? Why did not American officials publicly warn of the dangers of Islamist fundamentalism in the Balkans? An alternative explanation for American behavior is that the U.S. government was under pressure from its friends in the Muslim world, most notably Turkey and Saudi Arabia, and acceded to their wishes in order to maintain good relations with them. Those relations, however, are rooted in convergences of interests unrelated to

Bosnia and were unlikely to be significantly damaged by American failure to help Bosnia. In addition, this explanation would not explain why the United States implicitly approved huge quantities of Iranian arms going into Bosnia at a time when it was regularly challenging Iran on other fronts and Saudi Arabia was competing with Iran for influence in Bosnia.

While considerations of civilizational realpolitik may have played some role in shaping American attitudes, other factors appear to have been more influential. Americans want to identify the forces of good and the forces of evil in any foreign conflict and align themselves with the former. The atrocities of the Serbs early in the war led them to be portrayed as the "bad guys" killing innocents and engaging in genocide, while the Bosnians were able to promote an image of themselves as helpless victims. Throughout the war the American press paid little attention to Croat and Muslim ethnic cleansing and war crimes or the violations of U.N. safe areas and cease-fires by the Bosnian forces. For Americans, the Bosnians became, in Rebecca West's phrase, their "pet Balkan people established in their hearts as suffering and innocent, eternally the massacree and never the massacrer."[53]

American elites also were favorably disposed toward the Bosnians because they liked the idea of a multicultural country, and in the early stages of the war the Bosnian government successfully promoted this image. Throughout the war the American policy remained stubbornly committed to a multiethnic Bosnia despite the fact that the Bosnian Serbs and the Bosnian Croats overwhelmingly rejected it. Although creation of a multiethnic state was obviously impossible if, as they also believed, one ethnic group was committing genocide against another, American elites combined these contradictory images in their minds to produce widespread sympathy for the Bosnian cause. American idealism, moralism, humanitarian instincts, naivete, and ignorance concerning the Balkans thus led them to be pro-Bosnian and anti-Serb. At the same time the absence of both significant American security interests in Bosnia and any cultural connection gave the U.S. government no reason to do much to help the Bosnians except to allow the Iranians and Saudis to arm them. By refusing to recognize the war for what it was, the American government alienated its allies, prolonged the fighting, and helped to create in the Balkans a Muslim state heavily influenced by Iran. In the end the Bosnians felt deep bitterness toward the United States, which had talked grandly but delivered little, and profound gratitude toward their Muslim kin, who had come through with the money and weapons necessary for them to survive and score military victories.

"Bosnia is our Spain," observed Bernard-Henri Lévy, and a Saudi editor agreed: "The war in Bosnia and Herzegovina has become the emotional equivalent of the fight against fascism in the Spanish Civil War. Those who died there are regarded as martyrs who tried to save their fellow Muslims."[54] The comparison is apt. In an age of civilizations Bosnia is everyone's Spain. The Spanish Civil War was a war between political systems and ideologies, the

Bosnian War a war between civilizations and religions. Democrats, communists, and fascists went to Spain to fight alongside their ideological brethren, and democratic, communist, and, most actively, fascist governments provided aid. The Yugoslav wars saw a similar massive mobilization of outside support by Western Christians, Orthodox Christians, and Muslims on behalf of their civilizational kin. The principal powers of Orthodoxy, Islam, and the West all became deeply involved. After four years the Spanish Civil War came to a definitive end with the victory of the Franco forces. The wars among the religious communities in the Balkans may subside and even halt temporarily but no one is likely to score a decisive victory, and no victory means no end. The Spanish Civil War was a prelude to World War II. The Bosnian War is one more bloody episode in an ongoing clash of civilizations.

HALTING FAULT LINE WARS

"Every war must end." Such is the conventional wisdom. Is it true of fault line wars? Yes and no. Fault line violence may stop entirely for a period of time, but it rarely ends permanently. Fault line wars are marked by frequent truces, cease-fires, armistices, but not by comprehensive peace treaties that resolve central political issues. They have this off-again-on-again quality because they are rooted in deep fault line conflicts involving sustained antagonistic relations between groups of different civilizations. The conflicts in turn stem from the geographical proximity, different religions and cultures, separate social structures, and historical memories of the two societies. In the course of centuries these may evolve and the underlying conflict may evaporate. Or the conflict may disappear quickly and brutally if one group exterminates the other. If neither of these happens, however, the conflict continues and so do recurring periods of violence. Fault line wars are intermittent; fault line conflicts are interminable.

Producing even a temporary halt in a fault line war usually depends on two developments. The first is exhaustion of the primary participants. At some point when the casualties have mounted into tens of thousands, refugees into the hundreds of thousands, and cities — Beirut, Grozny, Vukovar — reduced to rubble, people cry "madness, madness, enough is enough," the radicals on both sides are no longer able to mobilize popular fury, negotiations which have sputtered along unproductively for years come to life, and moderates reassert themselves and reach some sort of agreement for a halt to the carnage. By the spring of 1994 the six-year war over Nagorno-Karabakh had "exhausted" both Armenians and Azerbaijanis and hence they agreed to a truce. In the fall of 1995 it was similarly reported that in Bosnia "All sides are exhausted," and the Dayton accords materialized.[55] Such halts, however, are self-limiting. They enable both sides to rest and replenish their resources. Then when one side sees the opportunity for gain, the war is renewed.

Achieving a temporary pause also requires a second factor: the involvement of nonprimary level participants with the interest and the clout to bring the fighters together. Fault line wars are almost never halted by direct negotiations between primary parties alone and only rarely by the mediation of disinterested parties. The cultural distance, intense hatreds, and mutual violence they have inflicted on each other make it extremely difficult for primary parties to sit down and engage in productive discussion looking toward some form of cease-fire. The underlying political issues, who controls what territory and people on what terms, keep surfacing and prevent agreement on more limited questions.

Conflicts between countries or groups with a common culture can at times be resolved through mediation by a disinterested third party who shares that culture, has recognized legitimacy within that culture, and hence can be trusted by both parties to find a solution rooted in the values of that culture. The Pope could successfully mediate the Argentine-Chilean boundary dispute. In conflicts between groups from different civilizations, however, there are no disinterested parties. Finding an individual, institution, or state whom both parties think trustworthy is extremely difficult. Any potential mediator belongs to one of the conflicting civilizations or to a third civilization with still another culture and other interests which inspire trust in neither party to the conflict. The Pope will not be called in by Chechens and Russians or by Tamils and Sinhalese. International organizations also usually fail because they lack the ability to impose significant costs on or to offer significant benefits to the parties.

Fault line wars are ended not by disinterested individuals, groups, or organizations but by interested secondary and tertiary parties who have rallied to the support of their kin and have the capability to negotiate agreements with their counterparts, on the one hand, and to induce their kin to accept those agreements, on the other. While rallying intensifies and prolongs the war, it generally is also a necessary although not sufficient condition for limiting and halting the war. Secondary and tertiary ralliers usually do not want to be transformed into primary level fighters and hence try to keep the war under control. They also have more diversified interests than primary participants, who are exclusively focused on the war, and they are concerned with other issues in their relations with each other. Hence at some point they are likely to see it in their interest to stop the fighting. Because they have rallied behind their kin, they have leverage over their kin. Ralliers thus become restrainers and halters.

Wars with no secondary or tertiary parties are less likely to expand than others but more difficult to bring to a halt, as are wars between groups from civilizations lacking core states. Fault line wars that involve an insurgency within an established state and that lack significant rallying also pose special problems. If the war continues for any length of time the demands of the insurgents tend to escalate from some form of autonomy to complete independence, which the government rejects. The government usually demands that the insurgents give up their arms as the first step toward stopping the fighting, which the insurgents reject. The government, also quite naturally, resists the involvement by outsiders in what it considers a purely internal problem involving "criminal elements." Defining it as an internal matter also gives other states an excuse for not becoming involved, as has been the case of the Western powers and Chechnya.

These problems are compounded when the civilizations involved lack core states. The war in Sudan, for instance, which began in 1956, was brought to a halt in 1972, when the parties were exhausted, and the World Council of Churches and the All African Council of Churches, in a virtually unique achievement for nongovernmental international organizations, successfully negotiated the Addis Ababa agreement providing autonomy for southern Sudan. A decade later, however, the government abrogated the agreement, the war resumed, the goals of the insurgents escalated, the position of the government hardened, and efforts to negotiate another halt failed. Neither the Arab world nor Africa had core states with the interest and the clout to pressure the participants. Mediation efforts by Jimmy Carter and various African leaders did not succeed nor did the efforts of a committee of East African states consisting of Kenya, Eritrea, Uganda, and Ethiopia. The United States, which has deeply antagonistic relations with Sudan, could not act directly; nor could it ask Iran, Iraq, or Libya, which have close relationships with Sudan, to play useful roles; hence it was reduced to enlisting Saudi Arabia, but Saudi influence over Sudan also was limited.[56]

In general, cease-fire negotiations are furthered to the extent that there is relative parallel and equal involvement of secondary and tertiary parties from both sides. In some circumstances, however, a single core state may be powerful enough to bring about a halt. In 1992 the Conference on Security and Cooperation in Europe (CSCE) attempted to mediate the Armenian-Azerbaijani war. A committee, the Minsk Group, was created that included the primary, secondary, and tertiary parties to the conflict (Nagorno-Karabakh Armenians, Armenia, Azerbaijan, Russia, Turkey) plus France, Germany, Italy, Sweden, the Czech Republic, Belarus, and the United States. Apart from the United States and France, with sizable Armenian diasporas, these latter countries had little interest in producing and little or no capability to produce an end to the war. When the two tertiary parties, Russia and Turkey, plus the United States agreed on a plan, it was rejected by the Nagorno-Karabakh Armenians. Russia, however, independently sponsored a long series of negotiations in Moscow between Armenia and Azerbaijan which "created an alternative to the Minsk Group, and . . . thus dissipated the effort of the international community."[57] In the end, after the primary contestants had become exhausted and the Russians had secured Iran's backing of the negotiations, the Russian effort produced a cease-fire agreement. As secondary parties, Russia and Iran also cooperated in the intermittently successful attempts to arrange a cease-fire in Tajikistan.

Russia will be a continuing presence in the Transcaucasus and will have the capability to enforce the cease-fire it sponsored so long as it has an interest in doing so. This contrasts with the situation of the United States with respect to Bosnia. The Dayton accords built on proposals that had been developed by the Contact Group of interested core states (Germany, Britain, France, Russia, and the United States), but none of the other tertiary parties were intimately involved in working out the final agreement, and two of the three primary parties to the war were on the margins of the negotiations. Enforcement of the agreement rests with an American-dominated NATO force. If the United States withdraws its troops from Bosnia, neither the European powers nor Russia will have incentives to continue to implement the agreement, the Bosnian government, Serbs, and Croats will have every incentive to renew the fighting once they have refreshed themselves, and the Serbian and Croatian governments will be tempted to seize the opportunity to realize their dreams of a Greater Serbia and a Greater Croatia.

Robert Putnam has highlighted the extent to which negotiations between states are "two level games" in which diplomats negotiate simultaneously with constituencies within their country and with their counterparts from the other country. In a parallel analysis, Huntington showed how reformers in an authoritarian government negotiating a transition to democracy with moderates in the opposition must also negotiate with or counter the hard-liners within the government while the moderates must do the same with the radicals in the opposition.[58] These two level games involve at a minimum four parties and at least three and often four relations between them. A complex fault line war, however, is a three level game with at least six parties and at least seven relations among them. (See Figure 11.1) Horizontal relations across the fault lines exist between pairs of primary, secondary, and tertiary parties. Vertical relations exist between the parties on different levels within each civilization. Achieving a halt in the fighting in a "full model" war thus is likely to require:

• active involvement of secondary and tertiary parties;
• negotiation by the tertiary parties of the broad terms for stopping the fighting;
• use by the tertiary parties of carrots and sticks to get the secondary parties to accept these terms and to pressure the primary parties to accept them;
• withdrawal of support from and, in effect, the betrayal of the primary parties by the secondary parties; and
• as a result of this pressure, acceptance of the terms by the primary parties, which, of course, they subvert when they see it in their interest to do so.

The Bosnian peace process involved all these elements. Efforts by individual actors, the United States, Russia, the European Union, to produce agreement were notably lacking in success. The Western powers were reluctant to include Russia as a full partner in the process. The Russians vigorously protested their exclusion, arguing that they had historic ties with the Serbs and also more direct interests in the Balkans than any other major power. Russia insisted that it be a full player in the efforts to resolve the conflicts and vigorously denounced the "tendency on the part of the United States to dictate its own terms." The need to include the Russians became clear in February 1994. Without consulting Russia, NATO issued an ultimatum to the Bosnian Serbs to remove their heavy weapons from around Sarajevo or face air attacks. The Serbs resisted this demand, and a violent encounter with NATO seemed likely. Yeltsin warned that "Some people are trying to resolve the Bosnian question without the participation of Russia" and "We will not allow this." The Russian government then seized the initiative and persuaded the Serbs to withdraw their weapons if Russia deployed peacekeeping troops to the Sarajevo area. This diplomatic coup prevented escalation of the violence, demonstrated to the West Russian clout with the Serbs, and brought Russian troops to the heart of the disputed area between Bosnian Muslims and Serbs.[59] Through this maneuver Russia effectively established its claim to "equal partnership" with the West in dealing with Bosnia.

In April, however, NATO again authorized the bombing of Serbian positions without consulting Russia. This produced an immense negative reaction across the Russian political spectrum and strengthened the nationalist opposition to Yeltsin and Kozyrev. Immediately thereafter, the relevant tertiary powers — Britain, France, Germany, Russia, and the United States — formed the Contact Group to devise a settlement. In June 1994 the group produced a plan which assigned 51 percent of Bosnia to a Muslim-Croat federation and 49 percent to the Bosnian Serbs and which became the basis of the subsequent Dayton agreement. The following year it was necessary to work out arrangements for the participation of Russian troops in the enforcement of the Dayton agreements.

Agreements among the tertiary parties have to be sold to the secondary and primary actors. The Americans, as Russian diplomat Vitaly Churkin said, must lean on the Bosnians, the Germans on the Croats, and the Russians on the Serbs.[60] In the early stages of the Yugoslav wars, Russia had made a momentous concession in agreeing to economic sanctions against Serbia. As a kin country which the Serbs could trust, Russia was also at times able to impose constraints on the Serbs and pressure them to accept compromises they would otherwise reject. In 1995, for instance, Russia along with Greece interceded with the Bosnian Serbs to secure the release of Dutch peacekeepers they held hostage. On occasion, however, the Bosnian Serbs reneged on agreements they had made under Russian pressure and thereby embarrassed Russia for not being able to deliver its kin. In April 1994, for example, Russia secured agreement from the Bosnian Serbs to end their attack on the Gorazde, but the Serbs then broke the agreement. The Russians were furious: the Bosnian Serbs have "become mad on war," declared one Russian diplomat, Yeltsin insisted that

"Serbian leadership must fulfill the obligation it has given to Russia," and Russia withdrew its objections to NATO air strikes.[61]

While supporting and strengthening Croatia, Germany and other Western states were also able to constrain Croatian behavior. President Tudjman was deeply anxious for his Catholic country to be accepted as a European country and to be admitted into European organizations. The Western powers exploited both the diplomatic, economic, and military support they provided Croatia and the Croatian desire to be accepted into the "club," to induce Tudjman to compromise on many issues. In March 1995 the case was made to Tudjman that if he wanted to be part of the West he had to allow the U.N. Protection Force to stay in Krajina. "Joining the West," one European diplomat said, "is very important to Tudjman. He doesn't want to be left alone with the Serbs and the Russians." He was also warned to restrict ethnic cleansing as his troops conquered territory in the Krajina and elsewhere peopled by Serbs and to refrain from extending his offensive into Eastern Slavonia. On another issue, the Croatians were told that if they did not join the federation with the Muslims, "the door to the West will be shut to them forever," as one U.S. official put it.[62] As the principal external source of financial support for Croatia, Germany was in a particularly strong position to influence Croatian behavior. The close relation that the United States developed with Croatia also helped to prevent, at least through 1995, Tudjman from implementing his oft-expressed desire to partition Bosnia-Herzegovina between Croatia and Serbia.

Unlike Russia and Germany, the United States lacked cultural commonality with its Bosnian client and hence was in a weak position to pressure the Muslims to compromise. In addition, apart from rhetoric, the United States only helped the Bosnians by turning a blind eye to the violations of the arms embargo by Iran and other Muslim states. The Bosnian Muslims, consequently, felt increasingly grateful to and increasingly identified with the broader Islamic community. Simultaneously they denounced the United States for pursuing a "double standard" and not repelling the aggression against them as it had against Kuwait. Their wrapping themselves in the victim guise made it still more difficult for the United States to pressure them to be accommodating. They thus were able to reject peace proposals, build up their military strength with help from their Muslim friends, and eventually take the initiative and regain a substantial amount of the territory they had lost.

Resistance to compromise is intense among the primary parties. In the Transcaucasus War, the ultranationalist Armenian Revolutionary Federation (Dashnak), which was very strong in the Armenian diaspora, dominated the Nagorno-Karabakh entity, rejected the Turkish-Russian-American peace proposal of May 1993 accepted by the Armenian and Azerbaijani governments, undertook military offensives that produced charges of ethnic cleansing, raised the prospects of a broader war, and aggravated its relations with the more moderate Armenian government. The success of the Nagorno-Karabakh offensive caused problems for Armenia, which was anxious to improve its relations with Turkey and Iran so as to ease the food and energy shortages resulting from the war and the Turkish blockade. "[T]he better things are going in Karabakh, the more difficult it is for Yerevan," commented one Western diplomat.[63] President Levon Ter-Petrossian of Armenia, like President Yeltsin, had to balance pressures from nationalists in his legislature against broader foreign policy interests in accommodating other states, and in late 1994 his government banned the Dashnak party from Armenia.

Like the Nagorno-Karabakh Armenians, the Bosnian Serbs and Croats adopted hard-line positions. As a result, as the Croatian and Serbian governments came under pressure to help in the peace process, problems developed in their relations with their Bosnian kin. With the Croats these were less serious, as the Bosnian Croats agreed in form if not in practice to join the federation with the Muslims. Spurred by personal antagonism, the conflict between President Milosevic and Bosnian Serb leader Radovan Karadzic, in contrast, became intense and public. In August 1994 Karadzic rejected the peace plan that had been approved by Milosevic. The Serbian government, anxious to bring sanctions to an end, announced that it was cutting off all trade with the Bosnian Serbs except for food and medicine. In return, the U.N. eased its sanctions on Serbia. The following year Milosevic allowed the Croatian army to expel the Serbs from Krajina and Croatian and Muslim forces to drive them back in northwest Bosnia. He also agreed with Tudjman to permit the gradual return of Serb-occupied Eastern Slavonia to Croatian control. With the approval of the great powers, he then in effect "delivered" the Bosnian Serbs to the Dayton negotiations, incorporating them into his delegation.

Milosevic's actions brought an end to the U.N. sanctions against Serbia. They also brought him cautious approbation from a somewhat surprised international community. The nationalist, aggressive, ethnic-cleansing, Greater Serbian warmonger of 1992 had become the peacemaker of 1995. For many Serbs, however, he had become a traitor. He was denounced in Belgrade by Serbian nationalists and the leaders of the Orthodox Church and he was bitterly accused of treason by the Krajina and Bosnian Serbs. In this, of course, they replicated the charges West Bank settlers levied at the Israeli government for its agreement with the P.L.O. Betrayal of kin is the price of peace in a fault line war.

Exhaustion with the war and the incentives and pressures of tertiary parties compel changes in the secondary and primary parties. Either moderates replace extremists in power or extremists, like Milosevic, find it in their interest to become moderate. They do so, however, at some risk. Those perceived as traitors arouse far more passionate hatred than enemies. Leaders of the Kashmiri Muslims, Chechens, and Sri Lankan Sinhalese suffered the fate of Sadat and Rabin for betraying the cause and attempting to work out compromise solutions with the archfoe. In 1914 a Serbian nationalist assassinated an Austrian archduke. In the aftermath of Dayton his most likely target would be Slobodan Milosevic.

An agreement to halt a fault line war will be successful, even if only temporarily, to the extent that it reflects the local balance of power among the primary parties and the interests of the tertiary and secondary parties. The 51 percent– 49 percent division of Bosnia was not viable in 1994 when the Serbs controlled 70 percent of the country; it became viable when the Croatian and Muslim offensives reduced Serbian control to almost half. The peace process was also helped by the ethnic cleansing which occurred, with Serbs reduced to less than 3 percent of the population of Croatia and members of all three groups being separated violently or voluntarily in Bosnia. In addition, secondary and tertiary parties, the latter often the core states of civilizations, need to have real security or communal interests in a war to sponsor a viable solution. Alone, primary participants cannot halt fault line wars. Halting them and preventing their escalation into global wars depend primarily on the interests and actions of the core states of the world's major civilizations. Fault line wars bubble up from below, fault line peaces trickle down from above.

V.

The

Future

of

Civilizations

Chapter 12

•

The West, Civilizations, and Civilization

THE RENEWAL OF THE WEST?

History ends at least once and occasionally more often in the history of every civilization. As the civilization's universal state emerges, its people become blinded by what Toynbee called "the mirage of immortality" and convinced that theirs is the final form of human society. So it was with the Roman Empire, the 'Abbasid Caliphate, the Mughal Empire, and the Ottoman Empire. The citizens of such universal states "in defiance of apparently plain facts . . . are prone to regard it, not as a night's shelter in the wilderness, but as the Promised Land, the goal of human endeavors." The same was true at the peak of the Pax Britannica. For the English middle class in 1897, "as they saw it, history for them, was over. . . . And they had every reason to congratulate themselves on the permanent state of felicity which this ending of history had conferred on them."[1] Societies that assume that their history has ended, however, are usually societies whose history is about to decline.

Is the West an exception to this pattern? The two key questions were well formulated by Melko:

First, is Western civilization a new species, in a class by itself, incomparably different from all other civilizations that have ever existed?

Second, does its worldwide expansion threaten (or promise) to end the possibility of development of all other civilizations?[2]

The inclination of most Westerners is, quite naturally, to answer both questions in the affirmative. And perhaps they are right. In the past, however, the peoples of other civilizations thought similarly and thought wrong.

The West obviously differs from all other civilizations that have ever existed in that it has had an overwhelming impact on all other civilizations that have existed since 1500. It also inaugurated the processes of modernization and industrialization that have become worldwide, and as a result societies in all other civilizations have been attempting to catch up with the West in wealth and modernity. Do these characteristics of the West, however, mean that its evolution and dynamics as a civilization are fundamentally different from the patterns that have prevailed in all other civilizations? The evidence of history and the judgments of the scholars of the comparative history of civilizations suggest otherwise. The development of the West to date has not deviated significantly from the evolutionary patterns common to civilizations throughout history. The Islamic Resurgence and the economic dynamism of Asia demonstrate that other civilizations are alive and well and at least potentially threatening to the West. A major war involving the West and the core states of other civilizations is not inevitable, but it could happen. Alternatively the gradual and irregular decline of the West which started in the early twentieth century could continue for decades and perhaps centuries to come. Or the West could go through a period of revival, reverse its declining influence in world affairs, and reconfirm its position as the leader whom other civilizations follow and imitate.

In what is probably the most useful periodization of the evolution of historical civilizations, Carroll Quigley sees a common pattern of seven phases.[3] (See p. 44.) In his argument, Western civilization gradually began to take shape between A.D. 370 and 750 through the mixing of elements of Classical, Semitic, Saracen, and barbarian cultures. Its period of gestation lasting from the middle of the eighth century to the end of the tenth century was followed by movement, unusual among civilizations, back and forth between phases of expansion and phases of conflict. In his terms, as well as those of other civilization scholars, the West now appears to be moving out of its phase of conflict. Western civilization has become a security zone; intra-West wars, apart from an occasional Cod War, are virtually unthinkable. The West is developing, as was argued in chapter 2, its equivalent of a universal empire in the form of a complex system of confederations, federations, regimes, and other types of cooperative institutions that embody at the civilizational level its commitment to democratic and pluralistic politics. The West has, in short, become a mature society entering into what future generations, in the recurring pattern of civilizations, will look back to as a "golden age," a period of peace resulting, in Quigley's terms, from "the absence of any competing units within the area of the civilization itself, and from the remoteness or even absence of struggles with other societies outside." It is also a period of prosperity which arises from "the ending of internal belligerent destruction, the reduction of internal trade barriers, the establishment of a common system of weights, measures, and coinage, and from the extensive system of government spending associated with the establishment of a universal empire."

In previous civilizations this phase of blissful golden age with its visions of immortality has ended either dramatically and quickly with the victory of an external society or slowly and equally painfully by internal disintegration. What happens within a civilization is as crucial to its ability to resist destruction from external sources as it is to holding off decay from within. Civilizations grow, Quigley argued in 1961, because they have an "instrument of expansion," that is, a military, religious, political, or economic organization that accumulates surplus and invests it in productive innovations. Civilizations decline when they stop the "application of surplus to new ways of doing things. In modern terms we say that the rate of investment decreases." This happens because the social groups controlling the surplus have a vested interest in using it for "nonproductive but ego-satisfying purposes . . . which distribute the surpluses to consumption but do not provide more effective methods of production." People live off their capital and the civilization moves from the stage of the universal state to the stage of decay. This is a period of

> acute economic depression, declining standards of living, civil wars between the various vested interests, and growing illiteracy. The society grows weaker and weaker. Vain efforts are made to stop the wastage by legislation. But the decline continues. The religious, intellectual, social, and political levels of the society began to lose the allegiance of the masses of the people on a large scale. New religious movements begin to sweep over the society. There is a growing reluctance to fight for the society or even to support it by paying taxes.

Decay then leads to the stage of invasion "when the civilization, no longer *able* to defend itself because it is no longer *willing* to defend itself, lies wide open to 'barbarian invaders,' " who often come from "another, younger, more powerful civilization."[4]

The overriding lesson of the history of civilizations, however, is that many things are probable but nothing is inevitable. Civilizations can and have re-formed and renewed themselves. The central issue for the West is whether, quite apart from any external challenges, it is capable of stopping and reversing the internal processes of decay. Can the West renew itself or will sustained internal rot simply accelerate its end and/or subordination to other economically and demographically more dynamic civilizations?*

---

* In a prediction which may be right but is not really supported by his theoretical and empirical analysis, Quigley concludes: "Western civilization did not exist about A.D. 500; it did exist in full flower about A.D. 1500, and it will surely pass out of existence at some time in the future, perhaps before A.D. 2500." New civilizations in China and India, replacing those destroyed by the West, he says, will then move into their stages of expansion and threaten both Western and Orthodox civilizations. Carroll Quigley, *The Evolution of Civilizations: An Introduction to Historical Analysis* (Indianapolis: Liberty Press, 1979; first published by Macmillan in 1961), pp. 127, 164–66.

In the mid-1990s the West had many characteristics Quigley identified as those of a mature civilization on the brink of decay. Economically the West was far richer than any other civilization, but it also had low economic growth rates, saving rates, and investment rates, particularly as compared with the societies of East Asia. Individual and collective consumption had priority over the creation of the capabilities for future economic and military power. Natural population growth was low, particularly compared with that of Islamic countries. Neither of these problems, however, would inevitably have catastrophic consequences. Western economies were still growing; by and large Western peoples were becoming better off; and the West was still the leader in scientific research and technological innovation. Low birth rates were unlikely to be cured by governments (whose efforts to do so are generally even less successful than their efforts to reduce population growth). Immigration, however, was a potential source of new vigor and human capital provided two conditions were met: first, if priority were given to able, qualified, energetic people with the talents and expertise needed by the host country; second, if the new migrants and their children were assimilated into the cultures of the country and the West. The United States was likely to have problems meeting the first condition and European countries problems meeting the second. Yet setting policies governing the levels, sources, characteristics, and assimilation of immigrants is well within the experience and competence of Western governments.

Far more significant than economics and demography are problems of moral decline, cultural suicide, and political disunity in the West. Oft-pointed-to manifestations of moral decline include:

1. increases in antisocial behavior, such as crime, drug use, and violence generally;
2. family decay, including increased rates of divorce, illegitimacy, teen-age pregnancy, and single-parent families;
3. at least in the United States, a decline in "social capital," that is, membership in voluntary associations and the interpersonal trust associated with such membership;
4. general weakening of the "work ethic" and rise of a cult of personal indulgence;
5. decreasing commitment to learning and intellectual activity, manifested in the United States in lower levels of scholastic achievement.

The future health of the West and its influence on other societies depends in considerable measure on its success in coping with those trends, which, of course, give rise to the assertions of moral superiority by Muslims and Asians.

Western culture is challenged by groups within Western societies. One such challenge comes from immigrants from other civilizations who reject assimilation and continue to adhere to and to propagate the values, customs, and cultures of their home societies. This phenomenon is most notable among Muslims in Europe, who are, however, a small minority. It is also manifest, in lesser degree, among Hispanics in the United States, who are a large minority. If assimilation fails in this case, the United States will become a cleft country, with all the potentials for internal strife and disunion that entails. In Europe, Western civilization could also be undermined by the weakening of its central component, Christianity. Declining proportions of Europeans profess religious beliefs, observe religous practices, and participate in religous activities.[5] This trend reflects not so much hostility to religion as indifference to it. Christian concepts, values, and practices nonetheless pervade European civilization. "Swedes are probably the most unreligious people in Europe," one of them commented, "but you cannot understand this country at all unless you realize that our institutions, social practices, families, politics, and way of life are fundamentally shaped by our Lutheran heritage." Americans, in contrast to Europeans, overwhelmingly believe in God, think themselves to be religious people, and attend church in large numbers. While evidence of a resurgence of religion in America was lacking as of the mid-1980s the following decade seemed to witness intensified religious activity.[6] The erosion of Christianity among Westerners is likely to be at worst only a very long term threat to the health of Western civilization.

A more immediate and dangerous challenge exists in the United States. Historically American national identity has been defined culturally by the heritage of Western civilization and politically by the principles of the American Creed on which Americans overwhelmingly agree: liberty, democracy, individualism, equality before the law, constitutionalism, private property. In the late twentieth century both components of American identity have come under concentrated and sustained onslaught from a small but influential number of intellectuals and publicists. In the name of multiculturalism they have attacked the identification of the United States with Western civilization, denied the existence of a common American culture, and promoted racial, ethnic, and other subnational cultural identities and groupings. They have denounced, in the words of one of their reports, the "systematic bias toward European culture and its derivatives" in education and "the dominance of the European-American monocultural perspective." The multiculturalists are, as Arthur M. Schlesinger, Jr., said, "very often ethnocentric separatists who see little in the Western heritage other than Western crimes." Their "mood is one of divesting Americans of the sinful European inheritance and seeking redemptive infusions from non-Western cultures."[7]

The multicultural trend was also manifested in a variety of legislation that followed the civil rights acts of the 1960s, and in the 1990s the Clinton administration made the encouragement of diversity one of its major goals. The contrast with the past is striking. The Founding Fathers saw diversity as a reality and as a problem: hence the national motto, *e pluribus unum*, chosen by a committee of the Continental Congress consisting of Benjamin Franklin, Thomas Jefferson, and John Adams. Later political leaders who also were fearful of the dangers of racial, sectional, ethnic, economic, and cultural diversity (which, indeed, produced the largest war of the century between 1815 and 1914), responded to the call of "bring us together," and made the promotion of national unity their central responsibility. "The one absolutely certain way of bringing this nation to ruin, of preventing all possibility of its continuing as a nation at all," warned Theodore Roosevelt, "would be to permit it to become a tangle of squabbling nationalities."[8] In the 1990s, however, the leaders of the United States have not only permitted that but assiduously promoted the diversity rather than the unity of the people they govern.

The leaders of other countries have, as we have seen, at times attempted to disavow their cultural heritage and shift the identity of their country from one civilization to another. In no case to date have they succeeded and they have instead created schizophrenic torn countries. The American multiculturalists similarly reject their country's cultural heritage. Instead of attempting to identify the United States with another civilization, however, they wish to create a country of many civilizations, which is to say a country not belonging to any civilization and lacking a cultural core. History shows that no country so constituted can long endure as a coherent society. A multicivilizational United States will not be the United States; it will be the United Nations.

The multiculturalists also challenged a central element of the American Creed, by substituting for the rights of individuals the rights of groups, defined largely in terms of race, ethnicity, sex, and sexual preference. The Creed, Gunnar Myrdal said in the 1940s, reinforcing the comments of foreign observers dating from Hector St. John de Crèvecoeur and Alexis de Tocqueville, has been "the cement in the structure of this great and disparate nation." "It has been our fate as a nation," Richard Hofstader agreed, "not to have ideologies but to be one."[9] What happens then to the United States if that ideology is disavowed by a significant portion of its citizens? The fate of the Soviet Union, the other major country whose unity, even more than that of the United States, was defined in ideological terms is a sobering example for Americans. "[T]he total failure of Marxism . . . and the dramatic breakup of the Soviet Union," the Japanese philosopher Takeshi Umehara has suggested, "are only the precursors to the collapse of Western liberalism, the main current of modernity. Far from being the alternative to Marxism and the reigning ideology at the end of history, liberalism will be the next domino to fall."[10] In an era in which peoples everywhere define themselves in cultural terms what place is there for a society without a cultural core and defined only by a political creed? Political principles are a fickle base on which to build a lasting community. In a multicivilizational world where culture counts, the United States could be simply the last anomalous holdover from a fading Western world where ideology counted.

Rejection of the Creed and of Western civilization means the end of the

United States of America as we have known it. It also means effectively the end of Western civilization. If the United States is de-Westernized, the West is reduced to Europe and a few lightly populated overseas European settler countries. Without the United States the West becomes a minuscule and declining part of the world's population on a small and inconsequential peninsula at the extremity of the Eurasian land mass.

The clash between the multiculturalists and the defenders of Western civilization and the American Creed is, in James Kurth's phrase, "the *real* clash" within the American segment of Western civilization.[11] Americans cannot avoid the issue: Are we a Western people or are we something else? The futures of the United States and of the West depend upon Americans reaffirming their commitment to Western civilization. Domestically this means rejecting the divisive siren calls of multiculturalism. Internationally it means rejecting the elusive and illusory calls to identify the United States with Asia. Whatever economic connections may exist between them, the fundamental cultural gap between Asian and American societies precludes their joining together in a common home. Americans are culturally part of the Western family; multiculturalists may damage and even destroy that relationship but they cannot replace it. When Americans look for their cultural roots, they find them in Europe.

In the mid-1990s new discussion occurred of the nature and future of the West, a renewed recognition arose that such a reality had existed, and heightened concern about what would insure its continued existence. This in part germinated from the perceived need to expand the premier Western institution, NATO, to include the Western countries to the east and from the serious divisions that arose within the West over how to respond to the breakup of Yugoslavia. It also more broadly reflected anxiety about the future unity of the West in the absence of a Soviet threat and particularly what this meant for the United States commitment to Europe. As Western countries increasingly interact with increasingly powerful non-Western societies they become more and more aware of their common Western cultural core that binds them together. Leaders from both sides of the Atlantic have emphasized the need to rejuvenate the Atlantic community. In late 1994 and in 1995 the German and British defense ministers, the French and American foreign ministers, Henry Kissinger, and various other leading figures all espoused this cause. Their case was summed up by British Defense Minister Malcolm Rifkind, who, in November 1994, argued the need for "an Atlantic Community," resting on four pillars: defense and security embodied in NATO; "shared belief in the rule of law and parliamentary democracy"; "liberal capitalism and free trade"; and "the shared European cultural heritage emanating from Greece and Rome through the Renaissance to the shared values, beliefs and civilization of our own century."[12] In 1995 the European Commission launched a project to "renew" the transatlantic relationship, which led to the signature of an extensive pact between the Union and the United States. Simultaneously many European political and business leaders endorsed the creation of a transatlantic free trade area. Although the AFL-CIO opposed NAFTA and other trade liberalization measures, its head warmly backed such a transatlantic free trade agreement which would not threaten American jobs with competition from low-wage countries. It was also supported by conservatives both European (Margaret Thatcher) and American (Newt Gingrich), as well as by Canadian and other British leaders.

The West, as was argued in chapter 2, went through a first European phase of development and expansion that lasted several centuries and then a second American phase in the twentieth century. If North America and Europe renew their moral life, build on their cultural commonality, and develop close forms of economic and political integration to supplement their security collaboration in NATO, they could generate a third Euroamerican phase of Western economic affluence and political influence. Meaningful political integration would in some measure counter the relative decline in the West's share of the world's people, economic product, and military capabilities and revive the power of the West in the eyes of the leaders of other civilizations. "With their trading clout," Prime Minister Mahathir warned Asians, "the EU-NAFTA confederation could dictate terms to the rest of the world." [13] Whether the West comes together politically and economically, however, depends overwhelmingly on whether the United States reaffirms its identity as a Western nation and defines its global role as the leader of Western civilization.

THE WEST IN THE WORLD

A world in which cultural identities — ethnic, national, religious, civilizational — are central, and cultural affinities and differences shape the alliances, antagonisms, and policies of states has three broad implications for the West generally and for the United States in particular.

First, statesmen can constructively alter reality only if they recognize and understand it. The emerging politics of culture, the rising power of non-Western civilizations, and the increasing cultural assertiveness of these societies have been widely recognized in the non-Western world. European leaders have pointed to the cultural forces drawing people together and driving them apart. American elites, in contrast, have been slow to accept and to come to grips with these emerging realities. The Bush and Clinton administrations supported the unity of the multicivilizational Soviet Union, Yugoslavia, Bosnia, and Russia, in vain efforts to halt the powerful ethnic and cultural forces pushing for disunion. They promoted multicivilizational economic integration plans which are either meaningless, as with APEC, or involve major unanticipated economic and political costs, as with NAFTA and Mexico. They attempted to develop close relationships with the core states of other civilizations in the form of a "global partnership" with Russia or "constructive engagement" with China, in the face of the natural conflicts of interest between the United States and those countries. At the same time, the Clinton administration failed to involve Russia wholeheartedly in the search for peace in Bosnia, despite Russia's major interest in that war as Orthodoxy's core state. Pursuing the chimera of a multi-civilizational country, the Clinton administration denied self-determination to the Serbian and Croatian minorities and helped to bring into being a Balkan one-party Islamist partner of Iran. In similar fashion the U.S. government also supported the subjection of Muslims to Orthodox rule, maintaining that "Without question Chechnya is part of the Russian Federation."[14]

Although Europeans universally acknowledge the fundamental significance of the dividing line between Western Christendom, on the one hand, and Orthodoxy and Islam, on the other, the United States, its secretary of state said, would "not recognize any fundamental divide among the Catholic, Orthodox, and Islamic parts of Europe." Those who do not recognize fundamental divides, however, are doomed to be frustrated by them. The Clinton administration initially appeared oblivious to the shifting balance of power between the United States and East Asian societies and hence time and again proclaimed goals with respect to trade, human rights, nuclear proliferation, and other issues which it was incapable of realizing. Overall the U.S. government has had extraordinary difficulty adapting to an era in which global politics is shaped by cultural and civilizational tides.

Second, American foreign policy thinking also suffered from a reluctance to abandon, alter, or at times even reconsider policies adopted to meet Cold War needs. With some this took the form of still seeing a resurrected Soviet Union as a potential threat. More generally people tended to sanctify Cold War alliances and arms control agreements. NATO must be maintained as it was in the Cold War. The Japanese-American Security Treaty is central to East Asian security. The ABM treaty is inviolate. The CFE treaty must be observed. Obviously none of these or other Cold War legacies should be lightly cast aside. Neither, however, is it necessarily in the interests of the United States or the West for them to be continued in their Cold War form. The realities of a multicivilizational world suggest that NATO should be expanded to include other Western societies that wish to join and should recognize the essential meaninglessness of having as members two states each of which is the other's worst enemy and both of which lack cultural affinity with the other members. An ABM treaty designed to meet the Cold War need to insure the mutual vulnerability of Soviet and American societies and thus to deter Soviet-American nuclear war may well obstruct the ability of the United States and other societies to protect themselves against unpredictable nuclear threats or attacks by terrorist movements and irrational dictators. The U.S.-Japan security treaty helped deter Soviet aggression against Japan. What purpose is it meant to serve in the post–Cold War era? To contain and deter China? To slow Japanese accommodation with a rising China? To prevent further Japanese militarization? Increasingly doubts are being raised in Japan about the American military presence there and in the United States about the need for an unreciprocated commitment to defend Japan. The Conventional Forces in Europe agreement was designed to moderate the NATO-Warsaw Pact confrontation in Central Europe, which has disappeared. The principal impact of the agreement now is to create difficulties for Russia in dealing with what it perceives to be security threats from Muslim peoples to its south.

Third, cultural and civilizational diversity challenges the Western and particularly American belief in the universal relevance of Western culture. This belief is expressed both descriptively and normatively. Descriptively it holds that peoples in all societies want to adopt Western values, institutions, and practices. If they seem not to have that desire and to be committed to their own traditional cultures, they are victims of a "false consciousness" comparable to that which Marxists found among proletarians who supported capitalism. Normatively the Western universalist belief posits that people throughout the world should embrace Western values, institutions, and culture because they embody the highest, most enlightened, most liberal, most rational, most modern, and most civilized thinking of humankind.

In the emerging world of ethnic conflict and civilizational clash, Western belief in the universality of Western culture suffers three problems: it is false; it is immoral; and it is dangerous. That it is false has been the central thesis of this book, a thesis well summed up by Michael Howard: the "common Western assumption that cultural diversity is a historical curiosity being rapidly eroded by the growth of a common, western-oriented, Anglophone world-culture, shaping our basic values . . . is simply not true."[15] A reader not by now convinced of the wisdom of Sir Michael's remark exists in a world far removed from that described in this book.

The belief that non-Western peoples should adopt Western values, institutions, and culture is immoral because of what would be necessary to bring it about. The almost-universal reach of European power in the late nineteenth century and the global dominance of the United States in the late twentieth century spread much of Western civilization across the world. European globalism, however, is no more. American hegemony is receding if only because it is no longer needed to protect the United States against a Cold War–style Soviet military threat. Culture, as we have argued, follows power. If non-Western societies are once again to be shaped by Western culture, it will happen only as a result of the expansion, deployment, and impact of Western power. Imperialism is the necessary logical consequence of universalism. In addition, as a maturing civilization, the West no longer has the economic or demographic dynamism required to impose its will on other societies and any effort to do so is also contrary to the Western values of self-determination and democracy. As Asian and Muslim civilizations begin more and more to assert the universal relevance of their cultures, Westerners will come to appreciate more and more the connection between universalism and imperialism.

Western universalism is dangerous to the world because it could lead to a major intercivilizational war between core states and it is dangerous to the West because it could lead to defeat of the West. With the collapse of the Soviet Union, Westerners see their civilization in a position of unparalleled dominance, while at the same time weaker Asian, Muslim, and other societies are beginning to gain strength. Hence they could be led to apply the familiar and powerful logic of Brutus:

> Our legions are brim-full, our cause is ripe.
> The enemy increaseth every day;
> We at the height, are ready to decline.
> There is a tide in the affairs of men,
> Which taken at the flood, leads on to fortune;
> Omitted, all the voyage of their life
> Is bound in shallows and miseries.
> On such a full sea are we now afloat,
> And we must take the current when it serves,
> Or lose our ventures.

This logic, however, produced Brutus's defeat at Philippi, and the prudent course for the West is not to attempt to stop the shift in power but to learn to navigate the shallows, endure the miseries, moderate its ventures, and safeguard its culture.

All civilizations go though similar processes of emergence, rise, and decline. The West differs from other civilizations not in the way it has developed but in the distinctive character of its values and institutions. These include most notably its Christianity, pluralism, individualism, and rule of law, which made it possible for the West to invent modernity, expand throughout the world, and become the envy of other societies. In their ensemble these characteristics are peculiar to the West. Europe, as Arthur M. Schlesinger, Jr., has said, is "the source — the *unique* source" of the "ideas of individual liberty, political democracy, the rule of law, human rights, and cultural freedom. . . . These are *European* ideas, not Asian, nor African, nor Middle Eastern ideas, except by adoption."[16] They make Western civilization unique, and Western civilization is valuable not because it is universal but because it *is* unique. The principal responsibility of Western leaders, consequently, is not to attempt to reshape other civilizations in the image of the West, which is beyond their declining power, but to preserve, protect, and renew the unique qualities of Western civilization. Because it is the most powerful Western country, that responsibility falls overwhelmingly on the United States of America.

To preserve Western civilization in the face of declining Western power, it is in the interest of the United States and European countries:

to achieve greater political, economic, and military integration and to coordinate their policies so as to preclude states from other civilizations exploiting differences among them;

to incorporate into the European Union and NATO the Western states of Central Europe that is, the Visegrad countries, the Baltic republics, Slovenia, and Croatia;

to encourage the "Westernization" of Latin America and, as far as possible, the close alignment of Latin American countries with the West;

to restrain the development of the conventional and unconventional military power of Islamic and Sinic countries;

to slow the drift of Japan away from the West and toward accommodation with China;

to accept Russia as the core state of Orthodoxy and a major regional power with legitimate interests in the security of its southern borders;

to maintain Western technological and military superiority over other civilizations;

and, most important, to recognize that Western intervention in the affairs of other civilizations is probably the single most dangerous source of instability and potential global conflict in a multicivilizational world.

In the aftermath of the Cold War the United States became consumed with massive debates over the proper course of American foreign policy. In this era, however, the United States can neither dominate nor escape the world. Neither internationalism nor isolationism, neither multilateralism nor unilateralism, will best serve its interests. Those will best be advanced by eschewing these opposing extremes and instead adopting an Atlanticist policy of close cooperation with its European partners to protect and advance the interests and values of the unique civilization they share.

CIVILIZATIONAL WAR AND ORDER

A global war involving the core states of the world's major civilizations is highly improbable but not impossible. Such a war, we have suggested, could come about from the escalation of a fault line war between groups from different civilizations, most likely involving Muslims on one side and non-Muslims on the other. Escalation is made more likely if aspiring Muslim core states compete to provide assistance to their embattled coreligionists. It is made less likely by the interests which secondary and tertiary kin countries may have in not becoming deeply involved in the war themselves. A more dangerous source of a global intercivilizational war is the shifting balance of power among civilizations and their core states. If it continues, the rise of China and the increasing assertiveness of this "biggest player in the history of man" will place tremendous stress on international stability in the early twenty-first century. The emergence of China as the dominant power in East and Southeast Asia would be contrary to American interests as they have been historically construed.[17]

Given this American interest, how might war between the United States and China develop? Assume the year is 2010. American troops are out of Korea, which has been reunified, and the United States has a greatly reduced military presence in Japan. Taiwan and mainland China have reached an accommodation in which Taiwan continues to have most of its de facto independence but explicitly acknowledges Beijing's suzerainty and with China's sponsorship has been admitted to the United Nations on the model of Ukraine and Belorussia in 1946. The development of the oil resources in the South China Sea has proceeded apace, largely under Chinese auspices but with some areas under Vietnamese control being developed by American companies. Its confidence boosted by its new power projection capabilities, China announces that it will establish its full control of the entire sea, over all of which it has always claimed sovereignty. The Vietnamese resist and fighting occurs between Chinese and Vietnamese warships. The Chinese, eager to revenge their 1979 humiliation, invade Vietnam. The Vietnamese appeal for American assistance. The Chinese warn the United States to stay out. Japan and the other nations in Asia dither. The United States says it cannot accept Chinese conquest of Vietnam, calls for economic sanctions against China, and dispatches one of its few remaining carrier task forces to the South China Sea. The Chinese denounce this as a violation of Chinese territorial waters and launch air strikes against the task force. Efforts by the U.N. secretary general and the Japanese prime minister to negotiate a cease-fire fail, and the fighting spreads elsewhere in East Asia. Japan prohibits the use of U.S. bases in Japan for action against China, the United States ignores that prohibition, and Japan announces its neutrality and quarantines the bases. Chinese submarines and land-based aircraft operating from both Taiwan and the mainland impose serious damage on U.S. ships and facilities in East Asia. Meanwhile Chinese ground forces enter Hanoi and occupy large portions of Vietnam.

Since both China and the United States have missiles capable of delivering nuclear weapons to the other's territory, an implicit standoff occurs and these weapons are not used in the early phases of the war. Fear of such attacks, however, exists in both societies and is particularly strong in the United States. This leads many Americans to begin to ask why they are being subjected to this danger? What difference does it make if China controls the South China Sea, Vietnam, or even all of Southeast Asia? Opposition to the war is particularly strong in the Hispanic-dominated states of the southwestern United States, whose people and governments say "this isn't our war" and attempt to opt out on the model of New England in the War of 1812. After the Chinese consolidate their initial victories in East Asia, American opinion begins to move in the direction that Japan hoped it would in 1942: the costs of defeating this most recent assertion of hegemonic power are too great; let's settle for a negotiated end to the sporadic fighting or "phony war" now going on in the Western Pacific.

Meanwhile, however, the war is having an impact on the major states of other civilizations. India seizes the opportunity offered by China's being tied down in East Asia to launch a devastating attack on Pakistan with a view to degrading totally that country's nuclear and conventional military capabilities. It is initially successful but the military alliance between Pakistan, Iran, and China is activated and Iran comes to Pakistan's assistance with modern and sophisticated military forces. India becomes bogged down fighting Iranian troops and Pakistani guerrillas from several different ethnic groups. Both Pakistan and India appeal to Arab states for support—India warning of the danger of Iranian dominance of Southwest Asia—but the initial successes of China against the United States have stimulated major anti-Western movements in Muslim societies. One by one the few remaining pro-Western governments in Arab countries and in Turkey are brought down by Islamist movements powered by the final cohorts of the Muslim youth bulge. The surge of anti-Westernism provoked by Western weakness leads to a massive Arab attack on Israel, which the much-reduced U.S. Sixth Fleet is unable to stop.

China and the United States attempt to rally support from other key states. As China scores military successes, Japan nervously begins to bandwagon with China, shifting its position from formal neutrality to pro-Chinese positive neutrality and then yielding to China's demands and becoming a cobelligerent. Japanese forces occupy the remaining U.S. bases in Japan and the United States hastily evacuates its troops. The United States declares a blockade of Japan, and American and Japanese ships engage in sporadic duels in the Western Pacific. At the start of the war China proposed a mutual security pact with Russia (vaguely reminiscent of the Hitler-Stalin pact). Chinese successes, however, have just the opposite effect on Russia than they had on Japan. The prospect of Chinese victory and total Chinese dominance in East Asia terrifies Moscow. As Russia moves in an anti-Chinese direction and begins to reinforce its troops in Siberia, the numerous Chinese settlers in Siberia interfere with these movements. China then intervenes militarily to protect its countrymen and occupies Vladivostok, the Amur River valley, and other key parts of eastern Siberia. As fighting spreads between Russian and Chinese troops in central Siberia, uprisings occur in Mongolia, which China had earlier placed under a "protectorate."

Control of and access to oil is of central importance to all combatants. Despite its extensive investment in nuclear energy, Japan is still highly dependent on oil imports and this strengthens its inclination to accommodate China and insure its flow of oil from the Persian Gulf, Indonesia, and the South China sea. During the course of the war, as Arab countries come under the control of Islamic militants, Persian Gulf oil supplies to the West diminish to a trickle and the West consequently becomes increasingly dependent on Russian, Caucasian, and Central Asian sources. This leads the West to intensify its efforts to enlist Russia on its side and to support Russia in extending its control over the oil-rich Muslim countries to its south.

Meanwhile the United States has been eagerly attempting to mobilize the full support of its European allies. While extending diplomatic and economic assistance, they are reluctant to become involved militarily. China and Iran, however, are fearful that Western countries will eventually rally behind the United States, even as the United States eventually came to the support of Britain and France in two world wars. To prevent this they secretly deploy intermediate-range nuclear-capable missiles to Bosnia and Algeria and warn the European powers that they should stay out of the war. As was almost always the case with Chinese efforts to intimidate countries other than Japan, this action has consequences just the opposite of what China wanted. U.S. intelligence perceives and reports the deployment and the NATO Council declares the missiles must be removed immediately. Before NATO can act, however, Serbia, wishing to reclaim its historic role as the defender of Christianity against the Turks, invades Bosnia. Croatia joins in and the two countries occupy and partition Bosnia, capture the missiles, and proceed with efforts to complete the ethnic cleansing which they had been forced to stop in the 1990s. Albania and Turkey attempt to help the Bosnians; Greece and Bulgaria launch invasions of European Turkey and panic erupts in Istanbul as Turks flee across the Bosporus. Meanwhile a missile with a nuclear warhead, launched from Algeria, explodes outside Marseilles, and NATO retaliates with devastating air attacks against North African targets.

The United States, Europe, Russia, and India have thus become engaged in a truly global struggle against China, Japan, and most of Islam. How would such a war end? Both sides have major nuclear capabilities and clearly if these were brought into more than minimal play, the principal countries on both sides could be substantially destroyed. If mutual deterrence worked, mutual exhaustion might lead to a negotiated armistice, which would not, however, resolve the fundamental issue of Chinese hegemony in East Asia. Alternatively the West could attempt to defeat China through the use of conventional military power. The alignment of Japan with China, however, gives China the protection of an insular cordon sanitaire preventing the United States from using its naval power against the centers of Chinese population and industry along its coast. The alternative is to approach China from the west. The fighting between Rusia and China leads NATO to welcome Russsia as a member and to cooperate with Russia in countering Chinese incursions into Siberia, maintaining Russian control over the Muslim oil and gas countries of Central Asia, promoting insurrections against Chinese rule by Tibetans, Uighurs, and Mongolians, and gradually mobilizing and deploying Western and Russian forces eastward into Siberia for the final assault across the Great Wall to Beijing, Manchuria, and the Han heartland.

Whatever the immediate outcome of this global civilizational war — mutual nuclear devastation, a negotiated halt as a result of mutual exhaustion, or the eventual march of Russian and Western forces into Tiananmen Square — the broader long-term result would almost inevitably be the drastic decline in the economic, demographic, and military power of all the major participants in the war. As a result, global power which had shifted over the centuries from the East to the West and had then begun to shift back from the West to the East would now shift from the North to the South. The great beneficiaries of the war of civilizations are those civilizations which abstained from it. With the West, Russia, China, and Japan devastated to varying degrees, the way is open for India, if it escaped such devastation even though it was a participant, to attempt to reshape the world along Hindu lines. Large segments of the American public blame the severe weakening of the United States on the narrow Western orientation of WASP elites, and Hispanic leaders come to power buttressed by the promise of extensive Marshall Plan–type aid from the booming Latin American countries which sat out the war. Africa, on the other hand, has little to offer to the rebuilding of Europe and instead disgorges hordes of socially mobilized people to prey on the remains. In Asia if China, Japan, and Korea are devastated by the war, power also shifts southward, with Indonesia, which had remained neutral, becoming the dominant state and, under the guidance of its Australian advisors, acting to shape the course of events from New Zealand on the east to Myanmar and Sri Lanka on the west and Vietnam on the north. All of which presages future conflict with India and a revived China. In any event, the center of world politics moves south.

If this scenario seems a wildly implausible fantasy to the reader, that is all to the good. Let us hope that no other scenarios of global civilizational war have greater plausibility. What is most plausible and hence most disturbing about this scenario, however, is the cause of war: intervention by the core state of one civilization (the United States) in a dispute between the core state of another civilization (China) and a member state of that civilization (Vietnam). To the United States such intervention was necessary to uphold international law, repel aggression, protect freedom of the seas, maintain its access to South China Sea oil, and prevent the domination of East Asia by a single power. To China that intervention was a totally intolerable but typically arrogant attempt by the leading Western state to humiliate and browbeat China, provoke opposition to China within its legitimate sphere of influence, and deny China its appropriate role in world affairs.

In the coming era, in short, the avoidance of major intercivilizational wars requires core states to refrain from intervening in conflicts in other civilizations. This is a truth which some states, particularly the United States, will undoubtedly find difficult to accept. This *abstention rule* that core states abstain from intervention in conflicts in other civilizations is the first requirement of peace in a multicivilizational, multipolar world. The second requirement is the *joint mediation rule* that core states negotiate with each other to contain or to halt fault line wars between states or groups from their civilizations.

Acceptance of these rules and of a world with greater equality among civilizations will not be easy for the West or for those civilizations which may aim to supplement or supplant the West in its dominant role. In such a world, for instance, core states may well view it as their prerogative to possess nuclear weapons and to deny such weapons to other members of their civilization. Looking back on his efforts to develop a "full nuclear capability" for Pakistan, Zulfikar Ali Bhutto justified those efforts: "We know that Israel and South Africa have full nuclear capability. The Christian, Jewish and Hindu civilizations have this capability. Only the Islamic civilization was without it, but that position was about to change."[18] The competition for leadership within civilizations lacking a single core state may also stimulate competition for nuclear weapons. Even though it has highly cooperative relations with Pakistan, Iran clearly feels that it needs nuclear weapons as much as Pakistan does. On the other hand, Brazil and Argentina gave up their programs aimed in this direction, and South Africa destroyed its nuclear weapons, although it might well wish to reacquire them if Nigeria began to develop such a capability. While nuclear proliferation obviously involves risks, as Scott Sagan and others have pointed out, a world in which one or two core states in each of the major civilizations had nuclear weapons and no other states did could be a reasonably stable world.

Most of the principal international institutions date from shortly after World War II and are shaped according to Western interests, values, and practices. As Western power declines relative to that of other civilizations, pressures will develop to reshape these institutions to accommodate the interests of those civilizations. The most obvious, most important, and probably most controversial issue concerns permanent membership in the U.N. Security Council. That membership has consisted of the victorious major powers of World War II and bears a decreasing relationship to the reality of power in the world. Over the longer haul either changes are made in its membership or other less formal procedures are likely to develop to deal with security issues, even as the G-7 meetings have dealt with global economic issues. In a multicivilizational world ideally each major civilization should have at least one permanent seat on the Security Council. At present only three do. The United States has endorsed Japanese and German membership but it is clear that they will become permanent members only if other countries do also. Brazil has suggested five new permanent members, albeit without veto power, Germany, Japan, India, Nigeria, and itself. That, however, would leave the world's 1 billion Muslims unrepresented, except in so far as Nigeria might undertake that responsibility. From a civilizational viewpoint, clearly Japan and India should be permanent members, and Africa, Latin America, and the Muslim world should have permanent seats, which could be occupied on a rotating basis by the leading states of those civilizations, selections being made by the Organization of the Islamic Conference, the Organization of African Unity, and the Organization of American States (the United States abstaining). It would also be appropriate to consolidate the British and French seats into a single European Union seat, the rotating occupant of which would be selected by the Union. Seven civilizations would thus each have one permanent seat and the West would have two, an allocation broadly representative of the distribution of people, wealth, and power in the world.

THE COMMONALITIES OF CIVILIZATION

Some Americans have promoted multiculturalism at home; some have promoted universalism abroad; and some have done both. Multiculturalism at home threatens the United States and the West; universalism abroad threatens the West and the world. Both deny the uniqueness of Western culture. The global monoculturalists want to make the world like America. The domestic mulitculturalists want to make America like the world. A multicultural America is impossible because a non-Western America is not American. A multicultural world is unavoidable because global empire is impossible. The preservation of the United States and the West requires the renewal of Western identity. The security of the world requires acceptance of global multiculturality.

Does the vacuousness of Western universalism and the reality of global cultural diversity lead inevitably and irrevocably to moral and cultural relativism? If universalism legitimates imperialism, does relativism legitimate repression? Once again, the answer to these questions is yes and no. Cultures are relative; morality is absolute. Cultures, as Michael Walzer has argued, are "thick"; they prescribe institutions and behavior patterns to guide humans in the paths which are right in a particular society. Above, beyond, and growing out of this maximalist morality, however, is a "thin" minimalist morality that embodies "reiterated features of particular thick or maximal moralities." Minimal moral concepts of truth and justice are found in all thick moralities and cannot be divorced from them. There are also minimal moral "negative injunctions, most likely, rules against murder, deceit, torture, oppression, and tyranny." What people have in common is "more the sense of a common enemy [or evil] than the commitment to a common culture." Human society is "universal because it is human, particular because it is a society." At times we march with others; mostly we march alone.[19] Yet a "thin" minimal morality does derive from the common human condition, and "universal dispositions" are found in all cultures.[20] Instead of promoting the supposedly universal features of one civilization, the requisites for cultural coexistence demand a search for what is common to most civilizations. In a multicivilizational world, the constructive course is to renounce universalism, accept diversity, and seek commonalities.

A relevant effort to identify such commonalities in a very small place occurred in Singapore in the early 1990s. The people of Singapore are roughly

76 percent Chinese, 15 percent Malay and Muslim, and 6 percent Indian Hindu and Sikh. In the past the government has attempted to promote "Confucian values" among its people but it has also insisted on everyone being educated in and becoming fluent in English. In January 1989 President Wee Kim Wee in his address opening Parliament pointed to the extensive exposure of the 2.7 million Singaporeans to outside cultural influences from the West which had "put them in close touch with new ideas and technologies from abroad" but had "also exposed" them "to alien lifestyles and values." "Traditional Asian ideas of morality, duty and society which have sustained us in the past," he warned, "are giving way to a more Westernized, individualistic, and self-centered outlook on life." It is necessary, he argued, to identify the core values which Singapore's different ethnic and religious communities had in common and "which capture the essence of being a Singaporean."

President Wee suggested four such values: "placing society above self, upholding the family as the basic building block of society, resolving major issues through consensus instead of contention, and stressing racial and religious tolerance and harmony." His speech led to extensive discussion of Singaporean values and two years later a White Paper setting forth the government's position. The White Paper endorsed all four of the president's suggested values but added a fifth on support of the individual, largely because of the need to emphasize the priority of individual merit in Singaporean society as against Confucian values of hierarchy and family, which could lead to nepotism. The White Paper defined the "Shared Values" of Singaporeans as:

> Nation before [ethnic] community and society above self;
> Family as the basic unit of society;
> Regard and community support for the individual;
> Consensus instead of contention;
> Racial and religious harmony.

While citing Singapore's commitment to parliamentary democracy and excellence in government, the statement of *Shared Values* explicitly excluded political values from its purview. The government emphasized that Singapore was "in crucial respects an Asian society" and must remain one. "Singaporeans are not Americans or Anglo-Saxons, though we may speak English and wear Western dress. If over the longer term Singaporeans became indistinguishable from Americans, British or Australians, or worse became a poor imitation of them [i.e., a torn country], we will lose our edge over these Western societies which enables us to hold our own internationally." [21]

The Singapore project was an ambitious and enlightened effort to define a Singaporean cultural identity which was shared by its ethnic and religous communities and which distinguished it from the West. Certainly a statement of Western and particularly American values would give far more weight to the rights of the individual as against those of the community, to freedom of expression and truth emerging out of the contest of ideas, to political participation and competition, and to the rule of law as against the rule of expert, wise, and responsible governors. Yet even so, while they might supplement the Singaporean values and give some lower priority, few Westerners would reject those values as unworthy. At least at a basic "thin" morality level, some commonalities exist between Asia and the West. In addition, as many have pointed out, whatever the degree to which they divided humankind, the world's major religions — Western Christianity, Orthodoxy, Hinduism, Buddhism, Islam, Confucianism, Taoism, Judaism — also share key values in common. If humans are ever to develop a universal civilization, it will emerge gradually through the exploration and expansion of these commonalities. Thus, in addition to the abstention rule and the joint mediation rule, the third rule for peace in a multicivilizational world is the *commonalities rule:* peoples in all civilizations should search for and attempt to expand the values, institutions, and practices they have in common with peoples of other civilizations.

This effort would contribute not only to limiting the clash of civilizations but also to strengthening Civilization in the singular (hereafter capitalized for clarity). The singular Civilization presumably refers to a complex mix of higher levels of morality, religion, learning, art, philosophy, technology, material well-being, and probably other things. These obviously do not necessarily vary together. Yet scholars easily identify highpoints and lowpoints in the level of Civilization in the histories of civilizations. The question then is: How can one chart the ups and downs of humanity's development of Civilization? Is there a general, secular trend, transcending individual civilizations, toward higher levels of Civilization? If there is such a trend, is it a product of the processes of modernization that increase the control of humans over their environment and hence generate higher and higher levels of technological sophistication and material well-being? In the contemporary era, is a higher level of modernity thus a prerequisite to a higher level of Civilization? Or does the level of Civilization primarily vary within the history of individual civilizations?

This issue is another manifestation of the debate over the linear or cyclical nature of history. Conceivably modernization and human moral development produced by greater education, awareness, and understanding of human society and its natural environment produce sustained movement toward higher and higher levels of Civilization. Alternatively, levels of Civilization may simply reflect phases in the evolution of civilizations. When civilizations first emerge, their people are usually vigorous, dynamic, brutal, mobile, and expansionist. They are relatively unCivilized. As the civilization evolves it becomes more settled and develops the techniques and skills that make it more Civilized. As the competition among its constituent elements tapers off and a universal state emerges, the civilization reaches its highest level of Civilization, its "golden age," with a flowering of morality, art, literature, philosophy, technology, and martial, economic, and political competence. As it goes into decay as a civilization, its level of Civilization also declines until it disappears under the onslaught of a different surging civilization with a lower level of Civilization.

Modernization has generally enhanced the material level of Civilization throughout the world. But has it also enhanced the moral and cultural dimensions of Civilization? In some respects this appears to be the case. Slavery, torture, vicious abuse of individuals, have become less and less acceptable in the contemporary world. Is this, however, simply the result of the impact of Western civilization on other cultures and hence will a moral reversion occur as Western power declines? Much evidence exists in the 1990s for the relevance of the "sheer chaos" paradigm of world affairs: a global breakdown of law and order, failed states and increasing anarchy in many parts of the world, a global crime wave, transnational mafias and drug cartels, increasing drug addiction in many societies, a general weakening of the family, a decline in trust and social solidarity in many countries, ethnic, religious, and civilizational violence and rule by the gun prevalent in much of the world. In city after city — Moscow, Rio de Janeiro, Bangkok, Shanghai, London, Rome, Warsaw, Tokyo, Johannesburg, Delhi, Karachi, Cairo, Bogota, Washington — crime seems to be soaring and basic elements of Civilization fading away. People speak of a global crisis in governance. The rise of transnational corporations producing economic goods is increasingly matched by the rise of transnational criminal mafias, drug cartels, and terrorist gangs violently assaulting Civilization. Law and order is the first prerequisite of Civilization and in much of the world — Africa, Latin America, the former Soviet Union, South Asia, the Middle East — it appears to be evaporating, while also under serious assault in China, Japan, and the West. On a worldwide basis Civilization seems in many respects to be yielding to barbarism, generating the image of an unprecedented phenomenon, a global Dark Ages, possibly descending on humanity.

In the 1950s Lester Pearson warned that humans were moving into "an age when different civilizations will have to learn to live side by side in peaceful interchange, learning from each other, studying each other's history and ideals and art and culture, mutually enriching each others' lives. The alternative, in this overcrowded little world, is misunderstanding, tension, clash, and catastrophe." [22] The futures of both peace and Civilization depend upon understanding and cooperation among the political, spiritual, and intellectual leaders of the world's major civilizations. In the clash of civilizations, Europe and America will hang together or hang separately. In the greater clash, the global *"real clash,"* between Civilization and barbarism, the world's great civilizations, with their rich accomplishments in religion, art, literature, philosophy, science, technology, morality, and compassion, will also hang together or hang separately. In the emerging era, clashes of civilizations are the greatest threat to world peace, and an international order based on civilizations is the surest safeguard against world war.

Notes

●

Chapter 1

1. Henry A. Kissinger, *Diplomacy* (New York: Simon & Schuster, 1994), pp. 23–24.

2. H. D. S. Greenway's phrase, *Boston Globe*, 3 December 1992, p. 19.

3. Vaclav Havel, "The New Measure of Man," *New York Times*, 8 July 1994, p. A27; Jacques Delors, "Questions Concerning European Security," Address, International Institute for Strategic Studies, Brussels, 10 September 1993, p. 2.

4. Thomas S. Kuhn, *The Structure of Scientific Revolutions*, (Chicago: University of Chicago Press, 1962), pp. 17–18.

5. John Lewis Gaddis, "Toward the Post–Cold War World." *Foreign Affairs*, 70 (Spring 1991), 101; Judith Goldstein and Robert O. Keohane, "Ideas and Foreign Policy: An Analytical Framework," in Goldstein and Keohane, eds., *Ideas and Foreign Policy: Beliefs, Institutions, and Political Change* (Ithaca: Cornell University Press, 1993), pp. 8–17.

6. Francis Fukuyama, "The End of History," *The National Interest*, 16 (Summer 1989), 4, 18.

7. "Address to the Congress Reporting on the Yalta Conference," 1 March 1945, in Samuel I. Rosenman, ed., *Public Papers and Addresses of Franklin D. Roosevelt* (New York: Russell and Russell, 1969), XIII, 586.

8. See Max Singer and Aaron Wildavsky, *The Real World Order: Zones of Peace, Zones of Turmoil* (Chatham, NJ: Chatham House, 1993); Robert O. Keohane and Joseph S. Nye, "Introduction: The End of the Cold War in Europe," in Keohane, Nye, and Stanley Hoffmann, eds., *After the Cold War: International Institutions and State Strategies in Europe, 1989–1991* (Cambridge: Harvard University Press, 1993), p. 6; and James M. Goldgeier and Michael McFaul, "A Tale of Two Worlds: Core and Periphery in the Post–Cold War Era," *International Organization*, 46 (Spring 1992), 467–491.

9. See F. S. C. Northrop, *The Meeting of East and West: An Inquiry Concerning World Understanding* (New York: Macmillan, 1946).

10. Edward W. Said, *Orientalism* (New York: Pantheon Books, 1978), pp. 43–44.

11. See Kenneth N. Waltz, "The Emerging Structure of International Politics," *International Security*, 18 (Fall 1993), 44–79; John J. Mearsheimer, "Back to the Future: Instability in Europe after the Cold War," *International Security*, 15 (Summer 1990), 5–56.

12. Stephen D. Krasner questions the importance of Westphalia as a dividing point. See his "Westphalia and All That," in Goldstein and Keohane, eds., *Ideas and Foreign Policy*, pp. 235–264.

13. Zbigniew Brzezinski, *Out of Control: Global Turmoil on the Eve of the Twenty-first Century* (New York: Scribner, 1993); Daniel Patrick Moynihan, *Pandaemonium:*

Ethnicity in International Politics (Oxford: Oxford University Press, 1993); see also Robert Kaplan, "The Coming Anarchy," *Atlantic Monthly*, 273 (Feb. 1994), 44–76.

14. See *New York Times*, 7 February 1993, pp. 1, 14; and Gabriel Schoenfeld, "Outer Limits," *Post-Soviet Prospects*, 17 (Jan. 1993), 3, citing figures from the Russian Ministry of Defense.

15. See Gaddis, "Toward the Post–Cold War World"; Benjamin R. Barber, "Jihad vs. McWorld," *Atlantic Monthly*, 269 (March 1992), 53–63, and *Jihad vs. McWorld* (New York: Times Books, 1995); Hans Mark, "After Victory in the Cold War: The Global Village or Tribal Warfare," in J. J. Lee and Walter Korter, eds., *Europe in Transition: Political, Economic, and Security Prospects for the 1990s* (LBJ School of Public Affairs, University of Texas at Austin, March 1990), pp. 19–27.

16. John J. Mearsheimer, "The Case for a Nuclear Deterrent," *Foreign Affairs*, 72 (Summer 1993), 54.

17. Lester B. Pearson, *Democracy in World Politics* (Princeton: Princeton University Press, 1955), pp. 82–83.

18. Quite independently Johan Galtung developed an analysis that closely parallels mine on the salience to world politics of the seven or eight major civilizations and their core states. See his "The Emerging Conflict Formations," in Katharine and Majid Tehranian, eds., *Restructuring for World Peace: On the Threshold of the Twenty-First Century* (Cresskill NJ: Hampton Press, 1992), pp. 23–24. Galtung sees seven regional-cultural groupings emerging dominated by hegemons: the United States, European Community, Japan, China, Russia, India, and an "Islamic core." Other authors who in the early 1990s advanced similar arguments concerning civilizations include: Michael Lind, "American as an Ordinary Country," *American Enterprise*, 1 (Sept./Oct. 1990), 19–23; Barry Buzan, "New Patterns of Global Security in the Twenty-first Century," *International Affairs*, 67 (1991), 441, 448–449; Robert Gilpin, "The Cycle of Great Powers: Has It Finally Been Broken?" (Princeton University, unpublished paper, 19 May 1993), pp. 6ff.; William S. Lind, "North-South Relations: Returning to a World of Cultures in Conflict," *Current World Leaders*, 35 (Dec. 1992), 1073–1080, and "Defending Western Culture," *Foreign Policy*, 84 (Fall 1994), 40–50; "Looking Back from 2992: A World History, chap. 13: The Disastrous 21st Century," *Economist*, 26 December 1992–8 January 1993, pp. 17–19; "The New World Order: Back to the Future," *Economist*, 8 January 1994, pp. 21–23; "A Survey of Defence and the Democracies," *Economist*, 1 September 1990; Zsolt Rostovanyi, "Clash of Civilizations and Cultures: Unity and Disunity of World Order," (unpublished paper, 29 March 1993); Michael Vlahos, "Culture and Foreign Policy," *Foreign Policy*, 82 (Spring 1991), 59–78; Donald J. Puchala, "The History of the Future of International Relations," *Ethics and International Affairs*, 8 (1994), 177–202; Mahdi Elmandjra, "Cultural Diversity: Key to Survival in the Future," (Paper presented to First Mexican Congress on Future Studies, Mexico City, September 1994). In 1991 Elmandjra published in Arabic a book which appeared in French the following year entitled *Premiere Guerre Civilisationnelle* (Casablanca: Ed. Toubkal, 1992, 1994).

19. Fernand Braudel, *On History* (Chicago: University of Chicago Press, 1980), pp. 210–211.

Chapter 2

1. "World history is the history of large cultures." Oswald Spengler, *Decline of the West* (New York: A. A. Knopf, 1926–1928), II, 170. The major works by these scholars analyzing the nature and dynamics of civilizations include: Max Weber, *The Sociology*

of Religion (Boston: Beacon Press, trans. Ephraim Fischoff, 1968); Emile Durkheim and Marcel Mauss, "Note on the Notion of Civilization," *Social Research*, 38 (1971), 808–813; Oswald Spengler, *Decline of the West*; Pitirim Sorokin, *Social and Cultural Dynamics* (New York: American Book Co., 4 vols., 1937–1985); Arnold Toynbee, *A Study of History* (London: Oxford University Press, 12 vols., 1934–1961); Alfred Weber, *Kulturgeschichte als Kultursoziologie* (Leiden: A. W. Sijthoff's Uitgerversmaatschappij N.V., 1935); A. L. Kroeber, *Configurations of Culture Growth* (Berkeley: University of California Press, 1944), and *Style and Civilizations* (Westport, CT: Greenwood Press, 1973); Philip Bagby, *Culture and History: Prolegomena to the Comparative Study of Civilizations* (London: Longmans, Green, 1958); Carroll Quigley, *The Evolution of Civilizations: An Introduction to Historical Analysis* (New York: Macmillan, 1961); Rushton Coulborn, *The Origin of Civilized Societies* (Princeton: Princeton University Press, 1959); S. N. Eisenstadt, "Cultural Traditions and Political Dynamics: The Origins and Modes of Ideological Politics," *British Journal of Sociology*, 32 (June 1981), 155–181; Fernand Braudel, *History of Civilizations* (New York: Allen Lane — Penguin Press, 1994) and *On History* (Chicago: University of Chicago Press, 1980); William H. McNeill, *The Rise of the West: A History of the Human Community* (Chicago: University of Chicago Press, 1963); Adda B. Bozeman, "Civilizations Under Stress," *Virginia Quarterly Review*, 51 (Winter 1975), 1–18, *Strategic Intelligence and Statecraft* (Washington: Brassey's (US), 1992), and *Politics and Culture in International History: From the Ancient Near East to the Opening of the Modern Age* (New Brunswick, NJ: Transaction Publishers, 1994); Christopher Dawson, *Dynamics of World History* (LaSalle, IL: Sherwood Sugden Co., 1978), and *The Movement of World Revolution* (New York: Sheed and Ward, 1959); Immanuel Wallerstein, *Geopolitics and Geoculture: Essays on the Changing World-system* (Cambridge: Cambridge University Press, 1992); Felipe Fernández-Armesto, *Millennium: A History of the Last Thousand Years* (New York: Scribners, 1995). To these works could be added the last, tragically marked work of Louis Hartz, *A Synthesis of World History* (Zurich: Humanity Press, 1983), which "with remarkable prescience," as Samuel Beer commented, "foresees a division of mankind very much like the present pattern of the post–Cold War world" into five great "culture areas": Christian, Muslim, Hindu, Confucian, and African. Memorial Minute, Louis Hartz, *Harvard University Gazette*, 89 (May 27, 1994). An indispensable summary overview and introduction to the analysis of civilizations is Matthew Melko, *The Nature of Civilizations* (Boston: Porter Sargent, 1969). I am also indebted for useful suggestions to the critical paper on my *Foreign Affairs* article by Hayward W. Alker, Jr., "If Not Huntington's 'Civilizations,' Then Whose?" (unpublished paper, Massachusetts Insitute of Technology, 25 March 1994).

2. Braudel, *On History*, pp. 177–181, 212–214, and *History of Civilizations*, pp. 4–5; Gerrit W. Gong, *The Standard of "Civilization" in International Society* (Oxford: Clarendon Press, 1984), 81ff., 97–100; Wallerstein, *Geopolitics and Geoculture*, pp. 160ff. and 215ff.; Arnold J. Toynbee, *Study of History*, X, 274–275, and *Civilization on Trial* (New York: Oxford University Press, 1948), p. 24.

3. Braudel, *On History*, p. 205. For an extended review of definitions of culture and civilization, especially the German distinction, see A. L. Kroeber and Clyde Kluckhohn, *Culture: A Critical Review of Concepts and Definitions* (Cambridge: Papers of the Peabody Museum of American Archaeology and Ethnology, Harvard University, Vol. XLVII, No. 1, 1952), passim but esp. pp. 15–29.

4. Bozeman, "Civilizations Under Stress," p. 1.

5. Durkheim and Mauss, "Notion of Civilization," p. 811; Braudel, *On History*,

326 Notes, pages 42–48

pp. 177, 202; Melko, *Nature of Civilizations*, p. 8; Wallerstein, *Geopolitics and Geoculture*, p. 215; Dawson, *Dynamics of World History*, pp. 51, 402; Spengler, *Decline of the West*, I, p. 31. Interestingly, the *International Encyclopedia of the Social Sciences* (New York: Macmillan and Free Press, ed. David L. Sills, 17 vols., 1968) contains no primary article on "civilization" or "civilizations." The "concept of civilization" (singular) is treated in a subsection of the article called "Urban Revolution," while civilizations (plural) receive passing mention in an article called "Culture."

6. Herodotus, *The Persian Wars* (Harmondsworth, England: Penguin Books, 1972), pp. 543–544.

7. Edward A. Tiryakian, "Reflections on the Sociology of Civilizations, "*Sociological Analysis*, 35 (Summer 1974), 125.

8. Toynbee, *Study of History*, I, 455, quoted in Melko, *Nature of Civilizations*, pp. 8–9; and Braudel, *On History*, p. 202.

9. Braudel, *History of Civilizations*, p. 35, and *On History*, pp. 209–210.

10. Bozeman, *Strategic Intelligence and Statecraft*, p. 26.

11. Quigley, *Evolution of Civilizations*, pp. 146ff.; Melko, *Nature of Civilizations*, pp. 101ff. See D. C. Somervell, "Argument" in his abridgment of Arnold J. Toynbee, A *Study of History*, vols. I–VI (Oxford: Oxford University Press, 1946), pp. 569ff.

12. Lucian W. Pye, "China: Erratic State, Frustrated Society," *Foreign Affairs*, 69 (Fall 1990), 58.

13. See Quigley, *Evolution of Civilizations*, chap. 3, esp. pp. 77, 84; Max Weber, "The Social Psychology of the World Religions," in *From Max Weber: Essays in Sociology* (London: Routledge, trans. and ed. H. H. Gerth and C. Wright Mills, 1991), p. 267; Bagby, *Culture and History*, pp. 165–174; Spengler, *Decline of the West*, II, 31ff; Toynbee, *Study of History*, I, 133; XII, 546–547; Braudel, *History of Civilizations*, passim; McNeill, *The Rise of the West*, passim; and Rostovanyi, "Clash of Civilizations," pp. 8–9.

14. Melko, *Nature of Civilizations*, p. 133.

15. Braudel, *On History*, p. 226.

16. For a major 1990s addition to this literature by one who knows both cultures well, see Claudio Veliz, *The New World of the Gothic Fox* (Berkeley: University of California Press, 1994).

17. See Charles A. and Mary R. Beard, *The Rise of American Civilization* (New York: Macmillan, 2 vols., 1927) and Max Lerner, *America as a Civilization* (New York: Simon & Schuster, 1957). With patriotic boosterism, Lerner argues that "For good or ill, America is what it is—a culture in its own right, with many characteristic lines of power and meaning of its own, ranking with Greece and Rome as one of the great distinctive civilizations of history." Yet he also admits, "Almost without exception the great theories of history find no room for any concept of America as a civilization in its own right" (pp. 58–59).

18. On the role of fragments of European civilization creating new societies in North America, Latin America, South Africa, and Australia, see Louis Hartz, *The Founding of New Societies: Studies in the History of the United States, Latin America, South Africa, Canada, and Australia* (New York: Harcourt, Brace & World, 1964).

19. Dawson, *Dynamics of World History*, p. 128. See also Mary C. Bateson, "Beyond Sovereignty: An Emerging Global Civilization," in R. B. J. Walker and Saul H. Mendlovitz, eds., *Contending Sovereignties: Redefining Political Community* (Boulder: Lynne Rienner, 1990), pp. 148–149.

20. Toynbee classifies both Therevada and Lamaist Buddhism as fossil civilizations, *Study of History*, I, 35, 91–92.

21. See, for example, Bernard Lewis, *Islam and the West* (New York: Oxford University Press, 1993); Toynbee, *Study of History*, chap. IX, "Contacts between Civilizations in Space (Encounters between Contemporaries)," VIII, 88ff; Benjamin Nelson, "Civilizational Complexes and Intercivilizational Encounters," *Sociological Analysis*, 34 (Summer 1973), 79–105.

22. S. N. Eisenstadt, "Cultural Traditions and Political Dynamics: The Origins and Modes of Ideological Politics," *British Journal of Sociology*, 32 (June 1981), 157, and "The Axial Age: The Emergence of Transcendental Visions and the Rise of Clerics," *Archives Europeennes de Sociologie*, 22 (No. 1, 1982), 298. See also Benjamin I. Schwartz, "The Age of Transcendence in Wisdom, Revolution, and Doubt: Perspectives on the First Millennium B.C.," *Daedalus*, 104 (Spring 1975), 3. The concept of the Axial Age derives from Karl Jaspers, *Vom Ursprung und Ziel der Geschichte* (Zurich: Artemisverlag, 1949).

23. Toynbee, *Civilization on Trial*, p. 69. Cf. William H. McNeill, *The Rise of the West*, pp. 295–298, who emphasizes the extent to which by the advent of the Christian era, "Organized trade routes, both by land and by sea, . . . linked the four great cultures of the continent."

24. Braudel, *On History*, p. 14: ". . . cultural influence came in small doses, delayed by the length and slowness of the journeys they had to make. If historians are to be believed, the Chinese fashions of the T'ang period [618–907] travelled so slowly that they did not reach the island of Cyprus and the brilliant court of Lusignan until the fifteenth century. From there they spread, at the quicker speed of Mediterranean trade, to France and the eccentric court of Charles VI, where hennins and shoes with long pointed toes became immensely popular, the heritage of a long vanished world — much as light still reaches us from stars already extinct."

25. See Toynbee, *Study of History*, VIII, 347–348.

26. McNeill, *Rise of the West*, p. 547.

27. D. K. Fieldhouse, *Economics and Empire, 1830–1914* (London: Macmillan, 1984), p. 3; F. J. C. Hearnshaw, *Sea Power and Empire* (London: George Harrap and Co, 1940), p. 179.

28. Geoffrey Parker, *The Military Revolution: Military Innovation and the Rise of the West* (Cambridge: Cambridge University Press, 1988), p. 4; Michael Howard, "The Military Factor in European Expansion," in Hedley Bull and Adam Watson, eds., *The Expansion of International Society* (Oxford: Clarendon Press, 1984), pp. 33ff.

29. A. G. Kenwood and A. L. Lougheed, *The Growth of the International Economy 1820–1990* (London: Routledge, 1992), pp. 78–79; Angus Maddison, *Dynamic Forces in Capitalist Development* (New York: Oxford University Press, 1991), pp. 326–27; Alan S. Blinder, reported in the *New York Times*, 12 March 1995, p. 5E. See also Simon Kuznets, "Quantitative Aspects of the Economic Growth of Nations — X. Level and Structure of Foreign Trade: Long-term Trends," *Economic Development and Cultural Change*, 15 (Jan. 1967, part II), pp. 2–10.

30. Charles Tilly, "Reflections on the History of European State-making," in Tilly, ed., *The Formation of National States in Western Europe* (Princeton: Princeton University Press, 1975), p. 18.

31. R. R. Palmer, "Frederick the Great, Guibert, Bulow: From Dynastic to National War," in Peter Paret, ed., *Makers of Modern Strategy from Machiavelli to the Nuclear Age* (Princeton: Princeton University Press, 1986), p. 119.

32. Edward Mortimer, "Christianity and Islam," *International Affairs*, 67 (Jan. 1991), 7.

33. Hedley Bull, *The Anarchical Society* (New York: Columbia University Press,

1977), pp. 9–13. See also Adam Watson, *The Evolution of International Society* (London: Routledge, 1992), and Barry Buzan, "From International System to International Society: Structural Realism and Regime Theory Meet the English School," *International Organization*, 47 (Summer 1993), 327–352, who distinguishes between "civilizational" and "functional" models of international society and concludes that "civilizational international societies have dominated the historical record" and that there "appear to be no pure cases of functional international societies." (p. 336).

34. Spengler, *Decline of the West*, I, 93–94.

35. Toynbee, *Study of History*, I, 149ff, 154, 157ff.

36. Braudel, *On History*, p. xxxiii.

Chapter 3

1. V. S. Naipaul, "Our Universal Civilization," The 1990 Wriston Lecture, The Manhattan Institute, *New York Review of Books*, 30 October 1990, p. 20.

2. See James Q. Wilson, *The Moral Sense* (New York: Free Press, 1993); Michael Walzer, *Thick and Thin: Moral Argument at Home and Abroad* (Notre Dame: University of Notre Dame Press, 1994), esp. chaps. 1 and 4; and for a brief overview, Frances V. Harbour, "Basic Moral Values: A Shared Core," *Ethics and International Affairs*, 9 (1995), 155–170.

3. Vaclav Havel, "Civilization's Thin Veneer," *Harvard Magazine*, 97 (July–August 1995), 32.

4. Hedley Bull, *The Anarchical Society: A Study of Order in World Politics* (New York: Columbia University Press, 1977), p. 317.

5. John Rockwell, "The New Colossus: American Culture as Power Export," and several authors, "Channel-Surfing Through U.S. Culture in 20 Lands," *New York Times*, 30 January 1994, sec. 2, pp. 1ff; David Rieff, "A Global Culture," *World Policy Journal*, 10 (Winter 1993–94), 73–81.

6. Michael Vlahos, "Culture and Foreign Policy," *Foreign Policy*, 82 (Spring 1991), 69; Kishore Mahbubani, "The Dangers of Decadence: What the Rest Can Teach the West," *Foreign Affairs*, 72 (Sept./Oct. 1993), 12.

7. Aaron L. Friedberg, "The Future of American Power," *Political Science Quarterly*, 109 (Spring 1994), 15.

8. Richard Parker, "The Myth of Global News," *New Perspectives Quarterly*, 11 (Winter 1994), 41–44; Michael Gurevitch, Mark R. Levy, and Itzhak Roeh, "The Global Newsroom: convergences and diversities in the globalization of television news," in Peter Dahlgren and Colin Sparks, eds., *Communication and Citizenship: Journalism and the Public Sphere in the New Media* (London: Routledge, 1991), p. 215.

9. Ronald Dore, "Unity and Diversity in World Culture," in Hedley Bull and Adam Watson, eds., *The Expansion of International Society* (Oxford: Oxford University Press, 1984), p. 423.

10. Robert L. Bartley, "The Case for Optimism — The West Should Believe in Itself," *Foreign Affairs*, 72 (Sept./Oct. 1993), 16.

11. See Joshua A. Fishman, "The Spread of English as a New Perspective for the Study of Language Maintenance and Language Shift," in Joshua A. Fishman, Robert L. Cooper, and Andrew W. Conrad, *The Spread of English: The Sociology of English as an Additional Language* (Rowley, MA: Newbury House, 1977), pp. 108ff.

12. Fishman, "Spread of English as a New Perspective," pp. 118–119.

13. Randolf Quirk, in Braj B. Kachru, *The Indianization of English* (Delhi: Oxford, 1983), p. ii; R. S. Gupta and Kapil Kapoor, eds., *English in India — Issues and Problems*

(Delhi: Academic Foundation, 1991), p. 21. Cf. Sarvepalli Gopal, "The English Language in India," *Encounter*, 73 (July/Aug. 1989), 16, who estimates 35 million Indians "speak and write English of some type or other." World Bank, *World Development Report 1985, 1991* (New York: Oxford University Press), table 1.

14. Kapoor and Gupta, "Introduction," in Gupta and Kapoor, eds., *English in India*, p. 21; Gopal, "English Language," p. 16.

15. Fishman, "Spread of English as a New Perspective," p. 115.

16. See *Newsweek*, 19 July 1993, p. 22.

17. Quoted by R. N. Srivastava and V. P. Sharma, "Indian English Today," in Gupta and Kapoor, eds., *English in India*, p. 191; Gopal, "English Language," p. 17.

18. *New York Times*, 16 July 1993, p. A9; *Boston Globe*, 15 July 1993, p. 13.

19. In addition to the projections in the *World Christian Encyclopedia*, see also those of Jean Bourgeois-Pichat, "Le nombre des hommes: État et prospective," in Albert Jacquard et al., *Les Scientifiques Parlent* (Paris: Hachette, 1987), pp. 140, 143, 151, 154–156.

20. Edward Said on V. S. Naipaul, quoted by Brent Staples, "Con Men and Conquerors," *New York Times Book Review*, 22 May 1994, p. 42.

21. A. G. Kenwood and A. L. Lougheed, *The Growth of the International Economy 1820–1990* (London: Routledge, 3rd ed., 1992), pp. 78–79; Angus Maddison, *Dynamic Forces in Capitalist Development* (New York: Oxford University Press, 1991), pp. 326–327; Alan S. Blinder, *New York Times*, 12 March 1995, p. 5E.

22. David M. Rowe, "The Trade and Security Paradox in International Politics," (unpublished manuscript, Ohio State University, 15 Sept. 1994), p. 16.

23. Dale C. Copeland, "Economic Interdependence and War: A Theory of Trade Expectations," *International Security* 20 (Spring 1996), 25.

24. William J. McGuire and Claire V. McGuire, "Content and Process in the Experience of Self," *Advances in Experimental Social Psychology*, 21 (1988), 102.

25. Donald L. Horowitz, "Ethnic Conflict Management for Policy-Makers," in Joseph V. Montville and Hans Binnendijk, eds., *Conflict and Peacemaking in Multiethnic Societies* (Lexington, MA: Lexington Books, 1990), p. 121.

26. Roland Robertson, "Globalization Theory and Civilizational Analysis," *Comparative Civilizations Review*, 17 (Fall 1987), 22; Jeffery A. Shad, Jr., "Globalization and Islamic Resurgence," *Comparative Civilizations Review*, 19 (Fall 1988), 67.

27. See Cyril E. Black, *The Dynamics of Modernization: A Study in Comparative History* (New York: Harper & Row, 1966), pp. 1–34; Reinhard Bendix, "Tradition and Modernity Reconsidered," *Comparative Studies in Society and History*, 9 (April 1967), 292–293.

28. Fernand Braudel, *On History* (Chicago: University of Chicago Press, 1980), p. 213.

29. The literature on the distinctive characteristics of Western civilization is, of course, immense. See, among others, William H. McNeill, *Rise of the West: A History of the Human Community* (Chicago: University of Chicago Press, 1963); Braudel, *On History* and earlier works; Immanuel Wallerstein, *Geopolitics and Geoculture: Essays on the Changing World-System*, (Cambridge: Cambridge University Press, 1991). Karl W. Deutsch has produced a comprehensive, succinct, and highly suggestive comparison of the West and nine other civilizations in terms of twenty-one geographical, cultural, economic, technological, social, and political factors, emphasizing the extent to which the West differs from the others. See Karl W. Deutsch, "On Nationalism, World Regions, and the Nature of the West," in Per Torsvik, ed., *Mobilization, Center-*

Periphery Structures, and Nation-building: A Volume in Commemoration of Stein Rok-kan (Bergen: Universitetsforlaget, 1981), pp. 51–93. For a succinct summary of the salient and distinctive features of Western civilization in 1500, see Charles Tilly, "Re-flections on the History of European State-making," in Tilly, ed., *The Formation of National States in Western Europe* (Princeton: Princeton University Press, 1975), pp. 18ff.

30. Deutsch, "Nationalism, World Regions, and the West," p. 77.

31. See Robert D. Putnam, *Making Democracy Work: Civil Traditions in Modern Italy* (Princeton: Princeton University Press, 1993), p. 121ff.

32. Deutsch, "Nationalism, World Regions, and the West," p. 78. See also Stein Rokkan, "Dimensions of State Formation and Nation-building: A Possible Paradigm for Research on Variations within Europe," in Charles Tilly, *The Formation of National States in Western Europe* (Princeton: Princeton University Press, 1975), p. 576, and Putnam, *Making Democracy Work*, pp. 124–127.

33. Geert Hofstede, "National Cultures in Four Dimensions: A Research-based The-ory of Cultural Differences among Nations," *International Studies of Management and Organization*, 13 (1983), 52.

34. Harry C. Triandis, "Cross-Cultural Studies of Individualism and Collectivism," in *Nebraska Symposium on Motivation 1989* (Lincoln: University of Nebraska Press, 1990), 44–133, and *New York Times*, 25 December 1990, p. 41. See also George C. Lodge and Ezra F. Vogel, eds., *Ideology and National Competitiveness: An Analysis of Nine Countries* (Boston: Harvard Business School Press 1987), passim.

35. Discussions of the interaction of civilizations almost inevitably come up with some variation of this response typology. See Arnold J. Toynbee, *Study of History* (London: Oxford University Press, 1935–61), II, 187ff., VIII, 152–153, 214; John L. Esposito, *The Islamic Threat: Myth or Reality* (New York: Oxford University Press, 1992), pp. 53–62; Daniel Pipes, *In the Path of God: Islam and Political Power* (New York: Basic Books, 1983), pp. 105–142.

36. Pipes, *Path of God*, p. 349.

37. William Pfaff, "Reflections: Economic Development," *New Yorker*, 25 Decem-ber 1978, p. 47.

38. Pipes, *Path of God*, pp. 197–198.

39. Ali Al-Amin Mazrui, *Cultural Forces in World Politics* (London: James Currey, 1990), pp. 4–5.

40. Esposito, *Islamic Threat*, p. 55, see generally, pp. 55–62; and Pipes, *Path of God*, pp. 114–120.

41. Rainer C. Baum, "Authority and Identity—The Invariance Hypothesis II," *Zeitschrift für Soziologie*, 6 (Oct. 1977), 368–369. See also Rainer C. Baum, "Authority Codes: The Invariance Hypothesis," *Zeitschrift für Soziologie*, 6 (Jan. 1977), 5–28.

42. See Adda B. Bozeman, "Civilizations Under Stress," *Virginia Quarterly Review*, 51 (Winter 1975), 5ff.; Leo Frobenius, *Paideuma: Umrisse einer Kultur- und Seelenlehre* (Munich: C.H. Beck, 1921), pp. 11ff; Oswald Spengler, *The Decline of the West* (New York: Alfred A. Knopf, 2 vols., 1926, 1928), II, 57ff.

43. Bozeman, "Civilizations Under Stress," p. 7.

44. William E. Naff, "Reflections on the Question of 'East and West' from the Point of View of Japan," *Comparative Civilizations Review*, 13/14 (Fall 1985 & Spring 1986), 222.

45. David E. Apter, "The Role of Traditionalism in the Political Modernization of Ghana and Uganda," *World Politics*, 13 (Oct. 1960), 47–68.

46. S. N. Eisenstadt, "Transformation of Social, Political, and Cultural Orders in Modernization," *American Sociological Review*, 30 (Oct. 1965), 659–673.

47. Pipes, *Path of God*, pp. 107, 191.

48. Braudel, *On History*, pp. 212–213.

Chapter 4

1. Jeffery R. Barnett, "Exclusion as National Security Policy," *Parameters*, 24 (Spring 1994), 54.

2. Aaron L. Friedberg, "The Future of American Power," *Political Science Quarterly*, 109 (Spring 1994), 20–21.

3. Hedley Bull, "The Revolt Against the West," in Hedley Bull and Adam Watson, eds., *Expansion of International Society* (Oxford: Oxford University Press, 1984), p. 219.

4. Barry G. Buzan, "New Patterns of Global Security in the Twenty-first Century," *International Affairs*, 67 (July 1991), 451.

5. *Project 2025*, (draft) 20 September 1991, p. 7; World Bank, *World Development Report 1990* (Oxford: Oxford University Press, 1990), pp. 229, 244; *The World Almanac and Book of Facts 1990* (Mahwah, NJ: Funk & Wagnalls, 1989), p. 539.

6. United Nations Development Program, *Human Development Report 1994* (New York: Oxford University Press, 1994), pp. 136–137, 207–211; World Bank, "World Development Indicators," *World Development Report 1984, 1986, 1990, 1994*; Bruce Russett et al., *World Handbook of Political and Social Indicators* (New Haven: Yale University Press, 1994), pp. 222–226.

7. Paul Bairoch, "International Industrialization Levels from 1750 to 1980," *Journal of European Economic History*, 11 (Fall 1982), 296, 304.

8. *Economist*, 15 May 1993, p. 83, citing International Monetary Fund, *World Economic Outlook*; "The Global Economy," *Economist*, 1 October 1994, pp. 3–9; *Wall Street Journal*, 17 May 1993, p. A12; Nicholas D. Kristof, "The Rise of China," *Foreign Affairs*, 72 (Nov./Dec. 1993), 61; Kishore Mahbubani, "The Pacific Way," *Foreign Affairs*, 74 (Jan./Feb. 1995), 100–103.

9. International Institute for Strategic Studies, "Tables and Analyses," *The Military Balance 1994–95* (London: Brassey's, 1994).

10. *Project 2025*, p. 13; Richard A. Bitzinger, *The Globalization of Arms Production: Defense Markets in Transition* (Washington, D.C.: Defense Budget Project, 1993), passim.

11. Joseph S. Nye, Jr., "The Changing Nature of World Power," *Political Science Quarterly*, 105 (Summer 1990), 181–182.

12. William H. McNeill, *The Rise of the West: A History of the Human Community* (Chicago: University of Chicago Press, 1963), p. 545.

13. Ronald Dore, "Unity and Diversity in Contemporary World Culture," in Bull and Watson, eds., *Expansion of International Society*, pp. 420–421.

14. William E. Naff, "Reflections on the Question of 'East and West' from the Point of View of Japan," *Comparative Civilizations Review*, 13/14 (Fall 1985 and Spring 1986), 219; Arata Isozaki, "Escaping the Cycle of Eternal Resources," *New Perspectives Quarterly*, 9 (Spring 1992), 18.

15. Richard Sission, "Culture and Democratization in India," in Larry Diamond, *Political Culture and Democracy in Developing Countries* (Boulder: Lynne Rienner, 1993), pp. 55–61.

16. Graham E. Fuller, "The Appeal of Iran," *National Interest*, 37 (Fall 1994), 95.

17. Eisuke Sakakibara, "The End of Progressivism: A Search for New Goals," *Foreign Affairs*, 74 (Sept./Oct. 1995), 8–14.

18. T. S. Eliot, *Idea of a Christian Society* (New York: Harcourt, Brace and Company, 1940), p. 64.

19. Gilles Kepel, *Revenge of God: The Resurgence of Islam, Christianity and Judaism in the Modern World* (University Park, PA: Pennsylvania State University Press, trans. Alan Braley 1994), p. 2.

20. George Weigel, "Religion and Peace: An Argument Complexified," *Washington Quarterly*, 14 (Spring 1991), 27.

21. James H. Billington, "The Case for Orthodoxy," *New Republic*, 30 May 1994, p. 26; Suzanne Massie, "Back to the Future," *Boston Globe*, 28 March 1993, p. 72.

22. *Economist*, 8 January 1993, p. 46; James Rupert, "Dateline Tashkent: Post-Soviet Central Asia; *Foreign Policy*, 87 (Summer 1992), 180.

23. Fareed Zakaria, "Culture Is Destiny: A Conversation with Lee Kuan Yew," *Foreign Affairs*, 73, (Mar./Apr. 1994), 118.

24. Hassan Al-Turabi, "The Islamic Awakening's Second Wave," *New Perspectives Quarterly*, 9 (Summer 1992), 52–55; Ted G. Jelen, *The Political Mobilization of Religious Belief* (New York: Praeger, 1991), pp. 55ff.

25. Bernard Lewis, "Islamic Revolution," *New York Review of Books*, 21 January 1988, p. 47; Kepel, *Revenge of God*, p. 82.

26. Sudhir Kakar, "The Colors of Violence: Cultural Identities, Religion, and Conflict" (Unpublished manuscript), chap. 6, "A New Hindu Identity," p. 11.

27. Suzanne Massie, "Back to the Future," p. 72; Rupert, "Dateline Tashkent," p. 180.

28. Rosemary Radford Ruther, "A World on Fire with Faith," *New York Times Book Review*, 26 January 1992, p. 10; William H. McNeill, "Fundamentalism and the World of the 1990s," in Martin E. Marty and R. Scott Appleby, eds., *Fundamentalisms and Society* (Chicago: University of Chicago Press, 1993), p. 561.

29. *New York Times*, 15 January 1993, p. A9; Henry Clement Moore, *Images of Development: Egyptian Engineers in Search of Industry* (Cambridge: M.I.T. Press, 1980), pp. 227–228.

30. Henry Scott Stokes, "Korea's Church Militant," *New York Times Magazine*, 28 November 1972, p. 68.

31. Rev. Edward J. Dougherty, S. J., *New York Times* 4 July 1993, p. 10; Timothy Goodman, "Latin America's Reformation," *American Enterprise*, 2 (July–August 1991), 43; *New York Times*, 11 July 1993, p. 1; *Time*, 21 January 1991, p. 69.

32. *Economist*, 6 May 1989, p. 23; 11 November 1989, p. 41; *Times* (London), 12 April 1990, p. 12; *Observer*, 27 May 1990, p. 18.

33. *New York Times*, 16 July 1993, p. A9; *Boston Globe*, 15 July 1993, p. 13.

34. See Mark Juergensmeyer, *The New Cold War? Religious Nationalism Confronts the Secular State* (Berkeley: University of California Press, 1993).

35. Zakaria, "Conversation with Lee Kuan Yew," p. 118; Al-Turabi, "Islamic Awakening's Second Wave," p. 53. See Terrance Carroll, "Secularization and States of Modernity," *World Politics*, 36 (April 1984), 362–382.

36. John L. Esposito, *The Islamic Threat: Myth or Reality* (New York: Oxford University Press, 1992), p. 10.

37. Régis Debray, "God and the Political Planet," *New Perspectives Quarterly*, 11 (Spring 1994), 15.

38. Esposito, *Islamic Threat*, p. 10; Gilles Kepel quoted in Sophie Lannes, "La revanche de Dieu — Interview with Gilles Kepel," *Geopolitique*,33 (Spring 1991), 14; Moore, *Images of Development*, pp. 214–216.

39. Juergensmeyer, *The New Cold War*, p. 71; Edward A. Gargan, "Hindu Rage Against Muslims Transforming Indian Politics," *New York Times*, 17 September 1993, p. A1; Khushwaht Singh, "India, the Hindu State," *New York Times*, 3 August 1993, p. A17.

40. Dore in Bull and Watson, eds., *Expansion of International Society*, p. 411; McNeill in Marty and Appleby, eds., *Fundamentalisms and Society*, p. 569.

Chapter 5

1. Kishore Mahbubani, "The Pacific Way," *Foreign Affairs*, 74 (Jan./Feb. 1995), 100–103; IMD Executive Opinion Survey, *Economist*, 6 May 1995, p. 5; World Bank, *Global Economic Prospects and the Developing Countries 1993* (Washington: 1993) pp. 66–67.

2. Tommy Koh, *America's Role in Asia: Asian Views* (Asia Foundation, Center for Asian Pacific Affairs, Report No. 13, November 1993), p. 1.

3. Alex Kerr, *Japan Times*, 6 November 1994, p. 10.

4. Yasheng Huang, "Why China Will Not Collapse," *Foreign Policy*, 95 (Summer 1995), 57.

5. *Cable News Network*, 10 May 1994; Edward Friedman, "A Failed Chinese Modernity," *Daedalus*, 122 (Spring 1993), 5; Perry Link, "China's 'Core' Problem," ibid., pp. 201–204.

6. *Economist*, 21 January 1995, pp. 38–39; William Theodore de Bary, "The New Confucianism in Beijing," *American Scholar*, 64 (Spring 1995), 175ff.; Benjamin L. Self, "Changing Role for Confucianism in China," *Woodrow Wilson Center Report*, 7 (September 1995), 4–5; *New York Times*, 26 August 1991, A19.

7. Lee Teng-hui, "Chinese Culture and Political Renewal," *Journal of Democracy*, 6 (October 1995), 6–8.

8. Alex Kerr, *Japan Times*, 6 November 1994, p. 10; Kazuhiko Ozawa, "Ambivalence in Asia," *Japan Update*, 44 (May 1995), 18–19.

9. For some of these problems, see Ivan P. Hall, "Japan's Asia Card," *National Interest*, 38 (Winter 1994–95), 19ff.

10. Casimir Yost, "America's Role in Asia: One Year Later," (Asia Foundation, Center for Asian Pacific Affairs, Report No. 15, February 1994), p. 4; Yoichi Funabashi, "The Asianization of Asia," *Foreign Affairs*, 72 (Nov./Dec. 1993), 78; Anwar Ibrahim, *International Herald Tribune*, 31 January 1994, p. 6.

11. Kishore Mahbubani, "Asia and a United States in Decline," *Washington Quarterly*, 17 (Spring 1994), 5–23; For a counteroffensive, see Eric Jones, "Asia's Fate: A Response to the Singapore School," *National Interest*, 35 (Spring 1994), 18–28.

12. Mahathir bin Mohamad, *Mare jirenma* (The Malay Dilemma) (Tokyo: Imura Bunka Jigyo, trans. Takata Masayoshi, 1983), p. 267, quoted in Ogura Kazuo, "A Call for a New Concept of Asia," *Japan Echo*, 20 (Autumn 1993), 40.

13. Li Xiangiu, "A Post–Cold War Alternative from East Asia," *Straits Times*, 10 February 1992, p. 24.

14. Yotaro Kobayashi, "Re-Asianize Japan," *New Perspectives Quarterly*, 9 (Winter 1992), 20; Funabashi, "The Asianization of Asia," pp. 75ff; George Yong-Soon Yee, "New East Asia in a Multicultural World," *International Herald Tribune*, 15 July 1992, p. 8.

15. Yoichi Funabashi, "Globalize Asia," *New Perspectives Quarterly*, 9 (Winter 1992), 23–24; Kishore M. Mahbubani, "The West and the Rest," *National Interest*, 28 (Summer 1992), 7; Hazuo, "New Concept of Asia," p. 41.

16. *Economist*, 9 March 1996, p. 33.

17. Bandar bin Sultan, *New York Times*, 10 July 1994, p. 20.

18. John L. Esposito, *The Islamic Threat: Myth or Reality* (New York: Oxford University Press, 1992), p. 12; Ali E. Hillal Dessouki, "The Islamic Resurgence," in Ali E. Hillal Dessouki, ed., *Islamic Resurgence in the Arab World* (New York: Praeger, 1982), pp. 9–13.

19. Thomas Case, quoted in Michael Walzer, *The Revolution of the Saints: A Study in the Origins of Radical Politics* (Cambridge: Harvard University Press, 1965), pp. 10–11; Hassan Al-Turabi, "The Islamic Awakening's Second Wave," *New Perspectives Quarterly*, 9 (Summer 1992), 52. The single most useful volume for understanding the character, appeal, limitations, and historical role of late-twentieth-century Islamic fundamentalism may well be Walzer's study of sixteenth- and seventeenth-century English Calvinist Puritanism.

20. Donald K. Emerson, "Islam and Regime in Indonesia: Who's Coopting Whom?" (unpublished paper, 1989), p. 16; M. Nasir Tamara, *Indonesia in the Wake of Islam, 1965–1985* (Kuala Lumpur: Institute of Strategic and International Studies Malaysia, 1986), p. 28; *Economist*, 14 December 1985, pp. 35–36; Henry Tanner, "Islam Challenges Secular Society," *International Herald Tribune*, 27 June 1987, pp. 7–8; Sabri Sayari, "Politicization of Islamic Re-traditionalism: Some Preliminary Notes," in Metin Heper and Raphael Israeli, eds., *Islam and Politics in the Modern Middle East* (London: Croom Helm, 1984), p. 125; *New York Times*, 26 March 1989, p. 14; 2 March 1995, p. A8. See, for example, reports on these countries in *New York Times*, 17 November 1985, p. 2E; 15 November 1987, p. 13; 6 March 1991, p. A11; 20 October 1990, p. 4; 26 December 1992, p. 1; 8 March 1994, p. A15; and *Economist*, 15 June 1985, pp. 36–37 and 18 September 1992, pp. 23–25.

21. *New York Times*, 4 October 1993, p. A8; 29 November 1994, p. A4; 3 February 1994, p.1; 26 December 1992, p.5; Erika G. Alin, "Dynamics of the Palestinian Uprising: An Assessment of Causes, Character, and Consequences," *Comparative Politics*, 26 (July 1994), 494; *New York Times*, 8 March 1994, p. A15; James Peacock, "The Impact of Islam," *Wilson Quarterly*, 5 (Spring 1981), 142; Tamara, *Indonesia in the Wake of Islam*, p. 22.

22. Olivier Roy, *The Failure of Political Islam* (London: Tauris, 1994), p. 49ff; *New York Times*, 19 January 1992, p. E3; *Washington Post*, 21 November 1990, p. A1. See Gilles Keppel, *The Revenge of God: The Resurgence of Islam, Christianity, and Judaism in the Modern World* (University Park, PA: Pennsylvania State University Press, 1994), p. 32; Farida Faouzia Charfi, "When Galileo Meets Allah," *New Perspectives Quarterly*, 11 (Spring 1994), 30; Esposito, *Islamic Threat*, p. 10.

23. Mahnaz Ispahani, "Varieties of Muslim Experience," *Wilson Quarterly*, 13 (Autumn 1989), 72.

24. Saad Eddin Ibrhahim, "Appeal of Islamic Fundamentalism," (Paper presented to the Conference on Islam and Politics in the Contemporary Muslim World, Harvard University, 15–16 October 1985), pp. 9–10, and "Islamic Militancy as a Social Movement: The Case of Two Groups in Egypt," in Dessouki, ed., *Islamic Resurgence*, pp. 128–131.

25. *Washington Post*, 26 October 1980, p. 23; Peacock, "Impact of Islam," p. 140; Ilkay Sunar and Binnaz Toprak, "Islam in Politics: The Case of Turkey," *Government*

and Opposition, 18 (Autumn 1983), 436; Richard W. Bulliet, "The Israeli-PLO Accord: The Future of the Islamic Movement," *Foreign Affairs*, 72 (Nov/Dec. 1993), 42.

26. Ernest Gellner, "Up from Imperialism," *New Republic*, 22 May 1989, p. 35; John Murray Brown, "Tansu Ciller and the Question of Turkish Identity," *World Policy Journal*, 11 (Fall 1994), 58; Roy, *Failure of Political Islam*, p. 53.

27. Fouad Ajami, "The Impossible Life of Muslim Liberalism," *New Republic*, 2 June 1986, p. 27.

28. Clement Moore Henry, "The Mediterranean Debt Crescent," (Unpublished manuscript), p. 346; Mark N. Katz, "Emerging Patterns in the International Relations of Central Asia," *Central Asian Monitor*, (No. 2, 1994), 27; Mehrdad Haghayeghi, "Islamic Revival in the Central Asian Republics," *Central Asian Survey*, 13 (No. 2, 1994), 255.

29. *New York Times*, 10 April 1989, p. A3; 22 December 1992, p. 5; *Economist*, 10 October 1992, p. 41.

30. *Economist*, 20 July 1991, p. 35; 21 December 1991–3 January 1992, p. 40; Mahfulzul Hoque Choudhury, "Nationalism, Religion and Politics in Bangladesh," in Rafiuddin Ahmed, ed., *Bangladesh: Society, Religion and Politics* (Chittagong: South Asia Studies Group, 1985), p. 68; *New York Times*, 30 November 1994, p. A14; *Wall Street Journal*, 1 March 1995, pp. 1, A6.

31. Donald L. Horowitz, "The Qur'an and the Common Law: Islamic Law Reform and the Theory of Legal Change," *American Journal of Comparative Law*, 42 (Spring and Summer, 1994), 234ff.

32. Dessouki, "Islamic Resurgence," p. 23.

33. Daniel Pipes, *In the Path of God: Islam and Political Power* (New York: Basic Books, 1983), pp. 282–283, 290–292; John Barrett Kelly, *Arabia, the Gulf and the West* (New York: Basic Books, 1980), pp. 261, 423, as quoted in Pipes, *Path of God*, p. 291.

34. United Nations Population Division, *World Population Prospects: The 1992 Revision* (New York: United Nations, 1993), table A18; World Bank, *World Development Report 1995* (New York: Oxford University Press, 1995), table 25; Jean Bourgeois-Pichat, "Le Nombre des Hommes: Etat et Prospective," in Albert Jacquard, ed., *Les Scientifiques Parlent* (Paris: Hachette, 1987), pp. 154, 156.

35. Jack A. Goldstone, *Revolution and Rebellion in the Early Modern World* (Berkeley: University of California Press, 1991), passim, but esp. 24–39.

36. Herbert Moeller, "Youth as a Force in the Modern World," *Comparative Studies in Society and History*, 10 (April 1968), 237–260; Lewis S. Feuer, "Generations and the Theory of Revolution," *Survey*, 18 (Summer 1972), pp. 161–188.

37. Peter W. Wilson and Douglas F. Graham, *Saudi Arabia: The Coming Storm* (Armonk, NY: M. E. Sharpe, 1994), pp. 28–29.

38. Philippe Fargues, "Demographic Explosion or Social Upheaval," in Ghassen Salame, ed., *Democracy Without Democrats? The Renewal of Politics in the Muslim World* (London: I. B. Tauris, 1994), pp. 158–162, 175–177.

39. *Economist*, 29 August 1981, p. 40; Denis Dragounski, "Threshold of Violence," *Freedom Review*, 26 (March/April 1995), 11.

Chapter 6

1. Andreas Papandreou, "Europe Turns Left," *New Perspectives Quarterly*, 11 (Winter 1994), 53; Vuk Draskovic, quoted in Janice A. Broun, "Islam in the Balkans," *Freedom Review*, 22 (Nov./Dec. 1991), 31; F. Stephen Larrabee, "Instability and

Change in the Balkans," *Survival*, 34 (Summer 1992), 43; Misha Glenny, "Heading Off War in the Southern Balkans," *Foreign Affairs*, 74 (May/June 1995), 102–103.

2. Ali Al-Amin Mazrui, *Cultural Forces in World Politics* (London: James Currey, 1990), p. 13.

3. See e.g., *Economist,*16 November 1991, p. 45, 6 May 1995, p. 36.

4. Ronald B. Palmer and Thomas J. Reckford, *Building ASEAN: 20 Years of Southeast Asian Cooperation* (New York: Praeger, 1987), p. 109; *Economist*, 23 July 1994, pp. 31–32.

5. Barry Buzan and Gerald Segal, "Rethinking East Asian Security," *Survival*, 36 (Summer 1994), 16.

6. *Far Eastern Economic Review*, 11 August 1994, p. 34.

7. An interview between Datsuk Seri Mahathir bin Mohamad of Malaysia and Kenichi Ohmae, pp. 3, 7; Rafidah Azia, *New York Times*, 12 February 1991, p. D6.

8. *Japan Times*, 7 November 1994, p. 19; *Economist*, 19 November 1994, p. 37.

9. Murray Weidenbaum, "Greater China: A New Economic Colossus?" *Washington Quarterly*, 16 (Autumn 1993), 78–80.

10. *Wall Street Journal*, 30 September 1994, p. A8; *New York Times*, 17 February 1995, p. A6.

11. *Economist*, 8 October 1994, p. 44; Andres Serbin, "Towards an Association of Caribbean States: Raising Some Awkward Questions," *Journal of Interamerican Studies*, 36 (Winter 1994), 61–90.

12. *Far Eastern Economic Review*, 5 July 1990, pp. 24–25, 5 September 1991, pp. 26–27; *New York Times*, 16 February 1992, p. 16; *Economist*, 15 January 1994, p. 38; Robert D. Hormats, "Making Regionalism Safe," *Foreign Affairs*, 73 (March/April 1994), 102–103; *Economist*, 10 June 1994, pp. 47–48; *Boston Globe*, 5 February 1994, p. 7. On Mercosur, see Luigi Manzetti, "The Political Economy of MERCOSUR," *Journal of Interamerican Studies*, 35 (Winter 1993/94), 101–141, and Felix Pena, "New Approaches to Economic Integration in the Southern Cone," *Washington Quarterly*, 18 (Summer 1995), 113–122.

13. *New York Times*, 8 April 1994, p. A3, 13 June 1994, pp. D1, D5, 4 January 1995, p. A8; Mahathir Interview with Ohmae, pp. 2, 5; "Asian Trade New Directions," *AMEX Bank Review*, 20 (22 March 1993), 1–7.

14. See Brian Pollins, "Does Trade Still Follow the Flag?" *American Political Science Review*, 83 (June 1989), 465–480; Joanne Gowa and Edward D. Mansfield, "Power Politics and International Trade," *American Political Science Review*, 87 (June 1993), 408–421; and David M. Rowe, "Trade and Security in International Relations," (unpublished paper, Ohio State University, 15 September 1994), passim.

15. Sidney W. Mintz, "Can Haiti Change?" *Foreign Affairs*, 75 (Jan./Feb. 1995), 73; Ernesto Perez Balladares and Joycelyn McCalla quoted in "Haiti's Traditions of Isolation Makes U.S. Task Harder," *Washington Post*, 25 July 1995, p. A1.

16. *Economist*, 23 October 1993, p. 53.

17. *Boston Globe*, 21 March 1993, pp. 1, 16, 17; *Economist*, 19 November 1994, p. 23, 11 June 1994, p. 90. The similarity between Turkey and Mexico in this respect has been pointed out by Barry Buzan, "New Patterns of Global Security in the Twenty-first Century," *International Affairs*, 67 (July 1991), 449, and Jagdish Bhagwati, *The World Trading System at Risk* (Princeton: Princeton University Press, 1991), p. 72.

18. See Marquis de Custine, *Empire of the Czar: A Journey Through Eternal Russia* (New York: Doubleday, 1989; originally published in Paris in 1844), passim.

19. P. Ya. Chaadayev, *Articles and Letters [Statyi i pisma]* (Moscow: 1989), p. 178 and N. Ya. Danilevskiy, *Russia and Europe [Rossiya i Yevropa]* (Moscow: 1991), pp.

267–268, quoted in Sergei Vladislavovich Chugrov, "Russia Between East and West," in Steve Hirsch, ed., *MEMO 3: In Search of Answers in the Post-Soviet Era* (Washington, D.C.: Bureau of National Affairs, 1992), p. 138.

20. See Leon Aron, "The Battle for the Soul of Russian Foreign Policy," *The American Enterprise*, 3 (Nov/Dec. 1992), 10ff; Alexei G. Arbatov, "Russia's Foreign Policy Alternatives," *International Security*, 18 (Fall 1993), 5ff.

21. Sergei Stankevich, "Russia in Search of Itself," *National Interest*, 28 (Summer 1992), 48–49.

22. Albert Motivans, " 'Openness to the West' in European Russia," *RFE/RL Research Report*, 1 (27 November 1992), 60–62. Scholars have calculated the allocation of votes in different ways with minor differences in results. I have relied on the analysis by Sergei Chugrov, "Political Tendencies in Russia's Regions: Evidence from the 1993 Parliamentary Elections" (Unpublished paper, Harvard University, 1994).

23. Chugrov, "Russia Between," p. 140.

24. Samuel P. Huntington, *Political Order in Changing Societies* (New Haven: Yale University Press, 1968), pp. 350–351.

25. Duygo Bazoglu Sezer, "Turkey's Grand Strategy Facing a Dilemma," *International Spectator*, 27 (Jan./Mar. 1992), 24.

26. Clyde Haberman, "On Iraq's Other Front," *New York Times Magazine*, 18 November 1990, p. 42; Bruce R. Kuniholm, "Turkey and the West," *Foreign Affairs*, 70 (Spring 1991), 35–36.

27. Ian Lesser, "Turkey and the West after the Gulf War," *International Spectator*, 27 (Jan./Mar. 1992), 33.

28. *Financial Times*, 9 March 1992, p. 2; *New York Times*, 5 April 1992, p. E3; Tansu Ciller, "The Role of Turkey in 'the New World,' " *Strategic Review*, 22 (Winter 1994), p. 9; Haberman, "Iraq's Other Front," p. 44; John Murray Brown, "Tansu Ciller and the Question of Turkish Identity," *World Policy Journal*, 11 (Fall 1994), 58.

29. Sezer, "Turkey's Grand Strategy," p. 27; *Washington Post*, 22 March 1992; *New York Times*, 19 June 1994, p. 4.

30. *New York Times*, 4 August 1993, p. A3; 19 June 1994, p. 4; Philip Robins, "Between Sentiment and Self-Interest: Turkey's Policy toward Azerbaijan and the Central Asian States," *Middle East Journal*, 47 (Autumn 1993), 593–610; *Economist*, 17 June 1995, pp. 38–39.

31. Bahri Yilmaz, "Turkey's new Role in International Politics," *Aussenpolitik*, 45 (January 1994), 94.

32. Eric Rouleau, "The Challenges to Turkey," *Foreign Affairs*, 72 (Nov./Dec. 1993), 119.

33. Rouleau, "Challenges," pp. 120–121; *New York Times*, 26 March 1989, p. 14.

34. Ibid.

35. Brown, "Question of Turkish Identity," p. 58.

36. Sezer, "Turkey's Grand Strategy," pp. 29–30.

37. Ciller, "Turkey in 'the New World,' " p. 9; Brown, "Question of Turkish Identity," p. 56; Tansu Ciller, "Turkey and NATO: Stability in the Vortex of Change," *NATO Review*, 42 (April 1994), 6; Suleyman Demirel, *BBC Summary of World Broadcasts*, 2 February 1994. For other uses of the bridge metaphor, see Bruce R. Kuniholm, "Turkey and the West," *Foreign Affairs*, 70 (Spring 1991), 39; Lesser, "Turkey and the West," p. 33.

38. Octavio Paz, "The Border of Time," interview with Nathan Gardels, *New Perspectives Quarterly*, 8 (Winter 1991), 36.

39. For an expression of this last concern, see Daniel Patrick Moynihan, "Free Trade

with an Unfree Society: A Commitment and its Consequences," *National Interest*, (Summer 1995), 28–33.

40. *Financial Times*, 11–12 September 1993, p. 4; *New York Times*, 16 August 1992, p. 3.

41. *Economist*, 23 July 1994, p. 35; Irene Moss, Human Rights Commissioner (Australia), *New York Times*, 16 August 1992, p. 3; *Economist*, 23 July 1994, p. 35; *Boston Globe*, 7 July 1993, p. 2; *Cable News Network*, News Report, 16 December 1993; Richard Higgott, "Closing a Branch Office of Empire: Australian Foreign Policy and the UK at Century's End," *International Affairs*, 70 (January 1994), 58.

42. Jat Sujamiko, *The Australian*, 5 May 1993, p. 18 quoted in Higgott, "Closing a Branch," p. 62; Higgott, "Closing a Branch," p. 63; *Economist*, 12 December 1993, p. 34.

43. Transcript, Interview with Keniche Ohmae, 24 October 1994, pp. 5–6. See also *Japan Times*, 7 November 1994, p. 19.

44. Former Ambassador Richard Woolcott (Australia), *New York Times*, 16 August 1992, p. 3.

45. Paul Kelly, "Reinventing Australia," *National Interest*, 30 (Winter 1992), 66; *Economist*, 11 December 1993, p. 34; Higgott, "Closing a Branch," p. 58.

46. Lee Kuan Yew quoted in Higgott, "Closing a Branch," p. 49.

Chapter 7

1. *Economist*, 14 January 1995, p. 45; 26 November 1994, p. 56, summarizing Juppé article in *Le Monde*, 18 November 1994; *New York Times*, 4 September 1994, p. 11.

2. Michael Howard, "Lessons of the Cold War," *Survival*, 36 (Winter 1994), 102–103; Pierre Behar, "Central Europe: The New Lines of Fracture," *Geopolitique*, 39 (English ed., August 1992), 42; Max Jakobson, "Collective Security in Europe Today," *Washington Quarterly*, 18 (Spring 1995), 69; Max Beloff, "Fault Lines and Steeples: The Divided Loyalties of Europe," *National Interest*, 23 (Spring 1991), 78.

3. Andreas Oplatka, "Vienna and the Mirror of History," *Geopolitique*, 35 (English ed., Autumn 1991), 25; Vytautas Landsbergis, "The Choice," *Geopolitique*, 35 (English ed., Autumn 1991), 3; *New York Times*, 23 April 1995, p. 5E.

4. Carl Bildt, "The Baltic Litmus Test," *Foreign Affairs*, 73 (Sept./Oct. 1994), 84.

5. *New York Times*, 15 June 1995, p. A10.

6. *RFE/RL Research Bulletin*, 10 (16 March 1993), 1, 6.

7. William D. Jackson, "Imperial Temptations: Ethnics Abroad," *Orbis*, 38 (Winter 1994), 5.

8. Ian Brzezinski, *New York Times*, 13 July 1994, p. A8.

9. John F. Mearsheimer, "The Case for a Ukrainian Nuclear Deterrent: Debate," *Foreign Affairs*, 72 (Summer 1993), 50–66.

10. *New York Times*, 31 January 1994, p. A8.

11. Quoted in Ola Tunander, "New European Dividing Lines?" in Valter Angell, ed., *Norway Facing a Changing Europe: Perspectives and Options* (Oslo: Norwegian Foreign Policy Studies No. 79, Fridtjof Nansen Institute et al., 1992), p. 55.

12. John Morrison, "Pereyaslav and After: The Russian-Ukrainian Relationship," *International Affairs*, 69 (October 1993), 677.

13. John King Fairbank, ed., *The Chinese World Order: Traditional China's Foreign Relations* (Cambridge: Harvard University Press, 1968), pp. 2–3.

14. Perry Link, "The Old Man's New China," *New York Review of Books*, 9 June 1994, p. 32.

15. Perry Link, "China's 'Core' Problem," *Daedalus*, 122 (Spring 1993), 205; Wei-

ming Tu, "Cultural China: The Periphery as the Center," *Daedalus*, 120 (Spring 1991), 22; *Economist*, 8 July 1995, pp. 31–32.

16. *Economist*, 27 November 1993, p. 33; 17 July 1993, p. 61.

17. *Economist*, 27 November 1993, p. 33; Yoichi Funabashi, "The Asianization of Asia," *Foreign Affairs*, 72 (Nov./Dec. 1993), 80. See in general Murray Weidenbaum and Samuel Hughes, *The Bamboo Network* (New York: Free Press, 1996).

18. Christopher Gray, quoted in *Washington Post*, 1 December 1992, p. A30; Lee Kuan Yew, quoted in Maggie Farley, "The Bamboo Network," *Boston Globe Magazine*, 17 April 1994, p. 38; *International Herald Tribune*, 23 November 1993.

19. *International Herald Tribune*, 23 November 1993; George Hicks and J.A.C. Mackie, "A Question of Identity: Despite Media Hype, They Are Firmly Settled in Southeast Asia," *Far Eastern Economic Review*, 14 July 1994, p. 47.

20. *Economist*, 16 April 1994, p. 71; Nicholas D. Kristof, "The Rise of China," *Foreign Affairs*, 72 (Nov./Dec. 1993), 48; Gerrit W. Gong, "China's Fourth Revolution," *Washington Quarterly*, 17 (Winter 1994), 37; *Wall Street Journal*, 17 May 1993, p. A7A; Murray L. Weidenbaum, *Greater China: The Next Economic Superpower?* (St. Louis: Washington University Center for the Study of American Business, Contemporary Issues Series 57, February 1993), pp. 2–3.

21. Steven Mufson, *Washington Post*, 14 August 1994, p. A30; *Newsweek*, 19 July 1993, p. 24; *Economist*, 7 May 1993, p. 35.

22. See Walter C. Clemens, Jr. and Jun Zhan, "Chiang Ching-Kuo's Role in the ROC-PRC Reconciliation," *American Asian Review*, 12 (Spring 1994), 151–154.

23. Koo Chen Foo, quoted in *Economist*, 1 May 1993, p. 31; Link, "Old Man's New China," p. 32. See "Cross-Strait Relations: Historical Lessons," *Free China Review*, 44 (October 1994), 42–52. Gong, "China's Fourth Revolution," p. 39; *Economist*, 2 July 1994, p. 18; Gerald Segal, "China's Changing Shape: The Muddle Kingdom?" *Foreign Affairs*, 73 (May/June 1994), 49; Ross H. Munro, "Giving Taipei a Place at the Table," *Foreign Affairs*, 73 (Nov./Dec. 1994), 115; *Wall Street Journal*, 17 May 1993, p. A7A; *Free China Journal*, 29 July 1994, p. 1.

24. *Economist*, 10 July 1993, pp. 28–29; 2 April 1994, pp. 34–35; *International Herald Tribune*, 23 November 1993; *Wall Street Journal*, 17 May 1993, p. A7A.

25. Ira M. Lapidus, *History of Islamic Societies* (Cambridge, UK: Cambridge University Press, 1988), p. 3.

26. Mohamed Zahi Mogherbi, "Tribalism, Religion and the Challenge of Political Participation: The Case of Libya," (Paper presented to Conference on Democratic Challenges in the Arab World, Center for Political and International Development Studies, Cairo, 22–27 September 1992, pp. 1, 9; *Economist*, (Survey of the Arab East), 6 February 1988, p. 7; Adlan A. El-Hardallo, "Sufism and Tribalism: The Case of Sudan," (Paper prepared for Conference on Democratic Challenges in the Arab World, Center for Political and International Development Studies, Cairo, 22–27 September 1992), p. 2; *Economist*, 30 October 1987, p. 45; John Duke Anthony, "Saudi Arabia: From Tribal Society to Nation-State," in Ragaei El Mellakh and Dorothea H. El Mellakh, eds., *Saudi Arabia, Energy, Developmental Planning, and Industrialization* (Lexington, MA: Lexington, 1982), pp. 93–94.

27. Yalman Onaran, "Economics and Nationalism: The Case of Muslim Central Asia," *Central Asian Survey*, 13 (No. 4, 1994), 493; Denis Dragounski, "Threshold of Violence," *Freedom Review*, 26 (Mar./April 1995), 12.

28. Barbara Daly Metcalf, "The Comparative Study of Muslim Societies," *Items*, 40 (March 1986), 3.

29. Metcalf, "Muslim Societies," p. 3.

30. *Boston Globe*, 2 April 1995, p. 2. On PAIC generally, see "The Popular Arab and Islamic Conference (PAIC): A New 'Islamist International'?" *TransState Islam*, 1 (Spring 1995), 12–16.

31. Bernard Schechterman and Bradford R. McGuinn, "Linkages Between Sunni and Shi'i Radical Fundamentalist Organizations: A New Variable in Middle Eastern Politics?" *The Political Chronicle*, 1 (February 1989), 22–34; *New York Times*, 6 December 1994, p. 5.

Chapter 8

1. Georgi Arbatov, "Neo-Bolsheviks of the I.M.F.," *New York Times*, 7 May 1992, p. A27.

2. North Korean views summed up by a senior U.S. analyst, *Washington Post*, 12 June 1994, p. C1; Indian general quoted in Les Aspin, "From Deterrence to Denuking: Dealing with Proliferation in the 1990's," Memorandum, 18 February 1992, p. 6.

3. Lawrence Freedman, "Great Powers, Vital Interests and Nuclear Weapons," *Survival*, 36 (Winter 1994), 37; Les Aspin, Remarks, National Academy of Sciences, Committee on International Security and Arms Control, 7 December 1993, p. 3.

4. Stanley Norris quoted, *Boston Globe*, 25 November 1995, pp. 1, 7; Alastair Iain Johnston, "China's New 'Old Thinking': The Concept of Limited Deterrence," *International Security*, 20 (Winter 1995–96), 21–23.

5. Philip L. Ritcheson, "Iranian Military Resurgence: Scope, Motivations, and Implications for Regional Security," *Armed Forces and Society*, 21 (Summer 1995), 575–576. Warren Christopher Address, Kennedy School of Government, 20 January 1995; *Time*, 16 December 1991, p. 47; Ali Al-Amin Mazrui, *Cultural Forces in World Politics* (London: J. Currey, 1990), pp. 220, 224.

6. *New York Times*, 15 November 1991, p. A1; *New York Times*, 21 February 1992, p. A9; 12 December 1993, p. 1; Jane Teufel Dreyer, "U.S./China Military Relations: Sanctions or Rapprochement?" *In Depth*, 1 (Spring 1991), 17–18; *Time*, 16 December 1991, p. 48; *Boston Globe*, 5 February 1994, p. 2; Monte R. Bullard, "U.S.-China Relations: The Strategic Calculus," *Parameters*, 23 (Summer 1993), 88.

7. Quoted in Karl W. Eikenberry, *Explaining and Influencing Chinese Arms Transfers* (Washington, D.C.: National Defense University, Institute for National Strategic Studies, McNair Paper No. 36, February 1995), p. 37; Pakistani government statement, *Boston Globe*, 5 December 1993, p. 19; R. Bates Gill, "Curbing Beijing's Arms Sales," *Orbis*, 36 (Summer 1992), p. 386; Chong-pin Lin, "Red Army," *New Republic*, 20 November 1995, p. 28; *New York Times*, 8 May 1992, p. 31.

8. Richard A. Bitzinger, "Arms to Go: Chinese Arms Sales to the Third World," *International Security*, 17 (Fall 1992), p. 87; Philip Ritcheson, "Iranian Military Resurgence," pp. 576, 578; *Washington Post*, 31 October 1991, pp. A1, A24; *Time*, 16 December 1991, p. 47; *New York Times*, 18 April 1995, p. A8; 28 September 1995, p. 1; 30 September 1995, p. 4; Monte Bullard, "U.S.-China Relations," p. 88, *New York Times*, 22 June 1995, p. 1; Gill, "Curbing Beijing's Arms," p. 388; *New York Times*, 8 April 1993, p. A9; 20 June 1993, p. 6.

9. John E. Reilly, "The Public Mood at Mid-Decade," *Foreign Policy*, 98 (Spring 1995), p. 83; *Executive Order 12930*, 29 September 1994; *Executive Order 12938*, 14 November 1994. These expanded on *Executive Order 12735*, 16 November 1990, issued by President Bush declaring a national emergency with respect to chemical and biological weapons.

10. James Fallows, "The Panic Gap: Reactions to North Korea's Bomb," *National Interest*, 38 (Winter 1994), 40–45; David Sanger, *New York Times*, 12 June 1994, pp. 1, 16.

11. *New York Times*, 26 December 1993, p. 1.

12. *Washington Post*, 12 May 1995, p. 1.

13. Bilahari Kausikan, "Asia's Different Standard," *Foreign Policy*, 92 (Fall 1993), 28–29.

14. *Economist*, 30 July 1994, p. 31; 5 March 1994, p. 35; 27 August 1994, p. 51; Yash Ghai, "Human Rights and Governance: The Asian Debate," (Asia Foundation Center for Asian Pacific Affairs, Occasional Paper No. 4, November 1994), p. 14.

15. Richard M. Nixon, *Beyond Peace* (New York: Random House, 1994), pp. 127–128.

16. *Economist*, 4 February 1995, p. 30.

17. Charles J. Brown, "In the Trenches: The Battle Over Rights," *Freedom Review*, 24 (Sept./Oct. 1993), 9; Douglas W. Payne, "Showdown in Vienna," ibid., pp. 6–7.

18. Charles Norchi, "The Ayatollah and the Author: Rethinking Human Rights," *Yale Journal of World Affairs*, 1 (Summer 1989), 16; Kausikan, "Asia's Different Standard," p. 32.

19. Richard Cohen, *The Earth Times*, 2 August 1993, p. 14.

20. *New York Times*, 19 September 1993, p. 4E; 24 September 1993, pp. 1, B9, B16; 9 September 1994, p. A26; *Economist*, 21 September 1993, p. 75; 18 September 1993, pp. 37–38; *Financial Times*, 25–26 September 1993, p. 11; *Straits Times*, 14 October 1993, p. 1.

21. Figures and quotes are from Myron Weiner, *Global Migration Crisis* (New York: HarperCollins, 1995), pp. 21–28.

22. Weiner, *Global Migration Crisis*, p. 2.

23. Stanley Hoffmann, "The Case for Leadership," *Foreign Policy*, 81 (Winter 1990–91), 30.

24. See B. A. Roberson, "Islam and Europe: An Enigma or a Myth?" *Middle East Journal*, 48 (Spring 1994), p. 302; *New York Times*, 5 December 1993, p. 1; 5 May 1995, p. 1; Joel Klotkin and Andries van Agt, "Bedouins: Tribes That Have Made it," *New Perspectives Quarterly*, 8 (Fall 1991), p. 51; Judith Miller, "Strangers at the Gate," *New York Times Magazine*, 15 September 1991, p. 49.

25. *International Herald Tribune*, 29 May 1990, p. 5; *New York Times*, 15 September 1994, p. A21. The French poll was sponsored by the French government, the German poll by the American Jewish Committee.

26. See Hans-George Betz, "The New Politics of Resentment: Radical Right-Wing Populist Parties in Western Europe," *Comparative Politics*, 25 (July 1993), 413–427.

27. *International Herald Tribune*, 28 June 1993, p. 3; *Wall Street Journal*, 23 May 1994; p. B1; Lawrence H. Fuchs, "The Immigration Debate: Little Room for Big Reforms," *American Experiment*, 2 (Winter 1994), 6.

28. James C. Clad, "Slowing the Wave," *Foreign Policy*, 95 (Summer 1994), 143; Rita J. Simon and Susan H. Alexander, *The Ambivalent Welcome: Print Media, Public Opinion and Immigration* (Westport, CT: Praeger, 1993), p. 46.

29. *New York Times*, 11 June 1995, p. E14.

30. Jean Raspail, *The Camp of the Saints* (New York: Scribner, 1975) and Jean-Claude Chesnais, *Le Crepuscule de l'Occident: Demographie et Politique* (Paris: Robert Laffont, 1995); Pierre Lellouche, quoted in Miller, "Strangers at the Gate," p. 80.

31. Philippe Fargues, "Demographic Explosion or Social Upheaval?" in Ghassan Salame, ed., *Democracy Without Democrats? The Renewal of Politics in the Muslim World* (London: I.B. Taurus, 1994), pp. 157ff.

Chapter 9

1. Adda B. Bozeman, *Strategic Intelligence and Statecraft: Selected Essays* (Washington: Brassey's [US], 1992), p. 50; Barry Buzan, "New Patterns of Global Security in the Twenty-first Century," *International Affairs*, 67 (July 1991), 448–449.

2. John L. Esposito, *The Islamic Threat: Myth or Reality* (New York: Oxford University Press, 1992), p. 46.

3. Bernard Lewis, *Islam and the West* (New York: Oxford University Press, 1993), p. 13.

4. Esposito, *Islamic Threat*, p. 44.

5. Daniel Pipes, *In the Path of God: Islam and Political Power* (New York: Basic Books, 1983), 102–103, 169–173; Lewis F. Richardson, *Statistics of Deadly Quarrels* (Pittsburgh: Boxwood Press, 1960), pp. 235–237.

6. Ira M. Lapidus, *A History of Islamic Societies* (Cambridge: Cambridge University Press, 1988), pp. 41–42; Princess Anna Comnena, quoted in Karen Armstrong, *Holy War: The Crusades and Their Impact on Today's World* (New York: Doubleday-Anchor, 1991), pp. 3–4 and in Arnold J. Toynbee, *Study of History* (London: Oxford University Press, 1954), VIII, p. 390.

7. Barry Buzan, "New Patterns," pp. 448–449; Bernard Lewis, "The Roots of Muslim Rage: Why So Many Muslims Deeply Resent the West and Why Their Bitterness Will Not Be Easily Mollified," *Atlantic Monthly*, 266 (September 1990), 60.

8. Mohamed Sid-Ahmed, "Cybernetic Colonialism and the Moral Search," *New Perspectives Quarterly*, 11 (Spring 1994), 19; M. J. Akbar, quoted *Time*, 15 June 1992, p. 24; Abdelwahab Belwahl, quoted ibid., p. 26.

9. William H. McNeill, "Epilogue: Fundamentalism and the World of the 1990's," in Martin E. Marty and R. Scott Appleby, eds., *Fundamentalisms and Society: Reclaiming the Sciences, the Family, and Education* (Chicago: University of Chicago Press), p. 569.

10. Fatima Mernissi, *Islam and Democracy: Fear of the Modern World* (Reading, MA: Addison-Wesley, 1992).

11. For a selection of such reports, see *Economist*, 1 August 1992, pp. 34–35.

12. John E. Reilly, ed., *American Public Opinion and U.S. Foreign Policy 1995* (Chicago: Chicago Council on Foreign Relations, 1995), p. 21; *Le Monde*, 20 September 1991, p. 12, cited in Margaret Blunden, "Insecurity on Europe's Southern Flank," *Survival*, 36 (Summer 1994), 138; Richard Morin, *Washington Post* (National Weekly Ed.), 8–14 November 1993, p. 37; Foreign Policy Association, National Opinion Ballot Report, November 1994, p. 5.

13. *Boston Globe*, 3 June 1994, p. 18; John L. Esposito, "Symposium: Resurgent Islam in the Middle East," *Middle East Policy* 3 (No. 2, 1994), 9; *International Herald Tribune*, 10 May 1994, pp. 1, 4; *Christian Science Monitor*, 24 February 1995, p. 1.

14. Robert Ellsworth, *Wall Street Journal*, 1 March 1995, p. 15; William T. Johnsen, *NATO's New Front Line: The Growing Importance of the Southern Tier* (Carlisle Barracks, PA: Strategic Studies Institute, U.S. Army War College, 1992), p. vii; Robbin Laird, *French Security Policy in Transition: Dynamics of Continuity and Change* (Washington, D.C.: Institute for National Strategic Studies, McNair paper 38, March 1995), pp. 50–52.

15. Ayatollah Ruhollah Khomeini, *Islam and Revolution* (Berkeley, CA: Mizan Press, 1981), p. 305.

16. *Economist*, 23 November 1991, p. 15.

17. Barry Buzan and Gerald Segal, "Rethinking East Asian Security," *Survival*, 36 (Summer 1994), 15.

18. *Can China's Armed Forces Win the Next War?*, excerpts translated and published in Ross H. Munro, "Eavesdropping on the Chinese Military: Where It Expects War — Where It Doesn't," *Orbis*, 38 (Summer 1994), 365. The authors of this document went on to say that the use of military force against Taiwan "would be a really unwise decision."

19. Buzan and Segal, "Rethinking East Asian Security," p. 7; Richard K. Betts, "Wealth, Power and Instability: East Asia and the United States After the Cold War," *International Security*, 18 (Winter 1993/94), 34–77; Aaron L. Friedberg, "Ripe for Rivalry: Prospects for Peace in Multipolar Asia," *International Security*, 18 (Winter 1993/94), 5–33.

20. *Can China's Armed Forces Win the Next War?* excerpts translated in Munro, "Eavesdropping on the Chinese," pp. 355ff.; *New York Times*, 16 November 1993, p. A6; Friedberg, "Ripe for Rivalry," p. 7.

21. Desmond Ball, "Arms and Affluence: Military Acquisitions in the Asia-Pacific Region," *International Security*, 18 (Winter 1993/94), 95–111; Michael T. Klare, "The Next Great Arms Race," *Foreign Affairs*, 72 (Summer 1993), 137ff.; Buzan and Segal, "Rethinking East Asian Security," pp. 8–11; Gerald Segal, "Managing New Arms Races in the Asia/Pacific," *Washington Quarterly*, 15 (Summer 1992), 83–102; *Economist*, 20 February 1993, pp. 19–22.

22. See, e.g., *Economist*, 26 June 1993, p. 75; 24 July 1995, p. 25; *Time*, 3 July 1995, pp. 30–31; and on China, Jacob Heilbrunn, "The Next Cold War," *New Republic*, 20 November 1995, pp. 27ff.

23. For discussion of the varieties of trade wars and when they may lead to military wars, see David Rowe, *Trade Wars and International Security: The Political Economy of International Economic Conflict* (Working paper no. 6, Project on the Changing Security Environment and American National Interests, John M. Olin Institute for Strategic Studies, Harvard University, July 1994), pp. 7ff.

24. *New York Times*, 6 July 1993, p. A1, A6; *Time*, 10 February 1992, pp. 16ff.; *Economist*, 17 February 1990, pp. 21–24; *Boston Globe*, 25 November 1991, pp. 1, 8; Dan Oberdorfer, *Washington Post*, 1 March 1992, p. A1.

25. Quoted *New York Times*, 21 April 1992, p. A10; *New York Times*, 22 September 1991, p. E2; 21 April 1992, p. A1; 19 September 1991, p. A7; 1 August 1995, p. A2; *International Herald Tribune*, 24 August 1995, p. 4; *China Post (Taipei)*, 26 August 1995, p. 2; *New York Times*, 1 August 1995, p. A2, citing David Shambaugh report on interviews in Beijing.

26. Donald Zagoria, American Foreign Policy Newsletter, October 1993, p. 3; *Can China's Armed Forces Win the Next War?*, in Munro, "Eavesdropping on the Chinese Military," pp. 355ff.

27. Roger C. Altman, "Why Pressure Tokyo? The US-Japan Rift," *Foreign Affairs*, 73 (May–June 1994), p. 3; Jeffrey Garten, "The Clinton Asia Policy," *International Economy*, 8 (March–April 1994), 18.

28. Edward J. Lincoln, *Japan's Unequal Trade*, (Washington, D.C.: Brookings Institution, 1990), pp. 2–3. See C. Fred Bergsten and Marcus Noland, *Reconcilable Differences? United States-Japan Economic Conflict* (Washington: Institute for International Economics, 1993); Eisuke Sakakibara, "Less Like You," *International Economy*, (April-May 1990), 36, who distinguishes the American capitalistic market economy from the Japanese noncapitalistic market economy; Marie Anchordoguy, "Japanese-American

Trade Conflict and Supercomputers," *Political Science Quarterly*, 109 (Spring 1994), 36, citing Rudiger Dornbush, Paul Krugman, Edward J. Lincoln, and Mordechai E. Kreinin; Eamonn Fingleton, "Japan's Invisible Leviathan," *Foreign Affairs*, 74 (Mar./April 1995), p. 70.

29. For a good summary of differences in culture, values, social relations, and attitudes, see Seymour Martin Lipset, *American Exceptionalism: A Double-Edged Sword* (New York: W. W. Norton, 1996), chapter 7, "American Exceptionalism — Japanese Uniqueness."

30. *Washington Post*, 5 May 1994, p. A38; *Daily Telegraph*, 6 May 1994, p. 16; *Boston Globe*, 6 May 1994, p. 11; *New York Times*, 13 February 1994, p. 10; Karl D. Jackson, "How to Rebuild America's Stature in Asia," *Orbis*, 39 (Winter 1995), 14; Yohei Kono, quoted in Chalmers Johnson and E. B. Keehn, "The Pentagon's Ossified Strategy," *Foreign Affairs*, 74 (July-August 1995), 106.

31. *New York Times*, 2 May 1994, p. A10.

32. Barry Buzan and Gerald Segal, "Asia: Skepticism About Optimism," *National Interest*, 39 (Spring 1995), 83–84; Arthur Waldron, "Deterring China," *Commentary*, 100 (October 1995), 18; Nicholas D. Kristof, "The Rise of China," *Foreign Affairs*, 72 (Nov./Dec. 1993), 74.

33. Stephen P. Walt, "Alliance Formation in Southwest Asia: Balancing and Bandwagoning in Cold War Competition," in Robert Jervis and Jack Snyder, eds., *Dominoes and Bandwagons: Strategic Beliefs and Great Power Competition in the Eurasian Rimland* (New York: Oxford University Press, 1991), pp. 53, 69.

34. Randall L. Schweller, "Bandwagoning for Profit: Bringing the Revisionist State Back In," *International Security*, 19 (Summer 1994), 72ff.

35. Lucian W. Pye, *Dynamics of Factions and Consensus in Chinese Politics: A Model and Some Propositions* (Santa Monica, CA: Rand, 1980), p. 120; Arthur Waldron, *From War to Nationalism: China's Turning Point, 1924–1925* (Cambridge: Cambridge University Press, 1995), pp. 48–49, 212; Avery Goldstein, *From Bandwagon to Balance-of-Power Politics: Structured Constraints in Politics in China, 1949–1978* (Stanford, CA: Stanford University Press: 1991), pp. 5–6, 35ff. See also, Lucian W. Pye, "Social Science Theories in Search of Chinese Realities," *China Quarterly*, 132 (December 1992), 1161–1171.

36. Samuel S. Kim and Lowell Dittmer, "Whither China's Quest for National Identity," in Lowell Dittmer and Samuel S. Kim, eds., *China's Quest for National Identity* (Ithaca, NY: Cornell University Press, 1991), p. 240; Paul Dibb, *Towards a New Balance of Power in Asia* (London: International Institute for Strategic Studies, Adelphi Paper 295, 1995), pp. 10–16; Roderick MacFarquhar, "The Post-Confucian Challenge," *Economist*, 9 February 1980, pp. 67–72; Kishore Mahbubani, " 'The Pacific Impulse,' " *Survival*, 37 (Spring 1995), 117; James L. Richardson, "Asia-Pacific: The Case for Geopolitical Optimism," *National Interest*, 38 (Winter 1994–95), 32; Paul Dibb, "Towards a New Balance," p. 13. See Nicola Baker and Leonard C. Sebastian, "The Problem with Parachuting: Strategic Studies and Security in the Asia/Pacific Region," *Journal of Strategic Studies*, 18 (September 1995), 15ff. for an extended discussion of the inapplicability to Asia of European-based concepts, such as the balance of power and the security dilemma.

37. *Economist*, 23 December 1995; 5 January 1996, pp. 39–40.

38. Richard K. Betts, "Vietnam's Strategic Predicament," *Survival*, 37 (Autumn 1995), 61ff, 76.

39. *New York Times*, 12 November 1994, p. 6; 24 November 1994, p. A12; *Interna-*

tional Herald Tribune, 8 November 1994, p. 1; Michel Oksenberg, *Washington Post*, 3 September 1995, p. C1.

40. Jitsuo Tsuchiyama, "The End of the Alliance? Dilemmas in the U.S.—Japan Relations," (Unpublished paper, Harvard University, John M. Olin Institute for Strategic Studies, 1994), pp. 18–19.

41. Ivan P. Hall, "Japan's Asia Card," *National Interest*, 38 (Winter 1994–95), 26; Kishore Mahbubani, "The Pacific Impulse," p. 117.

42. Mike M. Mochizuki, "Japan and the Strategic Quadrangle," in Michael Mandelbaum, ed., *The Strategic Quadrangle: Russia, China, Japan, and the United States in East Asia* (New York: Council on Foreign Relations, 1995), pp. 130–139; *Asahi Shimbon* poll reported in *Christian Science Monitor*, 10 January 1995, p. 7.

43. *Financial Times*, 10 September 1992, p. 6; Samina Yasmeen, "Pakistan's Cautious Foreign Policy," *Survival*, 36 (Summer 1994), p. 121, 127–128; Bruce Vaughn, "Shifting Geopolitical Realities Between South, Southwest and Central Asia," *Central Asian Survey*, 13 (No. 2, 1994), 313; Editorial, *Hamshahri*, 30 August 1994, pp. 1, 4, in *FBIS-NES-94-173*, 2 September 1994, p. 77.

44. Graham E. Fuller, "The Appeal of Iran," *National Interest*, 37 (Fall 1994), p. 95; Mu'ammar al-Qadhdhafi, Sermon, Tripoli, Libya, 13 March 1994, in *FBIS-NES-94-049*, 14 March 1994, p. 21.

45. Fereidun Fesharaki, East-West Center, Hawaii, quoted in *New York Times*, 3 April 1994, p. E3.

46. Stephen J. Blank, *Challenging the New World Order: The Arms Transfer Policies of the Russian Republic* (Carlisle Barracks, PA: U.S. Army War College, Strategic Studies Institute, 1993), pp. 53–60.

47. *International Herald Tribune*, 25 August 1995, p. 5.

48. J. Mohan Malik, "India Copes with the Kremlin's Fall," *Orbis*, 37 (Winter 1993), 75.

Chapter 10

1. Mahdi Elmandjra, *Der Spiegel*, 11 February 1991, cited in Elmandjra, "Cultural Diversity: Key to Survival in the Future," (First Mexican Congress on Future Studies, Mexico City, 26–27 September 1994), pp. 3, 11.

2. David C. Rapoport, "Comparing Militant Fundamentalist Groups," in Martin E. Marty and R. Scott Appleby, eds., *Fundamentalisms and the State: Remaking Polities, Economies, and Militance,* (Chicago: University of Chicago Press, 1993), p. 445.

3. Ted Galen Carpenter, "The Unintended Consequences of Afghanistan," *World Policy Journal*, 11 (Spring 1994), 78–79, 81, 82; Anthony Hyman, "Arab Involvement in the Afghan War," *Beirut Review*, 7 (Spring 1994), 78, 82; Mary Anne Weaver, "Letter from Pakistan: Children of the Jihad," *New Yorker*, 12 June 1995, pp. 44–45; *Washington Post*, 24 July 1995, p. A1; *New York Times*, 20 March 1995, p. 1; 28 March 1993, p. 14.

4. Tim Weiner, "Blowback from the Afghan Battlefield," *New York Times Magazine*, 13 March 1994, p. 54.

5. Harrison J. Goldin, *New York Times*, 28 August 1992, p. A25.

6. James Piscatori, "Religion and Realpolitik: Islamic Responses to the Gulf War," in James Piscatori, ed., *Islamic Fundamentalisms and the Gulf Crisis* (Chicago: Fundamentalism Project, American Academy of Arts and Sciences, 1991), pp. 1, 6–7. See also Fatima Mernissi, *Islam and Democracy: Fear of the Modern World* (Reading, MA: Addison-Wesley), pp. 16–17.

7. Rami G. Khouri, "Collage of Comment: The Gulf War and the Mideast Peace; The Appeal of Saddam Hussein," *New Perspectives Quarterly*, 8 (Spring 1991), 56.

8. Ann Mosely Lesch, "Contrasting Reactions to the Persian Gulf Crisis: Egypt, Syria, Jordan, and the Palestinians," *Middle East Journal*, 45 (Winter 1991), p. 43; *Time*, 3 December 1990, p. 70; Kanan Makiya, *Cruelty and Silence: War, Tyranny, Uprising and the Arab World* (New York: W. W. Norton, 1993), pp. 242ff.

9. Eric Evans, "Arab Nationalism and the Persian Gulf War," *Harvard Middle Eastern and Islamic Review*, 1 (February 1994), p. 28; Sari Nusselbeh, quoted *Time*, 15 October 1990, pp. 54–55.

10. Karin Haggag, "One Year After the Storm," *Civil Society* (Cairo), 5 (May 1992), 12.

11. *Boston Globe*, 19 February 1991, p. 7; Safar al-Hawali, quoted by Mamoun Fandy, *New York Times*, 24 November 1990, p. 21; King Hussein, quoted by David S. Landes, "Islam Dunk: the Wars of Muslim Resentment," *New Republic*, 8 April 1991, pp. 15–16; Fatima Mernissi, *Islam and Democracy*, p. 102.

12. Safar Al-Hawali, "Infidels, Without, and Within," *New Perspectives Quarterly*, 8 (Spring 1991), 51.

13. *New York Times*, 1 February 1991, p. A7; *Economist*, 2 February 1991, p. 32.

14. *Washington Post*, 29 January 1991, p. A10; 24 February 1991, p. B1; *New York Times*, 20 October 1990, p. 4.

15. Quoted in *Saturday Star* (Johannesburg), 19 January 1991, p. 3; *Economist*, 26 January 1991, pp. 31–33.

16. Sohail H. Hasmi, review of Mohammed Haikal, "Illusions of Triumph," *Harvard Middle Eastern and Islamic Review*, 1 (February 1994), 107; Mernissi, *Islam and Democracy*, p. 102.

17. Shibley Telhami, "Arab Public Opinion and the Gulf War," *Political Science Quarterly*, 108 (Fall 1993), 451.

18. *International Herald Tribune*, 28 June 1993, p. 10.

19. Roy Licklider, "The Consequences of Negotiated Settlements in Civil Wars, 1945–93," *American Political Science Review*, 89 (September 1995), 685, who defines communal wars as "identity wars," and Samuel P. Huntington, "Civil Violence and the Process of Development," in *Civil Violence and the International System* (London: International Institute for Strategic Studies, Adelphi Paper No. 83, December 1971), 12–14, who cites as the five major characteristics of communal wars a high degree of polarization, ideological ambivalence, particularism, large amounts of violence, and protracted duration.

20. These estimates come from newspaper accounts and Ted Robert Gurr and Barbara Harff, *Ethnic Conflict in World Politics* (Boulder: Westview Press, 1994), pp. 160–165.

21. Richard H. Shultz, Jr. and William J. Olson, *Ethnic and Religious Conflict: Emerging Threat to U.S. Security* (Washington, D.C.: National Strategy Information Center), pp. 17ff.; H. D. S. Greenway, *Boston Globe*, 3 December 1992, p. 19.

22. Roy Licklider, "Settlements in Civil Wars," p. 685; Gurr and Harff, *Ethnic Conflict*, p. 11; Trent N. Thomas, "Global Assessment of Current and Future Trends in Ethnic and Religious Conflict," in Robert L. Pfaltzgraff, Jr. and Richard H. Shultz, Jr., eds., *Ethnic Conflict and Regional Instability: Implications for U.S. Policy and Army Roles and Missions* (Carlisle Barracks, PA: Strategic Studies Institute, U.S. Army War College, 1994), p. 36.

23. See Shultz and Olson, *Ethnic and Religious Conflict*, pp. 3–9; Sugata Bose,

"Factors Causing the Proliferation of Ethnic and Religious Conflict," in Pfaltzgraff and Shultz, *Ethnic Conflict and Regional Instability,* pp. 43–49; Michael E. Brown, "Causes and Implications of Ethnic Conflict," in Michael E. Brown, ed., *Ethnic Conflict and International Security* (Princeton, NJ: Princeton University Press, 1993), pp. 3–26. For a counterargument that ethnic conflict has not increased since the end of the Cold War, see Thomas, "Global Assessment of Current and Future Trends in Ethnic and Religious Conflict," pp. 33–41.

24. Ruth Leger Sivard, *World Military and Social Expenditures 1993* (Washington, D.C.: World Priorities, Inc., 1993), pp. 20–22.

25. James L. Payne, *Why Nations Arm* (Oxford: B. Blackwell, 1989), p. 124.

26. Christopher B. Stone, "Westphalia and Hudaybiyya: A Survey of Islamic Perspectives on the Use of Force as Conflict Management Technique" (unpublished paper, Harvard University), pp. 27–31, and Jonathan Wilkenfeld, Michael Brecher, and Sheila Moser, eds., *Crises in the Twentieth Century* (Oxford: Pergamon Press, 1988–89), II, 15, 161.

27. Gary Fuller, " The Demographic Backdrop to Ethnic Conflict: A Geographic Overview," in Central Intelligence Agency, *The Challenge of Ethnic Conflict to National and International Order in the 1990's: Geographic Perspectives* (Washington, D.C.: Central Intelligence Agency, RTT 95-10039, October 1995), pp. 151–154.

28. *New York Times,* 16 October 1994, p. 3; *Economist,* 5 August 1995, p. 32.

29. United Nations Department for Economic and Social Information and Policy Analysis, Population Division, *World Population Prospects: The 1994 Revision* (New York: United Nations, 1995), pp. 29, 51; Denis Dragounski, "Threshold of Violence," *Freedom Review,* 26 (March-April 1995), 11.

30. Susan Woodward, *Balkan Tragedy: Chaos and Dissolution after the Cold War* (Washington, D.C.: Brookings Institution, 1995), pp. 32–35; Branka Magas, *The Destruction of Yugoslavia: Tracking the Breakup 1980–92* (London: Verso, 1993), pp. 6, 19.

31. Paul Mojzes, *Yugoslavian Inferno: Ethnoreligious Warfare in the Balkans* (New York: Continuum, 1994), pp. 95–96; Magas, *Destruction of Yugoslavia,* pp. 49–73; Aryeh Neier, "Kosovo Survives," *New York Review of Books,* 3 February 1994, p. 26.

32. Aleksa Djilas, "A Profile of Slobodan Milosevic," *Foreign Affairs,* 72 (Summer 1993), 83.

33. Woodward, *Balkan Tragedy,* pp. 33–35, figures derived from Yugoslav censuses and other sources; William T. Johnsen, *Deciphering the Balkan Enigma: Using History to Inform Policy* (Carlisle Barracks: Strategic Studies Institute, 1993), p. 25, citing *Washington Post,* 6 December 1992, p. C2; *New York Times,* 4 November 1995, p. 6.

34. Bogdan Denis Denitch, *Ethnic Nationalism: The Tragic Death of Yugoslavia* (Minneapolis: University of Minnesota Press, 1994), pp. 108–109.

35. Payne, *Why Nations Arm,* pp. 125, 127.

36. *Middle East International,* 20 January, 1995, p. 2.

Chapter 11

1. Roy Licklider, "The Consequences of Negotiated Settlements in Civil Wars, 1945–93," *American Political Science Review,* 89 (September 1995), 685.

2. See Barry R. Posen, "The Security Dilemma and Ethnic Conflict," in Michael E. Brown, ed., *Ethnic Conflict and International Security* (Princeton: Princeton University Press, 1993), pp. 103–124.

3. Roland Dannreuther, *Creating New States in Central Asia* (International Institute

for Strategic Studies/Brassey's, Adelphi Paper No. 288, March 1994), pp. 30–31; Dodjoni Atovullo, quoted in Urzula Doroszewska, "The Forgotten War: What Really Happened in Tajikistan," *Uncaptive Minds*, 6 (Fall 1993), 33.

4. *Economist*, 26 August 1995, p. 43; 20 January 1996, p. 21.

5. *Boston Globe*, 8 November 1993, p. 2; Brian Murray, "Peace in the Caucasus: Multi-Ethnic Stability in Dagestan," *Central Asian Survey*, 13 (No. 4, 1994), 514–515; *New York Times*, 11 November 1991, p. A7; 17 December 1994, p. 7; *Boston Globe*, 7 September 1994, p. 16; 17 December 1994, pp. 1ff.

6. Raju G. C. Thomas, "Secessionist Movements in South Asia," *Survival*, 36 (Summer 1994), 99–101, 109; Stefan Wagstyl, "Kashmiri Conflict Destroys a 'Paradise,'" *Financial Times*, 23–24 October 1993, p. 3.

7. Alija Izetbegovic, *The Islamic Declaration* (1991), pp. 23, 33.

8. *New York Times*, 4 February 1995, p. 4; 15 June 1995, p. A12; 16 June 1995, p. A12.

9. *Economist*, 20 January 1996, p. 21; *New York Times*, 4 February 1995, p. 4.

10. Stojan Obradovic, "Tuzla: The Last Oasis," *Uncaptive Minds*, 7 (Fall-Winter 1994), 12–13.

11. Fiona Hill, *Russia's Tinderbox: Conflict in the North Caucasus and Its Implications for the Future of the Russian Federation* (Harvard University, John F. Kennedy School of Government, Strengthening Democratic Institutions Project, September 1995), p. 104.

12. *New York Times*, 6 December 1994, p. A3.

13. See Mojzes, *Yugoslavian Inferno*, chap. 7, "The Religious Component in Wars"; Denitch, *Ethnic Nationalism: The Tragic Death of Yugoslavia*, pp. 29–30, 72–73, 131–133; *New York Times*, 17 September 1992, p. A14; Misha Glenny, "Carnage in Bosnia, for Starters," *New York Times*, 29 July 1993, p. A23.

14. *New York Times*, 13 May 1995, p. A3; 7 November 1993, p. E4; 13 March 1994, p. E3; Boris Yeltsin, quoted in Barnett R. Rubin, "The Fragmentation of Tajikistan," *Survival*, 35 (Winter 1993-94), 86.

15. *New York Times*, 7 March 1994, p. 1; 26 October 1995, p. A25; 24 September 1995, p. E3; Stanley Jeyaraja Tambiah, *Sri Lanka: Ethnic Fratricide and the Dismantling of Democracy* (Chicago: University of Chicago Press, 1986), p. 19.

16. Khalid Duran, quoted in Richard H. Schultz, Jr. and William J. Olson, *Ethnic and Religious Conflict: Emerging Threat to U.S. Security* (Washington, D.C.: National Strategy Information Center), p. 25.

17. Khaching Tololyan, "The Impact of Diasporas in U.S. Foreign Policy," in Robert L. Pfaltzgraff, Jr. and Richard H. Shultz, Jr., eds., *Ethnic Conflict and Regional Instability: Implications for U.S. Policy and Army Roles and Missions* (Carlisle Barracks, PA: Strategic Studies Institute, U.S. Army War College, 1994), p. 156.

18. *New York Times*, 25 June 1994, p. A6; 7 August 1994, p. A9; *Economist*, 31 October 1992, p. 38; 19 August 1995, p. 32; *Boston Globe*, 16 May 1994, p. 12; 3 April 1995, p. 12.

19. *Economist*, 27 February 1988, p. 25; 8 April 1995, p. 34; David C. Rapoport, "The Role of External Forces in Supporting Ethno-Religious Conflict," in Pfaltzgraff and Shultz, *Ethnic Conflict and Regional Instability*, p. 64.

20. Rapoport, "External Forces," p. 66; *New York Times*, 19 July 1992, p. E3; Carolyn Fluehr-Lobban, "Protracted Civil War in the Sudan: Its Future as a Multi-Religious, Multi-Ethnic State," *Fletcher Forum of World Affairs*, 16 (Summer 1992), 73.

21. Steven R. Weisman, "Sri Lanka: A Nation Disintegrates," *New York Times Magazine*, 13 December 1987, p. 85.

22. *New York Times*, 29 April 1984, p. 6; 19 June 1995, p. A3; 24 September 1995, p. 9; *Economist*, 11 June 1988, p. 38; 26 August 1995, p. 29; 20 May 1995, p. 35; 4 November 1995, p. 39.

23. Barnett Rubin, "Fragmentation of Tajikistan," pp. 84, 88; *New York Times*, 29 July 1993, p. 11; *Boston Globe*, 4 August 1993, p. 4. On the development of the war in Tajikistan, I have relied largely on Barnett R. Rubin, "The Fragmentation of Tajikistan," *Survival*, 35 (Winter 1993–94), 71–91; Roland Dannreuther, *Creating New States in Central Asia* (International Institute for Strategic Studies, Adelphi Paper No. 288, March 1994); Hafizulla Emadi, "State, Ideology, and Islamic Resurgence in Tajikistan," *Central Asian Survey*, 13 (No. 4, 1994), 565–574; and newspaper accounts.

24. Urszula Doroszewska, "Caucasus Wars," *Uncaptive Minds*, 7 (Winter-Spring 1994), 86.

25. *Economist*, 28 November 1992, p. 58; Hill, *Russia's Tinderbox*, p. 50.

26. *Moscow Times*, 20 January 1995, p. 4; Hill, *Russia's Tinderbox*, p. 90.

27. *Economist*, 14 January 1995, pp. 43ff.; *New York Times*, 21 December 1994, p. A18; 23 December 1994, pp. A1, A10; 3 January 1995, p. 1; 1 April 1995, p. 3; 11 December 1995, p. A6; Vicken Cheterian, "Chechnya and the Transcaucasian Republics," *Swiss Review of World Affairs*, February 1995, pp. 10–11; *Boston Globe*, 5 January 1995, pp. 1ff.; 12 August 1995, p. 2.

28. Vera Tolz, "Moscow and Russia's Ethnic Republics in the Wake of Chechnya," Center for Strategic and International Studies, *Post-Soviet Prospects*, 3 (October 1995), 2; *New York Times*, 20 December 1994, p. A14.

29. Hill, *Russia's Tinderbox*, p. 4; Dmitry Temin, "Decision Time for Russia," *Moscow Times*, 3 February 1995, p. 8.

30. *New York Times*, 7 March 1992, p. 3; 24 May 1992, p. 7; *Boston Globe*, 5 February 1993, p. 1; Bahri Yilmaz, "Turkey's New Role in International Politics," *Aussenpolitik*, 45 (January 1994), 95; *Boston Globe*, 7 April 1993, p. 2.

31. *Boston Globe*, 4 September 1993, p. 2; 5 September 1993, p. 2; 26 September 1993, p. 7; *New York Times*, 4 September 1993, p. 5; 5 September 1993, p. 19; 10 September 1993, p. A3.

32. *New York Times*, 12 February 1993, p. A3; 8 March 1992, p. 20; 5 April 1993, p. A7; 15 April 1993, p. A9; Thomas Goltz, "Letter from Eurasia: Russia's Hidden Hand," *Foreign Policy*, 92 (Fall 1993), 98–104; Hill and Jewett, *Back in the USSR*, p. 15.

33. Fiona Hill and Pamela Jewett, *Back in the USSR: Russia's Intervention in the Internal Affairs of the Former Soviet Republics and the Implications for the United States Policy Toward Russia* (Harvard University, John F. Kennedy School of Government, Strengthening Democratic Institutions Project, January 1994), p. 10.

34. *New York Times*, 22 May 1992, p. A29; 4 August 1993, p. A3; 10 July 1994, p. E4; *Boston Globe*, 25 December 1993, p. 18; 23 April 1995, pp. 1, 23.

35. Flora Lewis, "Between TV and the Balkan War," *New Perspectives Quarterly*, 11 (Summer 1994), 47; Hanns W. Maull, "Germany in the Yugoslav Crisis," *Survival*, 37 (Winter 1995–96), 112; Wolfgang Krieger, "Toward a Gaullist Germany? Some Lessons from the Yugoslav Crisis," *World Policy Journal*, 11 (Spring 1994), 31–32.

36. Misha Glenny, "Yugoslavia: The Great Fall," *New York Review of Books*, 23 March 1993, p. 61; Pierre Behar, "Central Europe: The New Lines of Fracture," *Geopolitique*, 39 (Autumn 1994), 44.

37. Pierre Behar, "Central Europe and the Balkans Today: Strengths and Weaknesses," *Geopolitique*, 35 (Autumn 1991), p. 33; *New York Times*, 23 September 1993, p. A9; *Washington Post*, 13 February 1993, p. 16; Janusz Bugajski, "The Joy of War,"

Post-Soviet Prospects, (Center for Strategic and International Studies), 18 March 1993, p. 4.

38. Dov Ronen, *The Origins of Ethnic Conflict: Lessons from Yugoslavia* (Australian National University, Research School of Pacific Studies, Working Paper No. 155, November 1994), pp. 23–24; Bugajski, "Joy of War," p. 3.

39. *New York Times,* 1 August 1995, p. A6; 28 October 1995, pp. 1, 5; 5 August 1995, p. 4; *Economist,* 11 November 1995, pp. 48–49.

40. *Boston Globe,* 4 January 1993, p. 5; 9 February 1993, p. 6; 8 September 1995, p. 7; 30 November 1995, p. 13; *New York Times,* 18 September 1995, p. A6; 22 June 1993, p. A23; Janusz Bugajski, "Joy of War," p. 4.

41. *Boston Globe,* 1 March 1993, p. 4; 21 February 1993, p. 11; 5 December 1993, p. 30; *Times* (London), 2 March 1993, p. 14; *Washington Post,* 6 November 1995, p. A15.

42. *New York Times,* 2 April 1995, p. 10; 30 April 1995, p. 4; 30 July 1995, p. 8; 19 November 1995, p. E3.

43. *New York Times,* 9 February 1994, p. A12; 10 February 1994, p. A1; 7 June 1995, p. A1; *Boston Globe,* 9 December 1993, p. 25; *Europa Times,* May 1994, p. 6; Andreas Papandreou, "Europe Turns Left," *New Perspectives Quarterly,* 11 (Winter 1994), 53.

44. *New York Times,* 10 September 1995, p. 12; 13 September 1995, p. A11; 18 September 1995, p. A6; *Boston Globe,* 8 September 1995, p. 2; 12 September 1995, p. 1; 10 September 1995, p. 28.

45. *Boston Globe,* 16 December 1995, p. 8; *New York Times,* 9 July 1994, p. 2.

46. Margaret Blunden, "Insecurity on Europe's Southern Flank," *Survival,* 36 (Summer 1994), 145; *New York Times,* 16 December 1993, p. A7.

47. Fouad Ajami, "Under Western Eyes: The Fate of Bosnia" (Report prepared for the International Commission on the Balkans of the Carnegie Endowment for International Peace and The Aspen Institute, April 1996), pp. 5ff.; *Boston Globe,* 14 August 1993, p. 2; *Wall Street Journal,* 17 August 1992, p. A4.

48. Yilmaz, "Turkey's New Role," pp. 94, 97.

49. Janusz Bugajski, "Joy of War," p. 4; *New York Times,* 14 November 1992, p. 5; 5 December 1992, p. 1; 15 November 1993, p. 1; 18 February 1995, p. 3; 1 December 1995, p. A14; 3 December 1995, p. 1; 16 December 1995, p. 6; 24 January 1996, pp. A1, A6; Susan Woodward, *Balkan Tragedy: Chaos and Dissolution After the Cold War* (Washington, D.C.: Brookings Institution, 1995), pp. 356–357; *Boston Globe,* 10 November 1992, p. 7; 13 July 1993, p. 10; 24 June 1995, p. 9; 22 September 1995, pp. 1, 15; Bill Gertz, *Washington Times,* 2 June 1994, p. A1.

50. *Jane's Sentinel,* cited in *Economist,* 6 August 1994, p. 41; *Economist,* 12 February 1994, p. 21; *New York Times,* 10 September 1992, p. A6; 5 December 1992, p. 6; 26 January 1993, p. A9; 14 October 1993, p. A14; 14 May 1994, p. 6; 15 April 1995, p. 3; 15 June 1995, p. A12; 3 February 1996, p. 6; *Boston Globe,* 14 April 1995, p. 2; *Washington Post,* 2 February 1996, p. 1.

51. *New York Times,* 23 January 1994, p. 1; *Boston Globe,* 1 February 1994, p. 8.

52. On American acquiescence in Muslim arms shipments, see *New York Times,* 15 April 1995, p. 3; 3 February 1996, p. 6; *Washington Post,* 2 February 1996, p. 1; *Boston Globe,* 14 April 1995, p. 2.

53. Rebecca West, *Black Lamb and Grey Falcon: The Record of a Journey through Yugoslavia in 1937* (London: Macmillan, 1941), p. 22 quoted in Charles G. Boyd, "Making Peace with the Guilty: the Truth About Bosnia," *Foreign Affairs,* 74 (Sept./Oct. 1995), 22.

54. Quoted in Timothy Garton Ash, "Bosnia in Our Future," *New York Review of Books,* 21 December 1995, p. 27; *New York Times,* 5 December 1992, p. 1.

55. *New York Times,* 3 September 1995, p. 6E; *Boston Globe,* 11 May 1995, p. 4.

56. See U.S. Institute of Peace, *Sudan: Ending the War, Moving Talks Forward* (Washington, D.C.: U.S. Institute of Peace Special Report, 1994); *New York Times,* 26 February 1994, p. 3.

57. John J. Maresca, *War in the Caucasus* (Washington: United States Institute of Peace, Special Report, no date), p. 4.

58. Robert D. Putnam, "Diplomacy and Domestic Politics: The Logic of Two Level Games," *International Organization,* 42 (Summer 1988), 427–460; Samuel P. Huntington, *The Third Wave: Democratization in the Late Twentieth Century* (Norman, OK: University of Oklahoma Press, 1991), pp. 121–163.

59. *New York Times,* 27 January 1993, p. A6; 16 February 1994, p. 47. On the Russian February 1994 initiative, see generally Leonard J. Cohen, "Russia and the Balkans: Pan-Slavism, Partnership and Power," *International Journal,* 49 (August 1994), 836–845.

60. *Economist,* 26 February 1994, p. 50.

61. *New York Times,* 20 April 1994, p. A12; *Boston Globe,* 19 April 1994, p. 8.

62. *New York Times,* 15 August 1995, p. 13.

63. Hill and Jewitt, *Back in the USSR,* p. 12; Paul Henze, *Georgia and Armenia — Toward Independence* (Santa Monica, CA: RAND P-7924, 1995), p. 9; *Boston Globe,* 22 November 1993, p. 34.

Chapter 12

1. Arnold J. Toynbee, *A Study of History* (London: Oxford University Press, 12 vols., 1934–1961), VII, 7–17; *Civilization on Trial: Essays* (New York: Oxford University Press, 1948), 17–18; *Study of History,* IX, 421–422.

2. Matthew Melko, *The Nature of Civilizations* (Boston: Porter Sargent, 1969), p. 155

3. Carroll Quigley, *The Evolution of Civilizations: An Introduction to Historical Analysis* (New York: Macmillan, 1961), pp. 146ff.

4. Quigley, *Evolution of Civilizations,* pp. 138–139, 158–160.

5. Mattei Dogan, "The Decline of Religious Beliefs in Western Europe," *International Social Science Journal,* 47 (Sept. 1995), 405–419.

6. Robert Wuthnow, "Indices of Religious Resurgence in the United States," in Richard T. Antoun and Mary Elaine Hegland, eds., *Religious Resurgence; Contemporary Cases in Islam, Christianity, and Judaism* (Syracuse: Syracuse University Press, 1987), pp. 15–34; *Economist,* 8 (July 1995), 19–21.

7. Arthur M. Schlesinger, Jr., *The Disuniting of America: Reflections on a Multicultural Society* (New York: W. W. Norton, 1992), pp. 66–67, 123.

8. Quoted in Schlesinger, *Disuniting of America,* p. 118.

9. Gunnar Myrdal, *An American Dilemma* (New York: Harper & Bros., 1944), I, 3. Richard Hofstadter quoted in Hans Kohn, *American Nationalism: An Interpretive Essay* (New York: Macmillan, 1957), p. 13.

10. Takeshi Umehara, "Ancient Japan Shows Post-Modernism the Way," *New Perspectives Quarterly,* 9 (Spring 1992), 10.

11. James Kurth, "The *Real* Clash," *National Interest,* 37 (Fall 1994), 3–15.

12. Malcolm Rifkind, Speech, Pilgrim Society, London, 15 November 1994 (New York: British Information Services, 16 November 1994), p. 2.

13. *International Herald Tribune*, 23 May 1995, p. 13.

14. Richard Holbrooke, "America: A European Power," *Foreign Affairs*, 74 (March/April 1995), 49.

15. Michael Howard, *America and the World* (St. Louis: Washington University, the Annual Lewin Lecture, 5 April 1984), p. 6.

16. Schlesinger, *Disuniting of America*, p. 127.

17. For a 1990s statement of this interest, see "Defense Planning Guidance for the Fiscal Years 1994–1999," draft, 18 February 1992; *New York Times*, 8 March 1992, p. 14.

18. Z. A. Bhutto, *If I Am Assassinated* (New Delhi: Vikas Publishing House, 1979), pp. 137–138, quoted in Louis Delvoie, "The Islamization of Pakistan's Foreign Policy," *International Journal*, 51 (Winter 1995–96), 133.

19. Michael Walzer, *Thick and Thin: Moral Argument at Home and Abroad* (Notre Dame: University of Notre Dame Press, 1994), pp. 1–11.

20. James Q. Wilson, *The Moral Sense* (New York: Free Press, 1993), p. 225.

21. Government of Singapore, *Shared Values* (Singapore: Cmd. No. 1 of 1991, 2 January 1991), pp. 2–10.

22. Lester Pearson, *Democracy in World Politics* (Princeton: Princeton University Press, 1955), pp. 83–84.

Index

●

Abdullah, Crown Prince of Saudi Arabia, 119
absolutism, 70, 233, 264
abstention rule, 316
Afghanistan, 112, 134, 168, 176, 210, 214, 247, 249, 255, 267, 271, 273, 274, 275, 276, 277, 287
African civilization, 45, 47, 49, 51, 61, 67, 183, 184–85, 192, 200, 204, 212, 241, 257, 263, 264, 275, 311, 315, 316, 317, 321
  cultural identities and values in, 33, 65, 128, 193, 196
  indigenization in, 94–95, 102
  modernization and, 75, 77
  political structure of, 135, 136, 157
  population of, 85–86
Ahmed, Akbar, 264
Ajami, Fouad, 114, 286
al-Assad, Hafiz, 250
Albania, 118, 119, 126, 127, 130, 138, 255, 260, 261, 284, 287, 315
Alexander II, Tsar of Russia, 140
Algeria, 90, 94, 101, 112, 113, 115, 118, 119, 126, 176, 177, 185, 188, 195, 198, 200, 202, 214, 215, 250, 273, 285, 287, 315
al-Hawali, Safar, 249, 250
Ali, Ben, 115, 250
Ali, Muhammad, 74
Aliyev, Gaider, 280
All African Council of Churches, 293
al-Qadhafi, Mu'ammar, 216, 239
al-Turabi, Hassan, 97, 100, 111, 176, 177
Andean Pact, 127, 131, 134, 240
Angola, 257
Apter, David E., 77
Arabic civilization, see Islamic civilization
Arabic language, 60, 62, 70, 269
Arab League, 176, 248, 250, 273

Arbatov, Georgi, 184
Argentina, 134, 136, 240, 292, 317
Armenia, 38, 64, 127, 144, 163, 164, 243, 255, 259, 272, 274, 277, 278–81, 291, 293, 296
Asia, 51, 77, 321
  Australian relations with, 151–54, 228, 235
  Chinese hegemony in, 218–38, 315
  clashes within, 28, 127, 131, 132, 218, 229–38
  cultural values pursued in, 32, 33
  economic development in, 102–9, 130, 132–33, 134, 151–53, 218, 219, 224, 228, 238, 302
  expanding strength of, 20, 21, 29, 33, 81, 82–83, 89, 93, 102–9, 120, 121, 194–95, 218–38, 311
  immigration from, 202, 203, 205
  military capabilities in, 38, 89, 90, 184, 186–90, 191–92, 218
  population of, 85–86
  superiority claimed by, 102, 104, 107–109, 224, 304, 310
  Western relations with, 102–9, 218–38, 307
  see also Japan, Japanese civilization; Sinic civilization; specific countries
Aspin, Les, 187, 190
Association for Relations Across the Taiwan Strait, 172
Association of Caribbean States, 133
Association of Southeast Asian Nations (ASEAN), 108, 128, 131, 132, 134, 194, 219, 235, 236
Associations of Croatians in the United States, 283
Ataturk, Mustafa Kemal, 74, 144, 147, 148, 149–50, 178
Australia, 38, 46, 84, 132, 133, 139, 151–154, 197, 199, 228, 235, 283, 319

Austria, 21, 126, 145, 157, 158, 160, 201,
281, 282, 287
Austro-Hungarian empire, 158, 165, 262
authoritarianism, 66, 105, 114, 138, 192,
219, 248, 270, 294
Azerbaijan, 38, 64, 127, 138, 146, 147,
240, 255, 268, 272, 277, 278, 279,
280, 281, 291, 293, 296

Bagby, Philip, 43, 44
Bairoch, Paul, 86–87
Baker, James, 193
Balancing, 232, 235
    see also Bandwagoning
Balladur, Edouard, 157
Bandaranaike, Solomon, 93–94
Bandwagoning, 235
    see also Balancing
Bangladesh, 115, 156, 248, 256, 286
Bashir, Tahsin, 174
Baum, Rainer, 76
Behar, Pierre, 160
Belarus, 127, 143, 158, 162, 163, 164, 293
Belgium, 129, 157, 201
Bhutto, Benazir, 239, 248
Bhutto, Zulfikar Ali, 317
Bolivia, 46, 282
Bolshevik Revolution, 141–42, 165
borrowing theory, 76
Bosnia, 28, 38, 64, 118, 126–27, 129, 138,
156, 176, 179, 184, 196, 212, 242,
251, 253, 254, 255, 257, 261–62, 263,
264, 267, 269–70, 271–72, 308, 215
    Dayton agreements and, 287, 289, 291,
295, 297, 298
    kin-country rallying and, 272, 281–96,
297–98
Boutros-Ghali, Boutros, 156, 286
Bozeman, Adda, 43, 76
Braudel, Fernand, 39, 41, 44, 47, 55, 68,
78
Brazil, 87, 99, 134, 136, 240, 317
Brzezinski, Zbignew, 35
Buddhism, 47–48, 49, 76, 94, 96, 98, 99,
102, 131, 132, 138, 176, 195, 219, 254,
255, 256, 263, 264, 268, 275, 320
Bulgaria, 126, 157, 160, 161, 162, 164,
284, 315
Bull, Hedley, 54, 58, 83
Bush administration, 31, 89, 191, 193,
221, 228, 249, 251, 308

Buzan, Barry, 83, 212
Byzantium, 50, 70, 95, 140, 141, 160,
210, 211

Canada, 34, 68, 126, 127, 132, 137, 150,
199, 200, 283, 308
Caribbean Community (CARICOM),
131, 133
Carter, Jimmy, 293
Catherine II, Empress of Russia, 140
Catholicism, 46, 68, 70, 99, 101, 126,
127, 138, 139, 150, 158, 160, 193,
200, 202, 240, 255, 256, 259, 269,
271–72, 281, 282, 282–83, 284, 296, 309
Central American Common Market, 127,
134
Central European Free Trade Area, 134
Chaadeyev, Pyotr Y., 141
chaos paradigm, 35, 321
Chechnya, 127, 129, 155, 175, 176, 243,
253, 255, 260, 264, 267, 268, 270–
271, 273, 274, 275, 276–78, 281,
292, 297, 309
Chesnais, Jean-Claude, 203–4
Chile, 109, 136, 282, 292
China, People's Republic of, 44, 47, 53,
85, 86, 99, 155–56, 177, 241, 258,
316, 321
    allies of, 39, 143, 168–74, 178, 185,
239–40, 244, 248
    co-prosperity sphere of, 168–74, 218–38
    cultural identities in, 126, 138, 169–70,
256
    economy of, 66, 87, 88, 103, 130, 132,
133, 134, 170–71, 195, 220, 223,
229, 230, 231, 236, 243, 256
    human rights in, 184, 194–95, 197,
221, 223, 224, 225, 228
    increasing assertiveness of, 31, 32, 38,
82–83, 168–74, 218–38, 244, 312–
314, 315
    indigenization in, 93–94, 95
    military capabilities of, 89, 90, 174,
186, 187, 188–90, 220, 223, 229–30,
236, 275, 313, 315
    Western relations with, 20, 29, 38, 51,
66, 95, 102–9, 190, 203, 207, 215,
218–38, 308, 309, 312–13
    see also Asia; Sinic civilization
China, Republic of, *see* Taiwan
Ch'ing dynasty, 74, 105

Chirac, Jacques, 201, 271
Christianity, Western, 28, 42, 46–47, 69,
    70, 177, 239, 311, 317, 320
  cultural identities and, 137, 138, 159,
    160, 176, 249, 254, 267, 278, 280,
    282–83, 286, 309
  economic and political development
    and, 29, 92–93, 132, 193, 196–97,
    237, 257, 262, 263, 264, 305
  spread of, 65–66, 72, 76, 96, 98–101,
    105, 106, 114, 137, 209–11, 249
  see also Western civilization
Christopher, Warren, 38, 188, 286
Churkin, Vitaly, 295
Ciller, Tansu, 145, 148, 149, 279
civilizational identities:
  in fault line wars, 266–72
  scope of, 43, 128
  torn countries and, 138–54, 306, 319
  see also cultural identities
civilizational paradigm, 36–39
civilizations:
  balance of power among, 20, 48–55,
    125, 129–30, 155, 183–206, 229,
    231–37, 241
  Civilization vs., 40–41, 320–21
  commonalities of, 318–21
  comprehensiveness of, 42–43, 56–57
  decline of, 301–8, 311
  defined, 40–44
  golden age of, 302–3, 320–21
  lone countries as, 136–37
  major, 44–48
  universal, *see* universal civilization
civil society, 71, 111–12
Classical civilization, 54, 69–70, 76–77,
    91, 139–40, 302
cleft countries, 137–38, 305
Clemenceau, Georges, 91
Clinton administration, 38, 89, 161, 162,
    188, 190, 191, 192, 193, 194, 203,
    209, 221, 222, 224, 251, 289, 305,
    308, 309
Cold War, 83, 88, 213, 217, 254–55
  alliances in, 126, 185, 197–98, 207,
    214, 218, 244, 272
  beginning of, 32, 161
  bipolar politics in, 21, 24–25, 30, 33,
    36, 39, 52–53, 54, 66, 82, 115, 128,
    135, 138, 151, 156, 157, 158, 168,
    218, 233, 238, 245, 255, 309

  end of, 21, 28, 31–32, 64, 67, 94, 99,
    100, 125, 127, 130, 133, 145, 147,
    150, 168, 219, 224, 228, 241, 244,
    246, 262, 310, 312
  ideological differences in, 219–20, 222
  nuclear weapons in, 187, 190, 192, 225
collectivism, 71, 108, 238
Colombia, 127, 134, 195
colonialism, 21, 33, 50, 63–64, 83, 91,
    135, 139, 205, 209–11, 212, 213
commonality rule, 320
Commonwealth of Independent States
    (CIS), 164, 165, 243, 280
communication, 61–62, 116, 129, 224
  technology for, 58–59, 67, 73, 78, 129,
    146, 171, 176, 199, 205, 254, 274
  see also language
communism, 32, 65, 66, 219, 270
  appeal of, 92, 105, 114, 137, 141–42
  collapse of, 31, 35–36, 100, 105, 138,
    142, 158, 160, 163, 183, 211, 215,
    246
  democratic conflicts with, 21, 35–36,
    52–53, 142, 215, 239; *see also* Cold
    War
  see also specific countries
Confederation of the Peoples of the
    Caucasus (KNK), 277
Conference on Security and Cooperation
    in Europe (CSCE), 293
Confucianism, 47, 94, 96, 99, 156, 168,
    264, 319, 320
  progress spurred by, 102, 106, 108, 225,
    234–35, 237–38
  see also Sinic civilization
Côte d'Ivoire, 136
Council of Europe, 219
Counter-Reformation, 70
Cresson, Edith, 201
Crimea, 167
Croatia, 38, 64, 127, 138, 156, 158, 161,
    212, 253, 255, 259, 260–62, 268–70,
    271–72, 309, 312, 315
  kin-country rallying in, 272, 281–91,
    295–96, 297, 298
Cuba, 136, 157, 193, 195, 196, 203, 216
cultural identities:
  cleft countries and, 137–38
  cooperation based on, 20, 28, 29, 34,
    125–35, 156
  crisis in, 125, 129, 252–54

cultural identities (*cont.*)
  means to definition of, 20, 21, 28, 67–
    68, 97–100, 116, 125, 126, 128
  multiplicity of, 128
  symbols of, 19–20, 116, 269–70, 271–
    272
  torn, 138–54, 306, 319
  see also civilizational identities
culture, 57
  appeal of, 92–93
  civilizations defined by, 41–42, 208
  power and, 91–92, 128, 129, 212, 310
  regionalism and, 82, 90, 130–35, 156,
    191
Cyprus, 161, 163, 164, 255
Czechoslovakia, 37, 137, 158
Czech Republic, 39, 126, 134, 145, 157,
    160, 161, 293

Danilevskiy, Nikolay Y., 141
Dawson, Christopher, 41, 47
Debray, Régis, 101
decolonization, 33, 53, 63–64, 83, 175,
    199, 210, 214, 241
de la Madrid, Miguel, 149–50
Delors, Jacques, 28
Demirel, Suleyman, 145, 147, 149
democracy, 29, 38, 114, 150, 153, 173,
    212–14, 237
  alliances and, 34, 160, 161, 162
  appeal of, 92–93, 105, 106, 114, 137,
    142, 183
  communist conflicts with, 21, 35–36,
    52–53, 142, 215, 239; *see also* Cold
    War
  human rights and, 184, 186, 192–98,
    225
  liberal, 53, 115, 130, 199, 212, 294,
    302, 305, 306
  paradox of, 94, 151, 248
  presumed triumph of, 31, 52–53, 142,
    183–84, 186, 193, 198
demography, 28, 303, 310, 315, 318
  population growth and, 20, 84, 86, 102,
    103, 109, 116–20, 175, 178, 198,
    200, 211, 242, 259–61, 265
  see also immigration
Deng Xiaoping, 91, 172, 207, 222, 224,
    229, 238
Denitch, Bogdan, 262
Dessouki, Ali E. Hillal, 110

Deutsch, Karl W., 70–71
diasporas, 272, 273, 274, 277, 280, 283,
    293
Dibdin, Michael, 20
distinctiveness theory, 67–68
Domenach, Jean Marie, 200
Dore, Ronald, 59, 93, 101
Dudayev, Dzhokhar, 267, 268
Durkheim, Emile, 41

East Asian Economic Caucus, 108, 32–
    33, 152
Eastern Europe:
  border of, 158–60
  economic and political development
    in, 29, 157–63, 193, 215
  see also specific countries
East Timor, 220, 253, 256, 257, 271
Economic Cooperation Organization
    (ECO), 133–34
economic development and power, 86–
    88, 92, 100, 211, 216, 241, 312, 316,
    317, 320–21
  cultural influences on, 29, 73, 92–93,
    95, 130–35, 141, 143, 144, 146, 150–
    153, 170, 177, 185
  East Asian model of, 102–9, 151–53
  immigration and, 198, 199, 202, 203,
    204
  regional associations and, 108, 127,
    130–35, 308
  shift in, 82, 175, 184, 191, 194, 208,
    218–38, 244, 301–8, 310
education, 85–86, 93, 116, 119, 144, 150,
    203, 220, 238, 320, 321
  Islamic, 110, 111, 112–13, 115, 147–
    148, 269
Egypt, 75, 101, 112, 113, 115, 119, 135,
    176, 177–78, 192, 198, 213, 214,
    215, 248, 249, 250, 251, 264, 287
Eisenstadt, Shmuel, 48, 77
Elchibey, Abulfez, 280
Eliot, T. S., 95
Elmandjra, Mahdi, 246
Engels, Friedrich, 142
English language, 59–60, 61, 62, 63, 64,
    73, 174, 202, 231, 319
Eritrea, 137, 275, 293
Esposito, John L., 110, 209
Estonia, 64, 138, 145, 158
Ethiopia, 47, 51, 136, 137, 256, 275, 293

Europe, 28, 46, 49, 83, 111, 114, 215–16, 220, 225, 232–34, 307–8, 310, 312, 315, 321
  cultural identities in, 126, 129, 130, 131–32, 157
  Eastern, *see* Eastern Europe
  immigration in, 199–202, 203–4, 205, 305
  international society in, 220, 233–34, 238
  Renaissance in, 50, 139, 218, 307
  West's border in, 157–63, 165, 218, 248, 296
  see also Western civilization; *specific countries*
European Community, 200
European Court of Justice, 163
European Parliament, 197
European Union, 28, 35, 54, 90, 126, 127, 131, 132, 133, 134, 145–47, 148, 152, 157, 158, 160–61, 162, 163, 168, 194, 202, 219, 242, 282, 284, 294, 308, 312, 318
Evans, Gareth, 151, 153
exclusionism, 72–73

fascism, 32, 52, 53, 282
fault line conflicts, 207–8, 245, 246–65, 266–98
  characteristics of, 252–54, 291
  demographic balance and, 259–61, 265
  escalation of, 272, 273, 289, 292–93, 295, 298, 312
  halting of, 291–98, 315–16
  levels of involvement in, 272–74, 281, 288–89, 291–93, 312
  moderates in, 266–67, 269, 270, 291, 294
  transitional, 246–52
feudalism, 139, 234
Finland, 126, 145, 157, 158, 160, 235
Fishman, Joshua, 62
France, 21, 71, 81, 89, 90, 129, 130, 135, 136, 148, 157, 163, 168, 186, 210, 215, 216, 229, 241, 262, 307, 315, 318
  immigration to, 67–68, 200, 201, 203–204
  kin-country rallying by, 293, 294, 295
Freedman, Lawrence, 187
French language, 60, 61, 62
French Revolution, 52, 109n

Friedberg, Aaron, 220, 238
Frobenius, Leo, 76
Fukuyama, Francis, 31
Fuller, Gary, 259
Fuller, Graham, 239
fundamentalism, 32, 73, 98, 99, 111, 175, 198, 213, 217, 247, 249, 271, 283, 285
  rise of, 37, 64, 94, 96–97, 101, 103, 110, 112–13, 115, 119, 147, 148, 178, 185, 215, 243, 256; *see also* Islamic Resurgence

Gaddis, John Lewis, 30
Gandhi, Rajiv, 275
Gellner, Ernest, 113
General Agreement on Tariffs and Trade (GATT), 222
Georgia, 64, 155, 163–64, 165, 277, 278, 279
Germany, unified, 28, 63, 81, 89, 90, 103, 135, 145, 156, 157, 163, 168, 229, 307, 317
  cultural identity of, 126, 127, 129
  in fault line conflicts, 272, 281, 282, 283, 287, 293, 294, 295, 296
  immigration to, 39, 147, 199, 200, 201, 202
Ghanoushi, Sheik, 214
Giscard d'Estaing, Valery, 201
Glenny, Misha, 271
globalization theory, 68
Goldstein, Avery, 234
Goldstone, Jack, 117
Gorbachev, Mikhail, 94, 141, 143, 279–280
government:
  church's relations with, 70, 72, 94, 109–20, 139, 210–11
  responsibilities of, 44, 184, 225
  structure of, 70–71, 139, 140
Grachev, Pavel, 243
Granada, 210
Great Britain, 21, 51, 70, 74, 81, 89, 126, 135, 157, 186, 197, 202, 209, 210, 216, 219, 229, 236, 251, 258, 262, 285, 294, 295, 301, 307–8, 315, 318, 319
Greece, 119, 126, 128, 144, 145, 146, 157, 162–63, 164, 198, 199, 243, 255, 274, 281, 283–84, 295, 307, 315
Greek civilization, ancient, 42, 52, 54, 62, 69, 76–77, 209

Greenway, H.D.S., 254
Gulf Cooperation Council, 252
Gulf War, 115, 145, 148, 176, 186, 216,
    217, 221, 246, 247–52
Gurr, Ted Robert, 256–57

Haiti, 50, 133, 136–37
Hanseatic League, 133
Hashmi, Sohail H., 251
Hassan, King of Morocco, 115, 248
Havel, Vaclav, 28, 57
Hawke, Robert, 153
Hekmatyar, Gulbuddin, 247
Hill, Fiona, 278
Hindu civilization, 33, 51, 52, 54, 127,
    183, 188, 218, 259, 316, 317
  cultural identities in, 135, 137, 138,
    176, 252, 255, 256, 268, 275
  modernization and, 72, 76, 77, 99
  political structure of, 70, 94, 135, 137,
    156
  power and influence of, 58, 84, 109
  Western relations with, 66, 102, 185,
    193, 250–51
Hinduism, 47, 96, 98, 101, 130, 131, 177,
    264, 320
Hitler, Adolf, 185, 231
Hoffmann, Stanley, 200
Hofstader, Richard, 306
Hong Kong, 63, 84, 97, 103, 106, 108,
    127, 132, 134, 168, 169, 170, 171,
    173, 194, 197, 219, 230, 238
Horowitz, Donald, 68
Hosokawa, Morihiro, 228
Howard, Michael, 158, 310
human rights, 70, 71–72, 92, 146, 153,
    184, 185, 186, 192–98, 199, 205,
    212, 221, 223, 224, 225, 228, 230,
    239, 241, 244, 283, 305, 309
  Western standards of, 184, 186, 192–
    198, 199, 205, 212, 221, 223, 224,
    225, 228, 230, 241, 283
Hungary, 39, 50, 92, 126, 134, 145, 157,
    158, 160, 161, 282
Hussein, Saddam, 145, 177, 186, 247–49,
    251, 252, 268
Hussein, King of Jordan, 115, 249

identities:
  level of, 43, 128, 129, 267–68
  modernization and, 76, 116, 125, 129

  oppositional definitions of, 67–68, 97,
    129, 270–72
  see also civilizational identities; cultural
    identities
ideology, 100
  appeal of, 92–93, 249
  divisions based on, 28, 33, 52–53, 125,
    129–30, 138, 142, 219–20, 222, 249,
    252–54
immigration, 103, 113, 148, 198–205,
    211, 230, 240, 241, 303, 305
  economic conditions and, 198, 199,
    202, 203, 204
  hostility toward, 19–20, 39, 67–68, 147,
    150, 186, 200–205, 212, 253
India, 28, 44, 49, 50, 72, 76, 86, 87, 90,
    126, 127, 187, 191, 192, 209, 212, 220,
    229, 239, 259, 313, 315, 316, 317
  allies of, 39, 156, 157, 244, 248, 268,
    271, 272, 274, 275
  cultural identities and values in, 33, 48,
    61, 94, 98, 101, 128, 137–38, 195,
    252, 254, 255–56, 268, 271
  economic and political development
    in, 82, 103, 109, 198
  language use in, 61, 62, 63–64
  see also Hindu civilization
indigenization, 91–95, 101, 102, 106, 107,
    112–13, 147–49, 183
individualism, 71–72, 108, 139, 184, 214,
    225, 238, 305, 306, 311, 319
Indonesia, 89, 95, 103, 113, 115–16, 121,
    133, 138, 168, 170, 171, 174, 194,
    195, 215, 219, 230, 235–36, 248,
    256, 264, 271, 314, 316
industrialization, 51, 68, 69, 87, 100, 175,
    302
institutions, international, 35, 100, 126,
    173, 178, 184, 185, 208, 223, 235,
    240, 292, 293, 312, 313, 317
intellectuals, 57–58, 114, 142–43, 175–
    176, 248, 261, 304
  indigenization and, 93–94, 101, 106,
    112–13
  language use of, 57–58, 63–64, 112–13
International Monetary Fund (IMF), 100,
    184, 208
international relations theory, 231
international system, international
    society vs., 54
invariance hypothesis, 76

investment, international, 52, 67, 169–71, 208, 224, 230, 238, 244

Iran, 28, 38, 39, 77, 82, 90, 97, 101, 109, 111, 126, 127, 133, 136, 146, 176, 178, 195, 198, 210, 214, 215, 216, 224, 239, 240, 248, 249–50, 264, 309
  kin-country rallying by, 272, 273, 275, 276, 277, 278, 279, 281, 285, 286, 287–88, 289, 290, 293, 297
  military capabilities of, 184, 185, 188, 189–90, 192, 223, 243, 267, 275, 314, 315, 317

Iranian Revolution, 113, 114, 118, 216

Iraq, 90, 177, 188, 189, 192, 257
  Western conflict with, 38, 39, 59, 145, 148, 184, 185, 214, 215, 216, 240, 246, 247–52, 293

Ireland, 157

Islam, 42, 47, 130, 160, 200, 209, 320; *see also* Islamic civilization
resurgence of, *see* Islamic Resurgence

Islamic civilization, 45, 54, 143, 144, 315
  cultural identities and values in, 19, 28, 70, 101, 110–20, 126, 127, 129, 131, 132, 137–38, 139, 185, 252, 254–65
  democracy in, 29, 212–14
  fault line conflicts in, 208, 247–52, 254–65, 267–72, 281–91
  immigration from, 200, 201, 203, 204, 211
  indigenization in, 94, 95, 101, 147–49
  kin-country rallying by, 272, 275–91, 309
  language use in, 64, 74
  military capabilities in, 184, 188–90, 192, 212, 242, 243–45, 310, 317
  modernization and, 73–74, 76–78, 99, 116, 175, 178
  political structure of, 135, 136, 137, 155, 156–57, 174–79, 185
  population growth in, 20, 84, 86, 102, 103, 109, 116–20, 211, 238, 259–61, 265, 304–5
  resources and influence of, 28, 50, 102, 109–21, 183, 209–17, 247–52, 254–265, 311, 312
  Sinic relations with, 185, 188–90, 195–196, 197, 219, 238–40, 241, 244–45
  social mobilization in, 102, 110, 111–112, 115, 116
  spiritual and temporal authority in, 70, 72, 94, 210–11
  superiority claimed by, 102, 183, 185, 211, 213, 217, 246, 304, 310
  violence in, 256–58, 285–86
  Western relations with, 20, 38, 39, 50, 51, 59, 66, 82, 102, 110–20, 121, 126, 144–46, 148, 158, 167, 178, 183, 184, 185, 193, 207, 209–19, 238, 239–40, 244, 246, 247–52, 264–65, 283, 312
  youth bulge in, 116–19, 121, 148, 211, 259–61, 265, 314

Islamic Resurgence, 65–66, 94, 96, 102, 109–21, 137, 144, 175, 193, 302
  political manifestations of, 110, 112, 113–15, 147–49, 209–18, 263, 267–272, 275–76, 283
  social manifestations of, 110, 111–12, 115, 147–49, 211

Israel, 71, 90, 115, 119, 157, 184, 186, 188, 192, 251, 254, 263, 267, 272, 274, 314, 317

Italy, 111, 119, 135, 157, 199–200, 201, 210, 282, 293

Izetbegovic, Alija, 267, 269, 270

James, William, 29

Japan, Japanese civilization, 32, 33, 44, 45, 47, 48, 49, 51, 89, 203, 228, 314, 315, 316, 317, 321
  Chinese hegemony and, 218–19, 220, 229, 230, 232, 233, 235, 236–27, 241, 243
  cultural identity of, 126, 128, 132–33
  economic power of, 38, 68, 83, 87, 103, 106–8, 120, 121, 132, 134–35, 170, 171, 186, 218–19, 221–22, 225–26, 243
  increased strength of, 28, 81, 82, 83, 86, 87, 88, 90, 103, 106–7, 186, 218–19, 230, 232–33, 236, 247
  indigenization in, 93–94, 95, 107
  lone country status of, 134–35, 137, 156
  modernization and, 72, 73, 74, 77, 105, 154
  political structure of, 70, 135
  U.S. military presence in, 221, 222, 230, 313
  Western relations with, 38, 68, 102–9, 134–35, 157, 185, 194, 207, 221, 224, 232–33, 236–37, 241, 250, 309, 312

Jewish civilization, Judaism, 48n, 96, 130,
    188, 198, 200, 211, 239, 254, 256,
    259, 263, 317, 320
Jiang Zemin, 223, 224, 240
Jinnah, Mohammad Ali, 93–94
John Paul II, Pope, 114, 282, 292
joint mediation rule, 316–17
Jordan, 112, 115, 192, 247, 248, 249,
    277–78
Juppé, Alain, 157–58

Karadzic, Radovan, 271, 297
Kashmir, 28, 127, 195, 244, 252, 253,
    256, 260, 264, 268, 271, 273, 274,
    297
Kazakhstan, 134, 138, 146, 163, 240, 276
Keating, Paul, 151, 152
Kelly, John B., 116
Kemalism, 73–75, 77, 93, 105, 115, 138,
    147, 154
Kenya, 137, 256, 293
Kepel, Gilles, 95–96, 98, 101
Khmelnytsky, Bohdan, 165, 166
Khomeni, Ayatollah Ruhollah, 91, 111,
    114, 216
kin-country rallying, 20, 28, 156, 208,
    217, 231, 248, 254, 268, 272–91,
    293, 294–96, 297–98, 309
    see also fault line conflicts
Kissinger, Henry, 28, 307
Koh, Tommy, 104
Kohl, Helmut, 91, 202
Koran, 72, 77, 112, 263, 268
Korea, North, 28, 38, 39, 45, 47, 90, 97,
    128, 157, 168, 170, 194, 195, 203,
    216, 219–20, 235, 243, 313, 316
    military capabilities of, 185, 186–87,
    188, 190, 191, 192
Korea, South, 28, 45, 47, 65, 89, 97, 98–
    99, 101, 103, 108, 128, 132–33, 134,
    157, 168, 170, 191, 192, 193, 203,
    219–20, 228, 235, 237, 243, 313,
    316
Kozyrev, Andrei, 271, 285, 295
Kravchuck, Leonid, 39, 166
Kuchma, Leonid, 166, 167
Kuhn, Thomas, 29–30
Kurth, James, 307
Kuwait, 184, 186, 215, 221, 248, 251,
    296
Kyrgyzstan, 64, 146, 271, 276

language, 21, 59–64, 70, 112–13, 126,
    133, 139, 174, 175, 202, 231, 253,
    319
    power and, 62–64, 73, 74, 269
Language of Wider Communication
    (LWC), 60–63, 231
Laos, 48, 132
Lapidus, Ira, 174
Latin American civilization, 45, 46, 70,
    99, 114, 200, 282, 317, 321
    cultural identities in, 127, 131–32,
    139
    economics and political development
    in, 33, 127, 131–32, 134, 192, 193,
    195, 196
    immigration from, 200, 202–3, 204,
    205, 305
    political structure of, 135–36
    population of, 85–86
    Western relations with, 50–51, 102,
    139, 184–85, 192, 193, 195, 196,
    240–41, 312
Latin language, 60–61, 62, 69, 70
Latvia, 64, 138, 145, 158
law, 70, 92, 139, 184, 305, 311, 321
    international, 52, 283
    Islamic, 110, 115–16, 144
Lawrence, Bruce B., 100
Lebanon, 42, 101, 214, 248, 254, 256,
    259, 273, 287
Lee Kuan Yew, 93–94, 97, 100, 106, 108,
    153, 170, 174, 197, 231
Lee Teng-hui, 106, 173, 223, 224
Lellouche, Pierre, 203–4
Lenin, V. I., 52–53, 140, 179, 212
Lévy, Bernard-Henri, 290
Lewis, Bernard, 98, 210, 212–13
Lewis, Flora, 282
liberal democracy, *see* democracy, liberal
Libya, 28, 38, 90, 116, 174, 176, 185, 188,
    192, 195, 214, 215, 216, 217, 248,
    273, 274, 281, 293
literacy, 85–86, 93, 116, 119
Lithuania, 64, 92, 158, 160, 165
Lloyd George, David, 91
lone countries, 134–35, 136–37, 156
Lord, Winston, 226

Macao, 171, 173
Macedonia, 138, 163, 284
MacFarquhar, Roderick, 234

McNeill, William H., 44, 92, 98, 101
Maghreb, 117, 120, 213, 216, 250
Mahathir, Mohammad, 109, 132–33, 152–53, 308
Mahbubani, Kishore, 59, 103, 237
Malaysia, 45, 89, 95, 103, 107, 116, 121, 137, 138, 168, 170, 171, 174, 192, 194, 195, 215, 219, 228, 230, 235–236, 249, 252, 256, 264, 274, 285, 286, 288
Malta, 161
Mandarin, 62, 63, 70, 94, 174, 231
Mao Tse-tung, 52–53, 105, 106
Marxist-Leninism, 52–53, 100, 105, 111, 130, 142, 209, 306, 310
  failure of, 31, 34, 53, 105–6, 138
Mauritania, 248
Mauss, Marcel, 41
Mazrui, Ali, 74, 75, 130, 188
Mearsheimer, John, 37
Meiji Restoration, 72, 105, 107
Melko, Matthew, 42, 44, 45, 301
Mercosur, 127, 131, 134, 240
Mernissi, Fatima, 214, 249, 251
Mexico, 19–20, 37, 46, 109, 134, 136, 192, 228, 308
  cultural identity of, 126, 127, 139, 149–151, 154
  immigration from, 202, 203, 204–5, 240, 305
  as torn country, 139, 149–51, 154
Middle East, 85, 91, 129, 130, 133, 135, 144, 177, 179, 188, 191, 204, 208, 212, 215, 217, 233, 252, 254, 263, 276, 311, 321
military capabilities, 51, 72, 88–90, 140, 161, 174, 177, 212, 243–45, 267, 275, 310, 312, 321
  nonproliferation of, 184, 185–92, 199, 208, 225, 228, 238–39, 242, 244, 315, 317
  nuclear, 37, 38, 90, 164, 167, 168, 186, 187–92, 199, 225, 230, 233, 241, 242, 243, 244, 309, 313, 314, 315, 317
  shifting strength in, 82, 83, 127, 178, 185, 186–92, 205, 208, 218–38, 303, 312–18
  spending on, 89–90, 186, 190–91, 214, 230, 239, 242
Milosevic, Slobodan, 261, 288, 297, 298

Minsk Group, 293
Mintz, Sidney, 136
Mitterrand, Francois, 91, 201
Miyazawa, Kiichi, 194
Mladic, Ratko, 285
modernism, 96, 100
modernization, 68–78, 88, 95, 97, 99, 154, 175, 178, 199, 306, 320–21
  acceptance of, 73–75, 105, 110, 140–141, 144–45
  identity crises and, 76, 116, 125, 129
  industrialization in, 68, 69, 302
  rejection of, 72–73, 74–75
  traditional cultures vs., 68–69
  Westernization conflated with, 20, 47, 68, 72, 73–74, 76, 78, 92n, 144–45, 302
Moldova, 127, 162, 163, 165
Mongolia, 48, 139, 140, 168, 220, 230, 243, 314, 315
Moore, Clement Henry, 114
Morocco, 113–14, 115, 119, 126, 176, 200, 248, 250, 285
Moro-Philippine conflict, 266–67, 273, 274
Morrison, John, 168
Mortimer, Edward, 54
Moynihan, Daniel Patrick, 35
Muslim Brotherhood, 112
Muslim countries, *see* Islamic civilization
Muslim World League, 176
Myanmar, 132, 194, 195, 220, 244, 256, 316
Myrdal, Gunnar, 306

Nagorno-Karabakh, 252, 272, 278, 279, 280, 291, 293, 296–97
Naipaul, V. S., 56
Nanking, Treaty of, 229
Nasser, Gamal Abdel, 176
National Endowment for Democracy, 193
nationalism, 53, 66, 94, 100, 105, 106, 114, 115, 150, 162, 164, 198, 246, 249, 268–72, 283, 297
nation states, 56, 135, 252
  anarchical relations among, 33–35, 36
  balancing vs. bandwagoning by, 231–235, 314
  borders of, 35, 37, 248, 271

nation states (*cont.*)
    declining influence of, 35, 36, 321
    identities of, 21, 43, 51, 125–26, 175,
        305, 306
    multiple interests of, 33–35
    principal role played by, 21, 35, 36,
        174
Netherlands, 129, 157, 262, 295
New Zealand, 46, 84, 132, 133, 316
Nigeria, 28, 136, 137, 192, 256, 317
Nixon administration, 168, 195
North America, 46, 50, 84, 130
    Mexican relations with, 127, 134, 139,
        149, 150–51
    see also Canada; United States
North American Free Trade Agreement
    (NAFTA), 127, 131, 134, 150, 151,
    154, 240, 308
North Atlantic Treaty Organization
    (NATO), 19, 38, 39, 89, 90, 126,
    128, 131, 132, 133, 144, 145, 148,
    215, 219, 307, 308, 309, 310, 312
    in fault line conflicts, 279, 283, 284,
        285, 286, 289, 294, 295, 315
    membership in, 158, 161–62, 163, 242,
        317
Norway, 145, 198
Nuclear Nonproliferation Treaty, 192,
    195
nuclear weapons, 37, 38, 90, 164, 167,
    168, 186, 187–92, 199, 225, 230,
    233, 241, 242, 243, 244, 309, 313,
    314, 315, 317
Nye, Joseph, 92

oil resources, 28, 116, 146, 147, 175, 178,
    184, 186, 212, 240, 243, 251–52,
    280, 313, 314–15, 316
Oksenberg, Michael, 236
Olympic Games, 38, 197, 223
one-world paradigm, 31–32
Opium War, 72
Organization for Security and
    Cooperation in Europe, 131, 219
Organization of African Unity, 317
Organization of American States, 317
Organization of the Islamic Conference
    (OIC), 137, 176, 273, 286, 287, 317
Organization on Security and
    Cooperation, 161
Orientalism, 32, 33, 109, 203

Orthodox Russian civilization, 45, 54, 91,
    183, 198, 219, 247, 259, 262
    cultural identities and values in, 70, 94,
        98, 100, 129, 132, 138, 255, 260,
        263, 276–80
    economic and political development
        in, 29, 86, 109, 140–44, 157–63,
        176, 193, 243
    kin-country rallying in, 281, 283–84,
        288–89, 291, 297
    political structure of, 70, 135, 143, 155,
        163–68, 176
    Western relations with, 28, 32, 37, 38,
        51, 52, 91, 100, 102, 126, 138, 139–
        144, 146–47, 154, 157, 158, 161–62,
        165, 166–68, 185, 193, 196, 242–43,
        283, 293, 308, 309, 312
    see also Russian Federation
Orthodoxy, 70, 90, 140, 166, 256, 264,
    269, 270–72, 320
Ottoman Empire, 51, 52, 64, 71, 74, 95,
    128, 141, 144, 147, 149, 158, 160,
    177, 178, 210, 260, 262, 263, 269,
    271, 272, 278, 287, 301
Özal, Turgut, 115, 145, 146, 147, 148,
    178–79, 279

Pakistan, 38, 90, 94, 97, 112, 113, 116,
    127, 128, 133, 156, 157, 176, 178,
    185, 187, 188, 189, 190, 191, 192,
    213, 215, 223, 239, 244, 247, 248,
    249, 250, 254, 255, 260, 264, 314,
    317
    in fault line conflicts, 268, 272, 273,
        274, 275, 276, 277, 286, 287
Palestine, 119, 176, 249, 256, 259, 264,
    267, 273, 274
Palestine Liberation Organization
    (PLO), 248, 249, 267, 297
Palmer, R. R., 52
Panama, 136, 282
Papandreou, Andreas, 284
paradigms, 29–39
    chaos, 35, 321
    civilizational, 36–39
    Cold War, 21, 24–25, 30, 33, 36, 39,
        52–53, 54, 66, 82, 115, 128, 135,
        138, 151, 156, 157, 158, 168, 218,
        233, 238, 245, 255, 309
    defined, 29–30
    one-world, 31–32

statist, 33–35, 37, 185
two-world, 32–33
Parker, Geoffrey, 51
Partnership for Peace, 161, 285
Pasqua, Charles, 201
Payne, James, 257
Paz, Octavio, 149
Pearson, Lester, 39, 321
Peloponnesian War, 209
Peres, Shimon, 133
Perry, Matthew Calbraith, 72
Persians, 42, 45, 64, 177
Peter the Great, Tsar of Russia, 138, 139, 140, 141, 144
Philippines, 103, 138, 157, 168, 169–70, 171, 176, 192, 193, 200, 202, 220, 230, 235, 236, 253, 256, 264
Moro conflict with, 266–67, 273, 274
Pipes, Daniel, 73–74, 77–78
pluralism, 70–71, 139, 140, 233, 237, 238, 302, 311
Poland, 39, 50, 68, 92, 114, 126, 134, 145, 157, 158, 160, 161, 165, 200, 282
Popular Arab and Islamic Conference (PAIC), 176
population growth, 20, 84, 86, 102, 103, 109, 116–20, 175, 178, 198, 200, 211, 238, 242, 259–61, 265, 304–5
Portugal, 50, 71, 150, 157, 192, 210, 216
Post Ministerial Conference (PMC), 132
power, 29, 34, 58, 318
bandwagoning and, 231–33
centralization of, 141
culture and, 91–92, 128, 129, 212, 310
defined, 83
diffusion of, 88, 90–91, 185, 192, 194
hard vs. soft, 92, 109
language use and, 62–64, 73, 784, 269
shifting balance of, 20, 48–55, 125, 129–30, 155, 183–206, 229, 231–37, 241, 312
Western decline in, 20–21, 29, 53–54, 63, 81–101, 103, 104, 105, 106, 107, 116, 184, 186, 191, 193–98, 205, 217, 228, 238, 242, 301–8, 311, 321
property rights, 70, 223, 228, 305
Proposition 187, 19–20, 203, 205
Protestantism, 46, 70, 99, 101, 126, 138, 160, 193, 202, 240, 256, 261
Protestant Reformation, 70, 109n, 111, 117, 139

Putnam, Robert, 294
Pye, Lucian, 44, 234

Quaid-i-Azam, 94
Quigley, Carroll, 44, 48, 302, 303, 304

Rafsanjani, Akhbar Hashemi, 188, 189, 239
Raspail, Jean, 203–4
Reagan administration, 91, 228, 246
realist paradigm, 33–35, 37, 185
Regional Cooperation for Development, 133–34
regions, 43
economic cooperation within, 108, 127, 130–35, 308
power distributed by, 82, 90, 130–35, 156, 191
relativism, 38, 98, 100, 196, 318
religion, 21, 64–66, 139
civilizations defined by, 42, 47–48, 59, 66, 174–79, 267–72, 320, 321
divisions based on, 28–29, 42, 43, 64, 125, 175, 209–17, 247–52, 253–54, 258–65
revitalization of, 28–29, 54, 64–65, 68, 94, 95–101, 102, 109–20, 305; *see also* Islamic Resurgence
state authority and, 70, 72, 94, 109–20, 139, 210–11
see also specific religions
Rifkind, Malcolm, 307
Rodinson, Maxine, 78
Roman civilization, 69, 70, 91, 92, 139–140, 158, 160, 301
Romania, 126, 157, 158, 160, 161, 162, 165, 283–84
Roosevelt, Franklin D., 32, 248
Roosevelt, Kermit, 86
Roosevelt, Theodore, 306
Roy, Oliver, 113
Rubin, Barnett, 276
Russian civilization, *see* Orthodox Russian civilization
Russian Federation, 19, 87, 94, 158, 209, 239, 251, 260, 310, 316
allies of, 28, 38, 39, 156, 163–65, 207, 314–15
Chinese hegemony and, 218–19, 220, 229, 241, 243

Russian Federation (*cont.*)
  cultural identity of, 37, 98, 126, 127,
    130, 132, 179, 253, 255, 267, 268,
    270–71, 292, 308
  elections in, 39, 143–44
  kin-country rallying by, 272, 274, 275–
    278, 279–80, 283–85, 286, 293,
    294–96, 309
  military capabilities of, 89, 90, 186,
    186, 187, 242, 280
  torn cultural identity of, 138, 139–44,
    151, 154
  Western relations with, 28, 32, 38, 91,
    100, 146–47, 154, 161–62, 185, 283,
    308, 309, 312
Russian language, 60, 62, 63, 64, 70,
  166
Russian Revolution, 52, 109n, 149, 165
Rwanda, 28

Sagan, Scott, 317
Said, Edward, 33
Sakharov, Andrei, 142
Salinas, Carlos, 149–50, 228
Saudi Arabia, 19, 28, 77, 97, 107, 110,
  112, 113–14, 116, 118, 119, 127,
  146, 175, 176, 178, 184, 186, 188,
  198, 210, 215, 216, 240, 247, 248,
  250, 251, 252, 264, 267
  kin-country rallying by, 273, 281, 285,
    286, 287–88, 289, 290, 293
Savitsky, Peter, 143
Schlesinger, Arthur M., Jr., 305, 311
Schwartz, Benjamin, 48
Schweller, Randall, 232
Second World Chinese Entrepreneurs
  Conference, 170
secularism, 96, 98, 110, 115, 150, 213,
  249, 268
  see also religion
Septinac, Alojzieje, 282
Serbia, 28, 38, 59, 64, 119, 126, 129, 130,
  138, 143, 156, 162, 163, 164, 243,
  251, 252, 254, 255, 259, 260–62,
  263, 268–70, 271–72, 309, 315
  kin-country rallying around, 272, 281–
    291, 295–96, 297
Shaposhnikov, Yevgeny, 279
Shevardnadze, Eduard A., 165
Sicily, 209
Sid-Ahmed, Mohammed, 213

Silajdzic, Haris, 267, 270
Singapore, 77, 89, 95, 97, 99, 103, 106,
  108, 127, 138, 168, 169, 171, 172,
  174, 194, 195, 219, 221, 235, 238,
  318–20
Sinic civilization, 38, 44, 45, 54, 71, 198,
  318–19
  Buddhism in, 47–48, 49, 76, 138
  cultural identities and values in, 28, 33,
    52, 65, 77, 102, 106, 127, 129, 132,
    138, 169–70, 173, 185, 252
  influence of, 31, 32, 38, 50, 58, 70, 84,
    95, 168–74, 183, 194
  Islamic relations with, 185, 188–90,
    195–96, 197, 219, 238–40, 241,
    244–45
  modernization and, 72, 73, 74, 76, 77,
    105
  political structure of, 135, 155–56,
    168–74
  Western relations with, 20, 29, 38, 51,
    66, 95, 102–9, 170–71, 185, 190,
    194–97, 203, 207, 209, 215, 218–38,
    239–40, 241, 307, 308, 309, 312–13
  see also China, People's Republic of
Sivard, Ruth Leger, 257
Slavonia, 284, 296
Slovakia, 39, 126, 139, 145, 157, 160,
  161
Slovenia, 138, 145, 158, 161, 282, 312
socialism, 53, 100, 105, 142, 246
Solzhenitsyn, Aleksandr, 142, 143
Somalia, 28, 59, 257
South Africa, 47, 94–95, 126, 136, 179,
  188, 204, 240–41, 264, 317
South America, 50, 150, 203
  see also specific countries
South Asian Association for Regional
  Co-operation, 131
Soviet-Afghan War, 246–47, 275
Soviet Union, 141–43, 175, 222, 308,
  321
  allies of, 21, 31, 34, 105, 144, 157, 160,
    168, 244, 273–74
  dissolution of, 19, 28, 29, 31, 35, 53,
    64, 81, 83, 92, 105, 114, 126, 127,
    138, 142, 146, 148, 157, 163, 164,
    165, 193, 208, 210, 215, 262, 275,
    278, 279, 280, 306, 307, 309, 311
  fault line conflicts in, 208, 259, 275,
    278

military power and aggression of, 83, 88, 89, 90, 92, 142, 161, 190–91, 217, 220, 224, 225, 230, 233
  see also Orthodox Russian civilization
Spain, 21, 49, 50, 111, 119–20, 135, 150, 157, 192, 207, 215, 282, 290–91
Spengler, Oswald, 41–42, 44, 55, 76, 83
Sri Lanka, 28, 48, 94, 137, 138, 156, 253, 254, 255, 259, 274, 275, 297, 316
Stalin, Joseph, 140, 185, 314
Stankevich, Sergei, 143
statist paradigm, 33–35, 37, 185
Straits Exchange Foundation, 172
Sudan, 28, 39, 113, 137, 157, 176, 177, 195, 214, 216, 248, 249, 253, 254, 256, 257, 264
  fault line conflicts and, 267, 273, 274, 275, 277, 287, 293
Suharto, General, 91, 115, 248
Sweden, 126, 130, 145, 157, 160, 162, 195, 293, 305
Switzerland, 199, 287
Syria, 119, 126, 185, 188, 192, 195, 214, 216, 248, 249, 250, 251

Taiwan, Republic of China, 77, 89, 103, 106, 108, 127, 132, 134, 157, 168, 169, 171–74, 193, 194, 197, 209, 219–21, 223, 228, 230, 236, 237, 238, 313
Tajikistan, 64, 127, 243, 253, 255, 267, 268, 270, 272, 273, 274, 275–76, 278, 293
Tanzania, 137, 256
technology, 51, 87–88, 100, 191, 199, 211, 312, 320, 321
  communications, 58–59, 67, 73, 78, 129, 146, 171, 176, 199, 205, 254, 274
Ter-Petrossian, Levon, 297
terrorism, 103, 187–88, 212, 216, 217, 241, 287
Thailand, 48, 97, 103, 152, 157, 168, 170, 220, 230, 235–36, 256, 264
Third World, 85, 90, 168
  Cold War conflict in, 21, 156, 272
  post-Cold War conflict in, 31, 150
  see also specific countries
Tiananmen Square, 105, 170, 194

Tibet, 48, 155, 168, 220, 223, 228, 230, 253, 315
torn countries, 138–54, 306, 319
  redefinitions of, 139, 150–51
Toynbee, Arnold, 42, 43, 44, 48n, 55, 73, 301
trade, international, 51–52, 67, 103, 165, 169–71, 208, 238, 309
  controversies over, 218–19, 221–22, 224, 225–26, 230, 297
  regionalism in, 130–35, 307–8
Trans-Dniester Republic, 165
Truman, Harry, 30
Tudjman, Franjo, 282, 296
Tunisia, 101, 115, 119, 126, 176, 200, 215, 248, 250, 286
Turkey, 19, 28, 37, 38, 45, 50, 51, 70, 74, 109, 113, 115, 143, 152, 157, 161, 163, 165, 168, 176, 195, 198, 199, 200, 215, 239, 243, 250, 251, 259, 264, 269, 314, 315
  cultural identity of, 126–27, 128, 130, 133, 144–49, 150, 151, 154, 162, 178–79, 255
  kin-country rallying by, 272, 273, 277–278, 279, 280, 281, 286, 287, 288, 289, 293, 296–97
  as torn country, 139, 144–49, 150, 151, 154, 162, 178–79
Turkmenistan, 64, 146
two-world paradigm, 32–33

Uganda, 28, 275, 293
Ukraine, 37, 39, 64, 126, 127, 138, 143, 158, 162, 165–68, 187, 242, 277, 284, 313
Umehara, Takeshi, 306
United Arab Emirates, 287
United Nations, 19, 31, 163, 194, 208, 241, 287, 306, 313, 317
  failures of, 32, 156, 188, 195–96, 251, 284
  peacemaking efforts of, 37, 38, 195–96, 284, 285, 286, 288, 289, 290, 296, 297
United States, 19, 21, 37, 38, 39, 50–51, 68, 86, 90, 126, 132, 152, 217, 244, 258, 283, 288
  allies of, 34, 105, 127, 128, 130, 133, 134, 145, 150–51, 156, 157, 161, 162, 168, 185, 207, 214

United States (*cont.*)
  Chinese hegemony and, 218–38
  in fault line conflicts, 246, 248, 250–
    251, 252, 258, 262, 263–64, 267–68,
    279, 281, 285, 286, 289–90, 293,
    294, 295, 296, 309
  future of, 312–18, 321
  immigration to, 198, 199, 203, 204–5,
    240, 305
  moral decline in, 304, 320–21
  multiculturalism in, 290, 305–7, 318–
    321
  power of, 28, 82, 83, 89, 104, 105, 106,
    135, 156, 157, 178, 183–84, 186–87,
    190, 192, 193–95, 197–98, 218–38,
    239, 240, 247, 301–8, 310, 311
  trade relations of, 218–19, 221–22,
    225, 307–8
universal civilization, 56–78, 91, 109,
    211, 301–8, 318–21
  defined, 56–59
  Western belief in, 20–21, 38, 51–53,
    55, 57–59, 66, 183–86, 192–98, 211,
    217, 224, 225, 232, 242, 301–8, 310–
    312
Universal Declaration on Human Rights,
    194, 196
urbanization, 86, 100, 103, 113, 116, 175
Uzbekistan, 64, 134, 146, 271, 275–76

Vatican, 281, 282, 284
Venezuela, 127, 134, 136
Vietnam, 45, 47, 52–53, 100, 103, 132,
    155–56, 157, 168, 171, 195, 203,
    246, 313, 316
  Chinese hegemony and, 219, 220, 221,
    223, 230, 235
Vlahos, Michael, 59

Wallerstein, Immanuel, 41
Walt, Stephen, 231–32
Walzer, Michael, 318
Warsaw Pact, 89, 126, 157, 310
Weber, Max, 47
Wee Kim Wee, 319
Weidenbaum, Murray, 171
Weigel, George, 96
Weiner, Myron, 199
West, Rebecca, 290
Western civilization, 45–46, 67–68
  characteristics of, 69–72, 139, 318

declining influence of, 20–21, 29, 53–
    54, 63, 81–101, 103, 104, 105, 106,
    107, 116, 184, 186, 191, 193–98,
    205, 217, 228, 238, 242, 301–8, 311,
    321
  in early modern era, 21, 22–23, 50–52
  economic well-being in, 32, 51, 52, 58,
    66, 86–88, 91, 103, 170–71, 303
  in fault line conflicts, 274, 275, 276,
    278, 279, 281–91, 293, 296
  future of, 312–18
  Hindu relations with, 66, 102, 185,
    193, 250–51
  human rights standards in, 184, 186,
    192–98, 199, 205, 212, 221, 223,
    224, 225, 228, 230, 241, 283
  imperialism of, 21, 32, 50–52, 63–64,
    83, 91, 135, 139, 184, 192–98, 205,
    209–11, 212, 213, 229, 239, 241,
    247, 263–64, 271, 283, 310, 312, 318
  Islamic relations with, 20, 38, 39, 50,
    51, 59, 66, 82, 102, 110–20, 121,
    126, 144–46, 148, 158, 167, 178,
    183, 184, 185, 193, 207, 209–18,
    238, 239–40, 244, 246, 247–52,
    264–65, 283, 312
  Japanese relations with, 38, 68, 102–9,
    134–35, 157, 185, 194, 207, 221,
    224, 232–33, 236–37, 241, 250, 309,
    312
  Latin American relations with, 50–51,
    102, 139, 184–85, 192, 193, 195,
    196, 240–41, 312
  lingua franca of, 59–60, 61, 62, 63, 64,
    73, 174, 231, 319
  military capabilities of, 51, 82, 83, 88–
    90, 91, 184, 185–87, 190–92, 205,
    212, 242, 251, 252, 303, 312, 313
  Orthodox Russian relations with, 28,
    32, 37, 38, 51, 52, 91, 100, 102, 126,
    138, 139–44, 146–47, 154, 157, 158,
    161–62, 165, 166–68, 185, 193, 196,
    242–43, 283, 293, 308, 309, 312
  political structure of, 135, 155, 157–63,
    165, 176
  renewal of, 301–8
  rise of, 50–53, 81–82, 301–8
  Sinic relations with, 20, 29, 38, 51, 66,
    95, 102–9, 170–71, 185, 190, 194–
    197, 203, 207, 209, 215, 218–38,
    239–40, 241, 307, 308, 309, 312–13

technological superiority of, 51, 78, 312
territory and population of, 84–86, 91, 303
universalist pretensions of, 20–21, 38, 51–53, 55, 57–59, 66, 183–86, 192–198, 211, 217, 224, 225, 232, 242, 301–8, 310–12
wars within, 21, 52, 53, 82
see also specific countries
Western European Union, 219
Westernization:
acceptance of, 73–74, 75, 144–45, 149–51, 183
modernization conflated with, 20, 47, 68, 72, 73–74, 76, 78, 92n, 144–45, 302
paths to, 57–59, 75–76
rejection of, 72–73, 74–75, 102, 104, 105, 110, 183–92
torn countries and, 139–46, 149–51, 152, 153–54, 319
Westphalia, Treaty of, 35, 52, 54
Wilson, Pete, 203
Wilson, Woodrow, 91
World Assembly of Muslim Youth, 287
World Bank, 100, 103, 208
World Council of Churches, 293
World Economic Forum, 57–58, 59

World Health Organization, 228
World Muslim Congress, 176
World Trade Organization, 223, 228
World War I, 32, 52, 210, 243, 262, 315
World War II, 32, 87, 88, 105, 106, 107, 142, 144, 175, 185, 187, 196, 210, 222, 226, 232, 262, 276, 282, 291, 313, 315, 317

Xinjiang, 230, 255

Yeltsin, Boris, 39, 91, 94, 100, 143, 164, 207, 268, 271, 284, 285, 295–96, 297
Yemen, 195, 214, 248
youth, 83, 86
change led by, 103, 112–13, 116–19, 121, 148, 175–76, 211, 242, 259–61, 265, 267, 314
Yugoslavia, 126, 158, 163, 199, 308
fault line conflict in, 19, 28, 37, 42, 125, 127, 138, 156, 208, 255, 259, 260, 261–62, 267, 269–70, 271–72, 273, 274, 281–91

Zaire, 28
Zhirinovsky, Vladimir, 143, 164
Zia ul-Haq, Mohammad, 116
Zionism, 188, 249

Credits